THE
PHILOSOPHY
OF
LITERARY
FORM

Kenneth Burke

THE
PHILOSOPHY
OF
LITERARY
FORM

Studies in Symbolic Action

THIRD EDITION

UNIVERSITY OF CALIFORNIA PRESS
BERKELEY, LOS ANGELES, LONDON

University of California Press
Berkeley and Los Angeles, California
University of California Press, Ltd.
London, England

ISBN: 0-520-02484-6 (cloth bound)
0-520-02483-4 (paper-bound)
Library of Congress Catalog Card Number: 72-93526

Printed in the United States of America

2 3 4 5 6 7 8 9 0

TO J. S. WATSON, JR.

Out of these several years
Since the days of *The Dial*
Amicably indeed

INSTEAD OF A FOREWORD
to Third Edition

F O R a long time I have wanted to try my hand at a somewhat unprofessional kind of index. And this new edition of
a book originally published in 1941 (a collection of "Thirty-
minded" pieces) seems to me the ideal opportunity. Since it
already had so professional an index for locating authors and
works by title, I could feel free to add my loosely topical effort, that aims to be suggestive rather than pinpointingly
specific.

Though there are many entries such that, if you happen
to be looking for X, you may find it listed quite literally under "X," there is also a troublesome centrifugal tendency
towards items wholly out of line with alphabetical place-
ment. Since I was unable to present them formally as "topics," the best I could do was think of them informally and
semi-punningly as "spots." Here are the spottiest of such,
jumbled into one "analphabetic" paragraph:

"Down with politics, up with apocalypse," xiii; seeing
through to the end (of the line) 3, 38 n., 70, 83, 84, 86, 88;
"curse me with forgiveness," 53; animal experimenters, inserting an "i" in "salvation," 159; what to look for, what to
look out for, 68, 146, 164, 165, 167; hivn, hervn, heavenly,
Ivn, 53, 53 n.; "blackness of darkness," 88 ("withinness of
withinness," on same page, did get through); *Substantia
prior est natura suis affectionibus*, 166; long-pull investment
vs. in-and-out trader, vii–viii; people might go crooked, yet
be in order, 242; at the bottom of a spring, 429; knocks at the
door, 431, thorough 428; and really meant it, 265; by filling

v

it out, 124, 145 n., 398, 445–446; we can shift the rules, 130–131; in the name of, 3, 4, 6, 192, 386–388; in terms of, xx, 22, 208, 210; in the sign of, 86; under the aegis of 24, 28, 86, 288, 436; so be it, 7; putting in and taking out and, on page 368, "after we have gone all the way round the circle," and "should there be any of us left."

By citing these as evidence of the excesses which my index resisted, I hope to get the advantage of that grand rhetorical figure, paraleipsis (*praeteritio*): "I leave unmentioned my opponent's scandalous conduct. Far be it from me to say what a dismal wretch he is," etc. Also I hope that, by "omitting" the mention of such excesses, I can best suggest the tenor of the motive at the roots of my procedure.

The Index of Topics begins on page 456.

KB

FOREWORD
to Second Edition

AFTER many changes in our national life, between the time when this book was originally published and present conditions when it appears again in unabridged form, things are in many notable respects like things then. And to that extent, some kind of circling-back seems to have occurred. Yet, when one starts to say "This is where I came in," one is quickly admonished to add, "but with a difference!"

We are often told that the major difference is: In the Olden Days the great stress was upon "Ideology," but now that's out. Beyond question, whether or not the presence or absence of "Ideology" does mark the major difference between the kinds of social-mindedness prevailing then and now, much of the typical current "Beatnicist" ferment more closely resembles the stirrings of the twenties than of the thirties (and these essays were "thirty-minded," I say, at the risk of being pursued by a pun). I have in mind the looseness of alignment as regards the relation between political programs and cultural concerns in general.

Though I was primarily concerned with theories of method that, if I succeeded in doing what I aimed to do, should meet the tests of "long-pull investment," any advocate of anything soon learns that he must also, somehow, try to meet the demands of the "in-and-out trader." Hence, in my original Foreword I suggested that, "while everything flows," a collection such as mine should ideally have a kind of loose-leaf arrangement whereby *different* examples could be presented, from year to year, depending upon the changes of emphasis in the cultural marketplace.

Thinking along those lines, in keeping with the modes of the moment as I conceive of them, I'd put the issue thus: There is a quite understandable hankering after works that, if reduced to a slogan, are in effect saying "Down with politics, up with apocalypse." Ingenious writers such as Norman O. Brown in one groove and Marshall McLuhan in another are in their different ways feeding this appetite (the one by being Freudian in Utopian ways that would doubtless have vexed Freud sorely; the other by so talking of "communicative media" and principles like "circularity" or "lineality," that you'd find it hard to tell the difference between a wagon wheel and a rondo). A Foreword to next year's ideal loose-leaf arrangement would probably favor other examples.

Where are we, then? I beg the reader to grant that, however inadequately the book may embody them, it particularly proffered arguments and evidence for these basic propositions:

(1) A work is composed of implicit or explicit "equations" (assumptions of "what equals what"), in any work considered as one particular structure of terms, or symbol-system. The most obvious example of what I mean by "equations" is indicated in my reference to Gorki, on Andreev's notions of a "hero" (p. 439). If I were writing the book over again, I'd point out the similarity between

viii

"equations" as so conceived and what contemporary social scientists call "values," or what in Aristotle's *Rhetoric* are called "topics." The essay on Freud indicates how the same concept impinges upon "associations."

(1-a) In these pages I often overstressed the sheerly *imagistic* aspect of such "equations." Much that I once talked about in terms of "image" or "metaphor" I'd now deal with purely in terms of "terms." Yet I hope that my recurrent references to the works of Coleridge will indicate the salient role performed by purely *imagistic* "bridging." At the same time, as I learned from friendly differences with Robert Penn Warren on such matters, the intrinsic ambiguities of imagery can readily accommodate themselves to a considerable range of interpretations. (On this point, more later.)

(2) Though I would now considerably alembicate (as I have done, for instance, in my *Grammar of Motives*) my analysis of the relationship between literary "strategies" and extra-literary "situations," I can still abide by this earlier statement of the case; also, it has the advantage of the very simplicity which I later was forced to complicate. The situation-strategy design says in effect: The poet is not poetizing in the middle of nowhere; though his poem may be viewed purely within itself ("in terms of" its internal consistency), it is also the act of an agent in a non-literary scene; but by the nature of notation, it survives the *particulars* of the scene in which it was originally enacted.

(3) Despite the fact that anthropology and literary hisstory share the realm of "myth" in common, purists will often frown upon a word such as "scapegoat" on the grounds that it does not belong to the theory of tragedy

(which is, etymologically, the "goat-song"!). I would hold, on the other hand: Many sociological and anthropological concepts have their analogues in literary criticism proper. With the rise of aesthetics, such concepts got *unnecessarily* exiled; and they found a home in these supposedly alien fields.

If my references to the Mystery Poems of Coleridge were to be revised in the light of later developments, I'd find no reason to retract what I originally said. But in the interest of methodological precision I'd point things up differently.

I'd now make it clear that I was involved in three distinct kinds of observation: (1) things that could be said about any one of the poems, if you had only it, knew nothing of its author, and wanted to discuss it purely within itself, in its intrinsic, internal development from-what, through-what, to-what; (2) things that could be said if you had other poems by the same author, and discussed them as a body of poetry, with each bearing upon the others; (3) things that could be said if there was a great deal of information about the poet (from letters, diaries, biographies, and the like), if you had grounds to believe that much of this poetically extrinsic knowledge (about Coleridge purely as a citizen with personal problems) could be shown to throw light upon the works, considered not just as "poems in particular" but as instances of "symbolic action in general."

In connection with investigations I was commissioned to undertake for Colonel Arthur Woods (when he was head of the Rockefeller Foundation and an assessor to the League of Nations Advisory Committee on Traffic in Opium and Other Dangerous Drugs), I happened to have done quite a bit of research in the social, psychological, and physiological effects of drug addiction. This sheerly "nosological" dimension overlapped upon my special attachment to Coleridge as poet and critic. And when, in connection with a course I was to give on Coleridge at the University of Chicago in 1938, I began working in earnest on the "equations" in Coleridge's work, I couldn't help being struck by the close correlation between the imagery in his best poems and the symptoms of opium addiction (both in the euphoric stage and during the torments of "withdrawal").

I had taken a considerable collection of notes on the subject (they were more than two years in the taking, mainly at the New York Public Library, the American Medical Association, and the Library of Congress, along with interviews). And though this material has long since disappeared, I know of sufficient professional agreement regarding the syndrome of opium addiction in its different phases for me to feel sure that we can tell when the Ancient Mariner's highly personalized boat has had a new dose of "honey dew," or when it is badly in need of one. And I would particularly treat as "perturbations" (that is, moments in the poem not explicable in terms of poetics alone) these three striking motivational puzzles: (1) The Mariner's impulsive killing of the Albatross (a detail which, we know on wholly "extra-poetic" evidence, was inserted by Wordsworth to account for the Mariner's otherwise inexplicable sense of guilt, in Coleridge's original version); (2) the impulsive blessing of the snakes (the detail that so greatly worried Irving Babbitt, the apostle of the "inner check"); and (3) the *periodic recurrence* of the Mariner's need to find a listener for his confession (though I hold that the difficulties are removed as soon as we turn from the poem *qua* poem to the poem as the personal act of Coleridge in his particular burdensome situation).

All these elements are considered in my original account (which stands as was). But I did not place them with such schematic sharpness as is now possible. Thus, if one says something about the relation between Sun and Moon in "The Ancient Mariner," one can be talking about the work purely in its internality, without regard to the author. But surely, in our attempts to understand the full scope of "symbolic action," we should not allow the canons of poetics to keep us from considering the further fact that typical imagery of the poems is also applied by Coleridge when he is referring to the discomfitures placed upon him personally by the nature of his addiction.

I think that, in my later work, I have explicitly sharpened the statement of my case considerably, as regards the relation between the canons of poetics in particular and speculations on the nature of symbolic action in general. But I see no reason to abandon the scheme as it is implicitly embodied here. On the contrary! The issue is treated at some length in my recent collection of essays *Language as Symbolic Action.* Also there, in an essay on "Mind, Body, and the Unconscious," I tackle from other angles the problem of the difference between the "lexical" meaning of a term (its public meaning as defined in a dictionary) and the special connotations that may surround it in one particular poet's nomenclature.

When discussing "equations" on p. 75 of this text, I

state: Sometimes they are best indicated by noting that A *equals* B, but at other times by noting that A *leads to* B. Now looking back over my treatment of equations, as reseen in the light of further precisions that were forced upon me by Robert Penn Warren's different interpretation of Coleridge's Mystery Poems (or Poems of Fascination), I should add this bit of post-mortem (redivivus!) observation:

My original analysis of "The Ancient Mariner" *in its internal relations* was too strongly affected by Lane Cooper's suggestive but insufficiently complex analysis of the relationship between Sun and Moon, viewed as motivating forces in the poem. For in the poem itself, there are *two* Suns. In Part II, stanza 4, we read:

> Nor dim nor red, like God's own head,
> The glorious Sun uprist:
> Then all averred, I had killed the bird
> That brought the fog and mist.
> 'Twas right, said they, such birds to slay,
> That bring the fog and mist.

Then things turn bad, until

> All in a hot and copper sky,
> The bloody Sun, at noon,
> Right up above the mast did stand,
> No bigger than the Moon.

Note: This evil eye above them is a *moon*-sun, not "glorious" like the rising sun that was saluted earlier, the kind of sun that Coleridge, in his theological writings, equated with the *solace* of religion (as distinct from religion in terms of *punishment* and *control*)—or, otherwise put, the God of *mercy* as distinguished from the God of *justice*.

I hadn't looked closely enough at the *narrative* kind of equation, whereby A *equals* B because A *leads to* B.

Taking a second look thus, lo! we note how, at the end of Part I, the final stanza, disclosing that the Mariner had shot the Albatross, immediately follows a stanza ending: "Whiles all the night, through fog-smoke white, / Glimmered the white Moon-shine." In Part II, we are told that the *punishing* sun was "No bigger than the Moon." And the motivational turning-point (fittingly in the middle section, Part IV) takes place when "The moving Moon went up the sky." Similarly, in the relaxation of Part VI, we are told that the "bright eye" of the ocean "Up to the Moon is cast." And the accursed hermit returns to shore while ". . . on the bay the moonlight lay, / And the shadow of the Moon." Yes, as I ran across by another route (*cf.* an article on imagery in Yeats, originally published in the Winter, 1942 issue of *The Southern Review*, and now reissued in a paperback volume, *The Permanence of Yeats*, edited by James Hall and Martin Steinman), things can get poetically reversed, so that the sun's light is in effect a reflection of the moon's. Or otherwise put: There is an element of *mooniness* in the spell at all stages, from inception, through punishment, to transformation and partial cure.

I can't say for sure that this all comes out quite the way Mr. Warren would have had it. I would say only that his expert pressures on my thesis helped me to make it more exact.

In the Foreword to the first edition I have a paragraph (pp. xi-xii) on the "Power" family of terms. I discuss it in connection with what I refer to as "Richard Wright's disturbingly impressive novel, *Native Son,* a book that offers a whole new avenue to follow in developing my remarks on the ambiguities of power."

I should like to call attention to that passage because it bears upon a matter of terminology which I have since come upon in many ways. For instance, on p. 388, with reference to John Dewey's *Liberalism and Social Action,* I refer to the "cycle of virtues" with which the author there associated the cause of liberalism. In my *Rhetoric of Religion* I build around a "Cycle of Terms Implicit in the Idea of 'Order,' "—and if I were to rewrite my *Grammar of Motives* I'd lay explicit stress upon what is in effect there already; namely: a "Cycle of Terms Implicit in the Idea of an 'Act.' "

Elsewhere I have tentatively dealt with other such terministic dynasties. But it seems to me that the Power, Act, and Order sets are particularly to be isolated for study. And I would lay great stress upon a distinction between "Action" and "Motion." I take it that the latter kind of process would still prevail, in its sheer physicality, were all symbol-using animals and their symbols (that is, all persons and the record of their acts) to be erased from the face of the earth.

In any event, I take it that the symbolically tinged realms of Power, Act, and Order, singly or all three, are grounded in the realm of Motion, so far as empirical existence is concerned. And this realm is *non-symbolic,* except in the sense that man, as the symbol-using animal, necessarily endows everything with the spirit of his symbol-systems.

I have found it necessary to emphasize this point because, over the years, my constant concern with "symbolicity" has often been *interpreted* in the spirit *exactly contrary* to my notions of "reality." The greater my stress upon the role of symbolism in human behavior (and misbehavior!), the greater has been my realization of the inexorable fact that, as regards the realm of the empirical, one cannot live by the *word* for bread alone. And though the *thing* bread is tinged by the realm of symbolic *action*, its empirical nature is grounded in the realm of non-symbolic, or extra-symbolic motion.

There is a basic difference between metaphysical idealism and my concern with "the word." To say that you can't talk about anything except by exemplifying the rules of talk is not identical with saying that our world is "nothing but" the things we say about it. On the contrary, alas! There's many a time when what we call a "food" should have been called a "poison." And if our ancestors had but hit upon too many of such misnomers, we'd not be here now.

No. Over the years I become more and more convinced: Only by knowing wholly about our ways with symbols can we become piously equipped to ask, not only in wonder but in great fear, just what may be the inexorable laws of non-symbolic motion which our symbolizing so often "transcends," sometimes to our "spiritual" gain and sometimes to our great detriment.

KENNETH BURKE

ANDOVER, NEW JERSEY
AUGUST, 1966

FOREWORD

THESE pieces are selections from work done in the Thirties, a decade so changeable that I at first thought of assembling them under the title, "While Everything Flows."

Their primary interest is in speculation on the nature of linguistic, or symbolic, or literary action—and in a search for more precise ways of locating or defining such action.

Words are aspects of a much wider communicative context, most of which is not verbal at all. Yet words also have a nature peculiarly their own. And when discussing them as modes of action, we must consider *both* this nature as words in themselves *and* the nature they get from the nonverbal scenes that support their acts. I shall be happy if the reader can say of this book that, while always considering words as acts upon a scene, it avoids the *excess* of environmentalist schools which are usually so eager to trace the relationships between act and scene that they neglect to trace the structure of the act itself.

However, it is not my intention here to discuss the internalities of a work's structure in the sense of a reporter who would inform about a work's subject, plot, background, the relationships among its characters, etc. I am more concerned with the *general problems* of internal structure and act-scene relationships—and I introduce reference to particular poems, novels, or dramas as illustrative material rather than as central theme. Thus the reader who wants the specific criticism of books might be more disappointed than the reader who wants a theory of the criticism of books (a theory that should be applicable, *mutatis mutandis,* to any specific cases).

As for analysis focused upon one work, probably my article on Hitler's *Mein Kampf* is the most complete example in these pages, with the references to the writings of Coleridge (whom I hope to treat later at greater length in a separate volume) probably coming next. The study of *Julius Caesar* as a device for the arousing and fulfilling of expectations in an audience, might fall within this class, if the reader is not led by its tone to assign it the quality of a *tour de force.* And I have included in an appendix some reviews that, while selected because in my opinion they clarified some aspect or other of my position, are by the nature of the case centered about some one formal object.

I might give an illustration as to the way in which the two modes of literary substance (the substance of a literary act as placed upon a scene, and the substance of the act within itself) would be related. Think of some philosophic school whose members were using a given set of identical or synonymous terms. Now, upon analysis, we should find that there are certain purely internal relationships prevailing among these terms. By reason of such purely internal relationships, it is logically possible to make certain recombinations among the terms, or to reduce certain of the terms to others, or by reason of certain ambiguities or overlaps among the terms to so manipulate them as to derive many important changes of emphasis or conclusion from them. To discuss the intrinsic nature of such philosophies, and to do so in a penetrating way and not as a mere reporter, one should have to discuss these technical possibilities and relate the given philosopher's strategy to them. Such considerations would provide an active way of treating the work's nature in itself. However, on considering the work as placed in biological or historical contexts, we might well find that the given philosopher, by manipulating the possibilities of emphasis in one way rather than another, was able symbolically to enroll himself in one social alliance, with its peculiar set of expectancies, rather than another. Here we should see what participation in a Cause caused his work, by what Movement it was motivated, on what sub-stance it made its stand. The act being an act upon a scene, its placing by reference to scene would be needed for a complete substantiation of this philosophy as an act.

However, an act may be placed in many contexts, and when the character of the context changes, the character of the act changes accordingly. Thus, the same book may be in a supply-and-demand context for a bookseller, a morality-immorality context for a censor, a classicism-romanticism context for a literary historian, the "substance" of the book changing in accordance with the point of view from which we would consider it. Ideally, the substance of the work, "in itself," would probably require a statement that would fit the characterization of the book in any and every context. But in actuality there is a tendency for writers to feel that they have characterized a work intrinsically when they apply epithets of approval or disapproval to it (appreciation), or refer to it in tonalities meant to be in tune with the tonalities of the book itself (impressionism), or tell what it's about (reviewing), or classify it (bibliography). All of these ways have value—but the way primarily tried here, more explicitly in the pieces written towards the end of the decade (they are not arranged in chronological order) is this: To identify the substance of a particular literary act by a theory of literary action in general.

The quickest way to sloganize this theory is to say that it is got by treating the terms "dramatic" and "dialectical" as synonymous. So it is, as you prefer, to be called either "dialectical criticism" or "dramatic criticism methodized" (i. e., a reasoned method for treating art as act). I invite the reader, at this point in our exposition, to accept whichever of the two terms he feels more at home with, and to reserve until later his decision as to whether the proposed labels are just, and whether they can legitimately be treated as synonymous.

Wherever an author would use an example to illustrate a general statement, the best manufacturing arrangement would probably be a kind of loose-leaf volume. For since the only purpose of illustrations is to make things seem clear, and since those topics seem clearest which are foremost in the public's attention at the moment, one might hope to seem clearest by "opportunistically" changing his illustrations in accordance with the shifts of public attention. Some speculators may get around this by analyzing human acts in terms of animals, mechanisms, or picturable designs. Which is effective so far as it goes. For if you build your generalization about a chicken, people tend to feel that it is eternally valid; but if you build your generalization about some topic or controversy, they tend to feel that the generalization dies as the topic or controversy drops out of focus. Yet a "dramatic" or "dialectical" perspective would vow one to hold that generalizations getting their cues from animals, mechanisms, or picturable designs are not using examples sufficiently complex to be representative of human acts and meanings. And so far as I am concerned, I find nothing more "contemporary" than the records of heresies, sects, and schisms that flourished centuries ago, which are by no means gone with their times, but are *mutatis mutandis* all vigorous today.

But with a loose-leaf arrangement, I might, at this precise moment, for instance, seek to "point up" my distinction between realism and naturalism (as discussed in my section on "Ritual Drama as 'Hub' ") by trying to show how it might be applied in considering Archibald MacLeish's attack upon the war novelists. For I think that this distinction lies blurred beneath the altercation—and that, had it been made, much fury, unnecessary and off the subject, could have been avoided by both the outraged and the outrager. (My reference to MacLeish here, however, is not to be confused with my reference to him in the essay, "War, Response, and Contradiction," concerning an article on the subject written by MacLeish in 1933.)

I would also, in a loose-leaf arrangement, have wanted to weave in references to Richard Wright's disturbingly impressive novel, *Native Son,* a book that offers a whole new avenue to follow in developing my remarks on the ambiguities of power. Indeed, as I have spoken briefly of what might be called the "Stance" family (terms for location, support, placing, "substance"), so I might note this other major clan, the "Power" family. It is composed of many members: social power, sexual, physical, political, military, commercial, monetary, mental, moral, stylistic (powers of grace, grandeur, vituperation, precision)—powers of emancipation, liberalization, separation ("loosing"), powers of fascination and fascization ("binding," as in Mann's "Mario and the Magician")—and powers of wisdom, understanding, knowledge. There are ways whereby, owing to the nature of synecdoche, any member of this family may come to do vicarious service for any other member, or for the family as a whole—so that one may marry or rape by politics, wage war in argument, be mentally superior by the insignia of social privilege, bind or loose by knowledge, show one's muscle or enhance one's stature by financial income, etc., in whatever permutations and combinations one cares to contrive. In particular, in *Native Son,* I should have liked to discuss the author's treatment of the interrelationships among the powers: physical, sexual, social, and monetary—with at the end a transcendence into the powers of understanding.

However, there is no end to the possibilities of such "looseleafing." So, through wanting to change, or to make last-minute comment upon, nearly everything, I found it easy to compromise by changing almost nothing, and confining my additions to a few references in the hitherto unpublished matter, and in cases where the "pointing up" could be done briefly. Accordingly, the reader may encounter the same formulations put forward with a different attitude, or used for different purposes, at different points in our text. He may treat this as mere inconsistency (to be forgiven, in so far as it can be forgiven, on the grounds that the years were changeable and that the development of one's thought might be expected to change somewhat with them). For the most part, however, I should prefer not to be "forgiven" these "inconsistencies." For we may properly expect a form to function differently when it is a part of one context than when it is a part of some other context—and often, on closer inspection, the different functions will be found not to "refute" one another, but simply to be modified by their difference in position.

All of these items have been previously published, except

the first and longest, of which only a small excerpt appeared before (in *The Southern Review*). The publications in which the others appeared are listed herewith:

"Semantic and Poetic Meaning," *The Southern Review;* "The Virtues and Limitations of Debunking," *The Southern Review;* "The Rhetoric of Hitler's 'Battle,' " *The Southern Review;* "The Calling of the Tune," *The Kenyon Review;* "War, Response, and Contradiction," *The Symposium;* "Freud—and the Analysis of Poetry," *The American Journal of Sociology.*

"Literature as Equipment for Living," *Direction;* "Twelve Propositions on the Relation Between Economics and Psychology," *Science & Society;* "The Nature of Art Under Capitalism," *The Nation;* "Reading ·While You Run," *The New Republic;* "Antony in Behalf of the Play," *The Southern Review;* "Trial Translation (From *Twelfth Night*)," *The New Age Weekly;* "Caldwell: Maker of Grotesques," *The New Republic;* "The Negro's Pattern of Life," *The Saturday Review of Literature;* "On Musicality in Verse," *Poetry.*

"George Herbert Mead," *The New Republic;* "Intelligence as a Good," *The New Republic;* "Liberalism's Family Tree," *The New Republic;* "Monads—on the Make," *The New Republic;* "Quantity and Quality," *The New Republic;* "Semantics in Demotic," *The New Republic;* "Corrosive Without Corrective," *The New Masses;* "The Constants of Social Relativity," *The Nation;* "The Second Study of Middletown," *The New Masses;* "A Recipe for Worship," *The Nation.*

"Hypergelasticism Exposed," *Hound and Horn;* "Mainsprings of Character," *The New Republic;* "Exceptional Improvisation," *Poetry;* "Exceptional Book," *The New Re-*

public; "Permanence and Change," *The New Republic;* "By Ice, Fire, or Decay?" *The New Republic;* "Fearing's New Poems," *The New Masses;* "Growth Among the Ruins," *The New Republic;* "Letters to the Editor—On Psychology," *The American Journal of Sociology;* "Letters to the Editor—On Dialectic," *The American Teacher;* "Dialectician's Hymn," *The University Review.*

Above all, I wish to state here publicly my great debt of gratitude to Professor Leonard Brown, of the Department of English at Syracuse University, who obligingly and ingeniously found time in the midst of many activities to prepare the index of this volume. And I do regret that the state of the proofs at the time when these far too inadequate words were inserted required my acknowledgment to come at the end, rather than the beginning, of my Foreword. The titular monograph in the book was reworked from material I originally presented as a visiting lecturer in connection with a course conducted by Professor Brown at Syracuse.

KENNETH BURKE

CONTENTS

I. THE PHILOSOPHY OF LITERARY FORM

II. LONGER ARTICLES

III. SHORTER ARTICLES

IV. APPENDIX

INDEXES

THE
PHILOSOPHY
OF
LITERARY
FORM

THE PHILOSOPHY
OF LITERARY FORM

SITUATIONS AND STRATEGIES

LET us suppose that I ask you: "What did the man say?"
And that you answer: "He said 'yes.' " You still do not know
what the man said. You would not know unless you knew
more about the situation, and about the remarks that preceded his answer.

Critical and imaginative works are answers to questions
posed by the situation in which they arose. They are not
merely answers, they are *strategic* answers, *stylized* answers.
For there is a difference in style or strategy, if one says "yes"
in tonalities that imply "thank God" or in tonalities that
imply "alas!" So I should propose an initial working distinction between "strategies" and "situations," whereby we
think of poetry (I here use the term to include any work
of critical or imaginative cast) as the adopting of various
strategies for the encompassing of situations. These strategies size up the situations, name their structure and outstanding ingredients, and name them in a way that contains
an attitude towards them.

This point of view does not, by any means, vow us to personal or historical subjectivism. The situations are real; the
strategies for handling them have public content; and in so
far as situations overlap from individual to individual, or
from one historical period to another, the strategies possess
universal relevance.

1

Situations do overlap, if only because men now have the same neural and muscular structure as men who have left their records from past ages. We and they are in much the same biological situation. Furthermore, even the concrete details of social texture have a great measure of overlap. And the nature of the human mind itself, with the function of abstraction rooted in the nature of language, also provides us with "levels of generalization" (to employ Korzybski's term) by which situations greatly different in their particularities may be felt to belong in the same class (to have a common substance or essence).

Consider a proverb, for instance. Think of the endless variety of situations, distinct in their particularities, which this proverb may "size up," or attitudinally name. To examine one of my favorites: "Whether the pitcher strikes the stone, or the stone the pitcher, it's bad for the pitcher." Think of some primitive society in which an incipient philosopher, in disfavor with the priests, attempted to criticize their lore. They are powerful, he is by comparison weak. And they control all the channels of power. Hence, whether they attack him or he attacks them, he is the loser. And he could quite adequately size up this situation by saying, "Whether the pitcher strikes the stone, or the stone the pitcher, it's bad for the pitcher." Or Aristophanes could well have used it, in describing his motivation when, under the threats of political dictatorship, he gave up the lampooning of political figures and used the harmless Socrates as his goat instead. Socrates was propounding new values —and Aristophanes, by aligning himself with conservative values, against the materially powerless dialectician, could himself take on the rôle of the stone in the stone-pitcher ratio. Or the proverb could be employed to name the predicament of a man in Hitler's Germany who might come forward with an argument, however well reasoned, against Hitler. Or a local clerk would find the proverb apt, if he would make public sport of his boss. These situations are all distinct in their particularities; each occurs in a totally different texture of history; yet all are classifiable together under the generalizing head of the same proverb.

Might we think of poetry as complex variants and recombinations of such material as we find in proverbs? There are situations typical and recurrent enough for men to feel the need of having a name for them. In sophisticated work, this naming is done with great complexity. Think of how much modern psychology, for instance, might be placed as a highly alembicated way of *seeing through to the end* the formulation now become proverbial: "The wish is father to the thought." Or think of how much in the Hegelian dialectic might be summed up, as an over-all title, in the idealist Coleridge's favorite proverb, "Extremes meet." And in all work, as in proverbs, the naming is done "strategically" or "stylistically," in modes that embody attitudes, of resignation, solace, vengeance, expectancy, etc.

MAGIC AND RELIGION

In addition to the leads or cues, for the analysis of poetic strategy, that we get from proverbs, with their strongly realistic element, we may get leads from magic and religion.

Magic, verbal coercion, establishment or management by decree, says, in effect: " 'Let there be'—and there was." And men share in the magical resources of some power by speaking "in the name of" that power. As Ogden and Richards remind us in *The Meaning of Meaning,* modern Biblical

3

scholarship has disclosed that we should interpret in this wise the formula, "taking the name of the Lord in vain." The formula referred to the offense of conjuring for malign purposes by uttering one's magical decrees "in the name of" the Lord.

The device, in attenuated and alembicated variants, is not so dead, or even so impotent, as one might at first suppose. Today, for instance, we are facing problems that arise from an attempt to fit private enterprise with the requirements of the citizenry as a whole. Think of the difference in magic if you confront this situation *in the strategic name of* "planned economy" or, employing a different strategy, *in the name of* "regimentation."

The magical decree is implicit in all language; for the mere act of naming an object or situation decrees that it is to be singled out as such-and-such rather than as something-other. Hence, I think that an attempt to *eliminate* magic, in this sense, would involve us in the elimination of vocabulary itself as a way of sizing up reality. Rather, what we may need is *correct* magic, magic whose decrees about the naming of real situations is the closest possible approximation to the situation named (with the greater accuracy of approximation being supplied by the "collective revelation" of testing and discussion).

If magic says, *"Let there be* such and such," religion says, *"Please do* such and such." The decree of magic, the petition of prayer. Freud has discussed the "optative as indicative" in dreams (where "would that it were" is stylistically rephrased: "it is"—as when the dreamer, desiring to be rid of a certain person, dreams that this person is departing). Neo-positivism has done much in revealing the secret commands and exhortations in words—as Edward M. Maisel,

in *An Anatomy of Literature,* reveals in a quotation from
Carnap, noting how the apparent historical creed: "There
is only one race of superior men, say the race of Hottentots,
and this race alone is worthy of ruling other races. Members of these other races are inferior," should be analytically
translated as: "Members of the race of Hottentots! Unite
and battle to dominate the other races!" The "facts" of the
historical assertion here are but a strategy of inducement
(apparently describing the *scene* for the action of a drama,
they are themselves a dramatic *act prodding to a further
dramatic act*).

It is difficult to keep the magical decree and the religious
petition totally distinct. Though the distinction between
the coercive command and the conducive request is clear
enough in its extremes, there are many borderline cases.
Ordinarily, we find three ingredients interwoven in a given
utterance: the spell and the counter-spell, the curse; the
prayer and the prayer-in-reverse, oath, indictment, invective; the dream, and the dream gone sour, nightmare.

So, taking this ingredient as common to all verbal action,
we might make the following three subdivisions for the
analysis of an act in poetry:

> dream (the unconscious or subconscious factors in a
> poem—the factor slighted by the Aristotelians,
> though by no means left unconsidered, as John
> Crowe Ransom's chapters on "The Cathartic Prin-
> ciple" and "The Mimetic Principle" in *The World's
> Body* make apparent),
> prayer (the communicative functions of a poem, which
> leads us into the many considerations of form, since
> the poet's inducements can lead us to participate in

his poem only in so far as his work has a public, or communicative, structure—the factor slighted by the various expressionistic doctrines, the Art for Art's Sake school stressing the work solely as the poet's externalizing of himself, or naming of his own peculiar number),

chart (the realistic sizing-up of situations that is sometimes explicit, sometimes implicit, in poetic strategies—the factor that Richards and the psychoanalysts have slighted).

It may annoy some persons that I take the realistic chart to possess "magical" ingredients. That is, if you size up a situation in the name of regimentation you *decree* it a different essence than if you sized it up in the name of planned economy. The choice here is not a choice between magic and no magic, but a choice between magics that vary in their degree of approximation to the truth. In both these magics, for instance, there is usually an assumption (or implied *fiat*) to the effect that increased industrial production is itself a good. But when we recall that every increase in the *consumption* of natural resources could with equal relevance be characterized as a corresponding increase in the *destruction* of natural resources, we can glimpse the opportunity for a totally different magic here, that would size up the situation by a different quality of namings. And when I read recently of an estimate that more soil had been lost through erosion in the last twenty years than in all the rest of human history, I began to ask whether either the "regimentation" magic or the "planned economy" magic is a close enough approximate for the naming of the situation in which we now are. The "regimentation" magic is on its face by far the worse, since its implicit demand, "Let us have no collective control over production," calls for as much wastage as is possible in an ailing property structure. But this wastage is, ironically, curtailed mainly by the maladjustments of the very property structure that the "regimentation" magic would perpetuate. The "planned economy" magic is much superior, but only when corrected by a criticism of "new needs." It is a menace when combined, as it usually is, with a doctrine that increased industrial output is synonymous with "progress." The irony is that a readjusted property structure would make possible greater wastage (or "consumption") than our present ailing one. Hence, the magic that made greater production possible would be the worst of calamities unless corrected by another magic decreeing that many of our present kinds of industrial output are culturally sinister.

The ideal magic is that in which our assertions (or verbal decrees) as to the nature of the situation come closest to a correct gauging of that situation as it actually is. Any *approximate* chart is a "decree." Only a *completely accurate* chart would dissolve magic, by making the structure of names identical with the structure named. This latter is the kind of chart that Spinoza, in his doctrine of the "adequate idea," selected as the goal of philosophy, uniting free will and determinism, since the "So be it" is identical with the "It must be so" and the "It is so." A completely adequate chart would, of course, be possible only to an infinite, omniscient mind.

"It is (morally or technically) wrong" is a stylized variant of "Don't do it." However, to note this translation of a command into the idiom of realism must not be taken as identical with a "debunking" of the verbal assertion. For a command may be a good command, involving a strategy that is quite accurate for encompassing the situation. Science simultaneously admits and conceals the element of *fiat* in a calculus by Latinistic stylization, as when it explicitly states the commands basic to a calculus but couches these in terms of "postulates" (*postulatum:* command, demand), a kind of *"provisory* command," in keeping with the customary trend towards *attenuation* in scientific stylizations. It replaces "big commands" with a whole lot of "little commands" that fall across one another on the bias, quite as modern poetry has replaced the "big spell" with a lot of "little spells," each work pulling us in a different direction and these directions tending to cancel off one another, as with the conflicting interests of a parliament.

SYMBOLIC ACTION

We might sum all this up by saying that poetry, or any verbal act, is to be considered as "symbolic action." But though I must use this term, I object strenuously to having the general perspective labeled as "symbolism." I recognize that people like to label, that labeling *comforts* them by *getting things placed.* But I object to "symbolism" as a label, because it suggests too close a link with a particular school of poetry, the Symbolist Movement, and usually implies the unreality of the world in which we live, as though nothing could be what it is, but must always be something else (as though a house could never be a house, but must be, let us say, the concealed surrogate for a woman, or as though the woman one marries could never be the woman one marries, but must be a surrogate for one's mother, etc.).

Still, there is a difference, and a radical difference, between building a house and writing a poem about building

8

a house—and a poem about having children by marriage is not the same thing as having children by marriage. There are *practical* acts, and there are symbolic acts (nor is the distinction, clear enough in its extremes, to be dropped simply because there is a borderline area wherein many practical acts take on a symbolic ingredient, as one may buy a certain commodity not merely to use it, but also because its possession testifies to his enrollment in a certain stratum of society).

The symbolic act is the *dancing of an attitude* (a point that Richards has brought out, though I should want to revise his position to the extent of noting that in Richards' doctrines the attitude is pictured as too sparse in realistic content). In this attitudinizing of the poem, the whole body may finally become involved, in ways suggested by the doctrines of behaviorism. The correlation between mind and body here is neatly conveyed in two remarks by Hazlitt, concerning Coleridge:

> I observed that he continually crossed me on the way by shifting from one side of the foot-path to the other. This struck me as an odd movement; but I did not at that time connect it with any instability of purpose or involuntary change of principle, as I have done since. . . .
>
> There is a *chaunt* in the recitation both of Coleridge and Wordsworth, which acts as a spell upon the hearer, and disarms the judgment. Perhaps they have deceived themselves by making habitual use of this ambiguous accompaniment. Coleridge's manner is more full, animated, and varied; Wordsworth's more equable, sustained, and internal. The one might be

termed more *dramatic,* the other more *lyrical.* Coleridge has told me that he himself liked to compose in walking over uneven ground, or breaking through the straggling branches of a copse-wood; whereas Wordsworth always wrote (if he could) walking up and down a straight gravel-walk, or in some spot where the continuity of his verse met with no collateral interruption.[1]

We might also cite from a letter of Hopkins, mentioned by R. P. Blackmur in *The Kenyon Review* (Winter, 1939):

> As there is something of the "old Adam" in all but the holiest men and in them at least enough to make them understand it in others, so there is an old Adam of barbarism, boyishness, wildness, rawness, rankness, the disreputable, the unrefined in the refined and educated. It is that that I meant by tykishness (a tyke is a stray sly unowned dog).

Do we not glimpse the labyrinthine mind of Coleridge, the *puzzle* in its pace, "danced" in the act of walking—and do we not glimpse behind the agitated rhythm of Hopkins' verse, the conflict between the priest and the "tyke," with the jerkiness of his lines "symbolically enacting" the mental conflict? So we today seem to immunize ourselves to the arhythmic quality of both traffic and accountancy by a distrust of the lullaby and the rocking cradle as formative stylistic equipment for our children.

The accumulating lore on the nature of "psychogenic illnesses" has revealed that something so "practical" as a

---

[1] The quotations are lifted from Lawrence Hanson's excellent study, *The Life of S. T. Coleridge.*

bodily ailment may be a "symbolic" act on the part of the body which, in this materialization, *dances* a corresponding state of mind, reordering the glandular and neural behavior of the organism in obedience to mind-body correspondences, quite as the formal dancer reorders his externally observable gesturing to match his attitudes. Thus, I know of a man who, going to a dentist, was proud of the calmness with which he took his punishment. But after the session was ended, the dentist said to him: "I observe that you are very much afraid of me. For I have noted that, when patients are frightened, their saliva becomes thicker, more sticky. And yours was exceptionally so." Which would indicate that, while the man in the dentist's chair was "dancing an attitude of calmness" on the public level, as a social facade, on the purely bodily or biological level his salivary glands were "dancing his true attitude." For he *was* apprehensive of pain, and his glandular secretions "said so." Similarly I have read that there is an especially high incidence of stomach ulcers among taxi drivers—an occupational illness that would not seem to be accounted for merely by poor and irregular meals, since these are equally the lot of workers at other kinds of jobs. Do we not see, rather, a bodily response to the intensely arhythmic quality of the work itself, the irritation in the continual jagginess of traffic, all puzzle and no pace, and only the timing of the cylinders performing with regularity, as if all the *ritual* of the occupational act had been drained off, into the *routine* of the motor's explosions and revolutions?

In such ways, the whole body is involved in an enactment. And we might make up a hypothetical illustration of this sort: imagine a poet who, on perfectly rational grounds rejecting the political and social authority of the powers that be, wrote poems enacting this attitude of rejection. This position we might call his symbolic act on the abstract level. On the personal, or intimate level, he might embody the same attitude in a vindictive style (as so much of modern work, proud of its emancipation from prayer, has got this emancipation dubiously, by simply substituting prayer-in-reverse, the oath). And on the biological level, this same attitude might be enacted in the imagery of excretion, as with the scene of vomiting with which Farrell ends the second volume of his Studs Lonigan trilogy.

Sir Richard Paget's theory of gesture speech gives us inklings of the way in which such enactment might involve even the selection of words themselves on a basis of tonality. According to Paget's theory, language arose in this wise: If a man is firmly gripping something, the muscles of his tongue and throat adopt a position in conformity with the muscles with which he performs the act of gripping. He does not merely grip with his hands; he "grips all over." Thus, in conformity with the act of gripping, he would simultaneously grip with his mouth, by closing his lips firmly. If, now, he uttered a sound with his lips in this position, the only sound he could utter would be *m*. *M* therefore is the sound you get when you "give voice" to the posture of gripping. Hence, *m* would be the proper tonality corresponding to the act of gripping, as in contact words like "maul," "mix," "mammae," and "slam." The relation between sound and sense here would not be an onomatopoetic one, as with a word like "sizzle," but it would rather be like that between the visual designs on a sound track and the auditory vibrations that arise when the instrument has "given voice" to these designs (except that, in the case of human speech, the designs would be those of the tongue and throat, plastic rather than graphic).

The great resistance to Paget's theory doubtless arises in large part from the conservatism of philological specialists. They have an investment in other theories—and only the most pliant among them are likely to see around the corner of their received ideas (Paget cites remarks by Jespersen that hit about the edges of his theory). But some of the resistance, I think, also arises from an error in Paget's strategy of presentation. He offers his theory as a *philological* one, whereas it should be offered as a contribution to *poetics*. Philology, because of its involvement in historicism, really deals with *the ways in which, if Paget's theory were 100 per cent correct, such linguistic mimesis as he is discussing would become obscured by historical accretions.*

Let us suppose, for instance, that *f* is an excellent linguistic gesture for the *p* sound prolonged, and the lips take the posture of *p* in the act of *s*pitting—hence, the *p* is preserved in the word itself, in "spittle" and "puke," and in words of re*p*ulsion and re*p*ugnance. The close phonetic relation between *p* and *f* is observed in the German exclamation of repugnance, *"pfui."* Mencken, in *The American Language,* cites two synthetic words by Winchell that perfectly exemplify this faugh-*f:* "phfft" and "foofff." These are "nonsense syllables" Winchell has invented to convey, by tonality alone, the idea that is denoted in our word *"p*est." Here, since the inventor has complete freedom, there are no historical accidents of language to complicate his mimesis, so he can symbolically spit long and hard.

Imagine, however, a new movement arising in history—and, as is so often the case with new movements, imagine that it is named by the enemy (as "liberalism" was named by the Jesuits, to convey connotations of "licentiousness," in contrast with *"servile,"* to convey connotations of "loyal"). If we hypothetically grant the existence of a faugh-*f,* we should discover that the enemy danced the attitude towards this new movement with perfect accuracy in naming the new movement "phfftism" or "foofffism." However, as so often happens in history, the advocates of "foofffism" accepted the term, and set out to "live it down" (as with "liberalism"—and also "nihilism," which was named by the enemy, but in the late nineteenth century recruited nihilistic *heroes*). And let us finally imagine, as so often happens in history, that the new movement, beginning in great disrepute, finally triumphs and becomes the norm. Though the attitude towards the name is now changed, the name itself may be retained, and so we may find earnest fellows saying, "I hereby solemnly swear allegiance to the flag of foofffism."

Now, philology would deal with these historical developments whereby the originally accurate mimesis became *obscured*—and it is in this sense that, to my way of thinking, Paget's theory should be presented as a contribution not to philology, but to poetics. The greatest attempt at a *poetics* of sound is Dante's *De Vulgari Eloquio*, which is equally concerned with a *rational selection* of a poetic language, its systematic isolation from a common speech that had developed by the hazards of historical accretion. And Paget's theory should, I contend, be viewed as a corresponding enterprise, except that now, given the change of reference from Dante's day to ours, the theory is grounded on a *biological* or *naturalistic* base.

A possible way whereby these theories might be empirically tested is this: We should begin by asking whether our system of phonetic recording might be inaccurate. Might there, for instance, be at least *two* sounds of ʃ, whereas both were recorded in writing as the same sound (as in French three different sounds of *e* are explicitly indicated, whereas the English ways of recording *e* do not indicate such differences)? Why, in the light of such evidence, should we assume that there is but one ʃ simply because our mode of recording this sound indicates but one? Might there, let us say, be a faugh-ʃ and a flower-ʃ (with the second trying to bring out the smoothness of ʃ, as were one to recite sympathetically Coleridge's line, "Flowers are lovely, love is flowerlike," and the other trying to stress its expulsive quality, as when I once heard a reactionary orator, spewing forth a spray of spittle, fulminate against "fiery, frenzied fanatics")? I do not know how accurate the electric recordings of a sound-track are, or how close a microscopic analysis of them could be: but if these recordings are accurate enough, and if microscopic analysis can be refined to the point of discriminating very minute differences in the design of the sound-track, one could select flower-passages and faugh-passages, have them recited by a skilled actor (without telling him of the theory), take an electric recording of his recitation, and then examine the sound-track for *quantitative* evidence (in the design of the sound-track) of a distinction in ʃ not indicated by our present conventions of writing. We might perhaps more accurately use *two* symbols, thus: ʃ′ and ʃ″. *It should be noted, however, that such a difference would not be absolute and constant.* That is, one might pronounce a word like "of" differently if it appeared expressively in a "flower" context than if it appeared in a "faugh" context. Which would again take us out of philology into poetics.

Similarly, inasmuch as *b* is midway between mammal *m* and the repulsion *p,* we might expect it to have an *m*-like sound on some occasions and a *p*-like sound on others. Thus, in the lines

> O blasphemy! to mingle fiendish deeds
> With blessedness!

we could expect "*b*lasphemy" to approximate "*p*lasphemy," and "*b*lessedness" to be more like "*m*lessedness," the explosive possibilities of *b* being purposely coached in the first case and tempered in the second. (Incidentally, no words are more like home to an idealist philosopher than "subject" and "object"—and we are told that when Coleridge had fallen into one of his famous monologues, he pronounced them "sumject" and "omject.")

Our gradual change of emphasis from the spoken to the documentary (with many symbols of mathematics and logic having no tonal associations whatsoever, being hardly other than designs) has made increasingly for a purely ocular style—so that children now are sometimes even trained to read wholly by eye. And there are indeed many essayistic styles that profit greatly if one can master the art of reading them without hearing them at all. For they are as arhythmic as traffic itself, and can even give one a palpitation of the heart if he still reads with an encumbrance of auditory imagery, and so accommodates his bodily responses to their total tonal aimlessness. But whatever may be the value of such styles, for bookkeeping purposes, they have wandered far afield from the gesturing of heard poetic speech. Paradoxically, their greatest accuracy, from the standpoint of mimesis, is in their *very absence* of such, for by this absence

16

they conform with our sedentary trend from the bodily to the abstract (our secular variant of the spiritual). It is the style of men and women whose occupations have become dissociated from the bodily level, and whose expression accordingly does not arise from a physical act as the rhythms of a Negro work song arise from the rhythms of Negroes at work.

In any event, as regards the correlation between mind and body, we may note for future application in this essay, that the poet will naturally tend to write about that which most deeply engrosses him—and nothing more deeply engrosses a man than his *burdens,* including those of a physical nature, such as disease. We win by capitalizing on our debts, by turning our liabilities into assets, by using our burdens as a basis of insight. And so the poet may come to have a "vested interest" in his handicaps; these handicaps may become an integral part of his method; and in so far as his style grows out of a disease, his loyalty to it may reinforce the disease. It is a matter that Thomas Mann has often been concerned with. And it bears again upon the subject of "symbolic action," with the poet's burdens symbolic of his style, and his style symbolic of his burdens. I think we should not be far wrong if, seeking the area where states of mind are best available to empirical observation, we sought for correlations between styles and physical disease (particularly since there is no discomfiture, however mental in origin, that does not have its physiological correlates). So we might look for "dropsical" styles (Chesterton), "asthmatic" (Proust), "phthisic" (Mann), "apoplectic" (Flaubert), "blind" (Milton), etc. The one great objection to such a nosological mode of classification is that it leads to a Max Nordau mode of equating genius with degeneracy. This is not the case, however, if one properly discounts his terminology, reminding himself that the true locus of assertion is not in the *disease,* but in the *structural powers* by which the poet encompasses it. The disease, seen from this point of view, is hardly more than the *caricature* of the man, the oversimplification of his act—hence, most easily observable because it is an oversimplification. This oversimplifying indicator is deceptive unless its obviousness as a caricature is discounted.

ANOTHER WORD FOR "SYMBOLIC"

I respect the resistance to the notion of "symbolic action," since this resistance is based upon a healthy distrust of the irrational (the only question being whether we are rational enough in merely trying to outlaw the irrational by magical decree, and whether we might be more rational in confronting it). Respecting the resistance, I want to offer some considerations that may ease the pain. One of the most "rational" of words today is our word *statistical,* as applied for instance to the thorough rationality of an actuarial table. So I want to see whether we might be justified in borrowing this word for our purposes, in considering at least some aspects of "symbolic action." I propose to offer reasons why we might equate the word *symbolic* with the word *statistical.*

Mr. Q writes a novel. He has a score to settle with the world, and he settles it on paper, symbolically. Let us suppose that his novel is about a deserving individual in conflict with an undeserving society. He writes the work from the standpoint of his unique engrossments. However, as Malcolm Cowley has pointed out, there is a whole *class* of such novels. And if we take them all together, in the lump, "statistically," they become about as unique as various objects all going downstream together in a flood. They are "all doing the same"—they become but different individuations of a common paradigm. As so considered, they become "symbolic" of something—they become "representative" of a social trend.

Or consider the matter from another angle. One puts his arms on the table. This is a unique, real act—and one is perfectly conscious of what he is doing. There is, to be sure, a lot that he doesn't know: he is not conscious, for instance, of the infinite muscular and nervous adjustments that accompany the act. But he is perfectly conscious of the overall event: he knows what he is doing. Yet I have heard a portrait-painter exclaim at such a moment, when a man placed his arm on the table: "There—just like that—that's your characteristic posture." Thus, for this painter, the act had become "symbolic," "representative" of the man's character. There was a kind of informal fact-gathering that had been going on, as the painter had observed this man—and his exclamation was a kind of informally statistical conclusion.

But let's make one more try at taking the fearsomeness out of the word "symbolic." John Crowe Ransom, in *The World's Body*, makes some praiseworthy attempts to reaffirm a realistic basis for poetry; as part of his tactics, he would present even the lyric poem as the enactment of a dramatic rôle. The poet is "play-acting"—and so we must not consider his work as merely a symbolization of his private problems. Well and good. But let us suppose that a writer has piled up a considerable body of work; and upon inspecting the lot, we find that there has been great se-

19

lectivity in his adoption of dramatic rôles. We find that his rôles have not been like "repertory acting," but like "type casting." This "statistical" view of his work, in disclosing a *trend,* puts us upon the track of the ways in which his selection of rôle is a "symbolic act." He is like a man with a tic, who spasmodically blinks his eyes when certain subjects are mentioned. If you kept a list of these subjects, noting what was said each time he spasmodically blinked his eyes, you would find what the tic was "symbolic" of.

Now, the work of every writer contains a set of implicit equations. He uses "associational clusters." And you may, by examining his work, find "what goes with what" in these clusters—what kinds of acts and images and personalities and situations go with his notions of heroism, villainy, consolation, despair, etc. And though he be perfectly conscious of the act of writing, conscious of selecting a certain kind of imagery to reinforce a certain kind of mood, etc., he cannot possibly be conscious of the interrelationships among all these equations. Afterwards, by inspecting his work "statistically," we or he may disclose by objective citation the structure of motivation operating here. There is no need to "supply" motives. The interrelationships themselves *are* his motives. For they are his *situation;* and *situation* is but another word for *motives.* The motivation out of which he writes is synonymous with the structural way in which he puts events and values together when he writes; and however consciously he may go about such work, there is a kind of generalization about these interrelations that he could not have been conscious of, since the generalization could be made by the kind of inspection that is possible only *after the completion* of the work.

At present I am attempting such a "symbolic" analysis

of Coleridge's writings. His highly complex mind makes the job of charting difficult. The associational interweavings are so manifold as to present quite a problem in book-keeping. Thus, even if my method were hypothetically granted to be correct, it is as though one invented a machine for recovering the exact course each person had taken on passing through Times Square. Even if one's machine were completely trustworthy, he would have difficulty in trying to present, on a design, the different paths taken. The lines would merge into a blot.

However, there are two advantages about the case of Coleridge that make the job worth trying. In the first place, there is the fact that he left so full a record, and that he employed the same imagery in his poems, literary criticism, political and religious tracts, letters, lectures, and intro-spective jottings. Thus we have objective bridges for get-ting from one area to another; these images "pontificate" among his various interests, and so provide us with a maxi-mum opportunity to work out a psychology by objective citation, by "scissor work." If you want to say that this equals that, you have the imagery, explicitly shared by this and that in common, to substantiate the claim. In fact, a psychology of poetry, so conceived, is about as near to the use of objective, empirical evidence as even the physical sciences. For though there must be purely theoretical grounds for selecting some interrelationships rather than others as more significant, the interrelationships themselves can be shown *by citation* to be there.

The second advantage in the case of Coleridge is that, along with his highly complex mind (perhaps one of the most complex that has left us a full record) you have an easily observable *simplification*. I refer to the burden of his drug addiction. Criticism is usually up against a problem of this sort: The critic tries to explain a complexity in terms of a simplicity, and when he is finished, his opponent need but answer: "But you have explained a complexity in terms of a simplicity, and a simplicity is precisely what a complexity is *not*. So you have explained something in terms of what it isn't." Explanation entails simplification; and any simplification is open to the charge of "oversimplification." So we have tried to explain human beings in terms of mechanistic psychology, adults in terms of child psychology, sophisticates in terms of primitive psychology, and the normal in terms of abnormal psychology—with the opponent's categorical refutation of the effort implicit in the nature of the effort itself. In the case of Coleridge's enslavement to his drug, however, you get an observable simplification, a burden the manifestations of which can be trailed through his work—yet at the same time you have him left in all his complexity, and so may observe the complex ways in which this burden becomes interwoven with his many other concerns.

To note the matter of symbolic action, however, is by no means to involve oneself in a purely subjectivist position. There are respects in which the clusters (or "what goes with what") are private, and respects in which they are public. Thus, I think we can, by analysis of the "clusters" in Coleridge's work, find ingredients in the figure of the Albatross slain in "The Ancient Mariner" that are peculiar to Coleridge (i. e., the figure is "doing something for Coleridge" that it is not doing for anyone else); yet the introduction of the Albatross, as victim of a crime to motivate the sense of guilt in the poem, was suggested by Wordsworth. And as Lowes has shown amply, "The Ancient

Mariner" also drew upon legends as public as those of the Wandering Jew and the fratricide of Cain. There are many points at which we, as readers, "cut in"—otherwise the poem would not affect us, would not communicate. But to grasp the full nature of the symbolic enactment going on in the poem, we must study the interrelationships disclosable by a study of Coleridge's mind itself. If a critic prefers to so restrict the rules of critical analysis that these private elements are excluded, that is his right. I see no formal or categorical objection to criticism so conceived. But if his interest happens to be in the structure of the poetic act, he will use everything that is available—and would even consider it a kind of vandalism to exclude certain material that Coleridge has left, basing such exclusion upon some conventions as to the ideal of criticism. The main ideal of criticism, as I conceive it, is to use all that is there to use. And merely because some ancient author has left us scant biographical material, I do not see why we should confine our study of a modern author, who has left us rich biographical material, to the same coördinates as we should apply in studying the work of the ancient author. If there is any slogan that should reign among critical precepts, it is that "circumstances alter occasions."

However, I shall try to show, later in this essay, that the perspective which I employ can quite naturally include observations as to the structure of a poem, even considered in isolation, and regardless of the poem's bearing upon symbolic action peculiar to the poet.

Maybe we could clarify the relation between the public act and the private act in this way: Suppose that we began by analyzing the structure of "The Ancient Mariner" as though we did not know one single detail about the author, and had not one single other line written by this author. We would note such events as the peripety in the fourth part, where the water snakes become transubstantiated (removed from the category of the loathsome into the category of the beautiful and blessed). We would note that the Mariner suffered his punishments under the aegis of the Sun, and that his cure was effected under the aegis of the Moon. We would have some "equations" to work on, as the Sun is "like God's own head," and the "loon," whose cure began when "the moving Moon went up the sky," was laved by a curative rain that, in ending the state of drought, filled "silly buckets"; and when the Mariner entered the Pilot's boat the Pilot's boy, "who now doth crazy go," called him the Devil. We may also see inklings of a "problem of marriage," in the setting of the poem, and in the closing explicit statement as to a preference for church over marriage.

If we had other poems, we could trail down these equations farther. For instance, we would find the "guilt, Sun at noon, problem of marriage" equations recurring. If we had the letters and introspective jottings, we could by imagistic bridging disclose the part that Coleridge's struggles with his drug played in the "loon, Moon, silly, crazy" equations (as Coleridge in despair speaks of his addiction as idiocy, talks of going to an asylum to be cured, and also employs the snake image with reference to the addiction). Now, if we had the one poem alone, we could note something like a dramatized "problem of metaphysical evil" (much like the basis of *Moby Dick*). Given other poems, we could make this more precise. Given biographical reference, we could also show the part played by his drug addiction and his marital difficulties in giving this general problem explicit content for Coleridge.

This would not vow us to the assertion that "you cannot understand 'The Ancient Mariner' unless you know of Coleridge's drug addiction and marriage problems." You can give a perfectly accurate account of its structure on the basis of the one poem alone. But in studying the full nature of a symbolic act you are entitled, if the material is available, to disclose also the things that the act is doing for the poet and no one else. Such private goads stimulate the artist, yet we may respond to imagery of guilt from totally different private goads of our own. We do not have to be drug addicts to respond to the guilt of a drug addict. The addiction is private, the guilt public. It is in such ways that the private and public areas of a symbolic act at once overlap and diverge. The recording has omitted some of these private ingredients, quite as it has omitted the exact personal way in which Coleridge recited the poem. If we happened to have liked Coleridge's "chaunt," this necessary omission from the stage directions for its recital is a loss; otherwise, it is a gain.

OTHER WORDS FOR ''SYMBOLIC''

It may have been noted that, while equating "symbolic" with "statistical," I also brought in another word: "representative." "Statistical" analysis discloses the ways in which a "symbolic" act is "representative," as Lady Macbeth's washing of her hands after the crime is "representative" of guilt. This moves us into the matter of synecdoche, the figure of speech wherein the part is used for the whole, the whole for the part, the container for the thing contained, the cause for the effect, the effect for the cause, etc. Simplest example: "twenty noses" for "twenty men."

The more I examine both the structure of poetry and the structure of human relations outside of poetry, the more I become convinced that this is the "basic" figure of speech, and that it occurs in many modes besides that of the formal trope. I feel it to be no mere accident of language that we use the same word for sensory, artistic, and political representation. A tree, for instance, is an infinity of events—and among these our senses abstract certain recordings which "represent" the tree. Nor is there any "illusion" here. In so far as we see correctly, and do not mistake something else for a tree, our perceptions *do really* represent the tree. Stress upon synecdochic representation is thus seen to be a necessary ingredient of a truly realistic philosophy (as against a naturalistic one, that would tend to consider our sensory representations as "illusory"). As to artistic representation, the term needs no further comment: the colors and forms in the painting of a tree *represent* the tree. In theories of politics prevailing at different periods in history, there have been quarrels as to the precise vessel of authority that is to be considered "representative" of the society as a whole (chief, nobles, monarch, churchmen, parliamentary delegates, poet, leader, the majority, the average, the propertied, or the propertyless, etc.) but all agree in assuming that there is *some* part representative of the whole,[2] hence fit to stand for it.

A "fetish," usually thought of as belonging in a totally

[2] Periods of social crisis occur when an authoritative class, whose purpose and ideals had been generally considered as *representative* of the total society's purposes and ideals, becomes considered as *antagonistic*. Their class character, once felt to be a *culminating* part of the whole, is now felt to be a *divisive* part of the whole.

different category, is thus seen likewise to be an aspect of the synecdochic function, as when the beloved's shoe is proxy for the beloved. The "scapegoat" becomes another kind of "representative," in serving as the symbolic vessel of certain burdens, which are ritualistically delegated to it. And as regards our speculations upon the nature of "clusters" or "equations," would it not follow that if there are, let us say, seven ingredients composing a cluster, any one of them could be treated as "representing" the rest? It is in this way that such an image as a "house" in a poem can become a "house plus," as it does proxy for the other ingredients that cluster about it (e. g., for the beloved that lives in the house, and is thus "identified" with it). Usually, several of these other ingredients will appear surrounding the one temporarily featured.

Our introduction of the word "identified" suggests also the importance of the *name* as an important aspect of synecdoche (the name as fetishistic representative of the named, as a very revealing part of the same cluster). Thus, such protagonists as "He," or "Man," or "The Poet," or Kafka's "K——" indicate by their very labeling a "problem of identity." And you will often find a change of identity, signalized by a change of name (the "Saul—Paul" reversal, or Coleridge's shift of epithets for his water snakes; Hitler speaks of his early period as a time when he and his group were "nameless," and he proclaims with exulting the later period when they "had names"). Such identification by name has a variant in change of clothes, or a change of surroundings in general, a change of "environmental clothes." [3] Such

[3] The thought suggests a possible interpretation of nudism as a symbolic divesting (unclothing) of guilt, a symbolic purification arrived at thus: (1) There has been the hiding of the shameful, hence the clothing of the pudenda as the "essence" of guilt; (2) the covering, as synecdochic representative of the covered,

investing by environment may sometimes enlist the very heavens, as with the change of identity in "The Ancient Mariner" as we move from suffering under the aegis of the Sun to release under the aegis of the Moon. In Aeschylus we have an equally thorough variant, when guilt is transformed into charity (i. e., the Erinyes are renamed the Eumenides).

The synecdochic function may also be revealed in the form of a poem, from the purely technical angle. If event 2, for instance, follows from event 1 and leads into event 3, each of these events may synecdochically represent the others (the interwovenness often being revealed objectively in such processes as "foreshadowing"). If the Albatross is put there to be killed, it could be said to "participate in the crime" in the sense that the savage, after a successful hunt, thanks the quarry for its coöperation in the enterprise. In being placed there as a "motivation" of the Mariner's guilt, its function as something-to-be-murdered is synonymous with its function as incitement-to-murder (recall that among the functions of synecdoche is the substitution of cause for effect and effect for cause). And since "the very deep did rot" as a result of this murder, the Albatross should be expected also to contain, implicitly, by foreshadowing, the substance of the water snakes that grew in this rot. This may explain why the Mariner, who was to kill the Albatross, fed it "biscuit worms" (in a later version this fatal incipience was obscured: "It ate the things it ne'er had eat"). In totemic thought, as in the communion service, consubstanti-

---

has come to participate in the same set of equations, taking on the same quality or essence, literally "by contagion"; (3) hence, by removing the clothes, one may at the same time ritualistically remove the shame of which the clothes are "representative." The resultant identity is a *social* one, in that the nudists form a colony, but of strongly naturalistic cast.

ality is got by the eating of food in common. "Tell me what you eat, and I'll tell you what you are." And in the "what you are" there is implicit the "what you will be." Thus, the Albatross names simultaneously its identity, its fate, and the outcome of that fate, in eating a food that is of the same substance as that fate and its outcome. The relation between the slain Albatross and the "thousand thousand slimy things" that grew out of its destruction may be disclosed by some lines from *Remorse,* where another variant of the metaphysical battle between good and evil (and behind it, the battle between the benign and malign effects of opium) is being fought. Ordonio, the villain, speaks:

> Say, I had laid a body in the sun!
> Well! in a month there swarms forth from the corse
> A thousand, nay, ten thousand sentient beings
> In place of that one man.—Say, I had killed him!
> Yet who shall tell me, that each one and all
> Of these ten thousand lives is not as happy,
> As that one life, which being push'd aside,
> Made room for these unnumbered—

Valdez interrupts: "O mere madness!" (we should also note that the epithet "happy" is also applied by the Mariner to the water snakes, as he impulsively sees them in their transubstantiated identity, their evil origin transcended into goodness).

To sum up, as illustration of the way in which these various terms could, for our purposes, all be brought together as aspects of synecdoche: A house lived in by a woman loved, would be "representative" of the woman who was "identified" with it (i. e., it would be in the same "associational cluster" or "set of equations"). As such, it could be a "fetishistic surrogate" for the woman. It could serve as "scapegoat" in that some forbidden impulse of the lover could be enacted vicariously in a "symbolic act" towards the house (as were she virginal, and were he impulsively to break the window in its door). The equations could be disclosed by a "statistical" analysis of the correlations within the imagery, establishing by objective citation "what goes with what." And formally, as foreshadowing in a poem, the breaking of a window at the opening of the poem might *implicitly* contain a scene of rape to be enacted later in the poem.

This last point might go far to explain the increasing proportion of *fragmentary* poems to be noted since the beginning of the nineteenth century. This we should attribute to an increased emphasis upon lyrical associationism, and a decreased emphasis upon rationally extricated dramatic plot (as most clearly revealed in the elaborate *intrigues* that are usually the basis of plot structure in the plays of Shakespeare). We could make the distinction clear in this way: Imagine an author who had laid out a five-act drama of the rational, intricate, intrigue sort—a situation that was wound up at the start, and was to be unwound, step by step, through the five successive acts. Imagine that this plot was scheduled, in Act V, to culminate in a scene of battle. Dramatic consistency would require the playwright to "foreshadow" this battle. Hence, in Act III, he might give us this battle incipiently, or implicitly, in a vigorous battle of words between the antagonists. But since there was much business still to be transacted, in unwinding the plot to its conclusion, he would treat Act III as a mere foreshadowing of Act V, and would proceed with his composition until the promises emergent in Act III had been fulfilled in Act V.

On the other hand, imagine a "lyric" plot that had reduced the intrigue business to a minimum. When the poet had completed Act III, his job would be ended, and despite his intention to write a work in five acts, he might very well feel a loss of inclination to continue into Acts IV and V. For the act of foreshadowing, in Act III, would already *implicitly contain* the culmination of the promises. The battle of words would itself be the *symbolic equivalent* of the mortal combat scheduled for Act V. Hence, it would *serve as surrogate* for the *quality* with which he had intended to end Act V, whereat the poet would have no good reason to continue further. He would "lose interest"—and precisely because the quality of Act V had been "telescoped" into the quality of Act III that foreshadowed it (and in foreshadowing it, was of the same substance or essence). Act III would be a kind of ejaculation too soon, with the purpose of the composition forthwith dwindling.

In *The World's Body,* John Crowe Ransom treats associationism as *dramatic,* citing Shakespeare as an example, in contrast with Donne. That is: Donne continues *one* conceit throughout a poem, whereas Shakespeare leaps about from one image to another, using each to deliver a quick blow and then shifting to fresh images, with none maintained over a long duration, or rationally exploited. It is a very acute and suggestive distinction—though I should want to interpret it differently. Shakespeare, I should say, had the rational intrigue, or business of his plot, as the basis of his consistency. This *permitted* him great shiftiness of imagery, as he tried to convey the quality of the action by views from various angles. Also, I will agree that, in a plot of this sort, the attempt to carry one conceit

31

throughout would be more of an encumbrance than a help. Since the plot itself provided the groundwork of consistency, the explicit riding of one image would attain the effect by excess, which would be tiresome.

Later lyricists (of the non-Donne sort) adopted the Shakespearean associationism while dropping its proper corrective: a plot of pronounced intrigue, or business. But I should want to place Donne in this pattern as follows: His exploitation of *one* metaphor throughout an entire poetic unit was the *equivalent,* in the lyric, for the *plottiness* of drama. It pledged the poet to much *rational business* in the unwinding of the poem's situation.

Thus, I should want to place Shakespeare, Donne, and the romantic lyric with relation to one another as follows: Shakespeare uses rational intrigue with associationism; Donne's lyric compensates for the loss of rational intrigue by using an equivalent, the business of exploiting one metaphor; the romantic lyric uses Shakespeare's associationism without either Shakespeare's or Donne's tactics of rational counterweighting. It is "free." However, we should also note that there usually is, even in the free associational procedure, some underlying "key" image that recurs in varying exploitations. Caroline Spurgeon's *Shakespeare's Imagery* has disclosed this practice as an important factor making for consistency of effect in the plays of Shakespeare. And Lane Cooper has done similar work on "The Ancient Mariner," showing the many overt and covert variants of the fixing, magnetic eye that prevail throughout the poem. The surprising thing about Lane Cooper's study, however, is that the critic seems to have been "disillusioned" by his own discovery. He tells of it in the accents of "indictment," where he could with more justice have employed the accents of admiration.

EQUATIONS ILLUSTRATED IN *GOLDEN BOY*

An especially convenient work to use as illustration of "cluster" or "equations" is Clifford Odets' *Golden Boy,* since it is formed about two opposed principles symbolized as an opposition between "violin" and "prizefight." The total dramatic agon is broken down, by analytic dissociation, into "violin" as the *symbol* of the protagonist and "prizefight" as the *symbol* of the antagonist, with the two symbols competing in an over-all coöperative act, as teams competitively work together to make a game. Here the equations are especially easy to observe, as you find, by statistically charting the course of the plot, that prizefight equals competition, cult of money, leaving home, getting the girl, while violin equals coöperative social unity, disdain of money, staying home, not needing the girl. Obviously, "prizefight" and "violin" don't mean that for all of us. But that is the way the clusters line up, within the conditions of the drama.

I do not wish, at this time, to attempt an exhaustive analysis of the interrelationships peculiar to Odets. I shall simply indicate the kind of "leads" I think one should follow, if he wanted to complete such a chart by "statistical" or "symbolic" analysis. At one point, Moody says: "Monica, if I had fifty bucks I'd buy myself a big juicy coffin—what?—so throw me in jail." Surely, such an unusual adjective for "coffin" would justify watching. Nothing may come of it; but it is worth noting as a "cue," a hunch that puts us vaguely on the track of something, and that may or may not materialize. Particularly in view of the fact that pre-

PHILOSOPHY OF LITERARY FORM

viously, when the boy's father had presented him with the violin, another character present had remarked: "It looks like a coffin for a baby." [4] Another character makes a speech that proceeds from talk of bad world conditions, to talk of spring, to talk of war, to: "Where's Joe? Did you give him the fiddle yet?" As a "first approximation," this sequence might indicate either that these various subjects "equal" one another, all being consistently part of the same cluster, or that some are compensatory to the others.

When we recall the prizefight-violin opposition, however, we get indications for a "closer approximation" here, as prizefight is in the war cluster by consistency, whereas violin is in the opposing cluster. So, at this point, the hunches begin to take form as follows: That the violin, in its relations to home (it was presented to the boy by his father, against whom his plans to be a fighter are a treachery, and Joe says: "You don't know what it means to sit around here and watch the months go ticking by! Do you think that's a life for a boy of my age? Tomorrow's my birthday! I change my life!"—a *vita nuova* in opposition to the father's ideals)—this violin is "tied up with" death to babies, quite as it is tied up with the continuity of life from preadolescence, a period of unity with sexual partner omitted.

Were we to trail down these interrelationships of the playwright's "psychic economy" further, we might, for statistical assistance, borrow help from his other plays. The antagonism between violin and prizefight, for instance, has a common agonistic ground in the fate of the boy's hand, which is broken in the prizefight, thus also ruining him as

[4] When someone gives a gift, one may well ask himself what the gift "represents." What is going from the giver to the receiver? What relationship between them is being identified? Or we might put it this way: If the gift were to be accompanied by a verbal compliment, what compliment would be most appropriate?

a violinist. We might then examine Odets' Nazi play for cues, since the theme of the crushed hand also figures there.

As for violin, much of the action in *Paradise Lost* takes place to the playing of music off stage. The correspondence between this music and other contents might be got by looking for some common quality of action or speech that runs through all the events on the stage concurrent with the playing off stage (including entrances or exits of characters, a kind of break that often supplies significant cues). Ideally, however, this relation would require us to dig out an explicit "pontification" in Odets that justified us, by objective "scissor-work," as against subjective interpretation, in treating the piano music of *Paradise Lost* as the equivalent of the violin in *Golden Boy*. (As, for instance, were a character to refer to a piano as a "key-fiddle" or to a violin as a "portable piano," or to speak of "fiddling around with the piano.") I leave this analysis unfinished, since I am not now attempting to make an exhaustive analysis of Odets, but simply to illustrate the rules of thumb by which it might proceed.

The "symbolism" of a word consists in the fact that no one quite uses the word in its mere dictionary sense. And the overtones of a usage are revealed "by the company it keeps" in the utterances of a given speaker or writer. Odets' "prizefight" is not Joe Louis's. If you tracked down all interrelations as revealed by the cluster in which a word has active membership, you would dissolve symbolism into an infinity of particulars. The "symbolic" attribute is like the title of a chapter; the particulars are like the details that fill out a chapter. The title is a kind of "first approximation"; the detailed filling-out a kind of "closer approximation."

LEVELS OF SYMBOLIC ACTION

The various levels of symbolic action that we might look for, in the analysis of poem as enactment, might be categorized as follows:

(1) The bodily or biological level. Kinaesthetic imagery. Symbolic acts of gripping, repelling, eating, excreting, sleeping, waking (insomnia), even and uneven rhythms (pace and puzzle, as tentative thought corresponds somewhat to the arhythmic movements of an experimenter's animal in an unfamiliar maze, while assertive thought corresponds to the thoroughly coördinated movements of an animal that has learned the workings of the maze, and proceeds to freedom without hesitancy).

We may also include sensory imagery here, with natural objects or events treated as replicas of corresponding mental states. Thus, no matter how concrete and realistic the details of a book, they may be found, when taken in the lump, to "symbolize" some over-all quality of experience, as growth, decay, drought, fixity, ice, desiccation, stability, etc. (Contrast the medieval liking for the architectural metaphor, or for the stable tree in familistic descent, with the "America on wheels" emphasis in *The Grapes of Wrath*.)

Note that, by employing such a "level of abstraction," we might properly group works as different in their concrete details as "The Ancient Mariner," *The Waste Land*, the Dos Passos trilogy, and *The Grapes of Wrath*. It should be noted, however, that such a procedure is critically truncated if it stops at the inclusion of various works in a common *genus*. It must proceed to the discussion of the *differentiae*. For it would be absurd, on noting the imagery of drought common to Eliot's poem and Steinbeck's novel, to conclude:

36

"*The Grapes of Wrath* is just *The Waste Land* over again." [5]

(2) The personal, intimate, familiar, familistic level. Relationships to father, mother, doctor, nurse, friends, etc. In the mention of the "family tree" above, we see how the sensory imagery may overlap upon this level. The levels are, in fact, but conveniences of discourse, for analytic purposes, and the actual event in a work of art usually contains an intermingling of them all. And since both a father and a state may be "authorities," we see how readily this personal level merges into a third,

(3) The abstract level. Here we move into the concern with the part played by *insignia* in poetic action, their use by the poet as ways of enrolling himself in a band. Sometimes this kind of symbolic act is explicit, as with "proletarian" school today, where the choice of a certain kind of hero is in itself a kind of "literary vote," a statement of one's "stand."

Sometimes this *"Bundschuh"* ingredient in art is but *implicit,* as with Pope's stylistic ways of enrolling himself with a new propertied class eager for "correctness." His neat couplet served stylistically to get everything "placed" for them; his poetry was perhaps the most sensitive "Book of Etiquette" ever written. It was a kind of "landscape gardening of the mind"—and in Edgar Johnson's *One Mighty Torrent* we get an almost startling picture of the change in symbolic enrollment that took place as we turned from this deft way of sitting on the lid to the romantic's blowing off the lid—as we turn from landscape gardening

[5] Kinaesthetic imagery is probably more active, sensory imagery ("impressions") more passive. At least, the latter has gained stress under modern sedentary conditions, and its percentage is greatly decreased in work songs and songs for people on the march.

of the mind, to an imagery of crags, chasms, volcanoes, earthquakes, cataracts, dizzying vistas, upheavals, and cataclysms.[6]

Here we get a symbolic proclaiming and formation of identity—while again, it is worthy of note, that the romantic movement tended greatly to conceive of man's identity in nonsocial, purely naturalistic terms, specializing in such objective imagery as would most directly correspond in quality with subjective states. It was "neoprimitive" in its notions of rôle, or identity, as against the strong emphasis upon the labels of social status in Pope.

The *formation* of rôle, however, involves, in its working out, a *transformation* of rôle. Even if one would symbolically form a rôle by becoming "most thoroughly and efficiently himself," he must slough off ingredients that are irrelevant to this purpose (ingredients that are "impure," if only in the chemical sense). So we watch, in the structural analysis of the symbolic act, not only the matter of "what equals what," but also the matter of "from what to what." And we detect, under various guises, the abandonment of an old self, in symbolic suicide, parricide, or prolicide.

Psychologists, particularly Otto Rank, have characterized this manifestation of art as the result of a "death wish." But I should contend that this interpretation is not "dialectical"

---

[6] Think of Joseph and Josephine, a married couple, engaged in a caricatured quarrel. Josephine, in anger, seizes a plate and sends it smashing to the floor. This may sober Joseph. He may say, "Come now. This is going too far. Let's try to contain ourselves and talk the matter over." In this he would speak with the voice of Pope and Pope's etiquette. Or Joseph might respond quite differently, by "transcending" the old rules, as he seized a dozen plates, muttering, "So that's what we're in for! Plate smashing! Very well—here's going you a lot better!" whereat he splintered the whole dozen, and did a very thorough job of it. Joseph here would speak with the voice of romanticism. He would change the rules, and burn out temptation by efficient excess of it. He would start himself and Josephine on an uncompromising journey "to the end of the line," as Josephine's rejoinder was to smash more efficiently still, and he in his repartee again outbid her, and so on, progressively.

enough. Look closer at poetic examples of the "death wish," and you will see that the symbolic slaying of an old self is complemented by the emergence of a new self. In fact, even though every action and person in the plot led downwards, we should find an assertion of identity in the constructive act of the poem itself. I should want to treat even suicide in real life as but the act of rebirth reduced to its simplest and most restricted form (its least complex idiom of expression).

But however one may feel about that point, the act of will in poetic organization justifies our claim that a *symbolic* suicide (on the page) is an *assertion,* the *building* of a rôle and not merely the abandonment of oneself to the disintegration of all rôles. True, the rôle that is so built may, by social tests, not be a very wholesome one—and in much contemporary art, introducing into the act of poetic construction itself an aesthetic of disintegration unmatched by an aesthetic of reintegration, we come close, even in the poem, to a "pure" suicide. Rather, we come *closer* than in most art of the past; but there is still an appreciable margin of difference, inherent in the act of composition itself. Implicit in poetic organization *per se* there is the assertion of an identity.

ASPECTS OF THE SCAPEGOAT IN REIDENTIFICATION

Since the symbolic transformation involves a sloughing off, you may expect to find some variant of killing in the work. (I treat indictment, vituperation, vindictiveness against a "villain," etc., as attenuated aspects of this same function.) So we get to the "scapegoat," the "representative" or "vessel" of certain unwanted evils, the sacrificial animal upon whose back the burden of these evils is ritualistically loaded. He becomes "charismatic" (if we may incongruously extend this word beyond the purely "benign" category into the "malign" category). We are now brought into the area of tragedy, the "goat-song"—and may profitably recall that, whereas in primitive societies, the purifying function could be ritualistically delegated to an animal, as societies grew in social complexity and sophistication, the tendency was to endow the sacrificial animal with social coördinates, so that the goat became replaced by the "sacrificial King."

This vessel, delegated to the rôle of sacrifice, must obviously be "worthy" of sacrifice. A few basic strategies for making him so may be listed:

(1) He may be made worthy legalistically (i. e., by making him an offender against legal or moral justice, so that he "deserves" what he gets).

(2) We may make him worthy by leading towards sacrifice fatalistically (as when we so point the arrows of the plot that the audience comes to think of him as a marked man, and so prepares itself to relinquish him). Portents, auguries, meteorological omens, and prophecies have regularly been thus used for functional purposes—while the transition into the sacrifice may often employ an intermingling of this second kind of worthiness with the first, as when the Greek dramatists reinforced the fatalistic operations with a personal flaw, *hubris,* punishable pride, the pride that goes before a fall.

(3) We may make him worthy by a subtle kind of poetic justice, in making the sacrificial vessel "too good for this world," hence of the *highest* value, hence the *most perfect* sacrifice (as with the Christ theme, and its secular variants, such as little Hanno Buddenbrooks, whose exceptional sen-

sitivity to music made him worthy to be sacrificed to music).

Incidentally, when thinking of the sacrificial vessel from this point of view, we get a much more charitable explanation of the Oedipus complex than is usually given in psychoanalytic doctrine. That is, we should not have to consider the child's dream of a parent's death as symbolizing simply the child's desire for the parent's removal, as a rival for affection. In many cases, at least, such a dream might well symbolize some *fear of personal disaster* on the child's part, while the child in its dream places the burden of this fear upon the protective parent, whose shoulders are more able to bear it (the parent having already become identified with such a protective rôle). Rivalries might also enter, to reinforce such a solution with "legalistic" or "rationalized" ingredients, without thereby being the sole ingredient in the recipe of motivation.

We should also note that a change of identity, *to be complete from the familistic point of view,* would require nothing less drastic than the *obliteration of one's whole past lineage.* A total rebirth would require a change of *substance;* and in the overlapping realm of familistic and causal ancestry ("like father like son" and the "genetic fallacy" of evaluating a thing in terms of its causal descent) a thorough job of symbolic rebirth would require the revision of one's ancestral past itself—quite as mystics hold that in becoming wholly transformed one not only can alter the course of the future but can even remake the past (the crudest act of this sort being such revision of the past as we get in official Nazi historiography). Hence, from this point of view, we might interpret symbolic parricide as simply an extension of symbolic suicide, a more thoroughgoing way of obliterating the substance of one's old identity

—while, as we have said before, this symbolic suicide itself would be but *one* step in a process which was not completed until the substance of the abandoned identity had been replaced by the new substance of a new identity. Hitler's voting himself a "blood stream" distinct from that of the Hebrew patriarchs is a symbolic transubstantiation of this sort—while an attentuated social variant of reidentification is to be seen in the legal adoption of a new family name, or in pseudonyms, *noms de plume,* secret lodge names, etc.

Applying such a calculus to the interpretation of symbolic incest in much modern literature, we should have cause to admonish against a view of it as simply the symbolization of incestuous desire. Sometimes it may well be just that. But until such an interpretation is forced upon us by many other aspects of the plot's imagery, we might do well to watch for a totally different possibility: that symbolic incest is often but a roundabout mode of self-engrossment, a narcissistic independence, quite likely at the decadent end of individualism, where the poet is but expressing in sexual imagery a pattern of thought that we might call simply "communion with the self," and is giving this state of mind concrete material body in the imagery of sexual cohabitation with someone "of the same substance" as the self.

Such an explanation seems particularly applicable to the plays of O'Neill prior to his return to the collective frame of the Catholic Church. In the earlier plays, as a *renegade* Catholic, he symbolized tangential states of mind, homeless individualists who had broken "free," and in the immaturity of their freedom were usually infused with satanism (the character that prays to the Dynamo in *Dynamo,* for instance, is but making obeisance to the Catholic Devil, thus materialistically refurbished). In *Marco Millions* there is a home-coming, but it is cynical and brutal; no adequate home. In *Mourning Becomes Electra* we see most clearly the ways in which symbolic incest merges into self-engrossment, with Lavinia at the end throwing out the flowers and closing the shutters, the thorough dramatization of a turning inwards. In *The Hairy Ape* we see this narcissistic quality, without the roundabout complications of symbolic incest, as the lonely, quarrelsome individual, Yank, on confronting the Hairy Ape (his *alter ego* who is but a drastically efficient reflection of himself), proclaims their identity of substance ("Ain't we both members of de same club—de Hairy Apes?"), gives the Ape the "secret grip" ("Come on, Brother. . . . Shake—de secret grip of our order")—whereupon the Ape embraces him ("Hey, I didn't say kiss me")—and in this embrace Yank dies. (We might here introduce, as relevant gloss on this death, a sentence from "Three Revolutions in Poetry," by Cleanth Brooks, Jr., *The Southern Review*, Autumn, 1935: "He [F. C. Prescott] shows that the verb 'to die' was used in the seventeenth century with the meaning 'to experience the consummation of the sexual act.' " The structure of the plot in *The Hairy Ape* gives cause to believe that O'Neill is drawing upon a similar ambiguity, though doubtless without any intention of borrowing from a seventeenth-century usage, or probably without even knowledge of it, but arriving at it by the same associated processes, linking bodily and mental events, through which the pun originally arose.)

The incest motif also appears in Joyce's recent work, *Finnegans Wake*. And here also I should want to interpret it not on its face value but as a narcissistic pattern dramatized in the idiom of sexual imagery. And I should be led

43

here to place this interpretation upon the imagery because of its bearing upon the whole nature of Joyce's aesthetic. Language, of all things, is most public, most collective, in its substance. Yet Joyce has methodically set about to produce a private language, a language that is, as far as possible, the sheer replica of inturning engrossments. His medium is of the identical substance with himself—and with this medium he communes, devoting his life to the study of its internalities. Hence, the whole quality of his efforts would admonish us to look for such union of same substance with same substance as would be perfectly conveyed in the imagery of incest. Joyce seems to have taken the last step into chemical perfection, by symbolizing a homosexual incest, the identity of substance thus gaining its ultimate symmetry.[7]

Applying in another way this same general strategy of motivation (i. e., interpreting the malign as an inferior idiom of the benign, rather than interpreting the benign as the malign deceptively refurbished): we might note that the elements which the scapegoat process draws upon seem to be variants of a response essentially *charitable*. I have in

---

[7] This theory might throw some light upon exogamy among primitive tribes, a practice accompanied by concepts of incest that seem to our culture arbitrary. The savage considers incestuous any cohabitation with anyone who shares his totem, though there is no blood relationship involved. It is almost as though we were to call it incest if a man and woman of the same church, lodge, or political party cohabited. Now, in primitive tribes the individual very closely identifies himself with all members of the clan having the same totem. The whole clan is "consubstantial." Hence, he could "avoid himself" only by copulation with the partaker of a different totemic substance. Sexual union with a member of his own totem would be a "cohabitation or communion with the self." However, this theory is not offered as an alternative to economic explanations of exogamy, but as a theory of the psychological processes that go with the economic ones. So also with the period of servitude that accompanied marriage into another clan. Such marriage would require a change of identity, hence the elements of regression and guilt that go with symbolic rebirth. And the period of servitude, explainable economically as a form of purchase, would function psychologically as a symbolic redemption of guilt.

mind the sense of *familistic consubstantiality* by which parents take personal gratification in noting the delight of their child, when the child has been given some plaything or is engrossed in some event. The child is at once *outside* them and *of* them, so that their pleasure by identification could not properly be called either wholly self-regarding or wholly extra-regarding. Their act is as much a *giving* as an *appropriation*. It is a giving *from* them, whatever may be its satisfactions *to* them.

Similarly, the delegation of one's burden to the sacrificial vessel of the scapegoat is a giving, a socialization, albeit the socialization of a loss, a transference of something, deeply within, devoutly a part of one's own self—and perhaps in its relation to consubstantiality it draws more from the attitude of child to parent than from the attitude of parent to child. It delegates the personal burden to an external bearer, yet the receiver of this burden possesses consubstantiality with the giver, a pontification that is contrived (where the scapegoat is the "bad" father) by objectively attributing one's own vices or temptations to the delegated vessel.

An *explicit ritual* of such transference may, paradoxically, often be the best way of protecting the individual from the deceptions of this pseudoscientific objectivity. For in explicit ritual, the vessel is *formally appointed;* but in its concealed pseudoscientific variants, where one's vices are simply "projected" upon the scapegoat, and taken literally to be an objective, absolute, nonfunctional, intrinsic attribute of the scapegoat (a "scientific fact" about the scapegoat's "true nature"), there is less incentive to *discounting*. A ritualistic scapegoat is felt both *to have* and *not to have* the character formally delegated to it—but a pseudoscientific scapegoat, endowed by "projection" without an explicit

45

avowal of the process, is felt purely and simply *to have* the assigned character. We may discount the ritualistic scapegoat by knowing that there is an element of mummery in the process of transference; but pseudoscientific projection suggests no discount: the scapegoat is taken to possess intrinsically the qualities we assign to it.

THE SACRIFICE AND THE KILL

We should also note an important ambiguity in the scapegoat as a "suppurating" device (that brings the evil "to a head"). I refer to an ambiguity of sacrifice and kill. In the sacrifice there is a kill; in the kill there is a sacrifice. But one or the other of this pair may be stressed as the "essence" of the two. Hemingway, for instance, stresses the *kill* in the purifying rôle played by the sacrificial animal, as against the stress upon the *sacrifice* in the story of Christ. In both Hemingway and Malraux we get the kill as the act from which the purified vision follows. (We may perceive the distinction by contrasting the assassination in the opening pages of "Man's Fate" with the slaying of the uncle in *Hamlet,* where the play deals with a *long and cautious preparation for the kill,* with insight dramatically deduced from the *initiation* rather than from the *act.* Perhaps *Macbeth* is closer to the contemporary emphasis, as *Hamlet* was closer to the modalities of liberalism; indeed, we might call Hamlet the "perfect liberal Christ" whose agony inaugurated the liberal era.)

In the pattern of the Crucifixion itself, we find Christ surrounded by two criminals. Should we treat this merely as an instance of what Trotsky would call an "amalgam" (i. e., a stratagem for visually and dramatically saying, in effect, "The so-called King of the Jews is to be put in the same class with men obviously and unequivocally criminal")? Or should we not, even if we hypothetically granted that this was the motivation on the part of the local authorities who were behind the crucifixion, attribute its duration throughout nearly two thousand years of tradition to a much more deep-lying appeal? To me, the design suggests a featuring of good, with the threat of evil about the edges (a dramatically or dialectically contrasting frame that "points up" the goodness by "polarity"). But in our contemporary modes, we often find the design retained with the positions reversed: in the "criminal Christs" of gangster stories and "hard-boiled" fiction, it is the evil that is featured, with promise of good as the frame. These various forms of disreputable character "die that we may live." And the Hemingway emphasis upon the kill implicit in the sacrifice seems to be a variant of this reversed design. The sacrificial bulls and wild game die in behalf of the slayer (dying that he may "live more intensely").[8]

We are now in the thick of the problem of criminality in general, as it applies to the devices of tragedy and puri-

[8] In *Attitudes Toward History* (Vol. II, footnote, pp. 13–15) I propose a distinction between "factional" and "universal" tragedy that has bearing upon the scapegoat device as employed in a *politicalized* setting. In comparing and contrasting Mann's early "universal" tragedy, *Death in Venice*, with his later factional tragedy, "Mario and the Magician" (where the guilt is not that of "Everyman," but is dissociatively relegated to the fascist enemy), I tried to show that the later work is the earlier one rewritten. In Aeschylus we seem to find this order of development reversed. It is in an earlier play, his *Persae*, that we find "factional" tragedy (the crime of *hubris* being attributed to Xerxes, the royal representative of the political enemy). Later, the crime is removed from a politicalized to a universalized setting, becoming the temptation of Everyman.

A critic has recently used a similar mode of analysis in a polemic article on Hemingway, noting that the Hemingway of the hunt and the bull-fight mode shared sympathetically in the misfortunes of the sacrificed, whereas in his later political mode the fascist enemy takes over the rôle of quarry, and the poet confronts them from without, wholly antagonistically. By this approach, the political opposition becomes interpreted as a mere "rationalization" of cruelty, a façade of social purpose concealing in more "justified" guise the same sadistic impulses.

The whole problem of the scapegoat, I submit, is still not charted thoroughly

fication. A tragedy is not profound unless the poet *imagines* the crime—and in thus imagining it, he symbolically commits it. Similarly, in so far as the audience participates in the imaginings, it also participates in the offense. So we get Mann's "sympathy with the abyss," Gide's suggestion that in "thou shalt not" there is implicit "what would happen if . . . ," Hopkins' "tykishness," or Goethe's statement that the poet contains the capacity for all crime. We also discern the same concern behind Coleridge's distinction between "innocence" and "virtue," with the latter and more mature of these two states being possible only by reason of temptation.

However, though we may say that the tragic dramatist, to write an ideal tragedy, must meet the crime halfway (or that no work on the Crucifixion is complete unless the poet and the audience vicariously assist in the crucifying), this is far from vowing us to a simple psychoanalytic interpretation to the effect that the poet merely "sublimates" his

---

enough to be exploited thus simply for polemic or vindictive ends. At least, not until the critic has explicitly stated and explicitly disposed of an alternative account, that might run thus: The poet, in enlisting his services in the cause of the Loyalists in Spain, had perfectly rational grounds for his choice; but in the course of elaborating a poetic act that symbolized this enlistment, he necessarily drew on methods he had developed in the past. The selection of the fascist as enemy scapegoat would, by this interpretation, be not "rationalized" (in the psychoanalytic sense of the term), but *rational*. That is, the fascist was, in the most objective sense of the term, an enemy.

The matter is further complicated, in the religious sphere, by the fact that, whereas on its face, the emphasis upon the sacrifice is much superior to the emphasis upon the kill, in the dialectic of concrete historical situations important matters of *insignia* figure. Both history and anthropology supply us with plenty of instances in which a priesthood has exploited the sounder method for malign purposes (in consciously or unconsciously so interweaving it with essentially unrelated structures of ownership and special privilege that in actual practice its function becomes the very reverse of a religious one). The result is alienation and anguish that may lead, by the simplifications of dialectical pressure, to the adoption of a counter-method (saying in effect, in the words with which Virginia Woolf ended an early story: "You go this way; alas! I go that"). When the Devil quotes scripture, poets try to avoid the ambiguity by a Black Mass (B having replaced A, they would make amends by having A replace B).

criminality by aesthetic subterfuge. I have seen consterna-
tion on people's faces, for instance, when I have suggested
that Mann contains within his work all the errors to which
the Nazis are prone. The remark is but preparation for a
very important revision, namely: *He contains them, but
encompasses them within a wider frame—and as so encompassed, they act entirely differently than they would if "efficiently" isolated in their "purity."* They are but part of
a wider configuration, and their function in this wider configuration is not at all the same function as they would have,
if not thus harnessed.[9]

Obviously, vicarious crime requires vicarious modes of
expiation. William Troy has called attention to the fact
that, in the case of Lawrence, the score is settled by the

[9] There is, however, a pattern in Mann's work that must increasingly give him
trouble, if he continues with the Joseph story. I refer to the nature of his irony,
which is most clearly revealed in his early story, "Tonio Kröger." Here the form
is constructed about a flat antithesis between "bourgeois" and "Bohemian," with
Tonio Kröger's sympathies directly contrary to his position. When he is among
the burghers, he thinks yearningly of Bohemia; when he is among the Bohemians,
his nostalgic vote is for the burghers.

Applying this ironic ambiguity to Mann's present situation, we are led to
suspect a predicament of this sort: That Mann would be more likely to continue
his Joseph story from an anti-Nazi point of view if he had remained in Germany
than in his present situation as exile. For in so far as the Tonio Kröger pattern
of irony is characteristic of his method, his situation as an exile would dispose
him towards a greater measure of interpretation from the Nazi point of view; i. e.,
with an *anti-Semitic* emphasis.

Whatever may be Mann's method as an imaginative writer, however, we know
that, as a citizen, a critic, a writer of hortatory political pamphlets, he is wholly
the liberal in his attitude towards anti-Semitism. Hence, he would seem to have
a choice between leaving the Joseph story unfinished or radically altering his
characteristic mode of irony this late in life (for it is unthinkable that he would
consent to go on with the story in terms of a Nazi perspective). Incidentally, since
I first thought of this problem in strategy, I have been told that Mann has written
a piece to "Bruder Hitler" (which would be translatable, in our present co-
ordination, as "consubstantial Hitler"). I have not seen the piece, and the rumor
may be inaccurate, but the rumor goes that it is written in a mood of amicable
cajolery. If this is the case, it would seem to be an attempt, on Mann's part, to
retain his earlier pattern while modifying it for the exigencies of his present
situation. Another response may be noted in his turn to *The Beloved Returns*,
a theme politically ambiguous, in that Goethe's love affair can be shared by
Nazis and anti-Nazis alike.

poet's offering of himself as the victim, as sacrificial king-god (which is more commendable as efficiency than as modesty). I have heard a writer of fiction state a somewhat similar aesthetic position; it is her task, she told me, to undergo great discomfort in the pains of composition, that readers may in their reading be comforted.

Another variant is seen in the many strategies of satanism, the "Byronic" line that we see emerging in Milton, and that is handed down through Coleridge, Poe, Baudelaire, Rimbaud, and Gide (with novelists like Stendhal and Dostoevsky also to be included). Its purest form is perhaps revealed in the old heresy of the Iscariotae, who maintained that Judas, rather than Christ, should be our primary object of worship; for if the human race was given the possibility of redemption by the sacrifice of Christ, it was Judas' act of betrayal that brought about this sacrifice—and Christ is now with the Father, whereas Judas, for his rôle in the redemption of man, damned himself to rot in eternal hell. Gide's ingeniously perverted scrupulosity has perhaps given us some of the most interesting variations on this theme, culminating in his great sympathy with the *fils naturel* as the ideal type (the man of guilt-laden substance, like Lafcadio, whose father is vague, but whose mother was on surprisingly intimate terms with a surprisingly large number of "uncles"—precisely the familistic rôle that the Elizabethans, with their strong sense of feudalistic identity, would select for their "villains").

Perhaps the most normal mode of expiation is that of socialization (the "socialization of losses"). So the church founded the notion of brotherhood on the concept of original sin, the preoccupational basis of a guild of the guilty (such expressions as "misery loves company," "all in the same boat," "all doing the same" will suggest the motivating basis here). And the patriot may slay for his country, his act being exonerated by the justice of serving his group. I do not see how we could categorically accept or reject the strategy of expiation by the socialization of losses. In different concrete social textures, there are different modes of such socialization, with varying degrees of accuracy and scope. The gangster who slays an informer to protect his gang (i. e., out of *loyalty*) enacts this strategy just as truly as would the revolutionary emancipator, like Washington or Lenin. Thus, the strategy could not be categorically approved or condemned, but would require a place in a ladder or *hierarchy* of such strategies.[10]

THE CONCEALED OFFENSE

There are many depths still to be plumbed, in bringing up for conscious observation the many modes of criminality hidden beneath the surface of art (criminality, I repeat, that is not, in mature works, merely a criminal tendency re-

[10] In Schumann, we see a variant of the socializing strategy, in his fiction of a Bund, the *Davidsbündler*, in league with him against the Philistines. Here he socialized his sense of persecution by the notion of an imaginary union against a common enemy. Subsequently, in nervous exhaustion, he fell under the obsession of one relentlessly persistent note that pursued him like a gadfly, never ceasing its drastic oneness. (As the sacred syllable AUM was felt, by the mystic, to sum up all existence in a benign oneness, so we got here a reversed malign counterpart, concentrating all evil into a single vessel of sound.) In anguish, he turned to self-destruction, his own disintegration being the only "solution" for such perfect integration on the part of "the enemy."

Mystic theories of immediate communion between the Self as microcosm and the Universe as macrocosm (between the Self as a Universe *in parvo* and the Universe as the Self writ large) may lead to another variant of malignity in the socializing strategy. Where this communion is *direct* (i. e., felt to be without the intervention of institutions or other persons) we may get, through merger of subject and object, a merging of the two "secrets," the secret of the unutterable Self and the Enigma of the Universe. Here the vessel of the private secret has intercourse with the vessel of the universal secret. Hence, the Universe being conceived after the analogy of the private Self, and the private secret being guilt-laden, the Universe itself may become guilt-laden.

pressed by social norms and gratified by aesthetic subterfuge, but is actually *transformed, transcended, transubstantiated,* by incorporation into a wider context of symbolic action). Occasionally I seem to detect it behind a kind of unconscious punning in language, particularly where an author could supply directer words than the ones he uses, but encounters both external and internal resistance to their use. I might get at the point in this wise:

Recall the use of *ablaut* in the work of Hopkins: that is, the retaining of a fixed consonantal structure, with a variation of the vowels (*ablaut* referring in grammar to such transformations as "sing, sang, sung," where the change of vowel, in the unchanged consonantal structure, indicates a change in grammatical function with constancy of over-all meaning). There is also a relevant passage in Coleridge's *Table Talk,* where he says that the consonants are "the framework of the word," and cites an example of a simple shorthand, understandable without vowels: "Gd crtd th hvn nd th rth." We may also borrow a reference for our purposes from *The American Language,* the section of "Forbidden Words," where Mencken lists the Hollywood device for pronouncing the "four-letter words" euphemistically "by changing the vowel of each to *e* and inserting *r* after it," a phonetic alchemy for instance by which "nuts" became "nerts." Our point is difficult to make, however, since pudency forces us to employ circumlocutions in place of direct illustrations—but one may detect the kind of punning we have in mind in observing a passage from *The Hairy Ape,* where Yank is reminiscing on his hateful lusting after Mildred, and exclaims: "I'll fix her!" Altering the vowel experimentally by *ablaut,* we may with a little patience and not too innocent a past, come close upon a socially forbidden form that expresses perfectly the attitude of the character, "Yank," who had thrown his shovel at the girl.

Let us, however, illustrate the point by an elaborate and unwieldy subterfuge. Let us imagine that there is a socially forbidden four-letter word, "hivn." By the Hollywood device for euphemism, this could be refurbished with immunity as "hervn." But might a writer carry such subterfuge a step further, by *ablaut* punning, and when in his attitudes he meant "You are a very hivn," might he say actually, recording this upon his linguistic façade as, "You are heavenly"? [11]

The possibility of such concealed punning, where the pun is not however based on a tonal correspondence, may be glimpsed in the passage on the blessing of the snakes in "The Ancient Mariner." Where the objects of this act reveal such ambiguity, might we not look for a corresponding ambiguity in the act itself? That is: can one have an ambiguous object of a verb without having a corresponding ambiguity in the verb itself? Hence, might an act of blessing not be merely the act that is proclaimed on its face, but also contain an ingredient whereby the blessing was something quite different from a blessing? This possibility gains in precision where, in *Remorse,* Ordonio, the vessel of the malign, says to Alvar, the vessel of the benign: "Curse me with forgiveness." Following out this pattern, if "forgiveness" equals "curse," would not "bless" equal "accuse"? [12]

[11] Incidentally, several days after having made up this hypothetical illustration, I suddenly recalled an early story of mine, of mildly satanistic cast, in which I had named the protagonist "Ivn." At the time I had no idea whatsoever why this sound seemed to me appropriate. I believe that the above elucubrations reveal what was going on, in that apparently arbitrary construction of a name.

[12] Hawthorne, in *The Scarlet Letter,* touches upon the same ambiguity when he writes, of Hester Prynne: "She was patient,—a martyr indeed—but she forbore to pray for her enemies; lest, in spite of her forgiving aspirations, the words of the blessing should stubbornly twist themselves into a curse." We also

A prayer is a strategy for taking up the slack between what is wanted and what is got. Hence, a "prayerful" sanction implies that the thing sanctioned by the prayer is thus impulsively sanctioned because it is *not* of the essence prayerfully attributed to it. A new essence is being *delegated* to it; it is being ritualistically ordained as member in a new cluster because of the fact that it is not naturally a member of this cluster. Hence, in the ordination there is implied a recognition of its tendency to "fall" from the rôle assigned to it. If Coleridge's drug were an important ingredient in the evil thus being "blessed," we could well account for the ambiguity of the "blessing." For however thorough its *ritualistic* redemption might be, the fact remained that, in its material identity, it retained the full malignity of its effects.

However, there are two kinds of "unutterable," the unutterably good as well as the unutterably bad, with an ambiguous area containing something of both. We may recall the vast collation of material on this subject in Frazer's *Golden Bough,* illustrating the various linguistic subterfuges used by savages to avoid pronouncing the names of Kings, of certain socially superior relatives, and of the deceased. The process of circumlocution is frequently carried out with such thoroughness that, if the deceased happened to bear the name of some natural object, the tribe must rename this object, with the result that the tribal idiom is constantly changing, with a much higher percentage of neologisms than we find in sophisticated Western vocabularies where the invention of new words has been necessary for naming the many new objects, processes, and relation-

---

find the same kind of scruples lurking behind the motivations of religious sectarians who refuse to *swear* an *oath*, sensing the profanation behind the act, as implicit in the double usage of these two words themselves.

ships resulting from the industrial revolution. Frazer also points out that not only were the *same* words to be avoided, but words *similar* in tonality, or words in which the name appeared as an ingredient (as if the King or the deceased were named "cat," and we were accordingly to avoid the word "con*cat*enation").

The Latin *sacer*, we may recall, did not correspond simply to our word "sacred." The criminal was *sacer* (an **ambiguity** that was at least retained in the vocabulary of action if not that of explicit linguistic usage, as we see it in the "rite of sanctuary" whereby a fugitive from the law could not be molested while under the protection of the altar, or perhaps in the design of the Crucifixion, with Christ surrounded by thieves). *Sacer* might thus be more accurately translated as "untouchable," since the extremely good, the extremely bad, and the extremely powerful are equally "untouchable."

Or better still, we might use simply our word "power," for "power" suggests the motive behind "untouchability" itself, and contains the same ambiguity, as with the powers of electricity, that are "good" if properly channelized, but are "bad" if one does not guard himself against contact with them. Power is ambivalent, though we have in recent years seen philosophic attempts to proclaim either absolute goodness or absolute badness as the "essence" of power. Dewey's instrumentalism, equating technology with "good" (via the steps: [1] technology is intelligent; and [2] intelligence is a "good"), illustrates the first kind of essentializing; Russell seems recently to have voted for the contrary essentialization. The theme of fascination in Coleridge's Mystery Poems is that of an ambivalent power. He gives us, as it were, a poetic thesaurus dictionary of terms ranging from thoroughly "good" fascination to thoroughly "bad" fascination.

55

The name of Jehovah was "unspeakable," for it represented the Almighty Power. In Greek it was called the "Tetragrammaton," which by a cunning, punning accident means "four-letter word." And we find an interesting variant of such verbal deflection in Silone's *Bread and Wine,* where one character always refers to Mussolini obliquely as "Etc."

Freud has given us the classic study of the "bad" pun, including not merely the explicit verbal pun but the implicit pun, where the dream enacts the pun as in charades. He has dealt with the many variants of the *lapsus linguae* whereby, in giving A the name of B, we reveal that for us A is a representative of B. I would contend that he has overstressed the element of "suppressed desire" in such analogizing. We need not give A the name of B simply because we *want* him to enact the rôle that we attribute to B; we may also *fear* that his person is in the same bin as B's. Or we may simply be strongly convinced that his rôle is like B's rôle (in situations where the sameness of essence, even if true, would cause us neither gratification nor discomfort—as were we to think B a harmless bore, and were *implicitly* to call A a harmless bore by "erroneously" calling him B).

What I am trying to get at is this: the "bad" pun (arising from a conflict of impulses where one states an attitude despite himself) is the kind most amenable to study. But should we not look for "benignities" that correspond to such "malignities"? Should there not also be "good" puns? As there are cases where we, in roundabout ways, pronounce the unutterable "four-letter-words," might there not be corresponding cases where we, in roundabout ways, pronounce the unutterable "Tetragrammaton"?

Let us begin with an instance where the name of God is uttered (the Christian God being *kindly* in essence, as against the ambivalence of Jehovah as a "power god," His name is not in the pure unutterable class, and it is only in neurotics and the intensely religious that we find the unutterability of the Secret stressed—the "hermetic" styles of post-War poetry being our nearest aesthetic variant of this):

I recall a prayer, learned in childhood, which ran

> God loving me
> Guard me in sleep
> Guide me to Thee,

where, if we test this by the Hopkins method of *ablaut* punning, we find that the verbs of lines two and three, predicates of the noun in line one, merely restate the noun, thus:

> G——d
> G——d
> G——d.

In sum: "to guard" and "to guide" are pun-conjugations of the verb, "to god." I should thus here treat "guard" and "guide" as "god-words" in the psychic economy of the person who wrote this prayer. And if I knew who the writer was, and had other writings by him, I should inspect them from the standpoint of the possibility that "guard" and "guide" as used by him in other contexts were also roundabout ways of saying "God" (and possibly "forbidden" ways —as he might be saying "God" in contexts where his auditors would object if he explicitly motivated his statement by this "ground of proof").

If such correlations are true, however, we must be able to substantiate them by objective citation of contexts. An explicit slip of the tongue occurs when two conflicting notes are struck simultaneously, as with a chord in music. But in most cases there is no slip of the tongue; the two elements are drawn out in narrative sequence, as when the notes in a musical chord are not struck simultaneously, but in succession, in arpeggio, as you proceed from one subject to the other.

My favorite instance is that of Senator Carter Glass, who in his "inspired" defense of the gold standard would give us progression from talk of "gold" to talk of "God" (again our g——d structure with *ablaut*).

We have several stages "along the spectrum of yellow." We have excremental yellow (as in "yellow journalism"); we have its first transcendence in the "yellow metal"; we have its second transcendence in the yellow of sunlight; and its ultimate transcendence in that "super-radiance" of divinity, the blinding essence of light that infused Dante's heaven, making sunlight itself seem by comparison a shadow. Typical Freudian exegesis would "reduce" all these to the kind of "forbiddenness" that is contained in the taboos of stage one. Our method would require us to judge by the contexts alone. If "God" is but a circus front for "gold," this fact will be revealed by examining the author's work; and if "God" is imaginatively slighted and "gold" filled out with imaginative fullness, we may take "gold" as the essence and "God" as the accident. If we wished to reduce "gold" in turn to its lowest stage as "essence," we should have to reveal the *double-entendres* at every turn (as were we to show that certain pleas for "gold" make more sense if read as pleas for its "transcendence downward").

To sum up: if A is in the same chordal structure with B and C, its kindred membership must be revealed by narrative arpeggios. That is, its function as an associate will be revealed by associational progressions in the work itself (as you find a progression from A to B to C in one place, from A to C to B in another, from B to A in another, etc.). The *ambivalent* notion of *sacer* will be more fruitful for leads here than a less dialectical essentializing that reduces the whole matter of the ambivalence in the forbidden to either a "good" or "bad" alone. And the analysis of equational structures within a work should reveal terms that "represent" sometimes one, sometimes the other, of the two principles, as dissociated, and sometimes their interlocking, as Coleridge says of Prometheus: "Prometheus, in the old myths, and for the most part in Aeschylus, is the Redeemer and the devil jumbled together," a statement he repeats the other way round when discussing the Book of Job: "Satan, in the prologue, does not mean the devil, our Diabolus. There is no calumny in his words. He is rather the *circuitor,* the accusing spirit, a dramatic attorney-general."

As religions mature, there is the tendency to dissociate the ambivalence of power, by dramatic analysis, into a "good" principle vs. an "evil" principle. But there is a technical problem implicit in this very act of dissociation. For the dissociated principles could not come to grips without some ground common to both; and in this common ground the ambivalent factor is restored. We may glimpse the process behind the rôle of Milton's Satan. The Greek Lucifer had brought to man a part of divinity, but had brought it *divisively,* as an offense against the gods. In the Christian cosmology, Christ had become revised as an unambiguously benign Lucifer, bringing light as a *representative* of the Godhead. Thus the divisive part had become the synecdochic part: a part not broken from its source, but integral

59

with its source. Milton's rebellious angel, in his tendency to become a hero, moves us back into the original ambiguity, where the part fluctuates between its dialectical poles as associate and dissociate of the whole. A dissociate part might be called negatively synecdochic (as the villain is a negative representation of the hero). As an angel, Lucifer is in synecdochic relationship with God (i. e., he is a "messenger"). As a rebel, he is in negatively synecdochic relationship.

BEAUTY AND THE SUBLIME

I should now like to draw these various remarks on tragedy, sacrifice, the kill, criminality, and obscenity together by reference to a theory of beauty. If we placed a certain lozenge-like design on a cake, and called it "beautiful," we should mean by the epithet such kind of "beauty" as would be in the same bin with "pretty," "pleasant," and "appealing." If, however, we found this same lozenge-like design on a rattlesnake, and overcame our terror sufficiently to pronounce an aesthetic judgment upon it, we might again call it "beautiful," but the epithet would here be in the same bin with "sinister," "ominous," "dangerously fascinating." And were it on a woman's scarf, we should veer towards one or the other of these qualities, depending upon our attitude towards the woman herself (whether we thought of her as "likable" or as "fascinating").

The distinction is offered as a way of suggesting that the whole subject of "beauty" became obscured in much aesthetic theory of the nineteenth century because it tended to start from notions of *decoration* rather than from notions of the *sublime*. There are many possible ingredients behind this motivation, among them being the fact that aesthetic theorizing was largely done *by* people in comfortable situations *for* people in comfortable situations. But there is a subtler factor operating here: poetry *is* produced for purposes of comfort, as part of the *consolatio philosophiae*. It is undertaken as *equipment for living*, as a ritualistic way of arming us to confront perplexities and risks. It would *protect* us.

Let us remind ourselves, however, that implicit in the idea of protection there is the idea of something to be *protected against*. Hence, to analyze the element of *comfort* in beauty, without false emphasis, we must be less monistic, more "dialectical," in that we include also, as an important aspect of the recipe, the element of *discomfort* (actual or threatened) for which the poetry is "medicine," therapeutic or prophylactic. And I submit that if we retraced the course of aesthetic speculation, until we came to its earlier mode, we should get a much more accurate description of what is going on in poetry. I refer to the time when the discussion explicitly pivoted about the distinction between the *ridiculous* and the *sublime*.

As soon as we approach the subject in these terms, we have in the very terms themselves a constant reminder that the *threat* is the basis of beauty. Some vastness of magnitude, power, or distance, disproportionate to ourselves, is "sublime." We recognize it with awe. We find it dangerous in its fascination. And we equip ourselves to confront it by piety, by stylistic medicine, and by structural assertion (form, a public matter that symbolically enrolls us with allies who will share the burdens with us). The ridiculous, on the contrary, equips us by impiety, as we refuse to allow the threat its authority: we rebel, and courageously play pranks when "acts of God" themselves are oppressing us (as with the many courageous jests that the farmers of the Dust Bowl invented,

61

to cancel off the dread of earthen clouds sifting through the cracks of their windows, into their rooms, into their very lungs and flesh).

Should we not begin with this as our way into the subject —treating all other manifestations of symbolic action as *attenuated variants* of pious awe (the sublime) and impious rebellion (the ridiculous)? The paternity is clear enough in works that depict either the ominousness of war or the fun-making of soldiers. We discern it behind the social phenomenon called "earthquake love," at the time of San Francisco's disaster, when the whole city was for a time unified in brotherly exaltation by the common danger—while we had a chance to see the contrary response in the many humorous anecdotes following the tremor in New York a few years ago. Or we got a record of the two responses recently, when the radio hoax of the great "Martian invasion" divided the listeners into piously terrorized and the impious sophisticates.

We move into attenuated areas as we depart from manifestations of divine, natural, or astronomical powers to social aspects of authority: with kings and heroes partaking of both, and commercial or parliamentary figures, insignia of social classes, and the like leading us farther afield, into purely secular aspects of admiration and disobedience. We grasp the aesthetic motivation behind Corneille's tragedies of "admiration," and behind the satyr-plays in which the Greeks topped off their trilogies of pious awe by burlesques that depicted the great legendary heroes as buffoons and boastful asses. As we move into the aesthetic of social realism, and thence into naturalism, the "dangers" become those of hypocrisy, smugness, outworn tradition, material interests pumped up into idealistic balloons, wrong but powerful, with impiety taking the form of "indictment" and "debunking."

Recalling that a founder of modern aesthetic theory, Lessing, built his speculations about the snake-entangled Laocoön group, why should we not take this "underlying situation" into account as an important aspect of his doctrines? (For should we not always consider a work's starting point as a significant "lead" into our interpretation of the work's motivation? Thus, similarly, I would have the *Decameron* read, not as a series of hilarious stories, but as a series of hilarious stories *told during a plague*.) And we see Coleridge, among the greatest critics of world literature, likening the work of Shakespeare to the movements of a serpent, while in "The Ancient Mariner," a poem explicitly of fascination and terror, we have that fatal moment of re-creation when the loathsome water snakes are proclaimed blessed and beautiful.

The story of Orpheus and his voyage to Hades has much to tell us about the ways of poetry. But a still more basic myth, it seems to me, is that of Perseus and the Medusa— Perseus who could not face the serpent-headed monster without being turned to stone, but was immune to this danger if he observed it by reflection in a mirror. The poet's style, his form (a social idiom), is this mirror, enabling him to confront the risk, but by the protection of an indirect reflection. Begin with this, I suggest, and look at the many aspects of poetic expression as but departures from it, watered, or toned down, or farther from the center, but all best analyzed as attenuations of the sublime-ridiculous problem, rather than as idioms wholly disrelated to it.

As there is the sublime serpent of beauty, so there is also the sublime serpent of wisdom, thus restoring us, via the

63

sublime, to a unitary approach. However, it will force no "oversimplifications" upon you. You will not have to "analogize" (in saying that B is A because B has an ingredient in common with A or that B can serve synecdochically as representative of A). You can make all the subdistinctions of multiple motivation you want whereby you can avoid the necessity of treating some haphazard news report in the same bin with *Lear*. But by starting with "the sublime and the ridiculous," rather than with "beauty," you place yourself forthwith into the realm of the *act,* whereas "beauty" turns out to be too *inert* in its connotations, leading us rather to overstress the *scene* in which the act takes place. Confronting the poetic act in terms of "beauty," we are disposed to commit one or another of two heretical overemphases: either we seek to locate beauty in the object, as scene, or by dialectical overcompensation we seek to locate it in the subject, as agent. Confronting the poetic act in terms of the sublime and the ridiculous, we are disposed to think of the issue *in terms of a situation and a strategy for confronting or encompassing that situation,* a scene and an act, with each possessing its own genius, but the two fields interwoven.

The poet is, indeed, a "medicine man." But the situations for which he offers his stylistic medicine may be very real ones. Often, he so takes the situation for granted that his poem is almost wholly devoted to the working out of a strategy for its encompassment (this may be the state of affairs that leads some critics to understress the situational ingredient in his work, treating the work as a kind of *attitude without content*). But it is only in so far as his situation overlaps upon our situation, that his strategy of encompassment is felt by us to be relevant.

As "medicine man," he deals with "poisons." (Foods, drugs, medicines, and poisons are all to be stretched along a single series of gradients, for if you do not think that bread is a poison, try eating a barrel of it, while the whole theory of homoeopathy, so close to "homoeopathic magic," is based upon a technique for transforming poisons into medicines by attenuation of the dose). The poet, in his pious or tragic rôle, would immunize us by stylistically infecting us with the disease. As we move towards the impious response, on the other hand, we get an "allopathic" strategy of cure. We get the recourse to "antidote." The medical analogy may be justified by authority, as it has been employed in similar contexts by both a critic and a poet. I refer to Frazer's study of "homoeopathic magic" and to the opening lines of Milton's preface to *Samson Agonistes*:

> Tragedy, as it was anciently composed, hath ever been held the gravest, moralest, and most profitable of all other poems; therefore said by Aristotle to be of power, by raising pity and fear, or terror, to purge the mind of those and such-like passions—that is, to temper and reduce them to just measure with a kind of delight, stirred up by reading or seeing their passions well imitated. Nor is Nature wanting in her own effects to make good his assertion; for so, in physic, things of melancholic hue and quality are used against melancholy, sour against sour, salt to remove salt humours.

I might terminate this aspect of the discussion by a brave suggestion. In these utilitarian days, pure science must earn its way by serving applied science. So I shall try to "justify" my theory by showing that it might become "gainfully employed." In Hollywood, when a new star is found, the experts in publicity are charged with the duty of finding her a winsome name. Over the years, a happy choice may mean a difference of hundreds of thousands of dollars in box office receipts. Here is where my theory enters. I propose that the experts proceed as follows:

I propose that they select some "poisonous" word—some one of the many repellent "four-letter words" that are socially forbidden, owing to one or another kind of unpleasantness they suggest. Then I would have the experts experiment with slight transformations of this word, until they had produced a structure in which the original repellent word was retained as a barely audible overtone, flickering about its edges. I submit that, to an auditor who did not know the genesis of this word, but who did know and dislike the word from which it had been derived, this new synthetic product would be "exceptionally beautiful." [13]

ON METHODOLOGY

A critic's perspective implicitly selects a set of questions that the critic considers to be key questions. We usually think of *answers* as the primary pointers of direction in a conceptual writer's work; actually however the point about

[13] Phonetically, *m* is closely related to *p*, both being labials—and *k* is closely related to *r*, both being gutturals (the guttural relationship being closer in French *r* than in English *r*). But *m* is smoother than *p*, and *r* is smoother than *k*. "Molière," by this analysis, is seen as an acrostic of "Poquelin," with the nasal omitted. Molière's beautiful pseudonym is a revision of his original surname, in the direction of much greater musicality. "Poquelin," to be sure, is not an oath; but it is certainly unpleasant as compared with its phonetic revision—and the quality of Moliere's mind, with the intense melancholy underlying his comic genius, gives us good ground to suspect that "Poquelin" was identified with an unliked aspect of himself. We should place him in a category of writers-at-cross-purposes with Flaubert, who flayed "Bovary" and "Bouvard," names surprisingly like acrostics of "Flaubert," when we recalled that *v* is but a voiced *f*.

which the differences in critical schools pivot is not in answers, but in questions.

All questions are leading questions. For instance, suppose that you wanted to weaken a statesman's reputation in the most "scientific" manner. A very good method would be to found some bureau for the polling of public opinion, and to send forth investigators armed with questions that constantly harped upon the matter of the man's integrity. They would not have to be "leading questions" in the obvious sense. They would need no "weighting" other than the weighting implicit in the choice of topic itself. The man's integrity, which might otherwise have been taken for granted, becomes a "problem." Even those who come to his defense must, in this very act, themselves help to emphasize the element of doubtfulness. A dubious name is a name half ill, and "He that hath an ill name is half hanged."

Questions harping on the subject of personal integrity would have another "creative" function. They would automatically select the field of controversy—hence, they would automatically deflect the attention from other possible fields of controversy. Questions might have been asked, for instance, that bore wholly on the *measures* which the statesman advocated. And the whole tenor of the discussion would have changed accordingly. It is in this sense that an institute for the polling of public opinion could not avoid "leading questions" no matter how hard it tried (and I doubt whether such enterprises usually try very hard). Every question selects a field of battle, and in this selection it forms the nature of the answers.

In this sense, also, we could say that Marxist criticism in recent years "triumphed" over its most emphatic opponents.

Even those critics who had previously been answering questions about "pure form" now began answering questions about "the relation between art and society," i. e., *Marxist* questions.

Implicit in a perspective there are two kinds of questions: (1) what to look for, and why; (2) how, when, and where to look for it. The first could be called ontological questions; the second, methodological. A critic eager to define his position should attempt to make his answers to these questions as explicit as possible, even at the risk of appearing to "lay down the law." After all, there are "laws" (or at least, rules of thumb) implicit in the critic's perspective—and the critic should do what he can to specify them as a way of defining that perspective. I am particularly prodded to this attempt because my procedures have been characterized as "intuitive" and "idiosyncratic," epithets that make me squirm. For I believe that a critic should seek to develop not only a method, but a methodology—and that this methodology should be formed, at every turn, by reference to the "collective revelation" of accumulated critical lore.

However, as a student of strategies, I realize that there is no sure remedy for my discomfiture. What if one did succeed in proving, for anyone concerned, that his method is developed in coöperation with the work of other critics, and that he can *deduce* from his perspective a set of procedures for analyzing the structure of a work *inductively?* An opponent would then need but transubstantiate his epithets. And the charge that the critic is "too intuitive" or "idiosyncratic" in his methods could be happily revised into a charge that he is too "derivative" and is following an "overly mechanical routine." Our critical vocabulary is rich in such resourcefulness.

So I shall now assemble in one spot some basic rules of thumb—with diffidence; and not in the forlorn hope of silencing anyone, but only in the hope of defining a perspective by stating the what's, how's, when's, where's, and why's that go with it. In other words, I am asking no one to "obey these rules" (or rather, these rules of thumb). I assemble them simply as a convenient way of crystallizing my exposition. If we wanted to know "what is going on" in a work of art, in accordance with the notion of "symbolic action," how should we proceed? What kind of "leads" would we follow? I have touched upon this matter in passing, but should like now to discuss it focally.

First: We should watch for the dramatic alignment. What is vs. what. As per Odets: violin vs. prizefight. Or in Hitler's *Mein Kampf*, where we found the discordant principle of parliament, with its many voices in dispersion, placed in dramatic or dialectic opposition to the one voice of Hitler. (The structure is described at length in "The Rhetoric of Hitler's 'Battle,'" *The Southern Review*, Summer, 1939.) To fill out such a description, we must note, at the same time, the sets of "equations" that reinforce each of the opposing principles. I have given a long list of these in the Hitler analysis, and have previously in the present item suggested some of the main ones in the case of *Golden Boy*. We discover these inductively, obediently, by "statistical" inspection of the specific work to be analyzed. We should not "help the author out" here. Thus, if we want to say that one principle equals "light," and the other equals "darkness," we must be able to extract this interpretation by explicit quotation from the work itself. In Seaver's *Between the Hammer and the Anvil*, for instance (a novel inferior in literary merit to his earlier *The Company*, but written with

69

such earnestness and simplicity that it provides an excellent example for illustrating basic ritualistic processes), a character who is being "converted" to a new attitude appropriately undergoes the change during a ferry ride (a "crossing"), while the turn from "darkness" to "light" is explicitly there, in the imagery of the events, as the boat on which the change of heart takes place begins its journey by moving from the shadows of the buildings into full sunlight.

We may, eventually, offer "generalizations atop generalizations" whereby different modes of concrete imagery may be classed together. That is, one book may give us "into the night" imagery; another "to the bottom of the sea" imagery; another the "apoplectic" imagery of Flaubert's *Légende de St. Julien, l'Hospitalier*—and we may propose some over-all category (such as "books that take us to the end of the line," or "books that would seek Nirvana by burning something out") that would justify us in classing all these works together on the basis of a common strategy despite differences in concrete imagery. But this procedure must be judged on its merits, when the time comes. The first step, the step we are concerned with at the moment, requires us to get our equations inductively, by tracing down the interrelationships as revealed by the objective structure of the book itself.

I think that there are both quantitative and qualitative considerations involved here. Thus, in her *Shakespeare's Imagery*, Caroline Spurgeon has shown, by *quantitative* test, that a certain image predominates in a given work. Might there not also be the *qualitative* importance of beginning, middle, and end? That is: should we not attach particular significance to the situations on which the work opens and closes, and the events by which the peripety, or reversal is contrived? Hence, along with the distinction between opposing principles we should note the development *from what through what to what*. So we place great stress upon those qualitative points: the "laying of the cornerstone," the "watershed moment," and the "valedictory," or "funeral wreath."

On this basis, in looking for the equations underlying "The Ancient Mariner," I should tentatively lay emphasis upon the fact that the narrative takes place on the occasion of a marriage-feast, that the narrator throughout is deflecting the wedding-guest from attending this ceremony, and that, at the very end, the Mariner explicitly states his values:

> O sweeter than the marriage-feast,
> 'Tis sweeter far to me,
> To walk together to the kirk
> With a goodly company!—

And I should expect to see this strand, latently if not patently, maintained at any intermediary points crucial to the development, as with the killing of the Albatross and the blessing of the snakes. The Albatross, we are told, came through the fog "As if it had been a Christian soul," and the Sun that avenges the murder is said to be "like God's own head." In "The Eolian Harp" we are told that Sarah, the poet's wife, who biddeth the poet walk humbly with his God, is a "Meek Daughter in the family of Christ." Sarah and the Albatross are thus seen to be in the same equational cluster. The drug, however, is in a different cluster. As he tells us in his letters, it is responsible for "barbarous neglect of my family." As for its affinity with pure or metaphysical evil, we have that explicitly in his letters: "I used to think St. James's Text: 'He who offendeth in one part of the Law, offendeth in all,' very harsh; but my own sad experience has taught me it's aweful, dreadful Truth. What crime is there scarcely which has not been included in or followed from the one guilt of taking opium?" And when he suffered from its malign effects, we are told in the same letter, "An indefinite indescribable Terror as with a scourge of ever restless, ever coiling and uncoiling serpents, drove me on from behind" (as the Mariner's ship was driven). Its benign effects, on the other hand, are manic and integrative. When under its influence, Coleridge would pour forth vast encyclopaedic projects that encompassed the whole of experience. It had the unifying attribute of imagination, which (he tells us in *Table Talk*) would have as its excessive form "mania." While its benignity lasted, it gave the unitary effect that Coleridge celebrates in his communion with the universe ("The Eolian Harp"), a vision followed by his surprising apologies to Sarah. And we might introduce one last correlation: among Coleridge's notes taken when he was planning the poem that became "The Ancient Mariner," there is a note that punningly suggests a different kind of Christian: "Christian, the MUTINEER" (the capitalization is Coleridge's). Taking all these points together, do we not find good cause to line up, as one strand in the symbolic action of the poem, a sequence from marriage problem, through the murder of the Albatross as a synecdochic representative of Sarah, to the "blessing" of the snakes that synecdochically represented the drug and the impulsive premarital aesthetic (belonging in a contrary cluster) to an explicit statement of preference for church, prayer, and companionship over marriage (with the Mariner returning to shore under the aegis of the praying Hermit, and the poem itself ending on the prayerful, moralizing note that has annoyed many readers as a change in quality)?

In many cases, of course, I should lack the citational bridges for linking the imagery within a poem to the poet's life outside the poem. But in the case of Coleridge this aspect of the symbolic act can be explicitly filled out by the use of attendant material, both from biographical and from poetic sources.

Please get me straight: I am *not* saying that we need know of Coleridge's marital troubles and sufferings from drug addiction in order to appreciate "The Ancient Mariner" and other poems wherein the same themes figure. I am saying that, in trying to understand the psychology of the poetic act, we may introduce such knowledge, where it is available, to give us material necessary for discussing the full nature of this act. Many of the things that a poet's work does for *him* are not things that the same work does for *us* (i. e., there is a difference in act between the poem as being-written and the poem as being-read). Some of them are, some of them are not. The critic may quite legitimately confine himself within any rules of discussion he prefers. He may, if he prefers, treat the poem structurally as though it had not been written by a private individual at all, but had been made merely by the tossing of alphabets into the air, said alphabets having happened to fall into a meaningful order.

But my position is this: That if we try to discover what the poem is doing for the poet, we may discover a set of generalizations as to what poems do for everybody. With these in mind, we have cues for analyzing the sort of *eventfulness* that the poem contains. And in analyzing this eventfulness, we shall make basic discoveries about the *structure* of the work itself.

There is an infinite number of things that can be said about a poem's structure. You can, for instance, chart the periodicity of the recurrence of the definite article. You can contrast the versification with that of any other poem known to man. You can compare its hero with the hero of some work three centuries ago, etc. What I am contending is that the mode of analysis I would advocate will give you ample insight into the purely structural features of a work, but that the kind of observations you will make about structure will deal with the *fundamentals* of structure, and will deal with them *in relation to one another,* as against the infinite number of possible disrelated objective notations that can be made.

I shall even go further: I shall grant to our current neo-Aristotelian school (by far the most admirable and exacting group a critic can possibly select as his opponent) that the focus of critical analysis must be upon the structure of the given work itself. Unless this requirement is fulfilled, and amply, the critic has slighted his primary obligation. It is my contention, however, that the proposed method of analysis is equally relevant, whether you would introduce correlations from outside the given poetic integer or confine yourself to the charting of correlations within the integer. And I contend that the kind of observation about structure is more relevant when you approach the work as the *functioning* of a structure (quite as you would make more relevant statements about the distribution of men and postures on a football field if you inspected this distribution from the standpoint of tactics for the attainment of the game's purposes than if you did not know of the game's purposes). And I contend that some such description of the "symbolic act" as I am here proposing is best adapted for the disclosure of a poem's function.

The two main symbols for the charting of structural relationships would be the sign for "equals" and some such sign as the arrow ("from —— to ——"). Thus, in a jotting like "the sunny mist, the luminous gloom of Plato," I should have "sunny mist" = "luminous gloom" = (i. e., is in the same cluster with) "Plato." If these equations are found to be reinforced at many other points in Coleridge's work, I should begin to take this "trial" equation seriously (testing it, for instance, by inquiring how it might serve in discussing the turn from Sun to Moon in "The Ancient Mariner," and inquiring how our application here might fit with his equations for Sun and Moon elsewhere, as in his religious tracts). Since literature is a progressive form, the matter of "equations" always verges on the matter of the arrow. That is: what we have is "sunny mist" *to* "luminous gloom" *to* "Plato." "Equations," we might say, cause us to collapse into a single chord a series of events that, by the nature of the literary medium, must be strung out in arpeggio. (In music we may strike *do, mi, sol, do* simultaneously, chordally, or sequentially, in arpeggio). But although there are many borderline cases where we might employ either the sign of equation or the sign of sequence (as a reference to murder, followed by a reference to night, might be designed either as "murder = night" or "murder → night"), for charting a narrative sequence, the most convenient design is obviously "event A → event B → event C," etc. The "chordal collapsing" of a writer's total work obviously requires the sign of equality, as "Sun (in one place) = parental duty (in another place) = religion (in another)," etc.

The arrow is obviously required for noting an ambiguous dialectical operation whereby one event calls forth an event, not similar in quality, but compensatory. If we met a sequence, for instance, "murder to night to a vision of peace," here "murder" and "night" might be consistent in quality ("murder = night") while the third event might be of opposite, or compensatory quality (which would require "night → peace"). Thus, pain and weeping are consistent in quality; pain and medicine are compensatory, the one being involved "dialectically" in the other. Again, of course, we come upon a borderline area here: there are occasions, for instance, where the weeping is itself a kind of medicine, as there are occasions when "the cure takes on the quality of the disease." Particularly in the case of a poet like Coleridge, whose favorite proverb was "Extremes meet," we often have trouble in drawing a sharp line between the consistent and the compensatory.

The confusion might be approached in another way: A total drama, as the agon, is analytically subdivided into competing principles, of protagonist and antagonist. Their competition sums up to one over-all coöperative act (as the rôle of Iago and Othello "dovetail" with each other to compose the total progression of the tragedy). Also, each of the "principles" possesses satellites, or adjuncts, some strongly identified with one or another of the principles (as Antony was unequivocally the adjunct of Caesar); whereas other characters shade off into a general overlapping background, as with the indeterminate shifting rôle of the mob which Brutus and Antony alternately swayed. Such a set of "mediating" characters is necessary, as a common ground of persons through which the coöperation of the competing principles can take place. Hence, no matter which of the three the dramatist begins with (agon, protagonist, or antagonist) he cannot give us a full drama unless he imaginatively encompasses the other two. (The simpler forms of "proletarian" literature suffer from the fact that the poet, beginning with a strong attitude towards protagonist or antagonist, features this attitude throughout, hence does not bring his other two terms to imaginative maturity.)

But there is obviously a philosophic sense in which agon, protagonist, and antagonist can each be said to exist implicitly in the others. Hence, if we analyze a formally mature work closely enough, we are continually coming upon those points where the consistent and compensatory merge. If, in the case of *Othello*, we take sexual jealousy as the subject or idiom, we find it analytically (dialectically, dramatically) subdivided into opposed components: the "whispered at" and the "whisperer to." But "opposed components" is obviously an incongruity, even an oxymoron. And we isolate for study either their *op*position or their *com*position. We are back, in secular guise, to the old problem of the logical triad, which may be italicized two ways: either as *three* in one, or as three in *one*. Where we would stress the compensatory relationship in equations, we could use "vs." instead of "equals"; and for designating a compensatory sequence, we could use the arrow with a slanting line (/) drawn across it.

It should be understandable by now why we consider synecdoche to be the basic process of representation, as approached from the standpoint of "equations" or "clusters of what goes with what." To say that one can substitute part for whole, whole for part, container for the thing contained, thing contained for the container, cause for effect, or effect for cause, is simply to say that both members of these pairs belong in the same associational cluster. The Hegelian formula that "everything is its other" can be applied here in two ways: We have the *polar* kind of otherness, as a certain kind of villainy is implicit in a certain kind of heroism, and vice versa. And we have synecdochic otherness, as the beloved's house may represent the beloved (or, as the ship on which the Mariner voyages represents the Mariner's own mental and bodily symptoms). Polar otherness unites things that are *opposite to* one another; synecdochic otherness unites things that are simply *different from* one another. The beloved's house is not *opposite to* the beloved, but merely *different from* the beloved. Under dialectical pressures, however (as in political alignments) any difference may come to be felt as an antithesis, as in Marxist theory the differences between the "bourgeois" and the "proletarian" become dramatized as an antithesis (a stylistic strategy that often throws the more naïve kind of Marxist into confusion when he comes upon areas of overlap between his dramatically antithesized principles).

Returning to the main line of our subject (considering leads that give us a "way in" to the discovery of the motivation, or situation, of the poetic strategy): we should watch for "critical points" within the work, as well as at beginnings and endings. There are often "watershed moments," changes of slope, where some new quality enters. Sometimes these are obvious, even so obvious as to threaten the integrity of the work. There is such a moment in *Murder in the Cathedral,* where the medium shifts from verse to prose (with critics divided as to whether the change is successful or a fault). In Louis Aragon's *Bells of Basle,* such a break occurs where Clara Zetkin enters—and here the change of personality is so great (as the author shifts from his "aesthete" rôle, with its philandering attitude towards women, to a "political" rôle wherein the "woman as mother" is stressed) critics seem generally agreed that the form of the

work is impaired, in too greatly violating the kind of expectancies the poet had built up in his readers. Such a
moment is the scene in "The Ancient Mariner," where the
loathsome snakes become beautiful and blessed, an event
that is acceptable to most critics but that greatly annoyed
Irving Babbitt.

Above all, any weakness in motivation is revelatory in
this connection. For instance, though the Albatross was, at
Wordsworth's suggestion, introduced into "The Ancient
Mariner" in order that the Mariner's slaying of it might
motivate the Mariner's sense of guilt, what in turn motivates
the slaying of the Albatross? And though the sinking of the
ship motivates the Mariner's transference to the Pilot's boat,
what motivates the sinking of the ship? And though the
presence of a Pilot's boat motivates the presence of a Pilot's
boy, what motivates the drastic fate that suddenly befell the
boy, who was not introduced into the poem until this last
fatal moment (as Juvenal says that the censorious Cato entered the theater simply that he might be able to leave it)?

However, it may be objected, such "critical points" seem
most observable where the poet falters. Is there some equivalent "way in" to material that is unquestionably coördinated? I think so. For instance, in Robert Penn Warren's
Night Rider, the fourth chapter ends thus: "He reached out
and laid his hand paternally on Mr. Munn's shoulder. Then,
as though embarrassed at betraying his own feelings, he removed it." Here, at a point where the novelist is obviously
not at all concerned with the suggesting of religious parallels, we come upon the possibility that a kind of "ordination" is taking place, by "the laying on of hands." Maybe
so, maybe not. In any event, it seems to me a good "hunch,"
worth putting down for possible testing in the light of sub-

sequent developments, and when "all returns are in" as to the work's equational structure.

I think that, as it turns out, this particular "lead" can be corroborated. Examining the various equations implicit in the work, we find something like this: The paternal figure who laid his hands upon young Munn's shoulder was a Senator, Senator Tolliver. He was prominent in organizing a group of tobacco planters to counteract the low prices they were getting for their crops from the big corporations. It was a public organization, representative, as the book explicitly states, of a "day" self. Later, in order to enforce the requirements of this "day" organization, a secret, or "night" organization is formed. It is a kind of sinister holding company, managed by a restricted group of insiders. Tolliver is the personalization of the "day" organization, and hands down his rôle to Munn. When the "night" organization is formed, Tolliver drops out, leaving Munn, who enters the "night" organization, symbolically fatherless. At the end of the story, after the acts of the "night" organization have involved Munn in criminality, there is a scene in which Munn returns to shoot this vessel of his "day" or public self, and where Tolliver again explicitly states his close relationship to Munn. Munn departs without killing him, thus leaving the vessel of his "day" self living; but a few pages farther on, the "night" self commits suicide while being pursued by representatives of the law. The closing sentences of the book are:

> Lying on the ground, he fired once more, almost spasmodically, without concern for direction. He tried to pull the trigger again, but could not. Lying there, while the solid ground lurched and heaved beneath him in a

long swell, he drowsily heard the voices down the slope
emptily, like the voices of boys at a game in the dark.

So, all told, Tolliver's gesture, strategically placed at the
end of a chapter, is a materialization of this relationship
between himself and Munn. He is the paternal representative of Munn's "day" self—and the events of Munn's
"night" self are enacted in disobedience to him.[14]

As another example of an incident where a "critical
point" leading us into a glimpse of a dramatic organization
involves no impairment of formal integrity, we might consider *The Grapes of Wrath*. Tom Joad, who is returning
from prison with a land turtle, meets the ex-preacher, Casy
—after which, he releases the turtle, whereat Casy says he
is like the turtle (Tom had picked it up, on his way home
from prison). I thus noted tentatively, for possible development, that the turtle might serve as a mediating material
object for tying together Tom, Casy, and the plot, a kind
of externalizing vessel, or "symbol" of such a function.
Maybe, as Steinbeck had entitled an earlier work *Of Mice
and Men*, this novel might, from our point of view, have
been entitled *Of Land Turtles and Men*.

The whole thing works out quite neatly. The turtle's
(explicitly stated) aimless wandering, over the dry soil, "fore-

14 It has been called to my attention that Munn does not commit suicide in
the literal sense—and that, for the English edition of *Night Rider*, the novelist
revised the ending so as to remove the possibility of such misinterpretation. The
distinction does not greatly matter for present purposes, however. For though
the ending is not literally suicidal, it is clearly suicidal in quality. Munn's shot,
though not fired against himself, is sent aimlessly into the void, after which he
languishes, sinking from the rôle of agent into a rôle of complete passivity. The
state is not directly a slaying of volition, but invites the lapse of volition. As motive
(i. e., that-which-sets-in-motion) it is neither an action (as of a driver) nor a passion
(as of one driven) but is rather the suspension or transcendence of motion, an
internalizing of flight, as with those organisms that, when attacked, protect themselves by sheer immobility. It probably comes closest to that abeyance of motive
which psychologists call the "catatonic state."

shadows" (or implicitly prophesies) the drought-pervaded trek with which Tom and Casy will be identified. Its wandering across the parched earth is "representative" of the migration in a stream of traffic on the dry highways. It contains implicitly, in "chordial collapse," a destiny that the narrative will unfold explicitly, in "arpeggio." We have Tom's homecoming, after prison, with this turtle in his pocket (i. e., "bearing the future plot with him," as a Bellerophontic letter); Tom's release of the turtle (which is proclaimed by Casy to be another Casy—thereby interweaving Casy and Tom); when Casy dies (with a variant of Christ's "Forgive them, for they know not what they do" as his last words), Tom establishes the consubstantiality of his cause with Casy's, first by avenging Casy, next by voicing his same philosophy of new political awareness ("God, I'm talking like Casy"), and lastly by being a fugitive from the same vessels of authority that had killed Casy.

Relating these events with the question of "from what to what," we find the whole work shaped into a *strategy for the redemption of crime.* The "pilgrim's progress" of Tom is from the rôle of a man who had left prison after slaying a man in a drunken brawl to that of a man who is a fugitive from the law for having slain a man in a "just" cause, since he had slain the slayer of Casy, the charismatic and sacrificial vessel of emancipation. It is a progress from an inferior kind of crime to a "transcendent" kind of crime (even orthodox criminologists usually putting political crime in a different category from kinds more private in their motivation —a reservation made necessary by the fact that the "criminal" philosophy of one era so often becomes the "normal" philosophy of a later era). Perhaps the most effective condensation of this philosophy, still "criminal," is in the sentence: "For here 'I lost my land' is changed; a cell is split and from its splitting grows the thing you hate—'We lost *our* land.'" The symbolic crime is thus expiated by socialization, because it *is* socialization.

We might consider the legend of Christopher, the "Christ-bearer," from this point of view. Christopher, carrying the stranger across the stream—and as he nears the other shore feeling his burden grow heavier and heavier, since it was Christ he was bearing, hence all the burdens of the world. The sense of burden is here a socialized one, the guilt having been purified, in that it is the burden of bearing the Cross-bearer, a burden that is an honor.

Also, since works embody an agon, we may be admonished to look for some underlying imagery (or groupings of imagery) through which the agonistic trial takes place, such as: ice, fire, rot, labyrinth, maze, hell, abyss, mountains and valleys, exile, migration, lostness, submergence, silence, sometimes with their antidote, sometimes simply "going to the end of the line." It is such over-all terms, I repeat, that make even the most concrete of imageries "symbolic" or "representative" of one class or another.

But we should always, in thus classifying, remember to introduce matters of *differentiae* when particularizing our description of a poet's strategy. Consider the many significant variants of pilgrimage, for instance: we may get a journey to the Holy Grail, the migration of a Crusade, a quest for the golden fleece, the touristic kind of pilgrimage that is in Chaucer or with the international traveler of Henry James, the vindictive hunt of *Moby Dick*, the vagabondage of Gorki, or some spiritualized journey of development, as with Wilhelm Meister, apprentice and journeyman, with the ideal end contained implicitly or "prophetically" in his surname. It is obvious that such distinctions also lead us quickly back into ingredients of social texture operating in the situation behind the writer's strategy, as when we contrast Henry James' kind of homelessness with that of Gorki.[15]

I have spoken of Robert Penn Warren's *Night Rider*. And I should now like to round out this section on methodology by a protracted illustrative consideration of the symbolic acts exemplified in this exceptionally fluent and intelligent novel (a work that was well received by the Guild, but does not seem to have got the general recognition it deserves).

First, it seems to me an unusually beautiful novel written in what I would call the "to the end of the line" mode. At one point, for instance, the process of maturing is metaphorically described as the peeling away of the successive layers of an onion, which would perfectly suggest such development by introversion, by inturning towards a non-existent core, as I would consider typical of the "to the end of the line" kind of plot. Carrying out the search for equations, we find the following structure:

The "night" self has attained symbolic self-destruction, as a kind of will-lessness. Senator Tolliver, representative of the "day" self, in the rôle of father has been left alive. Is he, then, a "vessel of futurity"? Examining the work further, for equational filling-out, we find him explicitly described,

[15] The imagery of the trek in *The Grapes of Wrath* has an interesting effect, from the functional point of view. Thus, I heard a critic say that the book "had movement" up to the point where the Joads reach California, but from that time on, it wandered, "lacked movement." It occurred to me that the observation applied in the most literal sense: until they reached California, the Joads were moving in a *definite direction;* after they arrive, their destination becomes as vague as the land turtle's.

with Munn concurring, as "talking to people all his life; crowds, never being anything except when his voice was talking to crowds; if he had anything in him, any life, sucking it out of crowds, talking. Crowds and women. Never being anything except when he thought somebody else thought he was something. Just—." The day self is thus a kind of social shell—so, if it is left, as a "vessel of futurity," it is presented under very bad auspices.

There is another possibility. Munn has broken with his wife, but she bears him a child after leaving him. However, the identity of this child also is presented under bad auspices. Munn does not even know its name. Furthermore, in his adolescence Munn had lived with an eccentric, scatterbrained aunt in Philadelphia, to whom he read the scattered news. Also, when living there, he had gone to a museum, where he saw foetuses pickled in jars. And now, when he thinks of his child, this period of his life and the pickled foetuses recur to him.

There is one more possibility. Towards the end of the novel, there is a superb chapter of recapitulation, where Munn has gone into hiding with a certain Proudfit, and this man tells him the story of his life. It is a story in the Phoenix-out-of-the-ashes category: of a man who burns cruelty out of himself by an excess of cruelty; purification by excess, the "Blake strategy." After the excesses he falls ill, and in his fever he dreams of coming down a hill, to green, and shade, and coolness, and water, and a little church, with a girl sitting by it. It signalizes a change; he recovers, returns home, where he finds the spot he had dreamed of, and marries the girl that had been sitting under the tree by the church.

This episode is engrossingly written; good in itself, it

also serves an excellent functional purpose. For, in a new individuation, it recapitulates the pattern of the novel itself, up to this point, yet supplies a very effective pause, preparatory to the final drive of the plot. Now, since Munn has gone to hide with this man, I take it that Munn is "under the aegis" of Proudfit. As the astrologers would say, Munn is now "in the sign of" Proudfit. Hence, Proudfit's story is Munn's story. Munn, however, leaves Proudfit, and returns to complete his destruction. So even this, as a "vessel of futurity," is not good-omened, in the light of the plot's further development. And whereas Proudfit, in coming down the hill into the valley, had been on his way to cure, Munn dies as he hears his pursuers "down the slope calling emptily." The parallelism ends in a contrast. Proudfit's final state of rest, we might say, but serves as technical contrast to heighten our appreciation of Munn's failure.

There is "futurity," however, in a less literal sense: in the intelligence and suavity of the workmanship itself. How much weight we are to place upon this factor alone (i. e., a kind of "spirituality without embodiment in dogma") I am not prepared to say. What we can say is that the book is fascinating, and that we find here, as in much of the best in modern writing, an artistic scrupulousness that leads to a *sinister* kind of beauty, where a hack could be more "wholesome" in his concocting of poetic recipes by a mechanical insertion of an "upturning" theme.

In any event, we do note an ironic development when a critic of Marxist cast examines the work of the agrarians. For these men (a) frequently write in the "to the end of the line" mode, and (b) seek to recommend their region by the use of "local color." Whereupon the Marxist, rudely jamming these two tendencies together, can say: "In associating

his region with so sinister a kind of plot, does not the region-
alist thereby *indict* his region?" I am not trying to start a
quarrel, either between camps or within one camp. I am
interested in this matter because, although I incline to the
Marxist interpretation here, I feel that there may be some
important factor in the issue that is being overlooked.[16]

In Warren's case, I feel that the connotations surrounding
Tolliver, as the vessel of the social or political self, are not
the ones that need surround this rôle, if it is linked with a
sufficiently rational and well-developed political philosophy.
Yet I am also aware that our rôle in a group activity is not
a perfect fit with our rôle as an individual; that salvation,
no matter how collectively oriented, is still an individual
matter; and that poems, as rituals of redemption, are a kind
of "private mass" (made public in so far as others can par-

[16] *The Grapes of Wrath* opens itself to a corresponding embarrassment, as was
revealed by Heywood Broun's objections in *The New Republic*, and the many
letters by wrathful liberals that Broun's remarks called forth. The book is in the
"emancipation" line, and there is no principle of control natural to the "emancipation" line. Any attempt to halt a trend is "reactionary." Hence, if the public
has become used to a certain amount of obscenity this year, "progress" requires
the use of still more obscenity next year. Obviously, you must call a halt somewhere—but no matter at what point you call it, you are proposing a "reaction."
Now, I do not think that *The Grapes of Wrath* contains much that could by any
reader familiar with modern styles be called "obscene." However, as Botkin has
pointed out, its dialogue is written in the "hard-boiled" style rather than a "folk"
style. It is not realistic, but naturalistic. The general result is an encumbrance
from the propagandist point of view, since the "good" cause is identified with a
suspect trend that must itself continually be *defended*. The political cause has
to be defended; and if in the course of your defense you identify it with an aesthetic
cause that equally requires defense, you are as a propagandist simply taking on
two burdens in place of one. The ideal act of propaganda consists in imaginatively
identifying your cause with values that are unquestioned. The point may be
grasped when we contrast *The Grapes of Wrath* with Elizabeth Madox Roberts'
The Time of Man, where characters in a situation very similar to that of *The
Grapes of Wrath* are identified with speech and acts more realistic than naturalistic (though the realism is too "quaint" and local for broader aspects of the
contemporary scene). And something of the embarrassment implicit in Steinbeck's
mode may be grasped when we recall an earlier period where the rôles were
reversed, as with the writers of the Restoration, whose cult of obscenity was itself
an aspect of "reaction." As it turned out, this "entangling alliance" helped to
organize the resistance to the political stand they aesthetically represented.

ticipate in them), communion services developed perhaps by "private enterprise" in keeping with the similar economic modes.

We should also note a "serial" quality in the "to the end of the line" mode—a kind of "withinness of withinness," as the "night" company within the "day" company (paralleling the similar development, in the economic sphere, from operating companies to holding companies, controlled by "insiders"). One may get the pattern in Coleridge's line, "Snow-drop on a tuft of snow." And in *Moby Dick* there is an especially "efficient" passage of this sort, prophetically announcing the quality of Ishmael's voyage: after walking through "blocks of blackness," he enters a door where he stumbles over an ash box; going on, he finds that he is in a Negro church, and "the preacher's text was about the blackness of darkness."

Borrowing a hint from Borgese, we might suggest a distinction between "revolution" and "involution," with books in the "to the end of the line" mode exemplifying the serial, or "involute" method. I am embarrassed, however, in that Borgese applies the term to characterize "the fascist involution," in contrast with its "revolutionary" pretenses. And I do not want to be in the position of gratuitously calling any man a fascist, and least of all a writer for whom I have great respect. Why not handle the matter this way: It is the fascist involution which Warren has embodied and ritualistically slain. So much has been symbolically removed, hence "prophetically" removed. The social, public self has been ritualistically spared—and this vessel, Senator Tolliver, is a *parliamentary* self. This self, however, is left with an incomplete identity—and quite accurately so, since in our present structure of conflicts the parliamentary rôle is indeed vague and confused, usually being related to no such fundamental concepts of social purpose as might successfully merge individual and public integrity.

"FORM" AND "CONTENT"

I do not contend that the mode of analysis here proposed is automatically free of subjective interpretations. I do contend that an undiscussable dictionary is avoided (as were one to have a set of absolute meanings for every kind of symbol, and to simply "translate" a book from its exoteric idiom into the corresponding esoteric one). To know what "shoe, or house, or bridge" means, you don't begin with a "symbolist dictionary" already written in advance. You must, by inductive inspection of a given work, discover the particular contexts in which the shoe, house, or bridge occurs. You cannot, in advance, know in what equational structure it will have membership.

By inspection of the work, you propose your description of this equational structure. Your propositions are open to discussion, as you offer your evidence for them and show how much of the plot's development your description would account for. "Closer approximations" are possible, accounting for more. The method, in brief, can be built upon, in contrast with essentializing strategies of motivation that all begin anew.

The general approach to the poem might be called "pragmatic" in this sense: It assumes that a poem's structure is to be described most accurately by thinking always of the poem's function. It assumes that the poem is designed to "do something" for the poet and his readers, and that we can make the most relevant observations about its design by considering the poem as the embodiment of this act.

89

In the poet, we might say, the poetizing existed as a physiological function. The poem is its corresponding anatomic structure. And the reader, in participating in the poem, breathes into this anatomic structure a new physiological vitality that resembles, though with a difference, the act of its maker, the resemblance being in the overlap between writer's and reader's situation, the difference being in the fact that these two situations are far from identical.

The justification for this pragmatic view of the poem resides in the kind of observation that a functional perspective leads us to select, from among an infinite number of possible observations about poetic structure.

Such an approach through the emphasis upon the act promptly integrates considerations of "form" and "content." I recall, for instance, talking with the painter Henry Billings about a series of paintings he was doing. It was a series of "Arrests": called "Arrest No. 1," "Arrest No. 2," etc. I was enthusiastic about the idea, for I felt that here the artist had "struck a vein." Everyone, I felt, has shared in the "There but for the grace of God go I" attitude towards the criminal. And when an artist hits upon some such basic situation, he can reindividuate it in many different concrete embodiments, with a strong predisposing factor of appeal already there before he begins. Similarly, one strong factor of appeal in Steinbeck's novel is in the underlying situation that he exploits: a huntedness, that may be reannounced from chapter to chapter, with our own financial uneasiness always there to help us "meet it halfway." [17]

17 In fact, paradoxically, the strong factor of appeal in this situation *per se* may in the case of the Steinbeck book have been responsible for its not being a still better book. Had the situation been less alluring in itself, he could not have relied so greatly upon it for his appeal, and might have done more, to win us, by

However, though I had such thoughts in mind, when thinking of a "vein," I discovered that Billings was taking my remarks in a totally different way, purely from the standpoint of his technical problems as a painter. The "opportunity for exploitation" he saw in the theme arose from the fact that an arrest spontaneously organized all spectators about a point of focus. Whenever an arrest occurs, all onlookers "take a position" with reference to it, quite as do the victim and the men that seize him.

I was thinking of the matter from the standpoint of pure "content." I saw the possibility, for instance, of even working out a "class structure" of arrests—for, when looking at his picture of a miserable sneak thief caught, I remembered seeing a photograph of Richard Whitney on his way to prison after conviction; and I had been struck by his bearing, as he walked boldly and with dignity, while it was the officers accompanying him that seemed shrunken and apologetic. There was something *assertive* about his conviction, as though he had *willed* it. While I was thinking thus of "content," Billings had been thinking of the same subject from the standpoint of "form." [18]

---

the development of character. As it is, most of the characters derive their rôle, which is to say their personality, purely from their relationship ·ο the basic situation. They can but "be"; they cannot *do*. They are flotsam on a stream of traffic, the highways of "America on Wheels." Thus, it is generally agreed that "Ma" is the most fully developed character; and it is no accident in this respect that she is also the character who makes up her mind. Casy comes next; he has a certain vocal articulacy. But all the rest are hardly even distinct as "types," as with the usual Broadway drama. Grampa's troubles with the buttons on his pants are "characteristic" in the sense in which some farce character that always sneezed or stuttered or stumbled could be said to have characteristics. Even Tom, who is as important as the turtle in integrating the plot, is vague as a person.

[18] I recall another painter, engaged in doing the portrait of a family, whose predicament throws light upon the same issue. He was having great difficulty, he complained, in finding some act about which the family group could be organized. For the various members of the family seemed to do nothing together as a family. In fact, since one or another of them usually had his meals in his room, they did not, as a family, even eat together.

Yet, as seen from the standpoint of symbolic action, we do not have to choose between the artist's mode of consideration and my own. He was concerned with a unifying act, and so was I. I am merely suggesting that, when you begin to consider the situations behind the tactics of expression, you will find tactics that organize a work technically *because* they organize it emotionally. The two aspects, we might say Spinozistically, are but modes of the same substance. Hence, if you look for a man's *burden,* you will find the principle that reveals the structure of his unburdening; or, in attenuated form, if you look for his problem, you will find the lead that explains the structure of his solution. His answer gets its form by relation to the questions he is answering.

I should thus take evidences of guilt, with corresponding modes of purification, as the major cue leading us into the tactics of poetic socialization. And as regards the tactics of work written in our particular social structure, with the long and arduous period of adolescent celibacy (or socially distrusted flouting of it) that goes with our particular social structure, I should expect to see a sexual problem assuming a major rôle in our typical expiatory strategies. A major rôle, but by no means an exclusive rôle: it is merely one strong ingredient in the total recipe—and the critic must always be prepared to go beyond it, noting the ways in which it becomes interwoven with a much wider texture of motives.

Perhaps as the best way of indicating just how the notion of the "burden" or "problem" underlying the tactics of a symbolic act would be charted, I should offer an explicit example of "proportional" motivation, using the case of Coleridge, and summing up the exegesis scattered through the foregoing pages.

The motivation here could be divided for convenience into five main strands: the aesthetic problem, the marital problem, the political problem, the drug problem, the metaphysical problem. To consider them briefly, in this order:

(1) The aesthetic problem. Illustrated *par excellence* in "The Eolian Harp." The merger of subject and object, exemplified in his vision of perfect communion between the individual and the universe. The unity of the player, the playing, and the being-played-upon. The poet here exemplifies a thoroughly "impulsive" aesthetic: the giving-forth is one with a being-given. Necessity and will are one. Yet the aesthetic is presented in terms of "temptation"—and the poem closes with apologies to his wife, as the poet promises to reform, which is surprising indeed, in view of the fact that the poet has celebrated a state of ideal exaltation. The progression is: from "My pensive Sara! Thy soft cheek reclined/ Thus on mine arm . . ." to

> And that simplest Lute,
> Placed lengthwise in the clasping casement, hark!
> How by the desultory breeze caressed,
> Like some coy maid half yielding to her lover,
> It pours such sweet upbraiding as must needs
> Tempt to repeat the wrongs! . . .

to the vision of communion,

> O! the one Life within us and abroad,
> Which meets all motion and becomes its soul,
> A light in sound, a sound-like power in light,
> Rhythm in all thought, and joyance everywhere—

to changing of scene (from evening twilight to noon),

> And thus, my Love! as on the midway slope
> Of yonder hill I stretch my limbs at noon,

to restatement of communion,

> And what if all of animated nature
> Be but organic Harps diversely framed,
> That tremble into thought, as o'er them sweeps
> Plastic and vast, one intellectual breeze,
> At once the Soul of each, and God of All?

to the apology,

> But thy more serious eye a mild reproof
> Darts, O belovéd Woman! nor such thoughts
> Dim and unhallowed dost thou not reject
> And biddest me walk humbly with my God.
> Meek Daughter in the family of Christ!
> Well hast thou said and holily dispraised
> These shapings of the unregen'rate mind; . . .

This leads us into

(2) The marital problem. Already, we can begin to draw upon "imagistic bridging." We note that the poet's apologies to the wife, for instance, are offered under the aegis of noon. We have the deflection from the marriage-feast in "The Ancient Mariner," and the record of punishments inflicted upon the Mariner at high noon. We also discover, from references elsewhere, that Sun equals religion and parental duty. This leads us back into "The Eolian Harp" for further corroboration, in that the poet's apologies to his wife are explicitly stated to arise from his feeling that his exalted vision was un-Christian, and that she represents his Chris-

tian duties. We note a similar function of noon, as related to marriage, elsewhere in his works (notably in other ballads written at the same time). Such would be observable, from the poetic material alone; we also have, as I have said, plenty of biographical material bearing upon the marital problem. But to illustrate the way in which imagistic interrelationships are traced, I might say that, as soon as we center upon one image, such as the noon, we find other images repeatedly clustering about it. For instance, we find that the Sun in "The Ancient Mariner" breeds rot. At the end we find the Hermit (under whose aegis the Mariner is absolved) praying on a seat of moss covering a rotted old oak stump. With this new baggage added, we go back and find elsewhere an ill-fated marriage procession (in "The Three Graves") advancing over a mossy track. We find the hermit's prayer-above-moss-hiding-rot backed by the course of "The Ancient Mariner" itself, with the preference for a religiosity-without-marriage explicitly stated, while the poem ends on a sermonizing note that has with many readers been felt as a faulty change in quality. I am not trying here to establish the various interrelationships convincingly (that would require much quotation, and I plan to do this at length in a monograph on "The Particular Strategy of Samuel Taylor Coleridge" on which I am now engaged). I wish simply to indicate the way in which the tracking down of interrelationships should proceed. As the Hermit praying by the oak stump figures in "The Ancient Mariner," for instance, so we find that Christabel is a Hermitess praying by the oak, which would "tie in" that poem with the other. Or the rôle played by the fascinating eye in various poems of Coleridge would have to be tracked down, with relation to the natural and narrative imagery surrounding it. For, as Lane

95

Cooper has pointed out, not only do persons in Coleridge's poem have this glittering magnetic eye, but we find it in the Sun and in serpents (whereat we may recall the snakes that thrive in the rot of the Sun).

(3) Political problem. By now we have enough established to note how various ingredients of motivation interweave. In his years just prior to marriage, for instance, Coleridge was much exalted by his "Pantisocracy" project, a Utopian plan for a communistic colony in America. His notion was that in this colony, given an adequate property structure, virtue would be inevitable (which moves us back into the impulsive aesthetic of "The Eolian Harp" and into the impulsive blessing of the snakes in "The Ancient Mariner"). He was engineered into marriage because it was agreed that each of the colonists should be married. The project fell through soon after his marriage, so that the focal reason for his marrying Sarah at all was removed. His disappointment with the collapse of this project was extreme. Moving back again into the aesthetic problem, Pantisocracy perfectly exemplified his ideal of imaginative unification; and we find him in later life, having turned from libertarian to Tory, working out this project in a Tory revision, now by transcendentally conceiving the structure of contemporary British society from such an integrative point of view (by which the imperfect conditions of historical actuality become transubstantiated, in terms of the principles or ideals they were said to embody).

(4) The drug problem. By charting the imagery in his poems with relation to the imagery he employs in his letters when describing his drug, we can disclose the ways in which "The Ancient Mariner" is a ritual for the redemption of his drug. We find the dramatic transubstantiation of the

drug, effected by the alchemic change that takes place when
the snakes are transformed from malign to benign creatures.
Here the snakes are found to be synecdochic representatives
of the drug (as part of the same "psychic economy," as revealed by the imagistic charting of equations). We then find
the rôle of the drug played in "Christabel," "Kubla Khan,"
Remorse, "Ode to the Departing Year." We can note the
gradual change from the benign, "honeymoon stage" of addiction to the malign, "let-down" stage, depicted in "Dejection" and "The Pains of Sleep," a change that can be traced
quite neatly through the differing qualities of sound said
to be given forth by the harp, or lute, in various poems written along this graded series. I think that one can account
for a great many important features in the form of Coleridge's poems by noting their tactical function with reference to the drug. In "The Ancient Mariner," for instance,
we get a change from benign to malign. In *Remorse* the
benign and malign principles are dramatically dissociated,
they compete, and the benign triumphs. In "Kubla Khan"
(written automatically, when the favorable aspects of the
drug were in the ascendant) we find almost wholly the
"manic" stage, with the "dialectical opposite" but flickering about the edges, and the barest hint of the serpentine
observable, perhaps in the "mazy motion" of the river, or
in the suggestion of Medusa locks in the "floating hair"
that made the poet cry "Beware! Beware!" (In an earlier
poem, "Religious Musings," there is a "pontificating" line
useful for our purposes: "Bidding her serpent hair in mazy
surge. . . .") In " Christabel," unfinished, we find the two
aspects suspended at the moment of indecision, poised hesi-
tantly at the indeterminate "watershed moment," the consubstantiality of both the good and the bad effects of the

drug being expressed by the tenuous interchanging of rôle, as the pious Christabel at times takes on the traits of the ominous Geraldine (on the occasions of her snakelike hissing), while the good Bard Bracy dreams of the relation between them as that of dove and serpent, with the serpent entwined about the dove's neck, swelling each time the dove swelled. (Of all poems, "Christabel" is the one that would have the best grounds for being left unfinished. For it deals precisely with that state of indeterminacy wherein two conflicting principles are exactly balanced. No ending would be possible without violating the present structure of the poem's motivation.) I think it can even be shown that Coleridge's "Ode to the Departing Year," explicitly dealing with a political prophecy, takes on resonance by drawing upon imagery related to misgivings about the drug, and so is prophecy on two levels, ostensibly about political trends, implicitly about the course of internal psychological events that culminate in "Dejection." [19] We may tie up the drug problem with the aesthetic, by noting that, in its euphoric stages, it provides the same kind of impulsive oneness that the aesthetic of "The Eolian Harp" proclaims. Also, in his letters, Coleridge explicitly presents it as a treachery to his wife. Its interweaving with his famous distinction between imagination and fancy is to be disclosed in his suggestion that the extreme of imagination would be mania and the extreme of fancy would be delirium, which are precisely the two terms for distinguishing between the effects of the drug

[19] You could state it this way: The poet would convey a sense of political foreboding. To do so effectively, he draws upon his own deepest experiences with the sense of foreboding. Prominent among such experiences, are his forebodings engendered by the nature of his drug. Hence, in prophesying about trends without, he prophesies about trends within.

in its euphoric stage and the stage of "falling abroad" (his term) that goes with the withdrawal symptoms.

(5) The metaphysical problem. Coleridge has called poetry "a dim analogue of creation." In human activity, however, this process of creation involves not merely a *making*, but a *remaking*. Consider, for instance, the problem of ancestral substance. Coleridge, in his cosmogony of good and evil (in "Religious Musings"), gives us a lineage that draws good out of evil. Hence, by the "like father like son" formula of causal ancestry, good threatens to become consubstantial with evil, as its lineal descendant. Hence, the need of transubstantiation, of transcendence, of a radical change in quality.

In keeping with our chord-arpeggio distinction, the metaphysical problem could be stated thus: In the arpeggio of biological, or temporal, growth, good *does* come of evil (as we improve ourselves by revising our excesses, the excesses thus being a necessary agent in the drama, or dialectic, of improvement: they are the "villain" who "competitively coöperates" as "criminal Christ" in the process of redemption). But when you collapse the arpeggio of development by the nontemporal, nonhistorical forms of logic, you get simultaneous "polarity," which adds up to good and evil as consubstantial. Now if one introduces into a chord a note alien to the perfect harmony, the result is a discord. But if you stretch out this same chord into an arpeggio having the same components, the discordant ingredient you have introduced may become but a "passing note." "Transcendence" is the solving of the logical problem by stretching it out into a narrative arpeggio, whereby a conflicting element can be introduced as a "passing note," hence not felt as "discord." A logic is "flat," simultaneous, "chordal"; ideally, it is all done before you begin.[20] Thus, Hegel's "dialectic of history" attempted the union of contradictory aims, in trying to make the passing note of an arpeggio fit as concord in a simultaneity. A logic being ideally all done before you begin, anti-Hegelians get their opportunity to object that his logic of development, if true, would make development impossible. Thesis, antithesis, and synthesis would all exist simultaneously and in equal force. But by stretching them out into a temporal arpeggio, he can depict the thesis as prevailing in greater percentage at one time, the antithesis at another, and the synthesis as an act of transcendence at still another.[21]

This is no place for me to offer all the material evidence

[20] Think of a work so dualistic in nature as to deserve the title, "Yes—and No." One might, putting "yes" and "no" together, into a simultaneity, collapse them into the title, "Maybe." Now, suppose that one had started with "Maybe," which is not very dramatic, and which he would expand into a narrative or dramatic arpeggio. We could imagine a division into two slopes, the first emphatically asserting "Yes," whereupon, after a transubstantiating peripety, the second slope could just as emphatically assert "No." Thus, though this total form, as collapsed into a "simultaneity," still gives you the quality of "Maybe," as drawn out it gives you a transcendence, *from* quality "Yes" *to* quality "No."

[21] You might phrase this in another way: A "logic" of history would be a set of universal statements about history. And these statements would be at such a "high level of generalization" that they would apply to *all* historical development. In short, the "laws" of movement cannot themselves move, if they are correctly stated. The "laws" of movement are a kind of "unmoved mover." Hence, in so far as a "logic" of movement was correct, you would get not movement, but the motionless. And "generalizations about movement" is but a contemporary stylization of "laws of movement." (This observation would suggest that the *function* of unmoved move is ingrained in the very nature of language; and that John Dewey's program, as in *The Quest for Certainty*, for removing it by a verbal philosophy would be a contradiction in terms.)

The point is worth noting since it has bearing upon the disputes as to whether "human nature can change." If your discussion is on a low level of generalization, human nature can constantly change. For instance, people in some places wear rings in their noses and in other places don't. But if your discussion is on a high level of generalization, human nature can't change. A savage acts one way, for instance; a child another; a priest another; a doctor another; a mechanic another. But if I say "people must act," I have made a universal statement about people in history—and with regard to this statement "human nature can't change."

Similarly with the altercations about capitalist enterprise. If you say, on a high

with which I should try to fill out Coleridge's five problems. I offer them simply to indicate how one might, by the charting of equations, avoid reduction to one "cause." Thus, even if one were to begin his analysis by isolating an explicit sexual burden (such as the marital problem or the possibility that the unitary aesthetic, which proclaimed a completeness of identity with the wife omitted, might thereby reveal a kinship with adolescent patterns, a mental economy formed prior to the inclusion of the wife)—the chart of interrelationships, as ultimately developed, would by no means vow one to some such simple picture of the author as writing works "caused" by this specific sexual problem.

One would not have to consider the matter of "causation" at all. The main point is to note *what the poem's equational structure is*. This is a statement about its *form*. But to guide our observations about the form itself, we seek to discover the *functions* which the structure serves. This takes us into a discussion of purpose, strategy, the symbolic act. When one notes, for instance, that the Pilot's boy in "The Ancient Mariner" acts as the vessel that takes upon itself the most malign features of a cure effected under the aegis of moonlight (i. e., the worst features of the lunacy affecting the "greybeard loon"), one discerns his formal function in the drama—and, going further back, we may discern the formal function, as foreshadowing, of the "silly" buckets that are filled when the cure first begins to take effect. (A remarkably

level of generalization, that "people must forever compete with one another," I believe you have made a sound universal statement about mankind, that will apply in all historical periods, and so "prove men incapable of change." But if you would select a less comprehensive level of generalization, you have plenty of possible changes. People may compete in religious piety, in ritual dancing, in philosophy, in business enterprise, even in a kind of "competitive conformity." At this level of generalization, people can change enormously, as per the vast difference between the things the Westerner and the Polynesian boast about.

happy word, as all readers must feel, and one certainly worthy of a gloss inquiring into its synecdochic functioning, its implications, its rôle as a representative of more than it explicitly says.)

I have elsewhere called this approach to art "sociological," in that it can usefully employ coördinates bearing upon social acts in general. It is not sociological in the sense that one treats a book as a kind of unmethodical report on a given subject-matter, as Sinclair Lewis' novels might be sociologically treated as making the same kind of report about society (though in haphazard, intuitional ways) as the Lynds make in their systematic studies of Middletown. We are by no means confined to a stress upon "content" in this sense. At every point, the content is functional—hence, statements about a poem's "subject," as we conceive it, will be also statements about the poem's "form." [22]

[22] The same point of view would apply to the analysis of the structure in the strategies of theology or philosophy. A speculative thinker is not "frank" (when he is "frank") through some cult of "disinterested curiosity." He is frank in order that, by bringing himself to admit the real nature of obstacles and resistances, he may seek to construct a chart of meanings that will help himself and others adequately to encompass these obstacles and resistances. In the course of such work, he may often seem to wander far afield. This is due partly to the fact that each tactic of assertion may lead to a problem, the tactic of its solution may lead to a further problem, etc. And when these problems become traditional, men of lesser enterprise, forgetting that these various tactics originally arose out of the business of symbolic vengeance, or consolation, or encouragement, or protection (including the protection of special prerogatives) devote themselves mainly to the accumulated internalities of tactics, picking up a special philosophic jargon (with its corresponding set of issues local to the guild) simply as *insignia of membership in a lodge*. And this symbolic enrollment is sufficient to satisfy their sparse needs of "socialization," especially when it nets them emoluments, and so brings the necessary economic ingredient into their strategy as a social act.

Indeed, if there is a point whereat rationality degenerates into *hubris*, it must be the point whereat "pure" speculation becomes too great (a change in the proportions or quantity of ingredients that gives rise to a new quality). Curiosity properly makes its discoveries in the course of aiming at benefit (as logical devices are best discovered not by a cult of such, but in the course of making an assertion). Curiosity becomes malign when the kind of benefit sought, or the kind of assertion made, is too restricted from the standpoint of social necessities. Or it becomes malign when the incentive of *power* outweighs the incentive of *betterment* (this being another way of saying that knowledge is properly sought as a way to *cure*,

RITUAL DRAMA AS "HUB"

The general perspective that is interwoven with our methodology of analysis might be summarily characterized as a *theory of drama*. We propose to take *ritual drama* as the Ur-form, the "hub," with all other aspects of *human* action treated as spokes radiating from this hub. That is, the social sphere is considered in terms of situations and acts, in contrast with the physical sphere, which is considered in mechanistic terms, idealized as a flat cause-and-effect or stimulus-and-response relationship. Ritual drama is considered as the culminating form, from this point of view, and any other form is to be considered as the "efficient" overstressing of one or another of the ingredients found in ritual drama. An essayistic treatise of scientific cast, for instance, would be viewed as a kind of Hamletic soliloquy, its rhythm slowed down to a snail's pace, or perhaps to an irregular jog, and the dramatic situation of which it is a part usually being left unmentioned.[23]

The reference to Hamlet is especially appropriate, in view of the newer interpretation that has been placed upon Hamlet's quandaries. For more than a hundred years, we had been getting a German translation of Hamlet, a translation in terms of romantic idealism, a translation brought into English by Coleridge, who interpreted Hamlet as an Elizabethan Coleridge, the "man of inaction." The newer and juster interpretation, which Maurice Evans has done much to restore for us, largely by the simple expedient of

---

but becomes "proud" when the moralizing light of "cure" is hidden under the accumulated bushel of power).

23 The Paget theory of "gesture speech" obviously makes a perfect fit with this perspective by correlating the origins of linguistic action with bodily action and posture.

giving us the play uncut, is that of Hamlet as the "scientist," a man anxious to weigh all the objective evidence prior to the act. Among other things, it has been pointed out, there was the "scientific" problem (as so conceived within the beliefs current in Shakespeare's day) of determining whether the ghost was *really* the voice of his father or a satanic deception. And Hamlet, as preparation for his act, employed the stolid Horatio and the ruse of the play-within-a-play as "controls," to make sure that his interpretation of the scene was not fallacious, or as we might say, "subjective." [24]

The objection may be raised that "historically" the ritual

[24] An exceptionally good instance revealing the ways in which dramatic structure underlies essayistic material may be got by inspection of Max Lerner's article, "Constitution and Court as Symbols" (*The Yale Law Journal*, June, 1937). The essay is divided into four parts, or as we should say, four acts. (In modern playwriting, the four-act form has very often replaced the five-act form of earlier Western drama, the climax coming in the third act, with the aftermath of acts IV and V telescoped into one.)

Act I. "Symbols Possess Men." Here the dramatist acquaints us with the situation in which his tragedy is to be enacted. He describes the ways in which leaders prod people to desired forms of action by manipulating the symbols with which these people think. He then narrows the field to the "constitution as symbol," and places the Supreme Court as a personalized vessel of the Constitutional authority.

Act II. "Constitution into Fetich." The action is now under way. Reviewing American history, the dramatist develops in anecdotal arpeggio the proposition summed up by a timeless level of abstraction in Act I. The act ends on "evidence of the disintegration of the constitutional symbol," a theme that will be carried an important step farther in—

Act III. "Divine Right: American Plan." The Justices of the Supreme Court are here presented as our equivalent for kingship and godhead. And the act ends on the tragic crime, the symbolic slaying of the sacrificial king, as the author is attacking our "kings," (i.e., he advocates their deposition from authority). In a footnote, the symmetry is rounded out by a kind of "funeral oration" that gives the slain fathers their dues: "There seems to be something about the judicial robes that not only hypnotizes the beholder but transforms the wearer; Marshall and Taney are the principal, but not the only, instances of men whose capacities for greatness no one suspected until they faced the crucial tasks of the Court." Thus, in both their malign and benign functions, these offerings are "worthy" of sacrifice.

Act IV. "New Symbols for Old." The result of the slaying is indeed a surprise, if approached from other than the dramatic point of view. For a new vision emerges, a vision of the basic motives by which men are moved. And strangely enough, these "transcendent" motives are *hunger* and *fear*. They are *naturalistic* motives. The dramatist, released by the slaying of the fathers, has "gone primi-

drama is *not* the Ur-form. If one does not conceive of ritual drama in a restricted sense (allowing for a "broad interpretation" whereby a Greek goat-song and a savage dance to tom-toms in behalf of fertility, rain, or victory could be put in the same bin), a good argument could be adduced, even on the historical, or genetic, interpretation of the Ur-form. However, from my point of view, even if it were proved beyond all question that the ritual drama is not by any means the poetic prototype from which all other forms of poetic and critical expression have successively broken off (as dissociated fragments each made "efficient" within its own rights), my proposal would be in no way impaired. Let ritual drama be proved, for instance, to be the *last* form historically developed; or let it be proved to have arisen anywhere along the line. There would be no embarrassment: we could contend, for instance, that the earlier forms were but groping towards it, as rough drafts, with the ritual drama as the perfection of these trends—while subsequent forms could be treated as "departures" from it, a kind of "aesthetic fall."

The reason for our lack of embarrassment is that we are not upholding this perspective on the basis of historical or genetic material. We are proposing it as a *calculus*—a vocabulary, or set of coördinates, that serves best for the integration of all phenomena studied by the *social* sciences. We propose it as the logical alternative to the treatment of human acts and relations in terms of the mechanistic

---

tive." The coördinates of the previous acts had been distinctly *social;* and, as anyone acquainted with Lerner's brilliant studies is aware, the coördinates customary to this author are social; but here, for the moment, the symbolic slaying surprises him into a new quality, a "Saturnalian" vision. The episode is, of course, essayistically refurbished elsewhere so that social coördinates are regained. I am here but discussing the form of this one article, taken as an independent integer.

metaphor (stimulus, response, and the conditioned reflex). And we propose it, along with the contention that mechanistic considerations need not be *excluded* from such a perspective, but take their part in it, as a statement about the predisposing structure of the *ground* or *scene* upon which the drama is enacted.[25]

Are we in an "Augustine" period or a "Thomistic" one? "Faith" cannot act relevantly without "knowledge"— "knowledge" cannot act at all without "faith." But though each requires the other, there is a difference of emphasis possible. The great political confusion of the present, which

[25] In work on which I am now engaged, as a kind of "Prolegomena to any future imputation of motives," I have been applying coördinates that can, I think, carry a step further the ways of locating and distinguishing motivational elements. I now distinguish the three voices, active, passive, and middle (reflexive), as they show motivationally in theories stressing action, passion, and mediation. And instead of the situation-strategy pair, I now use five terms: act, scene, agent, agency, purpose.

These five terms, with a treatment of the purely internal or syntactic relationships prevailing among them, are I think particularly handy for extending the discussion of motivation so as to locate the strategies in metaphysical and theological systems, in accounts of the Creation, in theories of law and constitutionality, and in the shifts between logic and history, being and becoming, as these shifts occur in theories of motivation.

The use of this fuller terminology in the synopsizing of fictional works would require no major emendations in the methods discussed. But I might, as a result of it, be able to state the basic rules of thumb in a more precise way, thus:

The critic is trying to *synopsize* the given work. He is trying to synopsize it, not in the degenerated sense which the word "synopsis" now usually has for us, as meaning a mere "skeleton or outline of the plot or argument," but in the sense of "conveying comprehensively," or "getting at the basis of." And one can work towards this basis, or essence, from without, by "scissor-work" as objective as the nature of the materials permits, in focussing all one's attention about the *motivation*, which is identical with *structure*.

Hence, one will watch, above all, every reference that bears upon expectancy and foreshadowing, in particular every overt reference to any kind of "calling" or "compulsion" (i. e., active or passive concept of motive). And one will note particularly the *situational* or *scenic* material (the "properties") in which such references are contexts; for in this way he will find the astrological relationships prevailing between the plot and the background, hence being able to treat scenic material as representative of psychic material (for instance, if he has distinguished between a motivation in the sign of day and a motivation in the sign of night, as explicitly derivable by citation from the book itself, and if he now sees night falling, he recognizes that the quality of motivation may be changing, with a new kind of act being announced by the change of scene).

is matched in the poetic sphere by a profusion of rebirth rituals, with a great rise of adolescent characters as the bearers of "representative" rôles (adolescence being the transitional stage *par excellence*), gives reason to believe that we are in a kind of "neo-evangelical" era, struggling to announce a new conception of purpose. And we believe that such a state of affairs would require more of the "Augustine" stress upon the *agon,* the contest, with knowledge as the Hamletic preparation for the act required in this agon. Scientific pragmatism, as seen from this point of view, would be considered less as a philosophical assertion per se than as the lore of the "complicating factors" involved in any philosophic assertion. It would be a *necessary admonitory adjunct* to any philosophy, and thus could and should be engrafted as an essential corrective ingredient in any philosophy; its best service is in admonishing us *what to look out for* in any philosophic assertion.

The relation between the "drama" and the "dialectic" is obvious. Plato's dialectic was appropriately written in the mode of ritual drama. It is concerned with the maieutic, or midwifery, of philosophic assertion, the ways in which an idea is developed by the "coöperative competition" of the "parliamentary." Inimical assertions are invited to collaborate in the perfecting of the assertion. In fact, the greatest menace *to* dictatorships lies in the fact that, through their "efficiency" in silencing the enemy, they deprive themselves of competitive collaboration. Their assertion lacks the opportunity to mature through "agonistic" development. By putting the quietus upon their opponent, they bring themselves all the more rudely against the *unanswerable opponent,* the opponent who cannot be refuted, the nature of brute reality itself. In so far as their chart of meanings is inadequate as a description of the scene, it is not equipped to encompass the scene. And by silencing the opponent, it deprives itself of the full value to be got from the "collective revelation" to the maturing of which a vocal opposition radically contributes.

And there is a "collective revelation," a social structure of meanings by which the individual forms himself. Recent emphasis upon the great amount of superstition and error in the beliefs of savages has led us into a false emphasis here. We have tended to feel that a whole collectivity can be "wrong" in its chart of meanings. On the contrary, if a chart of meanings were ever "wrong," it would die in one generation. Even the most superstition-ridden tribe must have had many very accurate ways of sizing up real obstacles and opportunities in the world, for otherwise it could not have maintained itself. Charts of meaning are not "right" or "wrong"—they are relative *approximations* to the truth. And only in so far as they contain real ingredients of the truth can the men who hold them perpetuate their progeny. In fact, even in some of the most patently "wrong" charts, there are sometimes discoverable ingredients of "rightness" that have been lost in our perhaps "closer" approximations. A ritual dance for promoting the fertility of crops was absurd enough as "science" (though its absurdity was effectively and realistically corrected in so far as the savage, along with the mummery of the rite, planted the seed; and if you do not abstract the rite as the essence of the event, but instead consider the act of planting as also an important ingredient of the total recipe, you see that the chart of meanings contained a very important accuracy). It should also be noted that the rite, considered as "social science," had an accuracy lacking in much of our contemporary action, since it was highly *collective* in its attributes, a *group dance* in which *all* shared, hence an incantatory device that kept alive a much stronger sense of the group's consubstantiality than is stimulated today by the typical acts of private enterprise.

In equating "dramatic" with "dialectic," we automatically have also our perspective for the analysis of history, which is a "dramatic" process, involving dialectical oppositions. And if we keep this always in mind, we are reminded that every document bequeathed us by history must be treated as a *strategy for encompassing a situation*. Thus, when considering some document like the American Constitution, we shall be automatically warned not to consider it in isolation, but as the *answer* or *rejoinder* to assertions current in the situation in which it arose. We must take this into account when confronting now the problem of abiding by its "principles" in a situation that puts forth totally different questions than those prevailing at the time when the document was formed. We should thus claim as our allies, in embodying the "dramatic perspective," those modern critics who point out that our Constitution is to be considered as a rejoinder to the theories and practices of mercantilist paternalism current at the time of its establishment.[26]

[26] In this connection, we might note a distinction between positive and dialectical terms—the former being terms that do not require an opposite to define them, the latter being terms that do require an opposite. "Apple," for instance, is a positive term, in that we do not require, to understand it, the concept of a "counter-apple." But a term like "freedom" is dialectical, in that we cannot locate its meaning without reference to some concept of enslavement, confinement, or restriction. And "capitalism" is not a positive term, but a dialectical one, to be defined by reference to the concepts of either "feudalism" or "socialism."

Our courts consider the Constitution in accordance with theories of positive law—yet actually the Constitution is a dialectical instrument; and one cannot properly interpret the course of judicial decisions unless he treats our "guaranties of Constitutional rights" not as positive terms but as dialectical ones.

Where does the drama get its materials? From the "unending conversation" that is going on at the point in history when we are born. Imagine that you enter a parlor. You come late. When you arrive, others have long preceded you, and they are engaged in a heated discussion, a discussion too heated for them to pause and tell you exactly what it is about. In fact, the discussion had already begun long before any of them got there, so that no one present is qualified to retrace for you all the steps that had gone before. You listen for a while, until you decide that you have caught the tenor of the argument; then you put in your oar. Someone answers; you answer him; another comes to your defense; another aligns himself against you, to either the embarrass-

---

Our Bill of Rights, for instance, is composed of clauses that descended from two substantially different situations. First, as emerging in Magna Carta, they were enunciated by the feudal barons in their "reactionary" struggles against the "progressive" rise of central authority. Later, in the British Petition of Right and Bill of Rights, they were enunciated by the merchant class in their "progressive" struggles against the "reactionary" resistance of the Crown. It is in this second form that they came into our Constitution.

BUT:

Note this important distinction: in the British Bill of Rights, they were defined, or located, as a resistance of the *people* to the *Crown*. Thus they had, at this stage, a strongly collectivistic quality, as the people were united in a common cause against the Crown, and the rights were thus dialectically defined with relation to this opposition. The position of the Crown, in other words, was a necessary term in giving meaning to the people's counter-assertions.

In the United States document, however, the Crown had been abolished. Hence, the dialectical function of the Crown in giving meaning to the terms would have to be taken over by some other concept of sovereignty. And the only sovereign within the realm covered by the Constitution was the *government elected by the people*. Hence, since the opposite "coöperates" in the definition of a dialectical term, and since the sovereignty or authority against which the rights were proclaimed had changed from that of an antipopular Crown to that of a popularly representative government, it would follow that the quality of the "rights" themselves would have to change. And such change of quality did take place, in that the rights became interpreted as rights of the people as *individuals* or *minorities* against a government representing the will of the people as a *collectivity* or *majority*.

Eventually, this interpretation assisted the rise of the great super-corporations, linked by financial ties and interlocking directorates. And these super-corporations gradually come to be considered as a new seat of authority, placed outside the

ment or gratification of your opponent, depending upon the quality of your ally's assistance. However, the discussion is interminable. The hour grows late, you must depart. And you do depart, with the discussion still vigorously in progress.

It is from this "unending conversation" (the vision at the basis of Mead's work) that the materials of your drama arise.[27] Nor is this verbal action all there is to it. For all these words are grounded in what Malinowski would call "contexts of situation." And very important among these "contexts of situation" are the kind of factors considered by Bentham, Marx, and Veblen, the material interests (of private or class structure) that you symbolically defend or

---

direct control of parliamentary election. And as this kind of business sovereignty becomes recognized as *bona fide* sovereignty, you begin to see a new change taking place in the "dialectical" concept of Constitutional rights. For theorists begin now to think of these rights as assertions against the encroachments of the super-corporations (the New Crown). That is: the tendency is to think once more of the rights as claimed by the people as a *majority* against the rule of the super-corporations as a sovereign minority.

However, the statement that a term is "dialectical," in that it derives its meaning from an opposite term, and that the opposite term may be different at different historical periods, does not at all imply that such terms are "meaningless." All we need to do is to decide what they are *against* at a given period (in brief, to recognize that the Constitution cannot be interpreted as a positive document, but must continually be treated as an *act in a scene outside it,* hence to recognize that we must always consider "the Constitution *beneath* the Constitution," or "the Constitution *above* the Constitution," or "The Constitution around the Constitution," which may as you prefer be higher law, divine law, the laws of biology, or of big business, or of little business, etc.). Much of the cruder linguistic analysis done by the debunko-semanticist school (worst offender: Stuart Chase) involves the simple fallacy of failing to note the distinction between positive and dialectical terms, whereby, in applying to *dialectical* terms the instruments of analysis proper to *positive* terms, they can persuade themselves that the terms are meaningless.

[27] Also, it is in this "unending conversation" that the assertions of any given philosopher are grounded. *Strategically,* he may present his work as departing from some "rock-bottom fact" (he starts, for instance: "I look at this table. I perceive it to have. . . ." etc.). Actually, the very selection of his "rock-bottom fact" derives its true grounding from the current state of the conversation, and assumes quite a different place in the "hierarchy of facts" when the locus of discussion has shifted.

symbolically appropriate or symbolically align yourself with in the course of making your own assertions. These interests do not "cause" your discussion; its "cause" is in the genius of man himself as *homo loquax*. But they greatly affect the *idiom* in which you speak, and so the idiom by which you think. Or, if you would situate the genius of man in a *moral* aptitude, we could say that this moral aptitude is universally present in all men, to varying degrees, but that it must express itself through a medium, and this medium is in turn grounded in material structures. In different property structures, the moral aptitude has a correspondingly different idiom through which to speak.

By the incorporation of these social idioms we build ourselves, our "personalities," i. e., our *rôles* (which brings us again back into the matter of the drama). The movie version of Shaw's *Pygmalion* shows us the process in an almost terrifyingly simplified form, as we observe his heroine building herself a character synthetically, by mastering the insignia, the linguistic and manneristic labels of the class among whom she would, by this accomplishment, symbolically enroll herself (with the promise that this symbolic enrollment would culminate in objective, material fulfillment). In its simplicity, the play comes close to heresy, as might be revealed by matching it with a counter-heresy: Joyce's individualistic, absolutist, "dictatorial" establishment of a language from within. Shaw's heroine, in making herself over by artificially acquiring an etiquette of speech and manners, is "internalizing the external" (the term is Mead's). But Joyce is "externalizing the internal."

I call both of these "heresies" because I do not take a heresy to be a flat opposition to an orthodoxy (except as so made to appear under the "dialectical pressure" arising from the fact that the two philosophies may become insignia of opposed material forces); I take a heresy rather to be the isolation of one strand in an orthodoxy, and its following-through-with-rational-efficiency to the point where "logical conclusion" cannot be distinguished from *"reductio ad absurdum."* An "orthodox" statement here would require us to consider complementary movements: both an internalizing of the external and an externalizing of the internal. Heresies tend to present themselves as arguments rather than as dictionaries. An argument must ideally be consistent, and tactically must at least have the *appearance* of consistency. But a dictionary need not aim at consistency: it can quite comfortably locate a mean by terms signalizing contradictory extremes.[28]

28 An ideal philosophy, from this point of view, would seek to satisfy the requirements of a perfect dictionary. It would be a calculus (matured by constant reference to the "collective revelation" that is got by a social *body* of thought) for charting the nature of events and for clarifying all important relationships. As it works out in practice, however, a philosophy is developed partially *in opposition to other philosophies,* so that tactics of refutation are involved, thus tending to give the philosopher's calculus the stylistic form of a lawyer's plea.

The connection between philosophy and law (moral and political) likewise contributes to the "lawyer's brief" strategy of presentation. The philosopher thus is often led to attempt "proving" his philosophy by proving its "justice" in the abstract, whereas the only "proof" of a philosophy, considered as a calculus, resides in showing, by concrete application, the scope, complexity, and accuracy of its coördinates for charting the nature of events. Thus, the name for "house" would not be primarily tested for "consistency" with the names for "tree" or "money." One would reveal the value of the names by revealing their correspondence with some important thing, function, or relationship. This is what we mean by saying that a philosophy, as a "chart," is quite at home in contradictions.

I recall a man, for instance, of "heretical" cast, who came to me with a sorrow of this sort: "How can you ever have a belief in human rationality," he complained, "when you see things like this?" And he showed me a news clipping about a truck driver who had received a prize for driving his truck the maximum distance without an accident. When asked how he did it, the truck driver answered: "I had two rules: Give as much of the road as you can, and take as much as you can." I saw in this no grounds to despair of human reason; on the contrary, I thought that the prize winner had been a very moral truck driver, and I was glad to read that, for once at least, such great virtue had been rewarded. This was true Aristotelian truck driving, if I ever saw it; and whatever else one may say against Aristotle, I never heard him called "irrational."

What, in fact, is "rationality" but the desire for an *accurate chart for naming*

The broad outlines of our position might be codified thus:

(1) We have the drama and the scene of the drama. The drama is enacted against a background.

(2) The description of the scene is the rôle of the physical sciences; the description of the drama is the rôle of the social sciences.

(3) The physical sciences are a calculus of events; the social sciences are a calculus of acts. And human affairs being dramatic, the discussion of human affairs becomes dramatic criticism, with more to be learned from a study of tropes than from a study of tropisms.

(4) Criticism, in accordance with its methodological ideal, should attempt to develop rules of thumb that can be adopted and adapted (thereby giving it the maximum possibility of development via the "collective revelation," a development from first approximation to closer approximation, as against the tendency, particularly in impressionistic criticism and its many scientific variants that do not go by this name, to be forever "starting from scratch").

(5) The error of the social sciences has usually resided in the attempt to appropriate the scenic calculus for a charting of the act.

(6) However, there is an interaction between scene and

---

what is going on? Isn't this what Spinoza had in mind, when calling for a philosophy whose structure would parallel the structure of reality? We thus need not despair of human rationality, even in eruptive days like ours. I am sure that even the most arbitrary of Nazis can be shown to possess it; for no matter how inadequate his chart of meaning may be, as developed under the deprivations of the quietus and oversimplifying dialectical pressure, he at least *wants* it to tell him accurately *what is going on* in his world and in the world at large.

Spinoza perfected an especially inventive strategy, by this stress upon the "adequate idea" as the ideal of a chart, for uniting free will and determinism, with rationality as the bridge. For if one's meanings are correct, he will choose the wiser of courses; in this he will be "rational"; as a rational man, he will "want" to choose this wiser course; and as a rational man he will *"have* to want" to choose this wiser course.

rôle. Hence, dramatic criticism takes us into areas that involve the act as "response" to the scene. Also, although there may theoretically be a common scenic background for all men when considered as a collectivity, the acts of other persons become part of the scenic background for any individual person's act.

(7) Dramatic criticism, in the idiom of theology, considered the individual's act with relation to God as a personal background. Pantheism proclaimed the impersonality of this divine rôle. I. e., whereas theology treated the scenic function of Nature as a "representative" of God, pantheism made the natural background identical with God. It narrowed the circumference of the context in which the act would be located. Naturalism pure and simple sought to eliminate the rôle of divine participation completely, though often with theological vestiges, as with the "God-function" implicit in the idea of "progressive evolution," where God now took on a "historicist" rôle. History, however, deals with "events," hence the increasing tendency in the social sciences to turn from a calculus of the act to a "pure" calculus of the event. Hence, in the end, the ideal of stimulus-response psychology.

(8) Whatever may be the character of existence in the physical realm, this realm functions but as scenic background when considered from the standpoint of the human realm. I. e., it functions as "lifeless," as mere "property" for the drama. And an ideal calculus for charting this physical realm must treat it as lifeless (in the idiom of mechanistic determinism). But to adopt such a calculus for the charting of life is to chart by a "planned incongruity" (i. e., a treatment of something in terms of what it is *not*).

(9) The ideal calculus of dramatic criticism would re-

quire, not an incongruity, but an inconsistency. I. e., it would be required to employ the coördinates of *both* determinism *and* free will.

(10) Being, like biology, in an indeterminate realm between vital assertions and lifeless properties, the realm of the dramatic (hence of dramatic criticism) is neither physicalist nor anti-physicalist, but physicalist-plus.

Narrowing our discussion from consideration of the social drama in general to matters of poetry in particular, we may note that the distinction between the "internalizing of the external" and the "externalizing of the internal" involves two different functions of imagery: imagery as confessional and imagery as incantatory, the two elements that John Crowe Ransom has isolated from Aristotle's *Poetics* in his chapters on "The Cathartic Principle" and "The Mimetic Principle." Imagery, as confessional, contains in itself a kind of "personal irresponsibility," as we may even relieve ourselves of private burdens by befouling the public medium. If our unburdening attains an audience, it has been "socialized" by the act of reception. In its public reception, even the most "excremental" of poetry becomes "exonerated" (hence the extreme anguish of a poet who, writing "with maximum efficiency" under such an aesthetic, does not attain absolution by the suffrage of customers).

But we must consider also the "incantatory" factor in imagery: its function as a device for inviting us to "make ourselves over in the image of the imagery." Seen from this point of view, a thoroughly "confessional" art may enact a kind of "individual salvation at the expense of the group." Quite as the development of the "enlightenment" in the economic sphere was from a collective to an individual emphasis (with "private enterprise" as the benign phase of an attitude which has its malign counterpart in the philosophy of *"sauve qui peut—*and the devil take the hindmost"), so have mass rituals tended to be replaced by individualist revisions, with many discriminations that adjust them with special accuracy to the particular needs of their inventor and "signer"; while this mode in turn attains its logical conclusion or reduction to absurdity in poetry having the maximum degree of confessional efficiency, a kind of literary metabolistic process that may satisfy the vital needs of the poet well enough, but through poetic passages that leave offal in their train. Such puns seem to have been consciously exploited by Joyce when he is discussing his *ars poetica* in *Finnegans Wake,* hence should be considered by any reader looking for the work's motivations (i. e., the center about which its structure revolves, or the law of its development). Freud's "cloacal theory" would offer the simplest explanation as to the ways in which the sexually private and the excrementally private may become psychologically merged, so that this theme could be treated as consubstantial with the theme of incest previously mentioned.

For if we test the efficient confessional (as perhaps best revealed in a writer like Faulkner) from the standpoint of the incantatory (from the standpoint of its exhortation to "come on" and make ourselves over in the image of its imagery), we quickly realize its sinister function, from the standpoint of over-all social necessities. By the "incantatory" test, a sadistic poetry, when reinforced by the imaginative resources of genius, seems to be a perfect match, in the aesthetic sphere, to the "incantatory" nature of our mounting armament in the practical or political sphere, or the efficiency of newspaper headlines (got by the formation and training of worldwide organizations devoted to the culling of calamities,

117

cataclysms, and atrocities "rationally" selected from the length and breadth of all human society, and given as our "true" representation of "that day's news").

Confessional efficiency, in its range from poem to report, has given rise to an equally fallacious counter-efficiency which, recognizing the incantatory function of imagery, diligently selects for "reassuring" purposes. Hence, the confessional emphasis of the nineteenth century was "dialectically complemented" by an aesthetic of easy optimism, merging into the sentimental and hypocritical, making peace with the disasters in the world by flatly decreeing that "all's right with the world." I think that much of Whitman's appeal resides in this poetic alchemy, whereby the dangerous destruction of our natural resources could be exaltedly interpreted as an "advance"—while simple doctrines of automatic and inevitable progressive evolution were its replica in the "scientific" bin.

So, in sum, we had two opposite excesses: the "cathartic" poetry which would relieve the poet of his spell by transferring its malignities to his audience, in so far as he was capable of doing so (as the Ancient Mariner got a measure of relief from his curse by a magnetic transference from himself to the wedding-guest, and by the disasters besetting the Pilot's boy). It is an art that tries to "leave the spell upon us," an art that I would propose to sum up as the "aesthetic of the Poe story," a "monotonic" art, from which the reader can escape only by refusal, by being "wholesomely trivial" enough to respond but superficially to the poet's incantations. And we had a "mimetic" poetry that did proceed on the recognition of the incantatory quality in imagery (its function in inviting us to assume the attitudes corresponding to its gestures), but was disposed towards the strategy of the "idealistic lie," in simply renaming an evil as a good, establishing solace by magical decree.

Perhaps the situation is most clearly revealed in music, in the gradual change from "symphony" to "tone poem," with Liszt as an important fulcrum in the change. The symphonic form contained a "way in," "way through," and "way out." It sought to place a spell of danger upon us, and in the assertion of its *finale* to release us from this spell. But the tone poem sought *to lead us in and leave us there,* to have us sink beneath the ground with Alpheus and never to re-emerge with Arethusa. It sought to *bewitch* us—and our only protection against it was either triviality of response or infection by a hundred other witcheries, a general clutter of spells, so falling across one another on the bias, that in their confusion they somewhat neutralized the effects of one another.

As regards the borderline area, in which the symbolic act of art overlaps upon the symbolic act in life, I would now offer an anecdote illustrative of spells, and how one might serve the ends of freedom, not by the attempt to eliminate spells (which I consider impossible) but by a critical attempt to coach "good" spells:

A man is, let us say, subject to spells of alcoholic debauchery. For weeks he subsists, in a drugged stupor. After which he recovers, is "purified," and for varying lengths of time rigorously abstains from alcohol.

He also has a sporadic gift for writing. But he cannot sustain this happier kind of spell, and when he relapses into an alcoholic debauch, he has no greater powers of articulacy than a cabbage. His friends say that his weakness for alcohol is gradually destroying his gift for writing; and he also fears this to be the case. Their interpretation seems borne out

119

by a correlation between the two kinds of spell, the malign "gift for" alcoholism and the benign "relapses into" writing. For after he has ended a debauch, and has abstained from alcohol for a time, his literary aptness returns.

He is especially apt, let us say, in depicting the current scene by a felicitous twist of humor that gets things picturesquely awry. And when the benign spell is upon him, some very appealing squibs of this sort occur to him. Then he is happy—and his friends begin to renew their hopes for him. They bestir themselves to assist him in getting the items published.

But what if the correlation between the malign alcoholic spell and the benign literary spell should be differently interpreted? What if they are but different stages along the same graded series, different parts of the same spectrum?

The literary gift of felicitous distortion would thus be but an incipient manifestation of the extreme distortions got by alcohol. Hence, when our hero writes his squibs in the belief that they are the *opposite* of his alcoholism, he may really be turning to the kind of incantation that acts as the "way in" to his period of debauch. Precisely when he thinks he is on the road to recovery, he would have begun the first stage of yielding.

The squibs, that is, are in his psychic economy a representative of the alcohol; they are part of the same cluster; they function synecdochically, and thus contain implicitly, as "foreshadowing," the whole of the cluster. Hence, in writing them, he is taking alcohol vicariously. This is not to say that the squibs are a mere "sublimation" of alcoholism; you could with more justice say that the alcoholism is a more "efficient" embodiment of the aesthetic exemplified in the squibs. What is got by materialistic manipulation through the taking of the alcohol, *"ex opere operato,"* is but the attainment, in a simplified, restricted idiom, of the effects got in a more complex idiom through the writing of the squibs.

The Latin formula is borrowed from theological controversy about the nature of the sacrament. In pagan magic, the material operations of the sacrament were deemed enough to produce the purification. Ritual purification was a "scientific" process, with the purifying effects got simply by the *material operations* of the rite. No matter of conscience was involved; no private "belief" was thought necessary to the success of the rite. The purification was, rather, thought to operate like the cures of modern medicine (from the mere performing of the correct material acts themselves)—as the effects of castor oil are the same with "believer" and "nonbeliever" alike. Theological tacticians had the problem of taking over the "scientific" magic of paganism and introducing a religious emphasis upon the need of conscience or belief as a factor in the effectiveness of the rite, without thereby implying that the rite was purely "symbolic." The magical doctrine was "realistic"; and similarly, the religious sacrament was "realistic" (that is, the rite was held *really* to have transubstantiated the holy wafers and the wine into the body and blood of Christ: the act was not deemed merely "symbolical," except among schismatics; it was as materialistic a means of purification as castor oil, yet at the same time its effective operation required the collaboration of belief, as castor oil does not; the effect could not be got, as with pagan magic and scientific materialism, through the objective operation alone, i. e., *ex opere operato*). We find this delicate state of indeterminacy in the relation between the squibs and the alcoholism, though the "piety" here is

121

of a different sort than that considered as the norm by orthodox Christian theologians: a piety more in keeping perhaps with the genius of Bacchantic services, the cult of methodic distortion that stressed the element of Priapic obscenities and finally became sophisticated, alembicated, and attenuated in comedy. The writing of the squibs corresponds to the stage aimed at by the theologians: it is a material operation, yet at the same time it requires "belief." The alcoholic stage is purely materialistic, the results now being attained efficiently by the "real" power of the substance alone.

But note the ironic element here. If the writing of the squibs is in the same equational structure with the taking of the alcohol, in writing the squibs it is as though our hero had "taken his first drink." This is the one thing he knows he must not do. For he knows that he is incapable of moderation, once the first drink has been taken. But if the squibs and the alcohol are in the same cluster, he has vicariously taken the first drink in the very act which, on its social face, was thought by him and his friends to belong in an opposing cluster.

Thus, he has begun his "way in." He has begun infecting himself with a kind of incantation that synecdochically foreshadows, or implicitly contains, the progression from this less efficient, ritualistic yielding to an efficient, practical yielding: he has begun the chain of developments that finally leads into alcohol as the most direct means for embodying the same aesthetic of distortion as was embodied in his squibs.

The irony is that, if he wanted to guard properly against relapse, *instead of writing the squibs, he would resolutely refuse to write them.* He would recognize that, however it may be in the case of other men, in his case he conjures forth a djinn (or, if you will, gin) that will come at his beckoning but will develop powers of its own, once summoned. He may know the magical incantations that summon it; but he does not know the magical incantations that compel it to obey him, once it has been summoned; hence, let him not summon it.

Would this mean that our hero should not write at all? I do not think so. On the contrary, I think it means that he should *attempt to coach some other kind of writing, of a different incantatory quality.* From this kind he would rigorously exclude the slightest distortion, no matter how appealing such distortion might be. *For him,* such distortions are in the category of intemperance, regardless of what category they may be in *for others.* Only thus, by deliberately refusing to cultivate such incantatory modes, would he be avoiding a "way in" to a dangerous state of mind and utilizing a mode of incantation truly oppositional to his weakness.[29]

We are not proposing here a mere literary variant of Buchmanism. We take it for granted that our hero's alcoholism is also interwoven with a material context of situation,

---

[29] I should contend that our hero, in thus altering his incantatory methods, would get greater freedom by acting more rationally. Others, however, would consider any incantation as per se a sign of "irrationality." The issue probably resolves into two contrasting theories of consciousness. There is a one-way theory, which holds that freedom is got by a kind of drainage, drawing something ("energy"?) from the unconscious and irrational into the conscious and rational. I call it the "reservoir theory," according to which a "dark" reservoir is tapped and its contents are gradually pumped into a "light" reservoir, the quantities being in inverse proportion to each other. Against this, I should propose a two-way, "dialectical" theory, with "conscious" and "unconscious" considered as reciprocal functions of each other, growing or diminishing concomitantly. An infant, by this theory, would be sparse in "unconscious" (with sparse dreams) owing to the sparsity of its consciousness (that provides the material for dreams). And by this theory, the attempt to "drain off" the unconscious would be absurd. Instead, one would seek to "harness" it. I believe that this dialectical theory, as ultimately developed, would require that *charitas,* rather than "intelligence," be considered as the primary faculty of adjustment.

123

which has become similarly endowed with "incantatory" quality, and must be critically inspected from the standpoint of the possibility that many environmental ingredients would also require alteration. We do hold, however, that environmental factors which one is personally unable to change can be given a different incantatory quality by a change of one's relationship towards them (as with his change of allegiance from one band to another).

It is, then, my contention, that if we approach poetry from the standpoint of situations and strategies, we can make the most relevant observations about both the content and the form of poems. By starting from a concern with the various tactics and deployments involved in ritualistic acts of membership, purification, and opposition, we can most accurately discover "what is going on" in poetry. I contend that the "dramatic perspective" is the unifying hub for this approach. And that it is not to be "refuted," as a calculus, by introducing some "argument" from logic or genetics, or simply by listing a host of other possible perspectives; the only serviceable argument for another calculus would be its explicit proclamation and the illustrating of its scope by concrete application. I do not by any means maintain that no other or better calculus is possible. I merely maintain that the advocate of an alternative calculus should establish its merits, not in the abstract, but by "filling it out," by showing, through concrete applications to poetic materials, its scope and relevance.

Some students, however, seem to feel that this perspective vows us to a neglect of the "realistic" element in poetry. Its stress upon processes of ritual and stylization, it is felt, too greatly implies that the poet is making passes in the air, mere blandishments that look silly, as tested by the "realistic" criteria of science.

In the first place, I would recall my distinction between "realism" and "naturalism," as a way of suggesting that much we call "realism" in science should be more accurately called "naturalism." In the aesthetic field, "naturalism" is a mode of "debunking." Where some group ideal is being exploited for malign purposes (as when the scoundrel has recourse to patriotism in cloaking his unpatriotic acts), the "naturalist" will proceed "efficiently" by debunking not only the scoundrel but the patriotism he exploits in his scoundreldom. Or he will "debunk" the religious hypocrite by "debunking" religion itself. Thurman Arnold's "scientific" analysis of social relations in his *Folklore of Capitalism* is largely of this "naturalistic" cast, leading him finally to a flat dissociation between the "scientist" and the "citizen." To act as a "citizen," by his criteria, one must participate in certain forms of political mummery. But to diagnose as a "scientist," one should simply "expose" this mummery.

Now, I grant that there is much faulty mummery in the world (indeed, I propose to wind up this discussion with a little burlesque revealing some of it). But where a structure of analysis is found to vow one to a flat antithesis between one's rôle as scientist and one's rôle as citizen, we should at least consider the possibility that the structure of analysis itself may be at fault. And I think that the distinction between the strategies of "realism" and "naturalism" may provide us with a handy way in to this matter.

Scientific "naturalism," we have suggested, is a lineal descendant of nominalism, a school that emerged in the late Middle Ages as an opponent of scholastic realism. And we have sought to sum up the distinction between realism and nominalism, from the standpoint of strategies, by saying that *realism considered individuals as members of a group,* and that *nominalism considered groups as aggregates of individuals.* We thus observe that the nominalist controversy, finally incorporated in the Franciscan order, prepared for scientific skepticism in undermining the group coördinates upon which church thought was founded, and also prepared for the individualistic emphasis of private enterprise.

This individualistic emphasis led in turn to naturalism. Thus, I should call Dos Passos a naturalist rather than a realist. And I should call the "hard-boiled" style today a kind of "academic school of naturalism" (a characterization suggesting that Steinbeck's sociality is still encumbered by "nonrealistic" vestiges). As used by Arnold, the naturalist-nominalist perspective finally leads to the assumption that the devices employed in a *group* act are mere "illusions," and that the "scientific truth" about human relations is discovered from an individualistic point of view, from outside the requirements of group action. One reviewer, intending to praise the book, hit upon the most damning line of all, in calling it a "challenge to right, center, and left," which is pretty much the same as saying that it is a "challenge" to *any* kind of social action.

But let us try out a hypothetical case. Suppose that some disaster has taken place, and that I am to break the information to a man who will suffer from the knowledge of it. The disaster is a *fact,* and I am going to *communicate this fact.* Must I not still make a *choice of stylization* in the communication of this fact? I may communicate it "gently" or "harshly," for instance. I may try to "protect" the man somewhat from the suddenness of the blow; or I may so "strategize" my information that I reinforce the blow. Indeed, it may even be that the information is as much a blow to me as it is to him, and that I may obtain for myself a certain measure of relief from my own discomfiture by "collaborating with the information": I may so phrase it that I take out some of my own suffering at the information by using it dramatically as an instrument for striking him. Or I may offer a somewhat similar outlet for both of us, by also showing that a certain person "is to blame" for the disaster, so that we can convert some of our unhappiness into anger, with corresponding relief to ourselves.

Now, note that in every one of these cases I have communicated "the fact." Yet note also that there are many different *styles* in which I can communicate this "fact." The question of "realistic accuracy" is not involved; for in every case, after I have finished, the auditor knows that the particular disaster, about which I had to inform him, has taken place. I have simply made a choice among possible styles—*and I could not avoid such a choice.* There is no "unstylized" feature here except the disastrous event itself (and even that may have a "stylistic" ingredient, in that it might be felt as more of a blow if coming at a certain time than if it had come at a certain other time—a "stylistic" matter of timing that I, as the imparter of the information, may parallel, in looking for the best or worst moment at which to impart my information).

I should call it a "naturalistic" strategy of communication if I so stylized the informative act as to accept the minimum of "group responsibility" in my choice. If I communicated the fact, for instance, without sympathy for the auditor. Or even more so, if I did have sympathy for the auditor, and the fact was as disastrous to me as it was to him, but I "took it

127

out on" him by reinforcing the blow rather than softening it. And I should call it a "realistic" strategy if I stylized my statement with the maximum sympathy (or "group attitude").

Do not get me wrong. I am not by any means absolutely equating "science" with "naturalism." I am saying that there is a so-called science that identifies "truth" with "debunking"—and I am simply trying to point out that *such "truth" is no less a "stylization" than any other.* The man who embodies it in his work may be as "tender-minded" as the next fellow; usually, in fact, I think that he is even more so— as will be revealed when you find his "hard hitting" at one point in his communication compensated by a great humanitarian softness at another point (which, as I have tried to show elsewhere, is patly the case with Arnold).

Stylization is inevitable. Sometimes it is done by sentimentalization (saying "It's all right" when it isn't). Sometimes by the reverse, brutalization, saying it with an overbluntness, in "hard-boiled" or its "scientific" equivalents (sadism if you like to write it, masochism if you like to read it). I recall a surrealistic movie that revealed the kind of "protection" we may derive from this strategy, in the aesthetic field where the information to be imparted is usually not quite so "disastrous" as the hypothetical event we have been just considering. The movie opens with a view of a man sharpening his razor. We next see a close-up of his eye, an enormous eye filling the entire screen. And then, slowly and systematically, the blade of the razor is drawn across this eye, and in horror we observe it splitting open. Many other horrors follow, but we have been "immunized" by the first shock. We are calloused; we have already been through the worst; there is nothing else to fear; as regards further pain, we

have become *roués*. Sometimes the stylization is by neutral
description, the method more normal to scientific procedure.
And tragedy uses the stylization of ennoblement, making
the calamity bearable by making the calamitous situation
dignified.

From this point of view we could compare and contrast
strategies of motivation in Bentham, Coleridge, Marx, and
Mannheim. Bentham, as "debunker," discusses motives
"from the bottom up." That is: they are treated as "eulogistic
coverings" for "material interests." Coleridge's motivation
is "tragic," or "dignifying," "from the top down" (in his
phrasing: *"a Jove principium"*). He treats material interests
as a limited aspect of "higher" interests. Marx employs a factional strategy of motivation, in debunking the motives of the
bourgeois enemy and dignifying the motives of the proletarian ally. Since he has reversed the values of idealism, he
would not consider the material grounding of proletarian
interests as an indignity. The proletarian view is dignified
by being equated with truth, in contrast with the "idealistic
lie" of a class that has special prerogatives to protect by systematic misstatements about the nature of reality. Mannheim seeks to obtain a kind of "documentary" perspective on
the subject of motives, on a "second level" of generalization.
That is: he accepts not only the Marxist debunking of bourgeois motives, but also the bourgeois counter-debunking of
proletarian motives; and he next proceeds to attenuate the
notion of "debunking" ("unmasking") into a more neutral
concept that we might in English call "discounting" or
"making allowance for."

Or let us consider another hypothetical case. A man would
enroll himself in a cause. His choice may be justified on
thoroughly "realistic" grounds. He surveys the situation,

sizes it up accurately, decides that a certain strategy of action is required to encompass it and that a certain group or faction is organized to carry out this strategy. Nothing could be more "realistic." Yet suppose that he would write a poem in which, deliberately or spontaneously, he would "stylize" the processes of identification involved in this choice. His act, no matter how thoroughly attuned to the requirements of his times, will be a "symbolic act," hence open to the kind of analysis we have proposed for the description of a symbolic act. If his choice of faction is relevant to the needs of the day, its "realism" is obvious. If the chart of meanings into which he fits this choice of faction are adequate, the relevance is obvious. And to call his poetic gestures merely "illusory" would be like calling it "illusory" when a man, wounded, "stylizes" his response by either groaning or gritting his teeth and flexing his muscles.

There is, in science, a tendency to substitute for ritual, routine. To this extent, there is an antipoetic ingredient in science. It is "poetic" to develop method; it is "scientific" to develop methodology. (From this standpoint, the ideal of literary criticism is a "scientific" ideal.) But we can deceive ourselves if we erect this difference in aim into a distinction between "reality" and "illusion," maintaining that, as judged by the ideals of scientific routine or methodology, the ideals of poetic method, or ritual, become "illusions."

The body is an actor; as an actor, it participates in the movements of the mind, posturing correspondingly; in styles of thought and expression we embody these correlations—and the recognition of this is, as you prefer, either "scientific" or "poetic."

It will thus be seen that, in playing the game of life, we have at our command a resource whereby we can shift the rules of this game. It is as though someone who had been losing at checkers were of a sudden to decide that he had really been playing "give away" (the kind of checkers where the object is not to take as many of your opponent's men as possible, but to lose as many of your own as possible). Where our resources permit, we may piously encourage the awesome, and in so encompassing it, make ourselves immune (by "tolerance," as the word is used of drugs, by Mithridatism). Where our resources do not permit, where we cannot meet such exacting obligations, we may rebel, developing the stylistic antidote that would cancel out an overburdensome awe. And in between these extremes, there is the wide range of the mean, the many instances in which we dilute, attenuate, mixing the ingredient of danger into a recipe of other, more neutral ingredients, wide in their scope and complexity, a chart that concerns itself with the world in all its miraculous diverse plentitude. And for this plentitude of the Creation, being very grateful.

But our symbolic acts can vary greatly in relevance and scope. If we enact by tragedy a purificatory ritual symbolizing our enrollment in a cause shaped to handle a situation accurately, for instance, we may embody the same processes as if we enacted a purificatory ritual symbolizing our enrollment in a cause woefully inadequate to the situation. And the analyst of the two tragedies may, by reason of his over-all classificatory terms, find much in common between the two symbolic acts. The fact remains, however, that one of these acts embodies a chart of meanings superior to the other (and if the chart is too far out of accord with the nature of the situation, the "unanswerable opponent," the objective recalcitrance of the situation itself, will put forth its irrefutable rejoinder).

131

To illustrate the point, I will close this discussion by a burlesque in which a certain important faultiness of chart may be revealed. Our form here may be like that of the Greek drama, where the tragic trilogy was regularly topped off by a satyr-play exemplifying the same heroic processes in their caricatured equivalents. So we would offer a kind of "critical analogue" to such a program, rounding out our observations on the nature of tragic purification by a burlesque in which our democratic elections are charted by the same coördinates, but with the President in the rôle of the Sacrificial King.

ELECTIONEERING IN PSYCHOANALYSIA

Psychoanalysia, an island situated in a remote area of the Not-so-Pacific Ocean, was given this name by the Western sociologists who went there to study its customs. The natives call their island Hobo-i, which means nearly the same as "En Route" in our idioms, and is also the Psychoanalysians' word for "investment." The most striking characteristic of Psychoanalysia is the natives' vivacious interest in popular elections, which are conducted in a vocabulary strikingly similar to that of our Freudian and post-Freudian psychologies. The Psychoanalysians' social and political structure is quite similar to that of our capitalist democracies, and in much the same sort of disrepair. But their peculiar electioneering habits are here briefly described because of the light they shed upon the psychology of politics in general, as shaped by democratic institutions.

Perhaps the quickest way to acquaint the reader with the peculiar flavor of Hobo-i electioneering methods is to cite some typical political slogans of Psychoanalysia:

132

"Become reborn in the name of Blott."
"Choose Blott for father-symbol."
"Make Bloop the rejected father."

"Put Blott in bed, in place of Bloop" (a Psychoanalysian idiom difficult to translate with quite the right flavor. One might get the point somewhat by recalling that our own word, "incumbent," means literally "lying down" or "reclining." This slogan was matched by another of Blott's, promising that he wouldn't make his bed a berth).

An important feature of Psychoanalysian elections is their emphasis upon the *curative value of a landslide*. Psychoanalysian politicians of all parties are insistent that the full cathartic (or purifying) effect of an election is frustrated unless the voters switch *violently* from one candidate to another. They maintain that this violence of reaction is all the more necessary because there is very little real difference between the candidates. For the last hundred and fifty years, according to native tradition, Psychoanalysia has had a one-party government, which has kept itself in power by a practice locally known as "electoral obscenity." And it is in accordance with this strange doctrine of "electoral obscenity" (which the writer will explain in due time) that all Psychoanalysian politicians insist upon the landslide.

In fact, the native society has developed an elaborate structure of scientific forecasting, known as Galloping, that is helping make the catharsis by electoral obscenity more efficient, as it stimulates a wider swing in the votes from one candidate to another. Thus, for instance, a Galloping survey, taken in advance of election, disclosed that 400,002 Psychoanalysians were planning to vote for Blott, and 399,-

998 were planning to vote for Bloop, thus giving Blott a majority of four. But as soon as these authoritative forecasts were announced, many of the indicated minority, eager to be on the winning side, shifted to Blott. Thus, the final election returns showed 700,000 for Blott, as against but 100,000 for Bloop, this being about the usual proportion of normal to unstable citizens among the Psychoanalysian constituency. Also, since representation is not proportional, but by majority, even a faction that got 40 per cent of the votes might have practically no delegates in the Hobo-ian parliament, so that here again we get an opportunity for a "curative" result.

The tie-up between the "electoral obscenity" doctrine, the one-party government, and the "curative value of a landslide" may be summed up, and deprived of its apparent inconsistencies, in this wise: Psychoanalysia, for one hundred and fifty years, has been the victim of a disorderly property structure, "Hobo-i-ugha," which is pretty close to what you would get by putting together our words "liberty," "patriotism," "capitalism," "gravy," and "stinko." Factions have come and gone, raging over trifles, but always the same general policies of government have been maintained. Thus, you have one-party government cunningly maintained by a paradox, a constant succession of coronations and depositions. We might sum up in this way: Revolution is avoided by making revolution the norm. The people are regularly encouraged to make a palace revolution, which means that, when they get the old leader out, they merely put the same kind in his place.

Here enters the doctrine of "electoral obscenity," as related to the "curative value of a landslide" doctrine. Perhaps the point can be most easily made clear by citing some fur-

ther electioneering material characteristic of Psychoanalysian tradition (I again select my material from posters used
a few years back by Hobo-i Blott, a prominent figure who
both came in and went out with what we would call a
"Bang"):

Blott's posters: "Throw Bloop out of office *by a landslide,*
and you'll feel that all the ills of an ailing capitalism are put
on the skids with him" (we translate freely: "all the ills of an
ailing capitalism" is, in the native dialect, *Hobo-i-ugha dum-
bella*). "But remember: Nothing short of a landslide will do
this. Nothing less than a vote that is a *slaughter*. Remember
Hirsutus-Diaperus."

"Hirsutus-Diaperus" obviously requires a gloss. The
reference is to a local tradition much like our celebrations at
New Year's. At the final night of the old year, there is a
drama enacted between Hirsutus, a bearded old man, and
Diaperus, a vigorous young boy, just born, about five years
old. Hirsutus is a pathetic figure, well deserving the respect
due to advanced age—but instead, surprisingly, the Psychoanalysians hoot and shout at him, with the most obscene
revelry, and send him on his way to death with Saturnalian
ribaldry. The feeling is, of course, that by this show of dis-
respect for age and a correspondingly rowdy welcome to
youth they are *ending* a bad phase and *inaugurating* a much
better one. And by the next year Diaperus will have grown
to be Hirsutus with bowed head, ripe only for death; and
the surging mob will gather to mock at him in turn, as
Sacrificial King, and to set up a new Diaperus in his place.

It is this practice that the Psychoanalysian politician has
in mind when appealing for election by landslide, in accordance with the doctrine of electoral obscenity. The
justice of the reference is obvious: For it must be remem-

bered that, whereas Hirsutus is each year deposed with lewdness and mockery, the traditional structure of Hobo-i-ugha is left quite as it was. Hence, nothing is changed. Hence, since all the ills survive intact, there is nothing to do the following year but repeat the mummery all over again, thereby getting a *sense* of relief and promise and newness.

Accordingly, the local politician is but asking that a similar process be enacted in the election. Perhaps excerpts from a political oration by Blott will make the process most apparent:

"If you make Bloop the rejected father, and make me the new father-symbol of accepted authority, I promise to change nothing. I shall do well by the banker and industrialist uncles. Accordingly, when you feel the need of a new relief, a fresh catharsis, these uncles will still be there, with plenty of strength, and plenty of money to hire a journalistic priesthood. And this priesthood can transform me from an obeyed father into a disobeyed father. Make me your King Diaperus, and when the time comes, you can make me your sacrificial King Hirsutus. I'll be your delegated scapegoat, upon whose back you can, by the rituals of the vote, symbolically load all your ills, and drive me off into the wilderness of Has-Been. Usher me in, a New Year, by the landslide that obscenely hoots the departure of Old Year Bloop. But you can trust me, I'll change nothing. The same old ailing structure of Hobo-i-ugha will continue to ail. So the time will come when you will need relief again. And there I'll be, all primed for the hooting. And thus, you can always stay in the same place, throwing me out and putting another one like me in, and leaving the uncles as they were; this you can do, again and again, benignly getting nowhere, and always feeling that you are getting somewhere if only you don't fall too far behind."

There are new tides threatening to rise against the traditional Psychoanalysian manners. Groups have arisen who insist that the Hirsutus-Diaperus pattern is inadequate to the needs of modern Hobo-i-ugha. Other groups are seeking solutions whereby Diaperus may remain forever Diaperus, with Hirsutus split off into a separate, correspondingly permanent rôle. Criticism is also being directed against the uncles, whose one set of policies has prevailed throughout the dramatic flickerings of faction. Adherents of this school say it is bad enough for a child to be uncertain of his father. But it is still worse if, in addition, he has too many uncles.

SEMANTIC AND POETIC
MEANING

THIS essay may be taken as a rhetorical defense of rhetoric. It is intended to give support, sometimes directly and sometimes indirectly, to the thesis that the ideal of a purely "neutral" vocabulary, free of emotional weightings, attempts to make a totality out of a fragment, "till that which suits a part infects the whole."

The historian Toynbee, I am told, has laid stress upon the period of "withdrawal" undergone by founders of religious structures. It is a period of hesitancy, brooding, or even rot, prior to the formation of the new certainties they will subsequently evangelize and organize. Stated in secular terms, it marks a transition from a system of social values grown unfit for the situation they would encompass, to a new order of values felt, correctly or not, to be a more scrupulous fit for the situation. "Circumstances alter occasions," and for the altered occasions they would round out a new strategy.

In the semantic ideal, we get an attenuated variant of this "withdrawal" process. It would build up a technical mode of analysis that gave us permanently and constantly a kind of mitigated withdrawal, thereby converting a transitional stage into an institution. Like the monastic orders, it would "bureaucratize" a purgatorial mood, turning a "state of evanescence" into a fixity by giving it an established routine. It would prolong a moment into a "way of life."

138

While attempting to uphold the thesis that there is no basic opposition between the ideals of semantic and poetic naming, that they are different rather than antithetical in their ultimate realistic aims, I do grant that there is a "dialectical process" whereby a difference becomes converted into an antithesis. You have, for example, noted that when two opponents have been arguing, though the initial difference in their position may have been slight, they tend under the "dialectical pressure" of their drama to become eventually at odds in everything. No matter what one of them happens to assert, the other (responding to the genius of the contest) takes violent exception to it—and vice versa. Thus similarly we find the *differences* between "bourgeois" and "proletarian" treated, under dialectical pressure, as an *absolute antithesis*, until critics, accustomed to thinking by this pat schematization, become almost demoralized at the suggestion that there may be a "margin of overlap" held in common between different classes. And if a man has at one time been engrossed in music, and at a later time becomes engrossed in painting, he will probably evolve an emotional economy whereby music and painting become for him the *opposite* of each other (as in Odets' *Golden Boy* violin and prizefight are filled out as antitheses, the violin signifying home and harmony, the prizefight leaving-home and competition). And likewise with the semantics-poetry issue, where semantic meaning, that may be considered as a partial aspect of poetic meaning, tends to become instead the *opposite* of poetic meaning, so that a mere graded series, comprising a more-than and a less-than, changes instead into a blunt battle between poetry and antipoetry, or "poetry vs. science." Only by a kind of "synecdochic fallacy," mistaking a part for the whole, can this opposition appear to exist.

139

1. THE SEMANTIC IDEAL ILLUSTRATED. For our point of departure, let us take the address on an envelope:

M........ (name)
.... (street and number)
.... (city or town)
.... (state)
.... (nation)

By filling out those few lines, you can effectively isolate one man among two billion, quite as though each individual were identified by an automobile license, with a record kept in some central bureau, like the Bertillon measurements of known criminals.

Perhaps we have exaggerated the case. The formula wouldn't work for getting an advertisement to a mid-African chieftain. Yet it can effectively isolate one of the two billion, if he happens to be among the hundreds of millions available through postal organization. The matter to be emphasized is this: In whatever areas the postal organization prevails, this brief formula generally serves to isolate the desired individual.

The formula has no orientative value in itself. It depends for its significance upon the establishment of a postal structure, as a going concern. It is like the coin in a slot machine. Given the machine, in good order, the coin will "work." The address, as a counter, works in so far as it indicates to the postal authorities what kind of operation should be undertaken. But it *assumes* an organization. Its *meaning,* then, involves the established procedures of the mails, and is in the instructions it gives for the performance of desired operations within this going concern.

The man who writes the address on an envelope may know very little about the concreteness of these operations. Likewise, the sorter who first tosses the letter into the "state" or "nation" bin will not concretely envision the act of final delivery, after the letter has been sifted down through various sub-classifications, until it reaches the pouch of the mailman on his route. Any single worker, handling the letter in its various stages of transit, interprets the address as instructions for a different kind of operation. Its "totality" is in the organized interlocking of these operations themselves, whereby each "specialist," performing a "partial" act, yet contributes to the performing of a "total" act, the entire arc of the letter's transit, from insertion in the mailbox at the corner to delivery at the door.

This kind of meaning I should call a *semantic* meaning. And extending from that I should state, as the semantic ideal, the aim *to evolve a vocabulary that gives the name and address of every event in the universe.*

Such naming would require the kind of "operational" test put forward in Bridgman's theory of meaning, which has recently been overzealously advocated by Stuart Chase in his *The Tyranny of Words*.[1] It is also, I think, the ideal of the logical positivists. Logical positivism would *point* to events. It would attempt to describe events after the analogy of the chart (as a map could be said to describe America). And the significance of its pointing lies in the instructions implicit in the name.

An ideal semantic definition of a chair would be such

[1] However, Chase's book is so much closer to scissor-work than to composition that no characterization by a summarizing proposition is wholly adequate. We might, rather, classify the work by reference to its manner, thus: "A rhetorical farewell to rhetoric—or, the tyrannicide as tyrant." And we might attempt quickly to convey the quality of his "revolt" against words (done in the extreme debunking mode) by noting such chapter headings as "Promenade with the Philosophers,"

that, on the basis of the definition, people knew what you wanted when you asked for one, a carpenter knew how to make it, a furniture dealer knew how to get it, etc. An ideal definition of an electron is such that the specialist knows what to do (within the limits of his technique and equipment) to bring about the kind of manifestation called an electron.

On the other hand, when you have isolated your individual by the proper utilizing of the postal process, you have not at all adequately encompassed his "meaning." He means one thing to his family, another to his boss, another to his underlings, another to his creditors, etc. All such meanings are *real* enough, since at every point people act towards him on the basis of these meanings. And at many points they impinge upon purely semantic meanings. His meaning for his creditors, for instance, may be involved in a credit report from Dun and Bradstreet's. His meaning to his underlings may lead them to adopt certain proportions of familiarity and aloofness. His wife may have found out that, as the case may be, she can get him to buy a new refrigerator either by saying that the Joneses already have one or that the Joneses do not have one. His boss may have decided that he is especially good at certain kinds of business, and especially poor at certain other kinds of business. And much of this can actually be "tested," though in a less organized way than would apply to the instructions for the filling of a medical prescription.

But though this kind of meaning *impinges* upon semantic meaning, it cannot be encompassed with perfect fidelity to the *semantic ideal*. You can't give the names and addresses

---

"Swing Your Partners with the Economists," and "Round and Round with the Judges."

of all these subtle significances. There is no organization like the postal service or the laboratory or the factory, with a set of patly interlocking functions. This kind of meaning I shall call *poetic* meaning.

Seen from this angle, poetic meaning and semantic meaning would not be absolute antitheses. Poetic meaning would not be the *opposite* of semantic meaning. It would be different from, or other than, or more than, or even, if you want, less than, but not antithetical to.

2. POETIC MEANING. Semantic meaning would be a way of pointing to a chair. It would say, "That thing is a chair." And to a carpenter it would imply, in keeping with his organized technique, "By doing such and such, I can produce this thing, a chair." Poetic pointing, on the other hand, might take many courses, roughly summed up in these three sentences:

> "Faugh! a chair!"
> "Ho, ho! a chair!"
> "Might I call your attention to yon chair?"

Of these, the third style of pointing obviously comes nearest to the semantic ideal. The first two, most strongly weighted with emotional values, with *attitudes,* would be farther off. *Meaning* there would unquestionably be, since an attitude contains an implicit program of action. An attitude may be reasonable or unreasonable; it may contain an adequate meaning or an inadequate meaning—but in either case, it would contain a meaning.

In aesthetics, you find the word "art" used indeterminately in two ways. Sometimes the thinker appears to mean "art, any art, all art," and at other times, "good art." And similarly, in theories of meaning, the concept sometimes seems to imply "any meaning, whether right or wrong, sound or fallacious," and at other times "correct meaning."

Meaning, when used in the sense of "correct meaning," leads to an either-or approach. "New York City is in Iowa" could, by the either-or principles, promptly be ruled out. The either-or test would represent the semantic ideal. But I am sorry to have to admit that, by the poetic ideal, "New York City is in Iowa" could *not* be ruled out.

Has one ever stood, for instance, in some little outlying town, on the edge of the wilderness, and watched a train go by? Has one perhaps suddenly felt that the train, and its tracks, were a kind of arm of the city, reaching out across the continent, quite as though it were simply Broadway itself extended? It is in such a sense that New York City can be found all over the country—and I submit that one would miss very important meanings, meanings that have much to do with the conduct of our inhabitants, were he to proceed here by the either-or kind of test.

"New York City is in Iowa" is "poetically" true. As a metaphor, it provides valid insight. To have ruled it out, by strict semantic authority, would have been vandalism.

"Poetic" meanings, then, cannot be disposed of on the true-or-false basis. Rather, they are related to one another like a set of concentric circles, of wider and wider scope. Those of wider diameter do not categorically eliminate those of narrower diameter. There is, rather, a progressive *encompassment*. To say that "man is a vegetable" contains much soundness. There is a vegetative level of human response, and one can find out much about it (much more, in fact, than we now know, as more is to be learned, for instance, about the ways in which the biologic organism responds to seasonal periodicity, changes in solar radiation, and the like). Again: to say that "man is an ant" does not "refute" the vegetational metaphor. The ant may be "vegetation-plus," since it too vegetates. And to say that "man is a communicant" is more comprehensive still, including the other metaphors but not abolishing them. These are examples of progressive encompassment that does not admit of mutual exclusion—and they are examples of what we take poetic characterizations to do.

3. A DIFFERENT MODE PROPOSED FOR THE TEST OF POETIC MEANING. Hence, for the validity of "poetic" meanings, I should suggest that the "test" cannot be a formal one, as with the diagrams for testing a syllogism. Poetic characterizations do not categorically exclude each other in the either-true-or-false sense, any more than the characterizations "honest" or "tall" could categorically exclude the characterizations "learned," "unlearned," or "thin." The test of a metaphor's validity is of a much more arduous sort, requiring nothing less than the *filling-out, by concrete body, of the characterizations which one would test.* There is no formal procedure, for example, for choosing among the three metaphors:

> man a vegetable
> man an ant
> man a communicant.

One can simply ask that the contestants advocate their choice by *filling it out.* That is: *let each say all he can* by way of giving body to the perspective inherent in his choice. Let each show the scope, range, relevancy, accuracy, applicability of the perspective, or metaphor, he would advocate.

And only after each has been so filled out, can we evaluate among them. Thus, though there be no *formal* basis for a choice among the three metaphors offered above, the test of filling-out, of embodiment in concrete application, would, I think, demonstrate the greater value of the third for interpretative purposes. One could *do more* with it. He could integrate wider areas of human relationship. Hence, as so tested, it would be assigned a higher place than the other two in a hierarchy of possible perspectives. No perspective could be formally ruled out, but one could be shown to include another.

Such testing would also involve more than merely expository meaning, of the "graph" sort. The third metaphor would likewise be richer in hortatory significance. It would not merely give the names and addresses of events, but would also suggest exhortations for the promotion of *better* names and addresses. The metaphor would thus serve not only a descriptive function, but also a normative function.

4. THE MORAL ASPECT OF POETIC MEANING. Much of the *partial* descriptive matter now developed, as in the behaviorists' experiments with conditioning, would still be usable. But instead of being taken as the description of man's *essence,* it would be considered simply for its value in revealing *certain important things to look out for* in any attempt to plead for a more satisfactory communicative or coöperative structure. Thus, if the data on conditioning were presented as *an admonishment* about people, rather than as *the* "low down" on them, the interpretative enterprise would be restored to its proper *moralistic* basis, in contrast with the "neutral" or "non-moral" ideals of meaning implicit in the attempt to get merely descriptive labels

146

(an attempt that, if it succeeded, would find its very success a mockery, for it would describe social events in a way that led to no moral exhortation, and would then have simply to let moral purposes creep in as contraband, a kind of irrational weakness, or benign error).

In general, primitive magic tended to transfer an animistic perspective to the charting of physical events. And positivistic science, by antithesis, leads to an opposite ideal, the transferring of a physicalist perspective to human events. Each is the migration of a metaphor in ways that require correctives, though I am willing to admit that, of the two excesses, I consider the savages' tendency to consider natural forces as spirits less deceptive than the positivists' tendency to consider people after the analogy of physical behavior. Semantic ideals of meaning could not possibly provide a proper vocabulary in which to consider the complexities of moral growth, because there is here no pragmatic routine to be "learned by repetition," as with proficiency in a trade. There is nothing to be "practiced" in the sense that one may practice tennis or carpentry. Qualitative growth cannot be "practiced" any more than biological growth can be "practiced." Given the faculty of speech, one can by practice master a new language. But there is no way for a dumb animal to acquire this faculty itself by practice. There is no "operation" for seeing a joke—though there may be operations for removing obstructions to the seeing of the joke.

The difference between the semantic ideal and the poetic ideal of moralistic interpretation would, I think, get down to this:

The semantic ideal would attempt to *get a description*

by the *elimination* of attitude. The poetic ideal would attempt to *attain a full moral act* by attaining a perspective *atop all the conflicts of attitude.*

The first would try to *cut away,* to *abstract,* all emotional factors that complicate the objective clarity of meaning. The second would try to derive its vision from the maximum *heaping up* of all these emotional factors, playing them off against one another, inviting them to reinforce and contradict one another, and seeking to make this active participation itself a major ingredient of the vision.

This "poetic" meaning would contain much more than pragmatic, positivistic, futuristic values. A fully moral act is basically an act *now.* It is not promissory, it is not "investment for future profit." It is not the learning of a technique in the hopes this technique, when learned, will enable one to make wheels go or to add a few more metallurgical alloys to the 500,000 or so that "business" and "industry" have not yet found "use" for. A fully moral act is a total assertion at the time of the assertion. Among other things, it has a *style*—and this style is an integral aspect of its meaning. If it points to the chair by saying "faugh," it pledges itself to one program—to quite another if it adopts the style of "ho, ho" or "might I?" The style selected will mold the character of the selector. Each brand of imagery contains in germ its own "logic." If he says "faugh" and deeply means it, he thereby *vows* himself to "faugh"; he must go *through* the faughness, until he has either persisted by the buttressing of his choice or has burnt it out.

But I seem to be contradicting myself, since I called a stylistic act an act *now,* whereas I have been talking about its future implications. For there is a sense in which every act involves a future—but within this generalization there

148

is a distinction. The distinction may be suggested in this way: To name something in the style of "faugh" is symbolically to act out a present attitude towards it, in the naming. To label it "Q271-Vii" is to withhold my act as a total present expression. The value of such naming will not reside so much in the rewards at the time, but in the "uses" I may subsequently put my nomenclature to. The name "Q271-Vii," for instance, may be much more serviceable as tested by some actuarial requirement or some problem in traffic regulation. To call a man a son-of-a-bitch is symbolically to make a complete assertion of attitude towards him now; it is itself a culmination, a "total summing up." To call him "Q271-Vii," on the other hand, is to put the value of the name in its future alone. It depends solely upon what you do with it, "in our next." In this sense it is relying upon the "promissory," whether mistaken or real.

5. "BEYOND GOOD AND EVIL." The semantic ideal envisions a vocabulary that *avoids* drama. The poetic ideal envisions a vocabulary that *goes through* drama. In their ideal completion, they have a certain superficial resemblance, in that both are "beyond good and evil." But the first seeks to attain this end by the programmatic elimination of a weighted vocabulary at the start (the neutralization of names containing attitudes, emotional predisposition); and the second would attain the same end by exposure to the *maximum profusion* of weightings. The first would be aside from the battle, stressing the rôle of the observer, whose observations it is hoped will define situations with sufficient realistic accuracy to prepare an adequate *chart* for action; the second would contend, by implication, that true knowledge can only be attained through the battle, stressing the rôle of the participant, who in the course of his participation, it is

149

hoped, will define situations with sufficient realistic accuracy to prepare an *image* for action.

The poetic ideal being obviously aesthetic, we could in contrast call the semantic ideal "anesthetic"; for though *aesthetic,* in its etymological origins, derives from a word meaning "to perceive," it has come to include the idea of emotionality in the perception, whereas the semantic ideal would aim at perception without feeling. Perhaps, in view of the etymological difficulties, we should sacrifice our pun on *aesthetic-anesthetic,* and instead offer as the semantic counterpart of aesthetic, "analgesic."

We should also point out that, although the semantic ideal would eliminate the *attitudinal* ingredient from its vocabulary (seeking a vocabulary for events equally valid for use by friends, enemies, and the indifferent) the ideal is itself an attitude, hence never wholly attainable, since it could be complete only by the abolition of itself. To the logical positivist, logical positivism is a "good" term, otherwise he would not attempt to advocate it by filling it out in all its ramifications. This observation spoils the symmetry of our case, in suggesting that semantics itself may be considered as an attenuated form of poetry, that "Q271-Vii" may itself be a gesture, secretly saying in a very mild way what "fiend" or "darling" says eagerly.

It would seem fair to take the symbols of Russell and Whitehead's *Principia Mathematica,* or the formulae of Carnap, as the nearest approach we have to the vocabulary of the semantic ideal. Or one may feel that we are stacking the cards here. Perhaps the semantic ideal does not show up at its best in ultimate over-all theories, but in the specific vocabularies of technological specializations. The vocabulary of chemistry, for instance, may be much the same for communist, fascist, and liberal. A theory of ballistics may be couched in one set of symbols, whether it is to be studied by progressives or reactionaries. A topographical survey may be as "neutral" as the situation it surveys; it needs only to be *accurate*, and the soundings that the Japs are said to be taking of our Western coast line aim at precisely the same kind of description as would the soundings taken by strategists of the U.S. navy.

So, for our purposes, you may, as you prefer, consider the semantic ideal most fully embodied in either the vocabulary of any specific technique, or in the coördinating theory designed to make a body of generalizations that would *mutatis mutandis* cover all the specific techniques. In any case, even if you do prefer to insist that the vocabularies of the physical sciences represent the semantic ideal at its best, you must concede that it is the hope of the semanticist to build a vocabulary for the discussion of human, or social, events after the same model. A vocabulary that does not *judge*, but *describes* or *places*, as the psychologists' terminology is designed simply to name *how things are*, regardless of what you *want* them to be.

The coyness of the semantic strategy might be conveyed like this: A theory of ballistics, as a physical science, merely tells you how to shoot ammunition. As such, it is "neutral," capable of being taken over by friends or enemies. If, however, you extended the same kind of vocabulary to describe the situations of friends and enemies also, their enmity likewise would be neutralized. Leave the process half completed, develop neutrality in the vocabulary of the physical sciences while leaving prejudice in the vocabulary of social relations, and technology as a power becomes an ominous power. But extend the technological ideal throughout the social sciences as well, and technological power becomes equated with good power. If this account of the semantic hope is fair, it would justify us in saying that the over-all semantic theories, rather than the vocabularies of specific scientific disciplines, are to be taken as representative of the ultimate semantic ideal.[2]

6. LETTING IN AND KEEPING OUT. Plays like Shakespeare's *Tempest* or Aeschylus' *Eumenides* would represent the ideal poetic vocabulary. Lucretius' *De Rerum Natura* is a mixture of both ideals. Wedded, as a materialist ("philosophical scientist") to the aim of analgesia, Lucretius nonetheless builds up extremely emotional moments. For example, in trying to make us feel the great relief that would come to us from the abolition of the gods, Lucretius exposes himself to the full rigors of religious awe. He must make us realize *awe,* in the contemplation of heavenly distances and storms, in order to make us realize the full measure of the *relief* that would follow from the dissolution of this awe (by dissolving the gods which have become the symbols, the "charismatic vessels," of it). So he becomes somewhat an advocate against his own thesis. For in trying to build up a full realization of the awe, in order to build up a full realization of the freedom that would come of banishing this awe, he leaves us with an unforgettable image of the

[2] Enough has been said, incidentally, to suggest that the over-all semantic chart is itself the riding of a metaphor, quite as the poet may carry some underlying metaphor, as a theme with variations, throughout his sonnet or his play. In logical positivism, according to one expositor (Julius Rudolph Weinberg: *An Examination of Logical Positivism*), "propositions are pictures of possible empirical facts." Thus the controversy does not resolve itself into an opposition between poetry as metaphorical and semantics as nonmetaphorical. Every perspective requires a metaphor, implicit or explicit, for its organizational base (as I tried to make clear in the section on "Perspective by Incongruity" in *Permanence and Change*)—and semantics as a perspective cannot skirt this necessity. This point may well be borne in mind at those places where I would ask to have the semantic perspective encompassed within the poetic perspective (considering semantics as a kind of special "poetic school" that would seek to erect its *partial* truth into a *whole* truth).

awe itself. We are left with the suspicion that he has never really freed himself of awe, but that he has been fighting valiantly to repress it (thereby indirectly reinforcing our sense of its pressure). He has tried, by the magic of his incantations, to get analgesia (perception without emotion); but he builds up, aesthetically, the motivation behind his anesthetic incantatory enterprise, thereby making us tremble all over again at the lines in which he reconstructs the sublimity of natural vastnesses and power, a vision reinforced by the tonal suggestiveness of his sentences (that contribute in their musicality to violate the genius of "Q271-Vii").

The pure semantic ideal, on the other hand, would have avoided this strategic difficulty at the start. For one thing, it would never discuss awe in words that, by their incantatory power, themselves suggested awe. It would spare itself Lucretius' losing task of refutation by never once giving aesthetic embodiment to the sense of awe. By never letting awe in, it would skirt the embarrassing problem of trying to get it out again. From the very start, its mode of naming "simply wouldn't give awe a chance." This feeling might possibly be lying there, in the background, as a motive in the semanticist's enterprise, but only by highly dubious detective work, by modes of metaphorical analysis that the semanticist himself would question as science, could you disclose such a motive. What the semanticist would put out, he never lets in.

7. AESCHYLUS' *EUMENIDES* TO ILLUSTRATE FULL POETIC MEANING. In the *Eumenides*, I think, we see the poetic method in its completeness. Where the semanticist does not fight, and Lucretius fights while stacking the odds against himself, Aeschylus completely gives himself to aesthetic exposure, and surmounts the risk. Here, to be sure, is the ideal

of analgesia—but it appears at the *end* of a most painful trilogy, devoted to an aesthetic reconstruction of struggle, horror, and the tortures of remorse. And to comfort us, the dramatist undertakes nothing less than the *conversion of the gods themselves.*

In this respect the play parallels explicitly the change we get as we turn from the wrathful Jehovah of the Old Testament (a warrior god, like warrior gods partaking of the rage that is in the Grecian Furies and the Norse Valkyries) to the Living Logos of the New Testament. Here is a ritual for the conversion of the Furies from a malign identity (named the Erinyes, from *erinyo,* to be wrathful towards) to a benign identity (named the Eumenides, from *eumeneo,* to feel kindly towards). Henceforth, we are informed, the emphasis of their function will be radically altered. No longer will they devote their ingenuity and enterprise to the *punishment of evil,* but the stress henceforth will be upon the *protection of good.* Logically, the two functions are certainly not at odds, but psychologically they are in far different realms. Fittingly, for our analysis, the Furies are characterized as *older* gods; and their conversion from malign to benign emphasis was done under the persuasion of such *younger* gods as Apollo and Athena. (Incidentally, I am indebted, for the form of this thought, to John Crowe Ransom's *God Without Thunder,* a work that has not generally been given the recognition it deserves. Unfortunately, I also have a responsibility to bear in this matter, as I was assigned *God Without Thunder* for review, but became so tangled in various ramifications of the critic's thesis that my review was never finished. In particular, as I see it now, I was struggling between a desire to salute his basic observation and a muddled disagreement with the uses he made of it. In any case, the incident has been on my conscience, for works of such incision are too rare for us to afford their neglect, and I shall feel better in so far as I have here belatedly made amends.)

What went on, in this play? Recently I caught a glimpse, or at least thought I caught a glimpse, of the exhilaration that must have lifted up the Athenian audience when it first felt the medicinal action of this ritual. On the personal plane, we have the redemption of Orestes, with whose sufferings the audience had presumably been profoundly identified, so that they would also profoundly take part in his release. On the religious plane, this personal redemption is contrived by nothing less important than a reordering of divinity itself, as the persecutional gods of wrath relinquish their torture of Orestes only after they have been persuaded to change their very office, taking a new temple in Athens where, underground, they will zealously and jealously do well by Athenian virtue, if any. And to round out the pattern for this polisminded people (one of the names for Zeus was Zeus Agoraios, Zeus the forensic) Orestes' restoration from division to unity is the occasion for the solemnizing of a pact between Athens and Argos. When all this had been put together (the personal, the religious, and the social—while the quick convergence towards the close must have been breath-taking), there is one final stroke still to be delivered:

> *Attendants.* Then come, ye dread powers, kind and
> faithful to Athens, nor waken to wrath;
> Come hither, be cheered by the flame, pine-
> consuming, that lightens your path.

> *Herald.*   Shout, ye folk, a new age hath begun!
> *Attendants.*   Torch-illumined libations henceforward
> the people of Pallas shall bring
>   To your dwelling—so Fate hath made compact
> with Zeus the Olympian King.
> *Herald.*   Shout, ye people, the chanting is done!

"A new age!" Thus had the cornerstone been grandilo-
quently laid for an ancient structure of "modernity." May
one not also discern even a certain playwright's cunning
here? For is not the final exhortation of the Herald an invitation to let the stage flow over into the audience, making
participation between actors and audience complete, as
they are asked to weld their shout of approval *for* the play
with a shout that has meaning *within* the play? Could they
know quite what their applause would signify: whether it
was applause for Aeschylus, or stage applause, or applause
for the slogan that so deftly put the coming era of enlightenment under good auspices, thereby "filling a civic need"?
Thomas Mann, in his letter to the official of Bonn University, who had notified him of the retraction of his honorary
degree, begins by taking up this matter—but before he has
finished, the issue has been subtly transformed into something of much broader implications. It is hard to remember,
in retrospect, just when we shifted from a .point of controversy between Mann and the subservient official to a discussion of cultural trends in their most sweeping aspects.
Such are the persuasive ambiguities of identification. And
might we note something similar, as we cannot tell whether
the shout is within the play, for the play, for Athens or
for Aeschylus, for the tactics of the ritualistic compliment
whereby the "new age" is evangelically announced, or for

the "new age" itself? Such complexity is what I glimpsed, or thought I glimpsed, when this firm architecture of action was first unveiled before the Athenian audience. The play itself had offered its audience ample grounds to shout—and in its closing line it gives them explicitly a cue to shout.

8. "THROUGH" AND "AROUND." The particular "curve" of Aeschylus' development is to be caught perhaps as we contrast the Orestes trilogy with an earlier drama, *The Persae*, a "factional" drama where the crime is committed by "the enemy," the foreigner Xerxes, in contrast with the later work in the mode of "universal" tragedy, where the crime is committed by Everyman.

But, like or dislike this whole mode of assuagement, as you prefer: the important point to be stressed for our purposes is that it is accomplished by going *through* drama, not by going *around* drama, or perhaps more accurately, *forestalling* drama. Similarly in Socrates, both the man and the protagonist formalized by Plato, there is a "dialectical" approach (through the dramas of conflict) to the ultimate philosophic vision. With Aristotle, however, you move towards something different. Here there is somewhat the tendency "to take up where Plato left off," as though Plato were still living and were making a definitive revision of his own first draft. Aristotle's *Rhetoric* and *Poetics* are evidence that he still retained a strong appreciation of the dramatic experience. But the risk of attenuation, successfully weathered by him, becomes progressively greater as we move towards disciples who would, in turn, "take up where Aristotle left off." Such development operates to perfection in the quantitative realm, as in the successive improvements made atop a mechanical invention. But one may question whether it applies to the qualitative realm, as with some recent young composers who, impressed with the tonal inventions of Beethoven's last quartets, would attempt simply to "begin" where he had ended, as though there could be handed to them, on a platter, the imaginative grasp of this ultimate period, which Beethoven himself earned by all that had gone before it. They tend, of course, simply to "project" his last style with efficiency into a mannerism, quite as Western borrowers of Chinese or African art tend to get the shell without the egg, or as a child will "imitate" a workman by merely making the same kind of noise.

Now, there is a crucial difference between the peace of a warrior who lays down his arms (Aeschylus wanted to be remembered, not as a poet, but as a soldier), and the peace of those who are innocent of war (innocence untried being like snow fallen in the night; let us not praise it for not melting until the sun has been full upon it). And the semantic ideal, I submit, would attempt to give us the final rewards of *Versöhnung*, of atonement, before we had ever gone through the conflicts by which alone we could properly "earn" it.

No, we are here being too thorough. Let us revise the fable in this wise: Men, out of conflict, evolve projects for atonement, *Versöhnung*, assuagement. They hand these on to others. And the heirs must either make these structures of atonement the basis of a new conflict, or be emptied. Much of the best in thought is evolved to teach us how to die well; whereupon it is studied and built upon by those who have never lived well. Either anesthesia is earned by aesthesia, or it is empty. When philosophy advances beyond the quality of Lucretius, who builds up the fear as well as the antidote, it approaches inanition.

The best thing to be said in favor of the semantic ideal is that it is a fraud: one may believe in it because it is impossible. Because poetry has been so arrantly misused, in the sophistries of the press and of political demagogues, there is apparent justification for the attempt to eliminate it. But one could with as much logic abolish printing itself, since printing has been misused. To paraphrase Mallarmé: semantics would make us Promethean inventors, minus the vulture (*"égaux de Prométhée à qui manque un vautour"*).

A comprehensive vocabulary, for social purposes, will persistently outrage the norms of the semantic ideal. It will not be unweighted; rather, it will have a maximum complexity of weighting. It will strike and retreat, compliment and insult, challenge and grovel, sing, curse, and whimper, subside and recover. Repeatedly, it will throw forth observations that are as accurate, in the realistic charting of human situations, as any ideal semantic formula. Many proverbs are brilliantly so. It will "neutralize" a meaning at any desired point. But such behavior must be merely taken in its stride. And its test of a "true" meaning will be its ability to fit into a piece with all other meanings, which is something radically different from the sheer expectancy that comes with conditioned salivation at the sound of a bell. (I sometimes wonder whether all of human "progress" is to be summed up as the insertion of an "i" in the word "salvation.")

9. COMPLAINTS. *The semantic style is bad style,* except in those who violate its tenets, as Newton violated them in the resonance of the language in which he gave account of his "celestial mechanics." Charts, graphs, crop reports, "intelligence," editorial comment, low-powered description—

all such is justifiable only in so far as "we gotta live," justifiable in short by the real or hoped-for "return on the investment."

Perhaps it is unfair to attack all this in the name of semantics, yet it is more legitimate to characterize it as poor semantics than as poor poetry. Information is quite often "semantically" sound. But it is rarely resonant. The percentage of such stuff has become too high. Unawares, we have allowed ourselves to take it as the *norm,* thereby confusing a norm with an average.

Even in poetry itself, "the norm" has encroached. I wonder how long it has been since a poet has asked himself: "What would I say if I wanted to present Miss Q with a gift, accompanied by a deft verbal compliment?—or what would I say if I wanted to knife someone *neatly?*" Or since someone told himself: "Suppose I did not simply wish to load upon the broad shoulders of the public medium, my own ungainly appetites and ambitions? Suppose that, gnarled as I am, I did not consider it enough simply to seek payment for my gnarledness, the establishment of communion through evils held in common? Suppose I would also erect a structure of encouragement, for all of us? How should I go about it, in the sequence of imagery, not merely to bring us most poignantly *into* hell, but also *out* again? Should I leave the curse of a malign spell upon us, in so far as I am able, and in so far as my audience cannot shake it off of themselves by discounting and triviality? Must there not, for every flight, be also a return, before my work can be called complete as a moral act?"

The thought suggests what must have been going on when the symphonic form was vital. The opening allegro: calm before storm. The sorrows, risks, and the ingenious struggles of movements two and three. And the final celebration, as a "way out," the bright clapping of the hands that releases the hypnotic spell (or should we say, supplants it with a daylight spell?). Then, as we move from the symphony towards the tone poem, we turn from this *rounded* aesthetic to the aesthetic of the Poe story. The one corrosive spell, leaving it for the reader's own enterprise or superficiality to shake himself free of the burden it would shift from the writer's shoulders upon his, as sacrificial goat. Alpheus without Arethusa.

Is it possible that writers are forgetting what to ask of their paragraphs? And should we think all the more on this subject, since we seem threatened with a period of political gloom ranging anywhere from a repellent aimlessness to an even more repellent aim (and if we get the latter, men will give blows with twice the fury of blows, striking the external enemy with vengeance, and making him also the recipient of their rage against the past uncertainties within themselves, a double-duty form of assertion we may fear especially in our frustrated businessmen, whose businesses have got in each other's way, and who are looking earnestly for someone to serve as vessel of their rage). We must get sturdiness from somewhere—we must seek some kind of physical muscle and its mental counterparts.

If a dismal political season is in store for us, shall we not greatly need a campaign base for personal integrity, a kind of beneath-which-not? And I wonder whether we might find this beneath-which-not in a more strenuous cult of style. This effort has been made many times in the past—and as regularly has been despised at other times, when there was no longer any need for it. Style for its own sake? Decidedly, not at all. Style solely as the *beneath-which-not,* as the *ad-*

monitory and hortatory act, as the *example* that would prod continually for its completion in all aspects of life, and so, in Eliot's phrase, "keep something alive," tiding us over a lean season. And there is all the more reason for us to attempt doing what we can by *present* imagery, since the promissory, the rewards of "postponed consumption," hold out so little of encouragement for the political future within our lifetime. So might we, rather than living wholly by a future that threatens so strongly to refute us, do rather what we can to live in a present that may in good time spread into the future?

Do not get me wrong. I am pleading for no "retreat" to anything. No literary Buchmanism, no off-by-itself, no back-to. Let our enlistments remain as they are. I am asking simply that the *temper* of our enlistment undergo a change of emphasis. That the *norm* of our tone cease to be the insulting tone that "talks down" to people. Nor would it be a presumptuous tone, that laid claim to uplift them. But rather a tone that would plead with us all, with the writer-to as well as the written-to. In it there must also be disdain, for those who have been giving the final insult to democracy, as they contrive to suggest that one almost has a moral obligation to write trivially and superficially, as though one could only show a proper love of mankind by plying the citizenry with flimsy items, "to be used once and thrown away."

The editor was late. The paper was ready for the printer, all but the columns reserved for him. Yet he knocked off his opinions on the state of the world in time to beat the deadline. Reading them, one recalled: "Yours of the twelfth inst. to hand, and have noted same. In reply would beg to state that we . . . etc." This is "the norm." By it all else is tested. It has its place. And unquestionably, the opinions

162

of a trained opinionator, situated at a strategic point with relation to the channels of information and advice, may even thus haphazardly make better comment than could a man deprived of his advantages. The question is: have they done anything? Can they, in this form, possibly do anything? I submit that they cannot. And further, I submit that, in so far as they become "the norm," they serve to prevent the doing of anything. On the other hand, out of attempts to key up the values of style, there could emerge writers whose muscularity was a fit with the requirements of the people. As things now stand, "the norm" prevents even an attempt at such selectivity.

In keeping with this norm, bright boys are imported from the provinces, put through the mill, stamped with a method, and used hard until they are used up—whereupon other bright boys are imported to take their places, the whole being kept on its toes despite disgust and boredom by muscling in and the fear of muscling in, with financial hashish as the positive incentive.

Or imagine this hypothetical case: Imagine an investigator who confided: "I've finished collating my material; I have my findings; but I haven't been able to write them up; I can't get the right sentence to start the whole thing going." The notion seems almost impertinent. The fact is that he would say his say, without a qualm, though his sentences rattled like dice in a box. When considering the welter of minor investigations that are now taken as the normal output of the academic bureaucracy, arising from the fact that everybody is expected to codify something or other for his degree, while the disproportionate flow of incomes acts to support a vast quantity of such low-powered collations—when considering these stamp collections of an overly prolif-

erating priesthood, I have wondered whether we might legitimately try to introduce some new kind of Occam's Razor,
some new test for exclusion of the inessential. Suppose, for
example, that a man were permitted only to say something
that he could grow eloquent about. That is, suppose he were
to place this requirement upon himself. I grant that there
would be much persiflage released upon the world. But every
once in a while it wouldn't be persiflage. And much that
now gets "scientific immunity" by reason of its very pallor
(a kind of "protection by unnoticeableness") would in its
attempted keying-up expose itself the more readily to weed-
ing-out. As things now stand, its pallor enjoys protective col-
oration by its close likeness to the journalistic pallor, that is
"the norm."

10. CONCLUSION. It would be unfair to lay all these ills
to the "semantic ideal." It might be more just to say that the
semantic ideal is the *perfection* of trends which we find here
in their aggravatedly *imperfect* state. At its best, it has an
incisiveness, an accuracy of formulation, a nicety, that makes
it itself a style. But anything short of it becomes the mere
riding of a convenience. And even at its best, when isolated
from the total texture of language, it is insufficient, and
promotes the upbuilding of a fallacious equipment.

Above all, it fosters, sometimes explicitly, sometimes by
implication, the notion that one may comprehensively discuss human and social events in a nonmoral vocabulary, and
that perception itself is a nonmoral act. It is the moral
impulse that motivates perception, giving it both intensity
and direction, suggesting *what to look for* and *what to look
out for*. Only by wanting very profoundly to make improvement, can we get a glimpse into the devious personal and
impersonal factors that operate to balk improvement. Or,

stating this in reverse, we could say that the structural firmness in a character like Iago is in itself an evidence of Shakespeare's moral depth. For it was in knowing what to look for that Shakespeare also knew what to look out for. We might even say that Shakespeare constructed this archdemon by making him an ominous caricature of the playwright's own methods, so that he becomes an admonishment not only to us, but to his inventor. For that peculiarly subtle variant of the "confidence game" in which Iago was an adept, inciting Othello to participate by leading him always to complete the surmises for himself, never wholly saying them, but all-but-saying them, and saying them in such a way that there is only one course for Othello to follow in building "logically" upon them, and taking double precautions to keep him in this track by constant repetition of goatish imagery—are not these Shakespeare's own profoundest wiles, here made sinister? So let the poetic ideal be sloganized as *Iago-plus-Ariel*—and let the semantic ideal be sloganized as a *neutral realm eliminating both.*

By our choice here, we should seek for neutralization *at moments,* for given purposes, and not as a blanket program for vocabulary, since the loss in *action now* (that is, in full moral asseveration) would be too great were the semantic ideal to prevail. We can understand why adepts at any given specialization might want to erect these neutralizing moments into a whole trade, asking that the whole world be seen from the perspective of their "occupational psychosis." We can understand why, through living professionally with a neutral vocabulary, they should favor the thought of its ideal extension until it has encompassed all vocabulary. But merely because they have found a way of prolonging the insight of one moment through a life-work, giving it body in documentation and routine, even that is not argument enough to make us believe that the realm of the affections can or should be expressed *ordine geometrico* (an aim that Spinoza expressed explicitly, whereas the humane attractiveness of his Ethics owes much to the fact that he implicitly violated his own program repeatedly, beginning perhaps with his first proposition, *Substantia prior est natura suis affectionibus,* for "substance" has since been shown to be a very *resonant* word).

We have, as it happens, the "neutral" word *shoe,* capable of designating equally well the shoe worn by a communist and the shoe worn by a fascist. One can imagine that we had instead only two weighted words, *bims* and *bams,* so that the same object worn by a communist *had* to be called a bim that, if worn by a fascist, could only in the pieties of poetry be called a bam. A liberal shoe manufacturer, making footwear for export, might then label his consignments to Germany bams and his consignments to Russia bims. And he would be grateful for some "neutralizer" who helped him simplify the keeping of his ledgers by inventing a purely "scientific" word, *shoe,* that would include both classes. But I have purposely imagined inventing a neutral word that we already have, to replace two weighted words we don't have, as a way of suggesting that spontaneous speech can, and repeatedly does, neutralize, where the occasion requires.

So, the poetic vocabulary, when complete, will take us into-and-out-of (the complete play with its exhilaration at the close). When incomplete, it will take us into, and seek to leave us there (the "aesthetic of the Poe story"). While the semantic vocabulary would, I think, unintentionally cheat us, by keeping us without, providing a kind of quietus in advance, never even giving the dramatic opposition a chance, avoiding the error which Lucretius made, at the sacrifice of his work as "science" and to its great gain as "poetry."

Paradoxically, however, we may also judge the semantic vocabulary as "imagery," as "secular prayer," as itself exemplifying a form of consolational dance, all in the tone of perfect peacefulness. Judged as a refuge from something, that would not permit even the mere mention of that from which it was a refuge, it becomes itself an attenuated form of poetry, with its own modes of hypnosis. Or we may consider it valuable as a *stage*, a kind of purgatorial disembodiment helpful for transition from an old poetic vocabulary whose weightings are all askew to a new poetic vocabulary whose weightings will be better fitted to the situations it would encompass. As preparation, as discipline, as itself pointing out some important things "to look for and to look out for," it can be saluted. It is only when it is considered as an ideal in itself, rather than as a preparation for new and more accurate weighting, that one need turn against it.

The ideal word is in itself an act, its value contained in its use at the moment of utterance. Its worth does not reside in its "usefulness" and promise (though that is certainly a part of it) but in its *style* as morals, as petition, in the *quality* of the petition, not in the *success* of the petition. For preparations, anything may serve, everything does serve —but preparations must not usurp the guise of fulfillments.

THE VIRTUES AND
LIMITATIONS OF DEBUNKING

THE word "debunking" has gone into our language because it fills a need. It refers in general to that class of
literature designed to show that George Washington did not
cut down the cherry tree, and the highly alembicated variants of such. It counters the inflating of reputations by the
deflating of reputations. It is the systematic "let down" that
matches the systematic "build up." At one time in America
an aspect of it went by the name of "muckraking." It took
a notable step forward with the biographical methods of
Lytton Strachey. But it had been given an explicit methodology as far back as the utilitarian philosophy of Jeremy
Bentham, with his schemes for disclosing the ways in
which material interests are masked by "eulogistic coverings."

Among Bentham's ideological inventions was his "Pan-
opticon," a project for a model prison so arranged that an
overseer, centrally located, could at all times observe the
behavior of the prisoners. Reading of this project with
Bentham's critique of language in mind, one is tempted to
ask whether it was not the perfect symbolization of Bentham's attitude toward spontaneous human speech itself.
Moralizing words he looked upon as transgressors; if not to
be imprisoned, they were at least to be put on probation
—and Bentham, by his analysis of language, developed a

"panoptical" perspective from which he could constantly observe his verbal suspects for signs of ill behavior.

Going still further back, we may note the emergence of the debunking attitude in the works of Machiavelli and Hobbes. Machiavelli tended to consider the "ungrateful, deceitful, cowardly, and greedy" aspects of men not as an aspect of their "fall," but as the very *essence* of their nature. Lying was not a *deviation* from the norm, it *was* the norm. Beneath this strategy, to be sure, there was a humane motive. Machiavelli felt, I believe, that since virtues are by very definition rare, they are a frail structure upon which to build a state. But if you could found a state upon vice, you would have a firm foundation indeed. And in an age of marked instability, Machiavelli was searching vigorously for firmness, a kind of beneath-which-not. Similarly, Hobbes based his arguments for political authority upon the "nasty" and "brutish" nature of men, who required an absolute monarch to hold their essential meanness in check. You may trail this mode of thought down through the paradoxes of Mandeville. And finally, in Adam Smith, it becomes *benign,* as Smith worked out a structure whereby the sheer accumulations of mutually conflicting individual greeds added up to a grand total of social benefit.

In brief, the history of debunking is interwoven with the history of liberalism. As soon as men began methodically to question the Church's vocabulary of human motivation, they gravitated towards the debunking category. The productivity of this attitude has been astounding. We might even with justice attribute to it the growth of psychology as a science (or, if you don't like that, the growth of psychology as a body of documented speculations). Particularly when you get to psychoanalysis, with its polysyllabic ways of ramifying the notion that "the wish is father to the thought," you are close to the center of the debunking approach.

I want here to discuss the debunking line, using as my text a recent bright and stimulating example, Thurman W. Arnold's *The Folklore of Capitalism*, which Arnold describes in his preface as "an application to a broader field of the same point of view represented in my former book, *The Symbols of Government.*" I agree with Arnold that there is no fundamental difference between these two works, so far as the general strategy of the thinking is concerned. The newer book is the more popular, probably because of its much greater reliance upon anecdote as the basis of his exposition. These anecdotes, chosen mainly from representative political, economic, and judicial pronouncements and maneuvers of 1937, are extremely entertaining. Arnold tells his stories in a lightly running style, with a catchy seasoning of irony, and with a cunning sense of showmanship. And whatever I may say about his book, by way of reservations, I do not wish to belittle its accomplishments. I can imagine many a reader who would refuse to follow Veblen's *The Theory of Business Enterprise* yet would read *The Folklore of Capitalism* with engrossment. And it must be saluted for its ability thus to "tap" new areas of the public, drawing them closer to a skeptical attitude towards our ailing status quo, and giving this attitude documentary substance by examples chosen from the press and from current investigations.

Arnold himself, to be sure, disclaims the rôle of the debunker. He realizes that, in attributing human action to motives low in the scale of values, we tend unwittingly to cheat ourselves. For if all men are in the same boat, and that boat is sunk, we too are sunk in the general sinking. In a total slump of the market, one's own holdings must likewise slump. And since we are all stockholders in the corporation of mankind, the debunker and his allies suffer with the debunked. It is my contention here that, although Arnold *explicitly* disclaims membership in the debunking line, his two books are implicitly perfect examples of this line.

I think that the typical debunker is involved in a strategy of this sort: He discerns an evil. He wants to eradicate this evil. And he wants to do a thorough job of it. Hence, in order to be sure that he is *thorough enough,* he becomes *too thorough.* In order to knock the underpinnings from beneath the arguments of his opponents, he perfects a mode of argument that would, if carried out consistently, also knock the underpinnings from beneath his own argument. But at this important juncture he simply "pulls his punch," refusing to apply as a test of his own position the arguments by which he has dissolved his opponents' position. If anyone is to say *"tu quoque,"* he leaves it to his opponents to do so. And he makes the application of the *"tu quoque"* test more difficult for his opponents by unconscious subterfuges on his part, involving ambiguities that are hard to discover.

In short: in order to shatter his opponents' policies, he adopts a position whereby he could not logically advocate a policy of his own. And then, since there comes a point at which he too must advocate something or other, he *covertly* restores important ingredients of thought that he has *overtly* annihilated. In Arnold's case, the strategic use of ambiguities is quite simple. He realizes the many ways in which discussions about "principles" have been misused in the current battle of words. Noting how the reference to "principle," which should be a *guide* to social adjustment, has

171

been misused as a mere *obstruction* to social adjustment, he wishes to prevent this misuse. So, in order to prevent the *misuse*, he ridicules the *use*. This would seem analogous to the project of a doctor who would prevent heart trouble by getting rid of hearts. However, since Arnold himself is not interested in being merely the destroyer, but would also uphold exhortations of his own, he must refer his policies to some basis. And having outlawed such reference by his jibes at those who think by "principles," he reintroduces the same way of thinking under the strategically altered name of "propositions."

Again, he does much damage to those who would try to advocate policies by "rational" tests. Some of his most entertaining pages are devoted to a picture of men as being essentially "irrational" in their conduct. But when he would recommend some policies of government that he considers necessary, he pleads for them as "sensible." Hence, what is overtly thrown out as "rational," is covertly brought back under the disarming guise of the "sensible." This same homely appeal, incidentally, is also implicit in his use of "comfort" as the test of a policy. The test of "comfort" is not much of a variant on Bentham's test of "utility." Yet the shift seems to have had its strategic value in persuasiveness, as a reviewer in *The New Republic* presented Arnold's book as something challengingly new in Western thought (the newness at this point apparently residing in the fact that "comfort" has more of a book-and-carpet-slippers-in-an-armchair-by-the-radiator tone than Bentham's "utility").

Again, we find much guying of those who think by the use of "abstract ideals." Yet towards the end of *The Folklore of Capitalism*, where the author is summarizing his positive position, we come upon Proposition 20: "A social need which runs counter to an abstract ideal will always be incompetently met until it gets a philosophy of its own. The process of building up new abstractions to justify filling new needs is always troublesome in any society, and may be violent." This proposition, if I interpret it correctly, clearly shows a recognition of the fact that we must have abstract ideals as a basis of social judgment. The reader who does not know the book will find nothing bothersome about this proposition. But after reading more than three hundred pages devoted to the guying of those who think by reference to "ideals," I think he will tend, rather, to look upon these lines as distinctly contraband. As "ideals" such thinking is thrown out, so that the author may throw out the exhortations of the enemy. But since the author also would exhort, they are brought back, under the name of "abstractions" and "a philosophy of its own."

Arnold is very enlightened in his attitude towards word magic. He would show little mercy to such ritualistic manipulations as we get when Saul, changing his identity, becomes Paul. Yet I wonder whether, even beneath his enlightened essay, making sport of such procedures, there may not be something similar taking place. Maybe all we have here is not some fundamental difference between poetic and essayistic methods; maybe "word magic" is more easily disclosed in poetry, but also prevails in the essay. Maybe the turn from "principles" to "propositions" is but the turn from "Saul" to "Paul." Maybe the poet's shift from "Tantris" to "Tristan" equals the essayist's shift from "rational" to "sensible." I have praised Arnold's showmanship. Much of it is got by debunking the "dramatic" ingredient in human conduct. Maybe his own indictment is more "dramatic" in its texture than he himself suspects.

I have, then, suggested, as the first mark of the debunker, the fact that, in order to combat a *bad* argument, he develops a position so thorough that it would combat *all* arguments—and then must covertly so rework this position that he may spare his own argument from the general slaughter. This he generally does, I have suggested, by an unintentional ambiguity whereby he throws something out by *one* name and brings it back by *another* name.

The situation calling forth this strategy has, of course, much to make us sympathetic with the strategist. Matches may be used either to light our pipes or burn down our houses. And one can well understand why, if they were being used almost entirely for the purpose of burning down our houses, a thinker should arise to say: "Let us have no more matches." By preventing the use, he could prevent the misuse. And then, if he still had occasion to light his pipe, he might make an altered recommendation of this sort: "What we really need is *lighters*." He might go on to show that matches are largely derived from tradition, whereas lighters are modern. And in our eagerness for the solution, we might be willing to meet the thinker halfway, failing thereby to note that lighters could be misused in quite the same way as matches were.

If you think that this is an absurd analogy, I might draw a parallel from the book itself. Arnold plays havoc with courts, as distinct from "administrative tribunals." He shows the medieval aspects of the law court, its substitution of "trial by wit" for "trial by combat." He discloses the purely "dramatic" nature of its conflicts. And when he comes forward with his plea for "administrative tribunals" as the solution for all this, you are invited to think that some totally different kind of situation would operate here. In this particular instance, he has so strongly stressed the *ritualistic* ingredients of the law court, and so slighted the rôle played by the *clash of interests* in legal combat, that you are invited to believe in the superiority of tribunals over courts simply because tribunals, being new, lack traditionalistic ritual. The *real* issue underlying conflicts, whether in courts or in tribunals, is of course the matter of conflicting interests. But by stressing the fact that courts rely upon rituals and that tribunals would not, you are led to think that we could solve the problem by getting rid of the *ritual*.

In any event, we have at present a situation that makes us sympathetic with the debunker's efforts. For conservatives and reactionaries have developed a most disturbing strategy. It would seem that they are no longer bothering to seek *good* arguments; rather, they are content to seek *any* arguments, if only there be enough of them kept running through the headlines, an *avalanche* of arguments, condemnations, prophecies of dire calamity, "statistical proofs," pronouncements by private and institutional "authorities," a barrage, a snowing under, a purely *quantitative* mode of propaganda. Are there no eagles among their publicized utterances? Very well; then let them be instead a swarm of mosquitoes. Before you could refute this morning's, there is a new batch out this afternoon. Anything, everything, if only it all points in the same general direction—a truly cynical exemplification of the slogan that "in union there is strength," a kind of "idealistic collectivism," a fabulous state of affairs whereby free speech is preserved only to be mocked at, the "free speech" that permits whispering "no" to a few friends and cronies while the loudspeakers blast forth a rousing "yes" for millions.

Seeing this, one has sympathy with the man who would

work fast, seeking for some quick cure-all. Arnold's book approached from this angle, is something to be grateful for. At its best, its very liabilities become its assets. For he does picturesque work particularly in confounding the output of the right, that group whose slogan, when confronting the Constitution, might very properly be: "Made to help, used to hinder."

But here again, Arnold relies upon an ambiguity for his effects. "Why object to that?" you may ask. "Why sit up all night worrying lest unfairness be treated unfairly?" But the matter is not so simple. For unfairness does not only confound the enemy. It may also confound one's allies, since it may lead *both sides* into a wrong view of the situation. It might be satisfactory as mere vengeance; but it becomes more than vengeance, it becomes a guide by its own right, and as a guide it is fallacious. To be specific:

Arnold is attacking the tremendous contemporary breach between ideals and practices. He is attempting to deprive apologetics of that persuasive device whereby, in converting every controversial issue about a practical measure into a matter of the highest moral principle, the priesthood of the *status quo* does its best to make people fear the adoption of "sensible" measures. Thus, a given measure is not considered on the basis of whether or not it would take care of the problem at hand, but whether or not it leads to "regimentation," or "fascism," or "communism," or "destruction of the American system," etc. By such amplification, or in Bentham's term, "censorious" speech, practical issues are lifted to a moral plane that fills people with all sorts of irrelevant terrors. And only by underground political "horse-trading" does the work of the government get done at all. To combat these tactics, Arnold makes grotesque caricatures of such apologetics. The question is: does his caricature become *too* thorough, and in so doing, threaten to mislead us all?

Suppose, for instance, that you were to write a farce on mankind. Suppose you made up a composite character, called "Mr. Everybody," and you made this one character state all the divergent and mutually contradictory views held in real life by many different kinds and classes and ages of people. "Mr. Everybody" would obviously be the very opposite of the "consistent, logical or rational." He would be a hilarious bundle of contradictions. Now, in a way, it is just such a farce as this that Arnold works up, though on a smaller scale. When a given issue is being debated in the press, many different people come forward with their interpretation of this issue. Twenty different arguments, by twenty different kinds of spokesmen, may be offered, let us say, against "packing the Court." And though all these spokesmen may agree on the proposition that "the Court should not be packed," each may approach the issue from a different rationale. However, if you lumped all their arguments together, as though they were to be taken as aspects of a single argument, you could bring out all sorts of clashes among them. This is, I think, what Arnold does—thereby making people look much more irrational than they are in actuality.

He assembles his group with reference to an *interest* they share in common. But when interpreting the *motivation* behind their pronouncements, he drops the test of interests, by which he has selected his sitters for a composite portrait, and attributes their pronouncements instead to a love of *ritual*, of *ceremony*, of *parade*. Hence, the ambiguity here exploited for polemic, pamphleteering purposes resides in the fact that he simultaneously employs and discards the factor of interest, putting the group together on the basis of the interest they share in common, and then slighting this interest as an interpretation of their statements.

A man, to reach his destination, goes *up* the street one day; the next day, it is raining, so he reaches his destination by going *down* the street, to the corner where the bus stops. Now imagine a thinker who said to him, "Yesterday you went up the street, today you go down the street. What inconsistency!" He might answer by suggesting, "But look at the interests involved in each case." And looking, you would find no "inconsistency" whatsoever. The same is true, in a more complex way, of arguments that discuss policies in terms of principles. You advocate a policy by relating it to a different principle than you would select when attacking the policy. Thus, we heard business apologists, at the time when the controversy over social insurance was paramount, attributing all our "progress" to the capitalist "principle" of *insecurity,* that kept people on their toes, and so stimulated maximum production. Security, we were told, would destroy ambition. But recently these apologists have been concerned over a different issue. They would put a stop to any further legislative experiments at Washington. So we hear much about the "principle" of *security,* as we are reminded that businessmen must plan, and that they can intelligently plan only on the basis of expectancy, and that they cannot plan on the basis of expectancy while the future course of legislation in Congress is uncertain. Now, such shifting is cause enough for bewilderment, even if you introduce the doctrine of "interests." But if you deliberately omit it, or even worse, group the arguments for or against a measure on the basis of interests and then omit the factor of interests as a motive for explaining the nature of the arguments, you arrive at chaos itself. This is Arnold's strategy as a writer of farce. He builds up the picture of a fabulously irrational world by juxtaposing the shifts from up-the-street to down-the-street, leaving out matters of destination and attendant circumstance, and attributing the thought of his opponents to their sheer "irrational" penchant for "ritual."

We need not enter here into a defense of ritual. A play by a great dramatist may be shown to be quite "rational" in its organization. And though the use of "Dear Sir" as heading for a letter is a purely ritualistic "way in," given a society in which that is the accepted convention, I see nothing "irrational" in the conduct of an individual who began his letter by obeying it. For present purposes, however, it should be enough to point out that, whatever part the rituals of legalistic fiction may play in complicating contemporary procedure (as when the government incorporates a bureau in order to get the same advantages that private enterprises enjoy through incorporation), one deprives himself of a greatly needed interpretative weapon if, for ritualistic purposes of his own (in Arnold's case, the dramatic building of a "case" against legal and political drama), he slights the tremendous part played by the pressure of interests (whether correctly or incorrectly gauged) in shaping the tactics of political, judicial, or economic apologetics.

Surely, an overwhelming amount of our present legalistic confusion through profusion could be adequately accounted for by the *Zweck im Recht* mode of discounting, the search for *purpose* behind the law and behind the legislating of all ideologists (ranging from the crudest columnist-pamphleteer to the most scrupulous philosopher). A law is passed, for example, to put gangsters into prison, as a protection to prop-

179

erty. But a situation arises whereby the same law, if consistently applied, would also put some outstanding financier into prison. So, if said outstanding financier is influential enough, and can hire sufficiently able corporation lawyers, some saving loophole in the law is discovered. In short, the law becomes ambivalently interpreted by the courts, in such a way that the gangster-promoter stays in and the financial promoter stays out. Or conversely: A law is passed to help the financial promoter stay out. But if consistently applied, it would also allow the gangster-promoter to stay out. So some "subtilization" by the courts becomes necessary, whereby a "universal" law can be made "selective." Or a law made for the *protection* of labor is twisted, by ingenious lawyers, into a device for use *against* labor (quite as the Fourteenth Amendment has been interpreted in the interests of corporations). "Ritual" undoubtedly figures here. The judge may wear some special vestment, which has its equivalent in the judicial style itself. But obviously the major shaping influence behind such "living law" is due to interpretations made in accordance with the sympathies of the interpreters. As a result of it, an enormous body of legal casuistry piles up, with all kinds of internal contradictions. But to locate such a procedure by primary emphasis upon the rituals is to *deflect* accurate social criticism (serving, in Arnold's case, as an *apparent* argument for administrative tribunals, which are expected to solve our problems by eliminating the rituals, while the really basic matter of conflicting interests is slighted).

Arnold thereby manages to convey the idea that there is some fundamental difference between the "priestly" mind and the "organizational" mind that thinks in terms of "practical" going concerns. Yet he himself, after building up a picture of our businessmen, like Ford, as exemplars of the practical, organizational mind, is to be found at other points in his book attacking these same men for their tendency to judge proposed political measures from the "priestly" point of view. Such an approach to the issue seems to me as unwieldy and inaccurate in its way as the overemphasis upon the ritualistic. Ford sees problems of production in the Ford plant from the "organizational" point of view. But he cannot relate them to a *wider* frame of reference involving the organization of the entire state. Other people can—if only because they do not share Ford's relationship to the Ford organization. There is nothing "priestly" about it. Ford workers can see the "organizational problems" in a Ford plant in a way that Ford simply *cannot* see them. Theorists of labor can propose "rationalizations" of the workers' problem, with relation to a wider political context. Why introduce the "priestly" element here, as something categorically opposed to the "organizational"?

There is surely a great necessity for considering a crisis with relation to over-all political and economic necessities. People are building philosophic criticisms or defenses of Ford *because there is an organizational problem in the motor car industry.* I am not here using the word in its restricted sense, the "organizing" of labor. I am referring to the *organizational* problem involved in trying to use the productive capacity of Detroit's factories. One may, for polemic purposes, refer to the propaganda speeches broadcast during Ford's Sunday evening music hour as "priestly." But one cannot *dismiss*, as "priestly," every reasoned attempt to evaluate Ford's policies with reference to general social criteria, problems, necessities, etc. A reasoned political measure may, when carried into practice, encounter difficulties not foreseen at the time of the planning. But the same is true of an "organizational" decision of the sales strategists to price a car at a certain figure.

Of late, we have been hearing so much criticism of government by "blue prints," you might be led to think that architects no longer used blue prints. "Abstract ideals," I submit, are social blue prints. They are ways of shaping policies with relation to principles. They select measures with reference to directives. "Go two blocks north, and then one block east." The "two blocks" and "one block" are the "policy," the "north" and "east" the "principles." And let no barrister's indictment of the "priestly" mind as against the "organizational" mind lead you into thinking that you can locate things any differently.

It is very disarming to say that we should evaluate measures purely on the basis of their contribution to "comfort." But even "comfort," in this usage, is a *principle,* an abstract ideal. In fact, so far as I am concerned, it is much *too* abstract. Its danger resides in the fact that, because it *sounds* familiar, one thinks he knows what it means. Don't worry about such matters as the balancing of the budget, says Arnold. Yet some men demand it, because it would *comfort* them. Hence, it is not a matter merely of comfort, but of *whose* comfort, comfort spread over how large a section of the population, etc. Furthermore, though Arnold has said much about the part that drama plays in the activating of historic processes (a point in which I agree with him though I should want it all differently interpreted) one may legitimately be led to ask, by his test, what great dramatizations of comfort we have had to date. The "comfort" of spiritual solace, of social solidarity, etc.—but not "creature comfort," which is the brand that Arnold clearly has in mind, when he likens it to the kind of comfort provided by the doctors for the inmates of an asylum.

But that gets us to another point, the matter of "humanitarianism."

I believe that "humanitarianism" can also be singled out as an integral aspect of the debunking strategy. For, unless the thinker is totally antisocial, humanitarian elements *must* be engrafted upon modes of thinking that attribute human actions to motives low in the scale of values. The typical debunker might write a book to prove, for instance, that "all people are crooks." The logical conclusion from such a book would be, "So let's try to cheat them before they cheat us." But a purely humanitarian afterthought is usually added to the thesis. Out of nowhere comes a corrective, that seems to say, "Let's try to help them not to be crooks and not to be the victims of crooks."

Something of this sort was, I believe, at the basis of Peirce's differences with William James, differences that led Peirce to call his own philosophy by the slightly altered name, "pragmaticism." James said that efficacy was the test of truth. And then, as a humanitarian afterthought, he expressed the hope that we would apply this test only to "good" efficacy. Peirce resented this mere annexing of a corrective. He sought a test of truth whereby the moral evaluation would be an integral part of the test. James, as a humanitarian pragmatist, seemed to be saying in effect, "Truth is as truth does. But here's hoping that you'll only ask it to do nice things." Peirce, on the other hand, was demanding in his "pragmaticism" a test of truth that would contain, within itself, the proper moral exhortation.

Dewey's instrumentalism brings out James' problem even more clearly, in so far as instrumentalism becomes the philosophy of technology (a philosophy that tends to confront the rigidified routines of technology while interpreting them mainly in terms of liquidity). Technology is a coefficient of power. A power is something in itself "neutral," that can be used for either "good" or "evil." It is like ballistics, that can be employed to defend a good cause, or for Italian aggression in Ethiopia. Dewey's strategy was to make a power look like a good power—thereby replacing an ambivalence by an ambiguity. That technology is a power no one would deny; but a power is ambivalent, capable of good uses or bad; and Dewey's job was the "humanitarian" task of saying "Power is the test of truth," and then furtively annexing, "But let us mean *good* power."

The same device underlies his use of "intelligence," in *The Quest for Certainty*. For it is obvious that Iago used intelligence in obfuscating Othello, and that chemical warfare requires a high degree of intelligence. But by ambiguously equating power with good power, and intelligence with good intelligence, Dewey skirts the major philosophic issue. Again, in *Liberalism and Social Action*, he calls for a social program that will free us for the "development of our capacities," a plea that sounds persuasive because we are covertly invited to read, "the development of our good capacities." In this way, he need not explicitly consider the problem (which may, for all I know, be solvable) as to why the capacities should not, in this particular instance, be ambivalent. Beginning as a Hegelian, Dewey stressed ambivalence. But in proportion as his instrumentalism stood out in its own right, we get in place of overt ambivalence a covert humanitarian ambiguity.[1]

[1] In my *Attitudes Toward History* (Vol. I, pp. 21–23) I analyze Emerson's essay on "Compensation" as a strategy for combining ambivalence (that "every excess

A "nonhumanitarian" ideal of truth would, I think, require a perspective whereby the expository and the hortatory were contained in one. Arnold, on the other hand, must, as debunker, continually be making a distinction between himself as a scientific expositor (or "diagnostician") and himself as a civic personality. In *The Symbols of Government,* where his psychiatric tests of comfort are brought out most clearly, he writes:

> From a humanitarian point of view the best government is that which we find in an insane asylum. In such a government the physicians in charge do not separate the ideas of the insane into any separate sciences such as law, economics, sociology; nor then instruct the insane as to the soundness nor unsoundness of their ideas. Their aim is to make the inmates of the asylum as comfortable as possible.

He says, "The advantages of such a theory are that we escape the troublesome assumption that the human race is rational," and "This theory eliminates from our thinking the moral ideals which hamper us whenever a governmental institution takes practical action. . . . It frees us from the

---

causes a defect") with optimism (that "there is no penalty to virtue"). Emerson, who had great influence upon James, was presumably responding to the emergence of technological enterprise (power) while still confronting the issue in terms of good and evil. James' pragmatism moves us further into the purely optimistic emphasis, slighting the factor of ambivalence. Dewey's instrumentalism perfects the step away from transcendentalism to a strongly optimistic interpretation of power. I was wrong, however, in saying (in *Attitudes Toward History*) that Dewey at no point explicitly considers the factor of ambivalence. Ernest Sutherland Bates has referred me to several relevant sections in Dewey and Tuft's *Ethics* that deal with this matter. But applying the "method of difference," we note how this feature drops away, in proportion as Dewey's Hegelian beginnings are reshaped into an independent philosophy. And by the time we arrive at *Liberalism and Social Action,* it has dwindled to the vanishing point. Or we might put it this way: You are more likely to find the doctrine of ambivalence stressed in Dewey the philosopher of education than in Dewey the political advocate.

necessity about names, and arguing about the respective merits of communism, fascism, or capitalism."

These "advantages," of course, would be gained by outlawing any attempt at reasonable discussion. Such proscriptions would, to be sure, avoid the tricks whereby men combat a measure by converting it into false moral equivalents. Looking only so far, one can sympathize strongly with the intention, at least until one arrives at this, exemplifying the "humanitarian" breach between expository truth and hortatory truth:

> Thus the theory might work as a practical philosophy for politicians. Yet it will never work as a general political theory. The realism is too apparent, as also is its implied scorn of the human race. The reasons for its failure are the reasons for the failure of all common-sense theories of government in a rational world. In the first place, it cannot be an effective social force among the masses who want to believe that government is moral, rational, and symmetrical. Nor can it be satisfactory to intellectuals who want to believe that governmental theory is the product of ages of careful scholarly thought. Any theory based on a purely humanitarian ideal that any one can understand is too simple . . . to support complicated ratiocination. The detailed understanding of mechanical and social organization to carry out humanitarian ideals therefore does not inspire the intellectual.

> A curious dilemma confronts the social and economic sciences. These sciences must act as a kind of folklore, and to perform this function must be believed as truths. They must support a spiritual government, and to give

this support must depart from a real and enter into an ideal world. They must give practical institutions a logical place in that ideal world, without interfering with their freedom in practical affairs. These functions cannot be fulfilled by a mere theory that the world should be governed like an insane asylum. Therefore the illustration with which we began this chapter will never appear in the future as the guiding star of any human organization. Though it permits us to escape from the confusing consequences of calling men rational, it is defective as a working philosophy because of its contemptuous attitude toward the human race.

In sum, the author's proposed perspective, adopted for expository purposes, "does not endow mankind with the dignity, or the hope or the tragedy which most persons feel that it actually possesses." This kind of "enlightenment," then, would tell us a kind of *isolate* truth that is opposed to *social* truth. Indeed, when social truth is viewed from this perspective, it becomes little better than a kind of benign self-deception.

If such a drastic presentation of the case is necessary, there is no good ground for inveighing against it. But I question whether it is necessary. Must we take on such cumbersome baggage! And what a twisted picture of human conduct we get as a result, with the citizen's truth and the scientist's truth vastly at odds, and the scientist's truth about human conduct becoming something which the citizen must lie about, in order to act for any political ideal, whether of right, center, or left! It is obvious that, in a state like ours, where there are extreme conflicts of interests, a government that seeks to mediate somewhat among these conflicts must adopt measures somewhat at odds with one another. But need we leap from this to the conclusion that the whole basis of rationality is thereby swept away? Can there not be, in fact, rationales that discuss precisely this kind of conflict, its origin in the present structure of property relationships, and the organizational policies that would follow from such principles? In one's way of sizing up all this, one might very well be *wrong*—but must he necessarily be *irrational?* Or his rationale itself may take on nonrational, or even irrational ingredients, without obliging us to consider such accretions as the *essence* of his philosophy.

I personally contend that *there is no need* for such statement of the case as Arnold presents. There is no need for the humanitarian afterthought at all, making for the kind of breach between exposition and exhortation that offers you a "true" picture of mankind and then tells you that you must *act* on the basis of a different, "illusory" picture. There is no need for all this overt throwing-out and covert taking-back. People, taken by and large, are acting reasonably enough, *within their frame of reference.* This frame of reference may not be large enough to encompass all the important factors operating today. Hence, they need a *still wider* frame of reference. Admittedly, those who would uphold the *status quo,* and have a grip upon the channels of information and instruction, will make the establishment of a wider frame quite difficult, perhaps even impossible. But that is no ground for asking that we try to drop the whole attempt, substituting a purely cameralistic point of view towards administrative problems. It is precisely because our adepts at organizational activities have run into difficulties, precisely because the organizations do not fit properly with one another, that we must seek some more comprehensive rationale for discussing the situation in its broader aspects, and adopting measures accordingly.

Towards the end of *The Folklore of Capitalism*, Arnold seems to show some awareness of this more mature attitude towards his theme. The pure debunker begins to drop away, and propositions of hortatory cast emerge. I have tried to show how badly they fit with the farcical ingredients in his book. And I am trying to suggest that a *proper* presentation of his thesis would have required no such ambiguous tactics. I see no good reason, except perversities arising in response to the complexities of our times, why one should have to treat the *exposition* of human motives as synonymous with the *debunking* of human motives. And I hold that, if one refuses to accept this equation, one may seek rather such perspectives as interpret human events by making scientific diagnosis and moral exhortation integral aspects of one program.

Since I was here concerned primarily with bringing out the aspects of Arnold's book that had to do with the general subject of "motives," I have necessarily failed to give a total picture of the book itself. Hence, I should like to add a kind of "humanitarian afterthought" of my own, for correcting this special emphasis. The most valuable feature of Arnold's book, I think, resides in his evidence showing the nature of "business government" in the contemporary state. That is, he "debunks," by the amassing of much convincing evidence, the current tendency to believe that "business" and "government" are antithetical types. And he does this by showing the elements of feudal autocratic government operating in the conduct of business itself. Business enterprises, you come to realize, are hardly other than governments with-

189

out parliaments. However, the presentation of this thesis is interwoven with his logically unrelated account of human motives, with the *unnecessary* responsibilities of this view. Hence, we find interpreted as "ritual" the methods whereby the same management whose policies threw a concern into bankruptcy make additional profits out of its reorganization and are left afterwards in control. One might with as much justice treat as "ritual" a trained thief's technique for picking a man's pockets. Or, if you don't like that analogy, which is clear enough but prejudicial in its overtones, think up a kindlier one, along these lines: Certain men have been enjoying tenures of office that bring them material rewards, and they so use the current structure of law and representation as to perpetuate their enjoyment of such tenure. You may, if you will, maintain that the complex of meanings on the basis of which they act is inadequate in shaping a way of life for either themselves or their victims. You may say that the requirements of the state as a whole are at odds with the requirements of these minor groups. But that would be quite different from a claim that "abstract ideals" are in themselves purely a matter of ritual and illusion.

THE RHETORIC
OF HITLER'S "BATTLE"

THE appearance of *Mein Kampf* in unexpurgated translation has called forth far too many vandalistic comments.
There are other ways of burning books than on the pyre—
and the favorite method of the hasty reviewer is to deprive
himself and his readers by inattention. I maintain that it is
thoroughly vandalistic for the reviewer to content himself
with the mere inflicting of a few symbolic wounds upon this
book and its author, of an intensity varying with the resources of the reviewer and the time at his disposal. Hitler's
"Battle" is exasperating, even nauseating; yet the fact remains: If the reviewer but knocks off a few adverse attitu-
dinizings and calls it a day, with a guaranty in advance that
his article will have a favorable reception among the decent
members of our population, he is contributing more to our
gratification than to our enlightenment.

Here is the testament of a man who swung a great people
into his wake. Let us watch it carefully; and let us watch
it, not merely to discover some grounds for prophesying
what political move is to follow Munich, and what move to
follow that move, etc.; let us try also to discover what kind
of "medicine" this medicine-man has concocted, that we
may know, with greater accuracy, exactly what to guard
against, if we are to forestall the concocting of similar medicine in America.

191

Already, in many quarters of our country, we are "beyond" the stage where we are being saved from Nazism by our *virtues*. And fascist integration is being staved off, rather, by the *conflicts among our vices*. Our vices cannot get together in a grand united front of prejudices; and the result of this frustration, if or until they succeed in surmounting it, speaks, as the Bible might say, "in the name of" democracy. Hitler found a panacea, a "cure for what ails you," a "snakeoil," that made such sinister unifying possible within his own nation. And he was helpful enough to put his cards face up on the table, that we might examine his hands. Let us, then, for God's sake, examine them. This book is the well of Nazi magic; crude magic, but effective. A people trained in pragmatism should want to inspect this magic.

1

Every movement that would recruit its followers from among many discordant and divergent bands, must have some spot towards which all roads lead. Each man may get there in his own way, but it must be the one unifying center of reference for all. Hitler considered this matter carefully, and decided that this center must be not merely a centralizing hub of *ideas*, but a mecca geographically located, towards which all eyes could turn at the appointed hours of prayer (or, in this case, the appointed hours of prayer-in-reverse, the hours of vituperation). So he selected Munich, as the *materialization* of his unifying panacea. As he puts it:

> The geo-political importance of a center of a movement cannot be overrated. Only the presence of such a center and of a place, bathed in the magic of a Mecca

or a Rome, can at length give a movement that force which is rooted in the inner unity and in the recognition of a hand that represents this unity.

If a movement must have its Rome, it must also have its devil. For as Russell pointed out years ago, an important ingredient of unity in the Middle Ages (an ingredient that long did its unifying work despite the many factors driving towards disunity) was the symbol of a *common enemy*, the Prince of Evil himself. Men who can unite on nothing else can unite on the basis of a foe shared by all. Hitler himself states the case very succinctly:

> As a whole, and at all times, the efficiency of the truly national leader consists primarily in preventing the division of the attention of a people, and always in concentrating it on a single enemy. The more uniformly the fighting will of a people is put into action, the greater will be the magnetic force of the movement and the more powerful the impetus of the blow. It is part of the genius of a great leader to make adversaries of different fields appear as always belonging to one category only, because to weak and unstable characters the knowledge that there are various enemies will lead only too easily to incipient doubts as to their own cause.
>
> As soon as the wavering masses find themselves confronted with too many enemies, objectivity at once steps in, and the question is raised whether actually all the others are wrong and their own nation or their own movement alone is right.
>
> Also with this comes the first paralysis of their own strength. Therefore, a number of essentially different

enemies must always be regarded as one in such a way that in the opinion of the mass of one's own adherents the war is being waged against one enemy alone. This strengthens the belief in one's own cause and increases one's bitterness against the attacker.

As everyone knows, this policy was exemplified in his selection of an "international" devil, the "international Jew" (the Prince was international, universal, "catholic"). This *materialization* of a religious pattern is, I think, one terrifically effective weapon of propaganda in a period where religion has been progressively weakened by many centuries of capitalist materialism. You need but go back to the sermonizing of centuries to be reminded that religion had a powerful enemy long before organized atheism came upon the scene. Religion is based upon the "prosperity of poverty," upon the use of ways for converting our sufferings and handicaps into a good—but capitalism is based upon the prosperity of acquisitions, the only scheme of value, in fact, by which its proliferating store of gadgets could be sold, assuming for the moment that capitalism had not got so drastically in its own way that it can't sell its gadgets even after it has trained people to feel that human dignity, the "higher standard of living," could be attained only by their vast private accumulation.

So, we have, as unifying step No. 1, the international devil materialized, in the visible, point-to-able form of people with a certain kind of "blood," a burlesque of contemporary neo-positivism's ideal of meaning, which insists upon a *material* reference.

Once Hitler has thus essentialized his enemy, all "proof" henceforth is automatic. If you point out the enormous

amount of evidence to show that the Jewish worker is at
odds with the "international Jew stock exchange capitalist,"
Hitler replies with one hundred per cent regularity: That
is one more indication of the cunning with which the "Jewish plot" is being engineered. Or would you point to
"Aryans" who do the same as his conspiratorial Jews? Very
well; that is proof that the "Aryan" has been "seduced" by
the Jew.

The sexual symbolism that runs through Hitler's book,
lying in wait to draw upon the responses of contemporary
sexual values, is easily characterized: Germany in dispersion
is the "dehorned Siegfried." The masses are "feminine." As
such, they desire to be led by a dominating male. This male,
as orator, woos them—and, when he has won them, he commands them. The rival male, the villainous Jew, would on
the contrary "seduce" them. If he succeeds, he poisons their
blood by intermingling with them. Whereupon, by purely
associative connections of ideas, we are moved into attacks
upon syphilis, prostitution, incest, and other similar misfortunes, which are introduced as a kind of "musical" argument when he is on the subject of "blood-poisoning" by
intermarriage or, in its "spiritual" equivalent, by the infection of "Jewish" ideas, such as democracy.[1]

The "medicinal" appeal of the Jew as scapegoat operates
from another angle. The middle class contains, within the
mind of each member, a duality: its members simultaneously have a cult of money and a detestation of this cult.
When capitalism is going well, this conflict is left more or
less in abeyance. But when capitalism is balked, it comes to

[1] Hitler also strongly insists upon the total identification between leader and
people. Thus, in wooing the people, he would in a roundabout way be wooing
himself. The thought might suggest how the Führer, dominating the feminine
masses by his diction, would have an incentive to remain unmarried.

the fore. Hence, there is "medicine" for the "Aryan" members of the middle class in the projective device of the scapegoat, whereby the "bad" features can be allocated to the "devil," and one can "respect himself" by a distinction between "good" capitalism and "bad" capitalism, with those of a different lodge being the vessels of the "bad" capitalism. It is doubtless the "relief" of this solution that spared Hitler the necessity of explaining just how the "Jewish plot" was to work out. Nowhere does this book, which is so full of war plans, make the slightest attempt to explain the steps whereby the triumph of "Jewish Bolshevism," which destroys *all* finance, will be the triumph of *"Jewish"* finance. Hitler well knows the point at which his "elucidations" should rely upon the lurid alone.

The question arises, in those trying to gauge Hitler: Was his selection of the Jew, as his unifying devil-function, a purely calculating act? Despite the quotation I have already given, I believe that it was *not*. The vigor with which he utilized it, I think, derives from a much more complex state of affairs. It seems that, when Hitler went to Vienna, in a state close to total poverty, he genuinely suffered. He lived among the impoverished; and he describes his misery at the spectacle. He was *sensitive* to it; and his way of manifesting this sensitiveness impresses me that he is, at this point, wholly genuine, as with his wincing at the broken family relationships caused by alcoholism, which he in turn relates to impoverishment. During this time he began his attempts at political theorizing; and his disturbance was considerably increased by the skill with which Marxists tied him into knots. One passage in particular gives you reason, reading between the lines, to believe that the dialecticians of the class struggle, in their skill at blasting his muddled speculations, put him into a state of uncertainty that was finally "solved" by rage:

> The more I argued with them, the more I got to know their dialectics. First they counted on the ignorance of their adversary; then, when there was no way out, they themselves pretended stupidity. If all this was of no avail, they refused to understand or they changed the subject when driven into a corner; they brought up truisms, but they immediately transferred their acceptance to quite different subjects, and, if attacked again, they gave way and pretended to know nothing exactly. Wherever one attacked one of these prophets, one's hands seized slimy jelly; it slipped through one's fingers only to collect again in the next moment. If one smote one of them so thoroughly that, with the bystanders watching, he could but agree, and if one thus thought he had advanced at least one step, one was greatly astonished the following day. The Jew did not in the least remember the day before, he continued to talk in the same old strain as if nothing had happened, and if indignantly confronted, he pretended to be astonished and could not remember anything except that his assertions had already been proved true the day before.
>
> Often I was stunned.
>
> One did not know what to admire more: their glibness of tongue or their skill in lying.
>
> I gradually began to hate them.

At this point, I think, he is tracing the *spontaneous* rise of his anti-Semitism. He tells how, once he had discovered the "cause" of the misery about him, he could *confront it*. Where he had had to avert his eyes, he could now *positively welcome* the scene. Here his drastic structure of *acceptance* was being formed. He tells of the "internal happiness" that descended upon him.

> This was the time in which the greatest change I was ever to experience took place in me.
> From a feeble cosmopolite I turned into a fanatical anti-Semite,

and thence we move, by one of those associational tricks which he brings forth at all strategic moments, into a vision of the end of the world—out of which in turn he emerges with his slogan: "I am acting in the sense of the Almighty Creator: *By warding off Jews I am fighting for the Lord's work*" (italics his).

He talks of this transition as a period of "double life," a struggle of "reason" and "reality" against his "heart." [2] It was as "bitter" as it was "blissful." And finally, it was

[2] Other aspects of the career symbolism: Hitler's book begins: "Today I consider it my good fortune that Fate designated Braunau on the Inn as the place of my birth. For this small town is situated on the border between those two German States, the reunion of which seems, at least to us of the younger generation, a task to be furthered with every means our lives long," an indication of his "transitional" mind, what Wordsworth might have called the "borderer." He neglects to give the date of his birth, 1889, which is supplied by the editors. Again there is a certain "correctness" here, as Hitler was not "born" until many years later—but he does give the exact date of his war wounds, which were indeed formative. During his early years in Vienna and Munich, he foregoes protest, on the grounds that he is "nameless." And when his party is finally organized and effective, he stresses the fact that his "nameless" period is over (i. e., he has shaped himself an identity). When reading in an earlier passage of his book some generalizations to the effect that one should not crystallize his political views until he is thirty, I made a note: "See what Hitler does at thirty." I felt sure that, though such generalizations may be dubious as applied to people as a whole, they must, given the Hitler type of mind (with his complete identification between himself and his followers), be valid statements about himself. One *should* do what he *did*. The hunch was verified: about the age of thirty Hitler, in a group of seven, began working with the party that was to conquer Germany. I trace these steps particularly because I believe

"reason" that won! Which prompts us to note that those who attack Hitlerism as a cult of the irrational should emend their statements to this extent: irrational it is, but it is carried on under the *slogan* of "Reason." Similarly, his cult of war is developed "in the name of" humility, love, and peace. Judged on a quantitative basis, Hitler's book certainly falls under the classification of hate. Its venom is everywhere, its charity is sparse. But the rationalized family tree for this hate situates it in "Aryan love." Some deep-probing German poets, whose work adumbrated the Nazi movement, did gravitate towards thinking *in the name of* war, irrationality, and hate. But Hitler was not among them. After all, when it is so easy to draw a doctrine of war out of a doctrine of peace, why should the astute politician do otherwise, particularly when Hitler has slung together his doctrines, without the slightest effort at logical symmetry? Furthermore, Church thinking always got to its wars in Hitler's "sounder" manner; and the patterns of Hitler's thought are a bastardized or caricatured version of religious thought.

I spoke of Hitler's fury at the dialectics of those who opposed him when his structure was in the stage of scaffolding. From this we may move to another tremendously important aspect of his theory: his attack upon the *parliamentary*. For it is again, I submit, an important aspect of his medicine, in its function as medicine for him personally and as medicine for those who were later to identify themselves with him.

---

that the orator who has a strong sense of his own "rebirth" has this to draw upon when persuading his audiences that his is offering them the way to a "new life." However, I see no categorical objection to this attitude; its menace derives solely from the values in which it is exemplified. They may be wholesome or unwholesome. If they are unwholesome, but backed by conviction, the basic sincerity of the conviction acts as a sound virtue to reinforce a vice—and this combination is the most disastrous one that a people can encounter in a demagogue.

There is a "problem" in the parliament—and nowhere was this problem more acutely in evidence than in the pre-war Vienna that was to serve as Hitler's political schooling. For the parliament, at its best, is a "babel" of voices. There is the wrangle of men representing interests lying awkwardly on the bias across one another, sometimes opposing, sometimes vaguely divergent. Morton Prince's psychiatric study of "Miss Beauchamp," the case of a woman split into several sub-personalities at odds with one another, variously combining under hypnosis, and frequently in turmoil, is the allegory of a democracy fallen upon evil days. The parliament of the Habsburg Empire just prior to its collapse was an especially drastic instance of such disruption, such vocal diaspora, with movements that would reduce one to a disintegrated mass of fragments if he attempted to encompass the totality of its discordancies. So Hitler, suffering under the alienation of poverty and confusion, yearning for some integrative core, came to take this parliament as the basic symbol of all that he would move away from. He damned the tottering Habsburg Empire as a "State of Nationalities." The many conflicting voices of the spokesmen of the many political blocs arose from the fact that various separationist movements of a nationalistic sort had arisen within a Catholic imperial structure formed prior to the nationalistic emphasis and slowly breaking apart under its development. So, you had this Babel of voices; and, by the method of associative mergers, *using ideas as imagery*, it became tied up, in the Hitler rhetoric, with "Babylon," Vienna as the city of poverty, prostitution, immorality, coalitions, half-measures, incest, democracy (i. e., majority rule leading to "lack of personal responsibility"), death, internationalism, seduction, and anything else of thumbs-down sort the associative enterprise cared to add on this side of the balance.

Hitler's way of treating the parliamentary babel, I am sorry to say, was at one important point not much different from that of the customary editorial in our own newspapers. Every conflict among the parliamentary spokesmen represents a corresponding conflict among the material interests of the groups for whom they are speaking. But Hitler did not discuss the babel from this angle. He discussed it on a purely *symptomatic* basis. The strategy of our orthodox press, in thus ridiculing the cacophonous verbal output of Congress, is obvious: by thus centering attack upon the *symptoms* of business conflict, as they reveal themselves on the dial of political wrangling, and leaving the underlying cause, the business conflicts themselves, out of the case, they can gratify the very public they would otherwise alienate: namely, the businessmen who are the activating members of their reading public. Hitler, however, went them one better. For not only did he stress the purely *symptomatic* attack here. He proceeded to search for the "cause." And this "cause," of course, he derived from his medicine, his racial theory by which he could give a noneconomic interpretation of a phenomenon economically engendered.

Here again is where Hitler's corrupt use of religious patterns comes to the fore. Church thought, being primarily concerned with matters of the "personality," with problems of moral betterment, naturally, and I think rightly, stresses as a necessary feature, the act of will upon the part of the individual. Hence its resistance to a purely "environmental" account of human ills. Hence its emphasis upon the "person." Hence its proneness to seek a noneconomic explanation of economic phenomena. Hitler's proposal of a noneconomic "cause" for the disturbances thus had much to recommend it from this angle. And, as a matter of fact, it was Lueger's Christian-Social Party in Vienna that taught Hitler the tactics of tying up a program of social betterment with an anti-Semitic "unifier." The two parties that he carefully studied at that time were this Catholic faction and Schoenerer's Pan-German group. And his analysis of their attainments and shortcomings, from the standpoint of demagogic efficacy, is an extremely astute piece of work, revealing how carefully this man used the current situation in Vienna as an experimental laboratory for the maturing of his plans.

His unification device, we may summarize, had the following important features:

(1) Inborn dignity. In both religious and humanistic patterns of thought, a "natural born" dignity of man is stressed. And this categorical dignity is considered to be an attribute of *all* men, if they will but avail themselves of it, by right thinking and right living. But Hitler gives this ennobling attitude an ominous twist by his theories of race and nation, whereby the "Aryan" is elevated above all others by the innate endowment of his blood, while other "races," in particular Jews and Negroes, are innately inferior. This sinister secularized revision of Christian theology thus puts the sense of dignity upon a fighting basis, requiring the conquest of "inferior races." After the defeat of Germany in the World War, there were especially strong emotional needs that this compensatory doctrine of an *inborn* superiority could gratify.

(2) *Projection* device. The "curative" process that comes with the ability to hand over one's ills to a scapegoat, thereby getting purification by dissociation. This was especially medicinal, since the sense of frustration leads to a self-

questioning. Hence if one can hand over his infirmities to a vessel, or "cause," outside the self, one can battle an external enemy instead of battling an enemy within. And the greater one's internal inadequacies, the greater the amount of evils one can load upon the back of "the enemy." This device is furthermore given a semblance of reason because the individual properly realizes that he is not alone responsible for his condition. There *are* inimical factors in the scene itself. And he wants to have them "placed," preferably in a way that would require a minimum change in the ways of thinking to which he had been accustomed. This was especially appealing to the middle class, who were encouraged to feel that they could conduct their businesses without any basic change whatever, once the businessmen of a different "race" were eliminated.

(3) *Symbolic rebirth.* Another aspect of the two features already noted. The projective device of the scapegoat, coupled with the Hitlerite doctrine of inborn racial superiority, provides its followers with a "positive" view of life. They can again get the feel of *moving forward,* towards a *goal* (a promissory feature of which Hitler makes much). In Hitler, as the group's prophet, such rebirth involved a symbolic change of lineage. Here, above all, we see Hitler giving a malign twist to a benign aspect of Christian thought. For whereas the Pope, in the familistic pattern of thought basic to the Church, stated that the Hebrew prophets were the *spiritual ancestors* of Christianity, Hitler uses this same mode of thinking in reverse. He renounces this "ancestry" in a "materialistic" way by voting himself and the members of his lodge a different "blood stream" from that of the Jews.

(4) *Commercial use.* Hitler obviously here had something

to sell—and it was but a question of time until he sold it (i. e., got financial backers for his movement). For it provided a *noneconomic interpretation of economic ills.* As such, it served with maximum efficiency in deflecting the attention from the economic factors involved in modern conflict; hence by attacking "Jew finance" instead of *finance,* it could stimulate an enthusiastic movement that left "Aryan" finance in control.

Never once, throughout his book, does Hitler deviate from the above formula. Invariably, he ends his diatribes against contemporary economic ills by a shift into an insistence that we must get to the "true" cause, which is centered in "race." The "Aryan" is "constructive"; the Jew is "destructive"; and the "Aryan," to continue his *construction,* must *destroy* the Jewish *destruction.* The Aryan, as the vessel of *love,* must *hate* the Jewish *hate.*

Perhaps the most enterprising use of his method is in his chapter, "The Causes of the Collapse," where he refuses to consider Germany's plight as in any basic way connected with the consequences of war. Economic factors, he insists, are "only of second or even third importance," but "political, ethical-moral, as well as factors of blood and race, are of the first importance." His rhetorical steps are especially interesting here, in that he begins by seeming to flout the national susceptibilities: "The military defeat of the German people is not an undeserved catastrophe, but rather a deserved punishment by eternal retribution." He then proceeds to present the military collapse as but a "consequence of moral poisoning, visible to all, the consequence of a decrease in the instinct of self-preservation . . . which had already begun to undermine the foundations of the people and the Reich many years before." This moral decay derived from "a sin against the blood and the degradation of the race," so its innerness was an outerness after all: the Jew, who thereupon gets saddled with a vast amalgamation of evils, among them being capitalism, democracy, pacifism, journalism, poor housing, modernism, big cities, loss of religion, half measures, ill health, and weakness of the monarch.

2

Hitler had here another important psychological ingredient to play upon. If a State is in economic collapse (and his theories, tentatively taking shape in the pre-war Vienna, were but developed with greater efficiency in post-war Munich), you cannot possibly derive dignity from economic stability. Dignity must come first—and if you possess it, and implement it, from it may follow its economic counterpart. There is much justice to this line of reasoning, so far as it goes. A people in collapse, suffering under economic frustration and the defeat of nationalistic aspirations, with the very midrib of their integrative efforts (the army) in a state of dispersion, have little other than some "spiritual" basis to which they could refer their nationalistic dignity. Hence, the categorical dignity of superior race was a perfect recipe for the situation. It was "spiritual" in so far as it was "above" crude economic "interests," but it was "materialized" at the psychologically "right" spot in that "the enemy" was something you could *see*.

Furthermore, you had the desire for unity, such as a discussion of class conflict, on the basis of conflicting interests, could not satisfy. The yearning for unity is so great that people are always willing to meet you halfway if you will give it to them by fiat, by flat statement, regardless of the facts. Hence, Hitler consistently refused to consider internal political conflict on the basis of conflicting interests. Here again, he could draw upon a religious pattern, by insisting upon a *personal* statement of the relation between classes, the relation between leaders and followers, each group in its way fulfilling the same commonalty of interests, as the soldiers and captains of an army share a common interest in victory. People so dislike the idea of internal division that, where there is a real internal division, their dislike can easily be turned against the man or group who would so much as *name* it, let alone proposing to act upon it. Their natural and justified resentment against internal division itself, is turned against the diagnostician who states it as a *fact*. This diagnostician, it is felt, is the *cause* of the disunity he named.

Cutting in from another angle, therefore, we note how two sets of equations were built up, with Hitler combining or coalescing *ideas* the way a poet combines or coalesces *images*. On the one side, were the ideas, or images, of disunity, centering in the parliamentary wrangle of the Habsburg "State of Nationalities." This was offered as the antithesis of German nationality, which was presented in the curative imagery of unity, focused upon the glories of the Prussian Reich, with its mecca now moved to "folkish" Vienna. For though Hitler at first attacked the many "folkish" movements, with their hankerings after a kind of Wagnerian mythology of Germanic origins, he subsequently took "folkish" as a basic word by which to conjure. It was, after all, another noneconomic basis of reference. At first we find him objecting to "those who drift about with the word 'folkish' on their caps," and asserting that "such a Babel of opinions cannot serve as the basis of a political fighting movement." But later he seems to have realized, as he well should, that its vagueness was a major point in its favor. So it was incorporated in the grand coalition of his ideational imagery, or imagistic ideation; and Chapter XI ends with the vision of "a State which represents not a mechanism of economic considerations and interests, alien to the people, but a folkish organism."

So, as against the disunity equations, already listed briefly in our discussion of his attacks upon the parliamentary, we get a contrary purifying set; the wrangle of the parliamentary is to be stilled by the giving of *one* voice to the whole people, this to be the "inner voice" of Hitler, made uniform throughout the German boundaries, as leader and people were completely identified with each other. In sum: Hitler's inner voice, equals leader-people identification, equals unity, equals Reich, equals the mecca of Munich, equals plow, equals sword, equals work, equals war, equals army as midrib, equals responsibility (the personal responsibility of the absolute ruler), equals sacrifice, equals the theory of "German democracy" (the free popular choice of the leader, who then accepts the responsibility, and demands absolute obedience in exchange for his sacrifice), equals love (with the masses as feminine), equals idealism, equals obedience to nature, equals race, nation.[3]

[3] One could carry out the equations further, on both the disunity and unity side. In the aesthetic field, for instance, we have expressionism on the thumbs-down side, as against aesthetic hygiene on the thumbs-up side. This again is a particularly ironic moment in Hitler's strategy. For the expressionist movement was unquestionably a symptom of unhealthiness. It reflected the increasing alienation that went with the movement towards world war and the disorganization after the world war. It was "lost," vague in identity, a drastically accurate reflection of the response to material confusion, a pathetic attempt by sincere artists to make their wretchedness bearable at least to the extent that comes of giving it expression. And it attained its height during the period of wild inflation, when the capitalist world, which bases its morality of work and savings upon the soundness of its money structure, had this last prop of stability removed. The anguish, in short, reflected precisely the kind of disruption that made people *ripe* for a Hitler. It was the antecedent in a phrase of which Hitlerism was the consequent. But by

And, of course, the two keystones of these opposite equations were Aryan "heroism" and "sacrifice" vs. Jewish "cunning" and "arrogance." Here again we get an astounding caricature of religious thought. For Hitler presents the concept of "Aryan" superiority, of all ways, in terms of "Aryan humility." This "humility" is extracted by a very delicate process that requires, I am afraid, considerable "good will" on the part of the reader who would follow it:

The Church, we may recall, had proclaimed an integral relationship between Divine Law and Natural Law. Natural Law was the expression of the Will of God. Thus, in the middle age, it was a result of natural law, working through tradition, that some people were serfs and other people nobles. And every good member of the Church was "obedient" to this law. Everybody resigned himself to it. Hence, the serf resigned himself to his poverty, and the noble resigned himself to his riches. The monarch resigned himself to his position as representative of the people. And at times the Churchmen resigned themselves to the need of trying to represent the people instead. And the pattern was made symmetrical by the consideration that each traditional "right" had its corresponding "obligations." Similarly, the Aryan doctrine is a doctrine of resignation, hence of humility. It is in accordance with the laws of nature that the "Aryan blood" is superior to all other bloods. Also, the "law of the survival of the fittest" is God's law, working through natural law. Hence, if the Aryan blood has been vested with the awful responsibility of its inborn superiority, the bearers of this "culture-creating" blood must resign themselves to struggle in behalf of its triumph. Otherwise,

---

thundering against this *symptom* he could gain persuasiveness, though attacking the very *foreshadowings of himself.*

the laws of God have been disobeyed, with human decadence as a result. We must fight, he says, in order to "deserve to be alive." The Aryan "obeys" nature. It is only "Jewish arrogance" that thinks of "conquering" nature by democratic ideals of equality.

This picture has some nice distinctions worth following. The major virtue of the Aryan race was its instinct for self-preservation (in obedience to natural law). But the major vice of the Jew was his instinct for self-preservation; for, if he did not have this instinct to a maximum degree, he would not be the "perfect" enemy—that is, he wouldn't be strong enough to account for the ubiquitousness and omnipotence of his conspiracy in destroying the world to become its master.

How, then, are we to distinguish between the benign instinct of self-preservation at the roots of Aryanism, and the malign instinct of self-preservation at the roots of Semitism? We shall distinguish thus: The Aryan self-preservation is based upon *sacrifice*, the sacrifice of the individual to the group, hence, militarism, army discipline, and one big company union. But Jewish self-preservation is based upon individualism, which attains its cunning ends by the exploitation of peace. How, then, can such arrant individualists concoct the world-wide plot? By the help of their "herd instinct." By their sheer "herd instinct" individualists can band together for a common end. They have no real solidarity, but unite opportunistically to seduce the Aryan. Still, that brings up another technical problem. For we have been hearing much about the importance of the *person*. We have been told how, by the "law of the survival of the fittest," there is a sifting of people on the basis of their individual capacities. We even have a special chapter of pure Aryanism:

"The Strong Man is Mightiest Alone." Hence, another distinction is necessary: The Jew represents individualism; the Aryan represents "super-individualism."

I had thought, when coming upon the "Strong Man is Mightiest Alone" chapter, that I was going to find Hitler at his weakest. Instead, I found him at his strongest. (I am not referring to *quality*, but to *demagogic effectiveness*.) For the chapter is not at all, as you might infer from the title, done in a "rise of Adolph Hitler" manner. Instead, it deals with the Nazis' gradual absorption of the many disrelated "folkish" groups. And it is managed throughout by means of a spontaneous identification between leader and people. Hence, the Strong Man's "aloneness" is presented as a *public* attribute, in terms of tactics for the struggle against the *Party's* dismemberment under the pressure of rival saviors. There is no explicit talk of Hitler at all. And it is simply *taken for granted* that *his* leadership is the norm, and all other leaderships the abnorm. There is no "philosophy of the superman," in Nietzschean cast. Instead, Hitler's blandishments so integrate leader and people, commingling them so inextricably, that the politician does not even present himself as candidate. Somehow, the battle is over already, the decision has been made. "German democracy" has chosen. And the deployments of politics are, you might say, the chartings of Hitler's private mind translated into the vocabulary of nationalistic events. He says *what he thought* in terms of *what parties did*.

Here, I think, we see the distinguishing quality of Hitler's method as an instrument of persuasion, with reference to the question whether Hitler is sincere or deliberate, whether his vision of the omnipotent conspirator has the drastic honesty of paranoia or the sheer shrewdness of a demagogue trained in *Realpolitik* of the Machiavellian sort.[4] Must we choose? Or may we not, rather, replace the "either—or" with a "both—and"? Have we not by now offered grounds enough for our contention that Hitler's sinister powers of persuasion derive from the fact that he spontaneously evolved his "cure-all" in response to inner necessities?

3

So much, then, was "spontaneous." It was further channelized into the anti-Semitic pattern by the incentives he derived from the Catholic Christian-Social Party in Vienna itself. Add, now, the step into *criticism*. Not criticism in the "parliamentary" sense of doubt, of hearkening to the opposition and attempting to mature a policy in the light of counter-policies; but the "unified" kind of criticism that simply seeks for conscious ways of making one's position more "efficient," more thoroughly itself. This is the kind of criticism at which Hitler was an adept. As a result, he could *spontaneously* turn to a scapegoat mechanism, and he could, by conscious planning, perfect the symmetry of the solution towards which he had spontaneously turned.

---

[4] I should not want to use the word "Machiavellian," however, without offering a kind of apology to Machiavelli. It seems to me that Machiavelli's *Prince* has more to be said in extenuation than is usually said of it. Machiavelli's strategy, as I see it, was something like this: He accepted the values of the Renaissance rule as a *fact*. That is: whether you like these values or not, they were there and operating, and it was useless to try persuading the ambitious ruler to adopt other values, such as those of the Church. These men believed in the cult of material power, and they had the power to implement their beliefs. With so much as "the given," could anything in the way of benefits for the people be salvaged? Machiavelli evolved a typical "Machiavellian" argument in favor of popular benefits, on the basis of the prince's own scheme of values. That is: the ruler, to attain the maximum strength, requires the backing of the populace. That this backing be as effective as possible, the populace should be made as strong as possible. And that the populace be as strong as possible, they should be well treated. Their gratitude would further repay itself in the form of increased loyalty.

It was Machiavelli's hope that, for this roundabout project, he would be rewarded with a well-paying office in the prince's administrative bureaucracy.

This is the meaning of Hitler's diatribes against "objectivity." "Objectivity" is interference-criticism. What Hitler wanted was the kind of criticism that would be a pure and simple coefficient of power, enabling him to go most effectively in the direction he had chosen. And the "inner voice" of which he speaks would henceforth dictate to him the greatest amount of realism, as regards the tactics of efficiency. For instance, having decided that the masses required certainty, and simple certainty, quite as he did himself, he later worked out a 25-point program as the platform of his National Socialist German Workers Party. And he resolutely refused to change one single item in this program, even for purposes of "improvement." He felt that the *fixity* of the platform was more important for propagandistic purposes than any revision of his slogans could be, even though the revisions in themselves had much to be said in their favor. The astounding thing is that, although such an attitude gave good cause to doubt the Hitlerite promises, he could explicitly explain his tactics in his book and still employ them without loss of effectiveness.[5]

Hitler also tells of his technique in speaking, once the Nazi party had become effectively organized, and had its army of guards, or bouncers, to maltreat hecklers and throw them from the hall. He would, he recounts, fill his speech with *provocative* remarks, whereat his bouncers would promptly

[5] On this point Hitler reasons as follows: "Here, too, one can learn from the Catholic Church. Although its structure of doctrines in many instances collides, quite unnecessarily, with exact science and research, yet it is unwilling to sacrifice even one little syllable of its dogmas. It has rightly recognized that its resistibility does not lie in a more or less great adjustment to the scientific results of the moment, which in reality are always changing, but rather in a strict adherence to dogmas, once laid down, which alone give the entire structure the character of creed. Today, therefore, the Catholic Church stands firmer than ever. One can prophesy that in the same measure in which the appearances flee, the Church itself, as the resting pole in the flight of appearances, will gain more and more blind adherence."

swoop down in flying formation, with swinging fists, upon anyone whom these provocative remarks provoked to answer. The efficiency of Hitlerism is the efficiency of the one voice, implemented throughout a total organization. The trinity of government which he finally offers is: *popularity* of the leader, *force* to back the popularity, and popularity and force maintained together long enough to become backed by a *tradition*. Is such thinking spontaneous or deliberate —or is it not rather both? [6]

Freud has given us a succinct paragraph that bears upon the spontaneous aspect of Hitler's persecution mania. (A persecution mania, I should add, different from the pure product in that it was constructed of *public* materials; all the ingredients Hitler stirred into his brew were already rife, with spokesmen and bands of followers, before Hitler "took them over." Both the pre-war and post-war periods were dotted with saviors, of nationalistic and "folkish" cast. This proliferation was analogous to the swarm of barter schemes and currency-tinkering that burst loose upon the United States after the crash of 1929. Also, the commercial availability of Hitler's politics was, in a low sense of the term, a *public* qualification, removing it from the realm of "pure"

[6] Hitler also paid great attention to the conditions under which political oratory is most effective. He sums up thus:

"All these cases involve encroachments upon man's freedom of will. This applies, of course, most of all to meetings to which people with a contrary orientation of will are coming, and who now have to be won for new intentions. It seems that in the morning and even during the day men's will power revolts with highest energy against an attempt at being forced under another's will and another's opinion. In the evening, however, they succumb more easily to the dominating force of a stronger will. For truly every such meeting presents a wrestling match between two opposed forces. The superior oratorical talent of a domineering apostolic nature will now succeed more easily in winning for the new will people who themselves have in turn experienced a weakening of their force of resistance in the most natural way, than people who still have full command of the energies of their minds and their will power.

"The same purpose serves also the artificially created and yet mysterious dusk of the Catholic churches, the burning candles, incense, censers, etc."

paranoia, where the sufferer develops a wholly *private* structure of interpretations.)

I cite from *Totem and Taboo:*

> Another trait in the attitude of primitive races towards their rulers recalls a mechanism which is universally present in mental disturbances, and is openly revealed in the so-called delusions of persecution. Here the importance of a particular person is extraordinarily heightened and his omnipotence is raised to the improbable in order to make it easier to attribute to him responsibility for everything painful which happens to the patient. Savages really do not act differently towards their rulers when they ascribe to them power over rain and shine, wind and weather, and then dethrone them or kill them because nature has disappointed their expectation of a good hunt or a ripe harvest. The prototype which the paranoiac reconstructs in his persecution mania is found in the relation of the child to its father. Such omnipotence is regularly attributed to the father in the imagination of the son, and distrust of the father has been shown to be intimately connected with the heightened esteem for him. When a paranoiac names a person of his acquaintance as his "persecutor," he thereby elevates him to the paternal succession and brings him under conditions which enable him to make him responsible for all the misfortune which he experiences.

I have already proposed my modifications of this account when discussing the symbolic change of lineage connected with Hitler's project of a "new way of life." Hitler is sym-

214

bolically changing from the "spiritual ancestry" of the Hebrew prophets to the "superior" ancestry of "Aryanism," and has given his story a kind of bastardized modernization, along the lines of naturalistic, materialistic "science," by his fiction of the special "blood-stream." He is voting himself a new identity (something contrary to the wrangles of the Habsburg Babylon, a soothing national unity); whereupon the vessels of the old identity become a "bad" father, i. e., the persecutor. It is not hard to see how, as his enmity becomes implemented by the backing of an organization, the rôle of "persecutor" is transformed into the rôle of persecuted, as he sets out with his like-minded band to "destroy the destroyer."

Were Hitler simply a poet, he might have written a work with an anti-Semitic turn, and let it go at that. But Hitler, who began as a student of painting, and later shifted to architecture, himself treats his political activities as an extension of his artistic ambitions. He remained, in his own eyes, an "architect," building a "folkish" State that was to match, in political materials, the "folkish" architecture of Munich.

We might consider the matter this way (still trying, that is, to make precise the relationship between the drastically sincere and the deliberately scheming): Do we not know of many authors who seem, as they turn from the rôle of citizen to the rôle of spokesman, to leave one room and enter another? Or who has not, on occasion, talked with a man in private conversation, and then been almost startled at the transformation this man undergoes when addressing a public audience? And I know persons today, who shift between the writing of items in the class of academic, philosophic speculation to items of political pamphleteering, and whose entire style and method changes with this change of rôle. In their academic manner, they are cautious, pains-taking, eager to present all significant aspects of the case they are considering; but when they turn to political pam-phleteering, they hammer forth with vituperation, they sys-tematically misrepresent the position of their opponent, they go into a kind of political trance, in which, during its throes, they throb like a locomotive; and behold, a moment later, the mediumistic state is abandoned, and they are the most moderate of men.

Now, one will find few pages in Hitler that one could call "moderate." But there are many pages in which he gauges resistances and opportunities with the "rationality" of a skilled advertising man planning a new sales campaign. Politics, he says, must be sold like soap—and soap is not sold in a trance. But he did have the experience of his trance, in the "exaltation" of his anti-Semitism. And later, as he became a successful orator (he insists that revolutions are made solely by the power of the spoken word), he had this "poetic" rôle to draw upon, plus the great relief it pro-vided as a way of slipping from the burden of logical analysis into the pure "spirituality" of vituperative prophecy. What more natural, therefore, than that a man so insistent upon unification would integrate this mood with less ecstatic mo-ments, particularly when he had found the followers and the backers that put a price, both spiritual and material, upon such unification?

Once this happy "unity" is under way, one has a "logic" for the development of a method. One knows when to "spir-itualize" a material issue, and when to "materialize" a spiritual one. Thus, when it is a matter of materialistic interests that cause a conflict between employer and em-ployee, Hitler here disdainfully shifts to a high moral plane.

He is "above" such low concerns. Everything becomes a matter of "sacrifices" and "personality." It becomes crass to treat employers and employees as different *classes* with a corresponding difference in the classification of their interests. Instead, relations between employer and employee must be on the "personal" basis of leader and follower, and "whatever may have a divisive effect in national life should be given a unifying effect through the army." When talking of national rivalries, however, he makes a very shrewd materialistic gauging of Britain and France with relation to Germany. France, he says, desires the "Balkanization of Germany" (i. e., its breakup into separationist movements—the "disunity" theme again) in order to maintain commercial hegemony on the continent. But Britain desires the "Balkanization of *Europe*," hence would favor a fairly strong and unified Germany, to use as a counter-weight against French hegemony. *German* nationality, however, is unified by the *spiritual* quality of Aryanism (that would produce the national organization via the Party) while this in turn is *materialized* in the myth of the blood-stream.

What are we to learn from Hitler's book? For one thing, I believe that he has shown, to a very disturbing degree, the power of endless repetition. Every circular advertising a Nazi meeting had, at the bottom, two slogans: "Jews not admitted" and "War victims free." And the substance of Nazi propaganda was built about these two "complementary" themes. He describes the power of spectacle; insists that mass meetings are the fundamental way of giving the individual the sense of being protectively surrounded by a movement, the sense of "community." He also drops one wise hint that I wish the American authorities would take in treating Nazi gatherings. He says that the presence of a

217

special Nazi guard, in Nazi uniforms, was of great importance in building up, among the followers, a tendency to place the center of authority in the Nazi party. I believe that we should take him at his word here, but use the advice in reverse, by insisting that, where Nazi meetings are to be permitted, they be policed by the authorities alone, and that uniformed Nazi guards to enforce the law be prohibited.

And is it possible that an equally important feature of appeal was not so much in the repetitiousness per se, but in the fact that, by means of it, Hitler provided a "world view" for people who had previously seen the world but piecemeal? Did not much of his lure derive, once more, from the *bad* filling of a *good* need? Are not those who insist upon a purely *planless* working of the market asking people to accept far too slovenly a scheme of human purpose, a slovenly scheme that can be accepted so long as it operates with a fair degree of satisfaction, but becomes abhorrent to the victims of its disarray? Are they not then psychologically ready for a rationale, *any* rationale, if it but offer them some specious "universal" explanation? Hence, I doubt whether the appeal was in the sloganizing element alone (particularly as even slogans can only be hammered home, in speech after speech, and two or three hours at a stretch, by endless variations on the themes). And Hitler himself somewhat justifies my interpretation by laying so much stress upon the *half-measures* of the middle-class politicians, and the contrasting *certainty* of his own methods. He was not offering people a *rival* world view; rather, he was offering a world view to people who had no other to pit against it.

As for the basic Nazi trick: the "curative" unification by a fictitious devil-function, gradually made convincing by the sloganizing repetitiousness of standard advertising technique—the opposition must be as unwearying in the attack upon it. It may well be that people, in their human frailty, require an enemy as well as a goal. Very well: Hitlerism itself has provided us with such an enemy—and the clear example of its operation is guaranty that we have, in him and all he stands for, no purely fictitious "devil-function" made to look like a world menace by rhetorical blandishments, but a reality whose ominousness is clarified by the record of its conduct to date. In selecting his brand of doctrine as our "scapegoat," and in tracking down its equivalents in America, we shall be at the very center of accuracy. The Nazis themselves have made the task of clarification easier. Add to them Japan and Italy, and you have *case histories* of fascism for those who might find it more difficult to approach an understanding of its imperialistic drives by a vigorously economic explanation.

But above all, I believe, we must make it apparent that Hitler appeals by relying upon a bastardization of fundamentally religious patterns of thought. In this, if properly presented, there is no slight to religion. There is nothing in religion proper that requires a fascist state. There is much in religion, when misused, that does lead to a fascist state. There is a Latin proverb, *Corruptio optimi pessima,* "the corruption of the best is the worst." And it is the corruptors of religion who are a major menace to the world today, in giving the profound patterns of religious thought a crude and sinister distortion.

Our job, then, our anti-Hitler Battle, is to find all available ways of making the Hitlerite distortions of religion apparent, in order that politicians of his kind in America be unable to perform a similar swindle. The desire for unity is genuine and admirable. The desire for national unity, in

219

the present state of the world, is genuine and admirable. But this unity, if attained on a deceptive basis, by emotional trickeries that shift our criticism from the accurate locus of our trouble, is no unity at all. For, even if we are among those who happen to be "Aryans," we solve no problems even for ourselves by such solutions, since the factors pressing towards calamity remain. Thus, in Germany, after all the upheaval, we see nothing beyond a drive for ever more and more upheaval, precisely because the "new way of life" was no new way, but the dismally oldest way of sheer deception—hence, after all the "change," the factors driving towards unrest are left intact, and even strengthened. True, the Germans had the resentment of a lost war to increase their susceptibility to Hitler's rhetoric. But in a wider sense, it has repeatedly been observed, the whole world lost the War—and the accumulating ills of the capitalist order were but accelerated in their movements towards confusion. Hence, here too there are the resentments that go with frustration of men's ability to work and earn. At that point a certain kind of industrial or financial monopolist may, annoyed by the contrary voices of our parliament, wish for the momentary peace of one voice, amplified by social organizations, with all the others not merely quieted, but given the quietus. So he might, under Nazi promptings, be tempted to back a group of gangsters who, on becoming the political rulers of the state, would protect him against the necessary demands of the workers. His gangsters, then, would be his insurance against his workers. But who would be his insurance against his gangsters?

THE CALLING OF THE TUNE

THE complete autonomy of art could but mean its dissociation from other aspects of the social collectivity. Complete freedom to develop one's means of communication ends as an impairment of communicability (the dilemma of work done in the Joyce-Stein-*transition* school). There is a point at which freedom for the artist becomes an embarrassment of riches, since one of the forms of this freedom is freedom from revenues.

A piper who had insisted upon the right to call his own tune became unhappy when everyone began saying to him, "I don't care what tune you play." He discovered that he wanted them to care tremendously—and to make them do so, he even tried outrageous tunes. Though insisting upon his professional immunity, he didn't want to be too damned immune, since complete tolerance would imply the unimportance of his craft. He simultaneously wanted separation and integration. He wanted the joyous marriage of "you must" and "I will."

Two recent books, Grace Overmyer's *Government and the Arts* and Herbert Read's *Poetry and Anarchism,* give us an opportunity to consider some of the specific issues involved in this vacillating relationship between the artist's freedom and the society's commands. The commands are given, sometimes by the direct use of policing activities, more often by the indirect effects of patronage.

The first of these books "does not seek primarily either

221

to justify or to condemn state aid to art as an institution. Its chief object has been the assembling of such facts as must form the basis of a just or useful judgment." To this end the author gives us the result of library research, interviews, and questionnaires, bearing upon the kinds of assistance that are given to art and artists, in many countries, by the agencies of both national and local government.

In America, the book reveals quite large federal, state, and municipal expenditures in support of one aesthetic medium or another—although, until recently, the art got in exchange was not often very close to the typical experiences of our national life, but was rather in the spirit of the Greek temples our architects copied to house government bureaus and banks. The author's account of the federal arts projects presents a highly honorable aspect of the Roosevelt administration, whose sponsorship of the arts seems to have come as close as one could reasonably expect of any such large enterprise to fulfilling the ideal set by Miss Overmyer in her chapter, " 'Interfering' with Art":

> The problem of "government interference," as it may accompany state subsidy of the arts, was once discussed by the late John Drinkwater in connection with the moot question of England's national theater. His epigrammatic conclusion, which might serve as motto for any government in its relationship to art, was simply this: "The state should pay the piper, but should not call the tune."

A respect for the proverbial might reasonably make one doubt whether, should the federal projects become permanent, their comparative liquidity can be retained. Some of this liquidity may be due to the newness of the enterprises, which have not yet "got their stride" as regards the ways of political appointment; and some to the peculiarly tentative nature of the New Deal itself, a transitional phase of federal administration that could hardly be expected to continue indefinitely. In any event, were we to consider the subject of art patronage in general, we should have to go far beyond the confines of Miss Overmyer's book, broad as they are. Wholly private institutions and subsidies are not a part of her investigation, and that is a very large item.

Nor does she consider the extensive employment of literary, graphic, dramatic, and musical talent for advertising purposes, with the organized recruiting of aesthetic mercenaries (often of great virtuosity) in the service of commercial warfare. Surely it is our businessmen with a product to sell who provide the largest financial subsidy to art. And you would get the unwarranted impression that dictatorships abroad are the only institutions imposing restrictions upon the artist, unless you stopped to consider these Medicis among our economic dynasts, employing whole hordes of craftsmen to beautify and signalize their realms of action, and specifying the selection of subjects and the nature of treatment with a strictness unthinkable in the days of royal patronage or even in contemporary political dictatorships.

An art, to be most thoroughly integrated with the national life, must represent, form, confirm, utilize, and project the national values, ideals, and expectancies. And to do this, it must be integrated with the basic modes of livelihood. The distinction between "pure" and "applied" art, resulting from an extensive use of art in recommending goods, has tended to force the artist into a choice between advertising

(wherein he is spokesman for the values, ideals, and expectancies of commerce) and advertising-in-reverse (that usually
goes by the name of "propaganda").

There is an intermediate realm, that I might call the
"Whitmanesque." It focuses attention upon the "human
element" in our patterns of sociality, the typical situations
of home life, farming, manufacture, etc., in ballgames, prize-
fights, crap shootings, picnics, and even in the "picturesqueness" of poverty and slums. In so far as it stresses the lamen-
table rather than the picturesque, it is felt to move into the
suspect area of "propaganda." And even among the advocates of propagandist lamentation and its organizational
counterpart, the sinister threat, there are few who would
choose such work to "live with," whatever they may think
of it as an occasional exhibit.

Much valuable art is still to be done within the Whitmanesque strategy of idealization, or humanization. But
such idealization, unless corrected by a critique that moves
it into the suspect area of "propaganda," can come to function as little more than a promiscuous flattering of the *status
quo,* in its bad aspects as well as its good ones. For wherever
there are people, there is something to be "humanized." And
if, when the limits of humanization are reached, you allow
for a shift into the area of sheer picturesqueness (as in the
earlier work of Caldwell, for instance), you have a still wider
range of "free" artistic expression. Thus can the patron
subsidize in the "applied art" of his advertising copy the
representation of commercial values that indirectly bring
about the dispossession of a dirt farmer, and as a purchaser
of "pure" art he can buy a Whitmanesque picture "human-
izing" the work patterns of the dirt farmer who is to be
dispossessed. Add to humanization and picturesqueness a

concern with our incunabula, the retrospective recovery of key situations in our past history, and you see how vast the resources of the "Whitmanesque strategy" are. It will surely continue to be the favorite mode of "pure" art—and recently when I heard over the radio an announcement that an influential business organization was calling for an "open road," I realized how neatly the Whitmanesque succeeds in offering something for everybody, making the interests of piper and tune-caller identical, hence allowing the poet simultaneously to "be himself" and to act as public spokesman for his patrons, or customers.

2

Herbert Read is concerned with the ways in which the piperpayer calls the tune, not as with the spontaneous group-spokesmen of the Whitmanesque strategy, but divisively, with artists and patrons as conflicting classes. He vigorously attacks the effects of capitalism upon art, even proposing in his chapter, "Why We English Have No Taste," that English laughter be renamed, for purposes of accuracy, "capitalist laughter." Leaving unconsidered the area of non-political humanization, that might even provide a range of "free" aesthetic action for some "loving" type of artist in Hitler's Germany, he is concerned mainly to stress his disturbance at the rise of political authoritarianism. He places poetry as the opposite of authority (which seems to me at most but a half-truth); and approaching social problems as a lover of poetry, he sets out to affirm his ideals frankly undeterred by considerations of "practicability." He is against tune-calling. And since tune-callers are "authorities" of one sort or another, he widens his position into a general plea for anarchism, as the only completely non-authoritarian social

225

structure. He would not recognize the authority of the "leader principle," of political parties, or even of *mores*, traditional or newly arisen.

Ideal anarchy being, by definition, that state of affairs wherein the lion and the lamb shall lie down together, it would not be relevant for a reviewer to point out a "problem" or a "contradiction," even if he thought he saw one unmistakably. Mr. Read states a set of wants—and though wants may be refused, they cannot be refuted. Every want is sovereign in its ideality. Nor can there be any contradiction in the expression of one's wants, since one is also free to want the impossible. In the realm of the practical, a trend is "opposed to" its counter-trend; but in the realm of ideality, this trend is merely "balanced by" its counter-trend. Our author thus already enjoys the immunities of expression he expects of the hypothetical anarchistic world society in the future.

Mr. Read rightly, I think, hits upon "authority" as a focal word for his concerns. But I question whether the problems of authoritarianism and anti-authoritarianism, as they affect art, have been properly elucidated until the theorist has charted the nature of *identification* in art, a subject that Mr. Read leaves undiscussed. In his ingenious book, *Science and Sanity*, Alfred Korzybski represents a brand of the same atomistic thinking as is present in Mr. Read's vision of ideal anarchy, with its society of sovereign individuals. He, like Mr. Reed, seems to continue the nominalist line of thought that treats *a group as an aggregate of individuals*, in contrast with the realistic position (now being reaffirmed in many bungling and cumbersome ways, but with much soundness behind it nonetheless) that treats *individuals as members of a group*. Mr. Korzybski correctly rounds out his atomistic,

226

anti-authoritarian position by an explicit attack upon the processes of identification. And until Mr. Read does the same, one cannot accurately know just what his views on the relation between artist and society are.

By "identification" I have in mind this sort of thing: one's material and mental ways of placing oneself as a person in the groups and movements; one's ways of sharing vicariously in the rôle of leader or spokesman; formation and change of allegiance; the rituals of suicide, parricide, and prolicide, the vesting and divesting of insignia, the modes of initiation and purification, that are involved in the response to allegiance and change of allegiance; the part necessarily played by groups in the expectancies of the individual (as Mr. Read himself, in an unguarded moment, tells us that "a group, a sect, a party" is necessary for the triumph of a social movement, while he attributes the origin of the movement to one man, and such a founder must certainly have the rôle of leader, with followers who identify themselves with him as their spokesman, or with the individual or body they take to be his spiritual heir when he is gone); clothes, uniforms, and their psychological equivalents; one's ways of seeing one's reflection in the social mirror.

My call for an explicit treatment of identification, as necessary to the description of both positive and negative responses to authority, is all the more justified in Mr. Read's case, since he avowedly approaches social issues as a lover of art, and the psychology of artistic production and consumption involves identification processes at every turn. With Mr. Korzybski the situation is different, since he takes an antipoetic stand on the subject of meaning.

However, had Mr. Read begun with a study of identification, I doubt whether he could have maintained his flatly

227

anti-authoritarian position. And I believe that his book would have been a better one. To build one's statements around an absolutely anti-authoritarian wish is to let the authoritarians be master of the controversy. If someone said, for instance, "I maintain that art is made of green cheese," and you devoted your efforts to maintaining that it isn't, your own statements would be restricted by the nature of the question your opponent had forced upon you. And an absolute revolt against authority in all its forms is as enslaving to speculation as is the absolute worship of authority. In the case of Mr. Read, it seems to have shunted a very discriminating art critic into the most oversimplified of pamphleteering. He advocates a social philosophy in the name of art, yet tells us almost nothing about the nature of the activity in whose name his philosophy is advocated. He restates vehemently the ideal that John Drinkwater states mildly in the quotation by Miss Overmyer. But when you are through, you have learned nothing more about the intricacies of the issue than you get from this casual epigram proposing to unite the best possible features of two worlds.

3

God knows, there are ominous structures of authority taking form in the contemporary world. And as the farmer, under threat of invasion, might lay down his hoe and take up his rifle for a season, so might the writer, like Mr. Read in his present volume, feel that an act of propaganda is the kind of tithing he can do, at a time when personal sacrifices may be demanded of all. But if one approaches the situation from a categorical rejection of *all* authority, does he properly equip himself and his readers for a choice among the various real structures of authority that necessarily arise whenever a "vision" is given embodiment in the material organizations of "this imperfect world"?

You can make allowance for "necessary evils," but you have introduced a device that can be used to justify anything. Nor can you solve this problem by categorically refusing to make allowance for necessary evils. One need not consider authority as a necessary evil at all, but as a power, hence having the ambivalence of a power, to effect both good and evil. It is not only a necessary evil but also a necessary good. And even if you want pure anarchy, you'll only get it by forming "a group, a sect, a party," with all the aspects of cohesion and representation that Mr. Read seems to distrust. Again, if the ideal anarchist society were here, its perpetuation would be a custom—and a poetry such as Mr. Read demands, set categorically against the authority of custom, would become sheer satanism.

But should you object to my word "identification" above, try in its stead the word "representation." The artist, as spokesman, does not merely represent his subject; nor does he merely represent himself; he also represents his readers, in the sense in which a legislator is said to represent his constituents. He speaks for an audience, sometimes sharply demarcated, as in "addressed" writing, sometimes a hypothetical "Audience X," with whom he is identified. In the case of the commercial or political mercenary (the latter being paid mainly in terms of esteem and trouble in situations where he is at odds with an authoritative patron) his rôle as representative or spokesman places the maximum restrictions upon him. This is particularly true when, as with commercial and political dictatorship over the artist, he is not directly identified with the *bureau of patronage (and censorship)* that is interposed between himself and the public at large.

229

When this identification is lacking, he must rebel despite himself. He must produce a kind of involuntary sabotage, willy-nilly defacing his product: being ordered to glorify that in which he sees no glory, he cannot. He simply "lacks the talent." If great genius is required to write a great work embodying the values in which one does believe, think how much greater genius would be required to write a great work embodying values in which one did not believe! Hence, in proportion as dictatorship seeks to force and coach, the best art must either move into marginal areas that are not forced and coached, or must turn to the catacombs.

4

In our highly mobile world of today, the usual equivalent of the catacombs is exile. Exile or silence seem to be the only choices open to writers who, born and trained in the ways of liberalism, are suddenly compelled to meet situations of absolute dictatorship wholly alien to their training. Bred to one situation, with their methods formed by it, they find a totally alien situation abruptly forced upon them. Thus, even in remaining at home, they would be living in a kind of exile, a world with new deprivations and without new promises to match.

But I can imagine there gradually arising, among a younger generation of writers bred to the new situation, a new language of deployments and maneuvers, with sly sallies that have an implied weighting far in excess of their surface meanings. In short, I am suggesting that no political structure, if continued long enough for people to master its ways, is capable of preventing forms of expression that tug at the limits of patronage. A patronage may affect the conditions of expression, but cannot prevent this pressure against its limits. Even under the censorship of the Czar, for instance, there were circumlocutions, known to all informed readers, that referred to the day when the Czar would be deposed. Nor were these any less known to the censors than to the readers. They were allowed in part, perhaps, as a way of revealing to government agents those particular authors who might, by thus expressing their attitudes, provide the agents with valuable "leads" into more serious forms of conspiracy.

One could even imagine the emergence of a particular aesthetic school, in which not one single thought or image was "subversive" on its face, yet functioned as a *Bundschuh*. Nazis in Poland, for instance, wear white sox, harmless enough in themselves, yet significant enough as a *Bundschuh* to enrage a Polish patriot—and so there may be subtler aspects of a style, functioning like the white sox in Poland, even stylistic ways of wearing anti-white-sox in Hitler's Germany. So with "travel literature" like that of Tacitus, who wrote under conditions of dictatorship, and attacked the local political situation by an ambiguous device, in presenting an idealization of Germany that implied a criticism of Rome (the point is taken from Jacques Barzun's interesting book on *Race Theories*, which also notes some irony in the fact that Tacitus, for progressive purposes, here gave the first form to the doctrines of "Nordic" superiority that were subsequently to serve the ends of reactionaries). Utopias have regularly arisen in this way, as strategies for criticizing the *status quo* with immunity. And we might even say that the conditions are "more favorable" to satire under censorship than under liberalism—for the most inventive satire arises when the artist is seeking simultaneously to take risks and escape punishment for his boldness, and is never quite certain himself whether he will be acclaimed or punished. In proportion as you remove these conditions of danger, by liberalization, satire becomes arbitrary and effete, attracting writers of far less spirit and scantier resources.

But in these closing paragraphs I may seem to have been bearing out Mr. Read's feeling that authority is but something to revolt against, and that good art arises only in so far as it is revolted against. On the contrary. Though I would agree that the artist will tug at the limits of authority, I still insist that his work derives its strength as much from the structure of authority as from his modes of resistance. Authority provides the gravitational pull necessary to a work's firm location.

The artist's situation is most difficult when the authority is not directly that of his audience (their *mores*) but lies with a bureau interposed between him and his audience. Yet even here there is no flat antithesis, since the bureau itself is composed of officials who share, to varying degrees, the values of the citizenry they represent. Even where they would *force* certain political or social judgments, there may be a complete identity of judgment, among writer, citizenry, and bureau, about certain values that are considered heroic, villainous, desirable, undesirable, and the like. And when we are talking of a work as it is, realistically, we must consider it in its totality, not singling out some one feature and treating this, in its isolation, as the "essence" of art. If, instead of this "essentializing" approach (that abstracts one ingredient in a work as the significant element and overlooks the rest), you analyze the individual work as a recipe, with a *proportion of ingredients,* you will quickly discover that the proportion of revolt against authority is slight. And this is true especially of works that prod governments to be reformed or topple.

There is but one kind of art in which this proportion of revolt is great. I refer to the kind of art we get in the Joyce-Stein-*transition* school. It is almost 100 per cent anti-authoritarian (except, in the best of it, for a good slavishness to the dictates of the ear), and allows the artist maximum freedom of improvisation. Yet it is precisely here that we find, by the ambiguities of the *Bundschuh*, the kind of art most thoroughly preparatory to political authoritarianism in its strictest forms. For the greater the dissociation and discontinuity developed by the artist in an otherworldly art that leaves the things of Caesar to take care of themselves, the greater becomes the artist's dependence upon some ruler who will accept the responsibility for doing the world's "dirty work." Thus, a thoroughly anti-authoritarian aesthetic requires, as its logical complement, that its advocates accept (as a "necessary evil" to keep the material continuities of the world in operation) any structure of authority able to prove itself on a "Darwinian" basis, by success in prevailing over rival structures of authority. Begin by rejecting all authority, and you end by accepting any.

WAR, RESPONSE,
AND CONTRADICTION

THE various arguments in recent years as to the relation between art and propaganda may have struck some observers as purely a haggle among literary specialists. Yet the issue is a vital one, and carries far beyond a mere matter of literary fashions. Aesthetical values are intermingled with ethical values—and the ethical is the basis of the practical. Or, put more simply: our ideas of the beautiful, the curious, the interesting, the unpleasant, the boring are closely bound with our ideas of the good, the desirable, the undesirable— and our ideas of the desirable and undesirable have much to do with our attitudes towards our everyday activities. They make us ask ourselves, more or less consciously: Are we doing the things we want to do? to what extent is there a breach between what we must do and what we should like to do? Probably for this reason, even the most practical of revolutions will generally be found to have manifested itself first in the "aesthetic" sphere.

Then it is no academic matter to concern oneself with the *implications* of books. And however much one may disagree with the results of Michael Gold's patient search for the faintest chemical traces of fascism and anti-Semitism in the "pure" poetry of Archibald MacLeish, one must grant that the intention is justified. Points of view first make themselves apparent in the realm of "fancy." In time they come to be carried into the structure of our sciences, so that savants can train their telescopes upon the infinite or their microscopes upon the infinitesimal and find there what they were looking for. Even theories of psychology eventually succumb to the same pattern, the same "perspective"—and lastly, perhaps, the cultural lag of our social institutions themselves is made to budge somewhat, and the point of view which began as a poet's irresponsible "inkling" attains its embodiment in the very architecture of the state.

For such reasons, the question of the relationship between art and society is momentous—and the Battle of the Books now in progress is no mere tempest in a teapot. To an extent, books merely exploit our attitudes—and to an extent they may form our attitudes. The difference between exploitation and formation may be illustrated by war literature. A work picturing the "atrocities" of the enemy would *exploit* our attitude towards such atrocities. It would arouse our resentment by depicting the kind of incidents which we already hated prior to this specific work of art. Such a work might *form* our attitudes by picturing a certain specific people as committing these atrocities: it would serve to aggravate our vindictiveness towards this particular people.

The whole issue was revealed in some of its most perplexing aspects by the controversy (in *The New Republic* of September 20, 1933) between Archibald MacLeish and Malcolm Cowley on the subject of the volume, *The First World War*, edited by Laurence Stallings. MacLeish seems mainly concerned with the poet's response to experience, and Cowley with the public's response to the poet. There is thus some talking at cross-purposes; but the discussion is particularly vital, it seems to me, because it keeps so near to the heart of the problem. Art is a means of communication. As such it

235

is certainly designed to elicit a "response" of some sort. And the present article will attempt, by using the MacLeish-Cowley controversy as a *point de départ*, to offer some considerations as to the nature of human response in general, and to make deductions from them.

MacLeish begins by objecting because *The First World War* pictures only the repellent side of the War. The War was heroic and adventurous as well as horrible, MacLeish asserts, yet Stallings here omits the heroic and adventurous aspects entirely. Though we are today largely what the War made of us, MacLeish seems to feel that we owe the War some courtesy, some allegiance: we must be "truthful" about the War. Even now we must not use the War to our purposes, but must continue to be victimized by it. If it was a "human" war, the honest poet must say so, and will say so, regardless of the effects upon society. Such seems to be Mac-Leish's position—and on the face of it, it does not look very defensible. Artistic scrupulosity is an expensive luxury, if it is to be obtained at the expense of society as a whole.

MacLeish may be confusing two issues. He seems to take it for granted that the new book, edited by Stallings, is about the last war. Hence, recalling by personal experience that the War had its profoundly human side, he complains that the new book is an incomplete record, artistically dishonest. For the artist must record "those things, seen or unseen, which have actually occurred . . . regardless of their effect upon the minds of the young or the minds of the old." Thus, a picture of the War should also include its noble and adventurous side, be the final effect "immoral" or not. Yet it is highly questionable whether the true subject of *The First World War* is an actual war at all. The very title would suggest that it is about an anticipated war. And I think that

Cowley is more nearly correct on this point, since he is concerned with our responses to the possibility of war rather than with our responses to a war already gone into history. Now: anticipated events are quite properly idealized in art. It is a commonplace of psychology, human and universal enough for any poet to draw upon, that we expect things to be either much better or much worse than they turn out to be. Anticipation is by very nature an abstractive process, a simplification; as such, it has an interpretative or "philosophic" consistency which events in actuality do not have. The future itself is a "work of art" until it is actually upon us. Thus, one may be quite within his rights when picturing a future war either as all heroism and adventure or as all hideousness. Where indeed can MacLeish point to the authority of the events "as they actually occurred," when the occurrence is still confined to the poet's symbols themselves?

To be sure when writing of an anticipated war, the artist must select his material out of the past and the present. All anticipation is such selection, whether it involve one's forebodings about an international calamity or one's attempt to decide whether the red sky at night will be shepherd's delight and the red sky at morning shepherd's warning. For the poet, not all of such material is confined to objective events. Much of it lives in the memory, emphases, interests, preferences, and apprehensions of his contemporaries. In writing, he handles not merely a past situation, but also a present one. The Rosetta Stone was carved for the purpose of conveying certain information local to the times. It became important to us as a key for deciphering Egyptian. We owe the stone no allegiance. We use it for our purposes, for a "truth" which did not exist at the time of its erection.

Is there a kind of naïve realism lurking at the bottom of MacLeish's exhortation? Though at one point he complains against Marxian "absolutism," does he not himself grow absolutist in assuming that the War possesses one definite, absolute character which must remain unchanged throughout history? To the people on Morgan's preferred lists, Morgan has a different "character" than he has for the people not on his preferred lists. Yet it is one and the same Morgan in both relationships. The analogy might suggest that "character" is largely a matter of relationship, and is necessarily changed by a change in relationship. And if our relationship to war is different now from what it was in 1916, why must we attempt to uphold, by strange canons of "truth," the "1916 character" of war?

Are not wars what we make of them—like stones and trees, like Napoleon and the history of Greece? And might we not very humanly want to make a different thing of them in anticipation than in actuality? When we are inescapably in one, the only wise thing to do is to make it as decent as we can, thereby maintaining some continuity of our humaneness even under conditions of slaughter. But when we are not at war, no such grave psychological obligation is upon us —we are not vowed by the actualities of our predicament to tell ourselves that even war can be a cultural way of life.

Hence, I hold that MacLeish has been discussing a poet's response to a past actual war whereas the question is really about an audience's response to a future anticipated war. Yet strangely enough, when we consider the matter from this point of view, MacLeish's plea for a total picture of war has much to be said in its favor. There are some reasons for believing that the response to a *human* picture of war will be socially more wholesome than our response to an *inhuman*

one. It is questionable whether the feelings of horror, repugnance, hatred would furnish the best groundwork as a
deterrent to war. They are extremely militaristic attitudes,
being in much the same category of emotion as one might
conceivably experience when plunging his bayonet into the
flesh of the enemy. And they might well provide the firmest
basis upon which the "heroism" of a new war could be
erected. The greater the horror, the greater the thrill and
honor of enlistment. I can imagine an upstanding young fellow, when *Der Tag* is again upon us, pointing to photographs
of mutilated bodies, and saying quietly but firmly to his
sweetheart, who adores him: "See those? That is what war is.
Dearie, this day I have enlisted in the service of my country." The sly cartoonists of *The New Yorker* might possibly
do most to discourage militarism, while deeply pious tracts
are but the preparation for new massacres. They may be the
first stage of the next combat—the preparatory "aesthetic
barrage"—staunchly building by the collation of military
horrors the imagery which will be drawn upon in sharpening our concepts of heroism. In any event, we do know that
a batch of such material preceded the "conversion" of Germany from the psychology of Wandering Birds to the psychology of Brown Shirts.

Such possibilities bring us to a surprising state of affairs.
If, by picturing only the hideous side of war, we lay the
aesthetic groundwork above which a new stimulus to "heroism" can be constructed, might a picture of war as thoroughly human serve conversely as the soundest deterrent to
war? I have never seen anyone turn from *The Iliad* a-froth
with desire for slaughter. And might MacLeish, who fears
that he is being socially irresponsible when he pleads for a
"whole" war, with all its contradictions, really be pleading

for the most ethical presentation of all? He would recall "a war of parades, speeches, brass bands, *bistros,* boredom, terror, anguish, heroism, endurance, humor, death." He would have a "human war," recorded with "neither morality, nor text, nor lesson." And though he is humble at the thought, and even willing to damn the artist as "an enemy of society" (at least, so far as a society's temporal aberrations are concerned) is there not much to be said in favor of his "human" war as deterrent where a picture of an "inhuman" war might act as stimulant?

For one thing, a human war, picturing gentleness, companionship, humor, respect for courage (in the enemy as well as among one's own ranks), dignity in suffering, refusal to admire the jockeyings and elbowings for position which characterize so much of our efforts under conditions of capitalist peace—such a human picture might be less likely to encourage the hysteria which, in its intensity, can be converted into its antithesis at a moment's notice, becoming the counterhysteria of rabidity and ferocity. It may really serve to promote, not warlike zest, but a *cultural* approach towards the question of human happiness, a sense of critical appraisal, and incidentally, a realization that the purposes of humanity may best be attained through the machinery of peace. If there is any sound reason for discovering the cultural superiority of peace over war, the surest way to arrive at it would be through a total, restful attitude towards war itself. Sunday-school texts have ever been considered by sophisticated moralists the essential stimulus to "sin"—and I see no reason why the same fact should not apply to a Sunday-school simplification in dealing with the problems of war. On the other hand, let war be put forward *as a cultural way of life, as one channel of effort in which people can be profoundly human,* and you induce in the reader the fullest possible response to war, precisely such a response as might best lead one to appreciate the preferable ways of peace.

There is another paradoxical fact to be considered. A book wholly constructed of the repellent may partially close the mind to the repellent. It may call forth, as its response, a psychological callus, a protective crust of insensitiveness. Horrors strike deeper when they strike out of a sweet and gentle context, as the highly contradictory genius of Thomas Mann's *The Magic Mountain* testifies. And when they do strike, note how they strike: for one has been responding to the humanity of humans; one has been warmed; one presumably is aglow—and then of a sudden one sees these human concentration-points of courage and tenderness blasted into hell. What, in the end, would he carry away with him, if not a wincing, and a regret at the realization of how much is tossed away by war, the waste of full cultural possibilities which the way of culture-through-war really involves?

Is there not today in criticism the assumption that people are quite as direct as machines in their responses? Cowley, for instance, attributes MacLeish's difficulty to a very rudimentary kind of conditioning, a stimulus-response connection almost as simple and direct as the causal connection between pushbutton and doorbell. During the period of service in the last War, Cowley says, MacLeish saw many posters, proclaiming: "These dead shall not have died in vain." And now, still obedient to this stimulus, MacLeish responds automatically by insisting that the War was a noble war, in which men did not fight in vain, where "some few ridiculously believed in the thing for which (or so they thought) they died." Cowley suggests that "Echoing through

his mind must be those words so often printed on posters,"
and as MacLeish recalls dead friends, he recalls them hal-
lowed by this slogan.

The slogan, to begin with, seems hardly such a cunning one
as to have very deeply impressed a poet of MacLeish's stature,
and particularly a poet of MacLeish's sophistication. I can
even imagine that a great many real and very moving events
must have had to occur behind the lines and in the trenches
before the doubts raised by so blunt an advertisement could
have been erased from the poet's mind. But that is too "subjective" an approach. I shall turn to such matters of response
as are more accessible to discussion.

It is understandable that, in an age intensely characterized by the "rationality" of its machines, we should attempt
as much as possible to consider human psychology from the
interpretative point of view, the "perspective," furnished us
by the mechanistic metaphor. By this machine perspective,
things may do one of two things: they either "go straight"
or they "get out of order." Extending this metaphorical
usage to people, we necessarily eliminate any intermediate
position, such as the possibility that people might go crooked
and yet be in order. Is it possible that the assumption of
a rational psychology for explaining human responses is
based too faithfully upon an analogy with the procedures
of our masters, the machines? Do we tend to imagine a human psychology patterned too literally after the best factory
models, a schema of stimulus and response whereby you put
in leather and take out leather goods, or put in iron and
take out iron pots? Or, returning to the issues of war: you
put in war-horrors and take out antimilitarism, put in "human" pictures of war and take out war-spirit. It may be that
the assumption is justified, that the approach to man from

the perspective supplied by the processes of the machine really does yield all that we have to know about his ways of assimilation. Yet biological analogies would suggest that the putting-in and the taking-out are often qualitatively different. For the present, I wish merely to raise the question. Does a book act precisely as it seems to do on the face of it—a pro-this book making one pro-this, an anti-that book making one anti-that? Is the machine metaphor, the assumption that we have only a choice between "rationality" and "breakdown," enough to describe the ways of biologic response? And, if we do use the perspective of the factory, can we use it in this way: put humanity in, and you take culture out; put inhumanity in, and you take ferocity out?

Imagine setting a lamp on the very edge of a table. Suppose that it gave you better light there for your purposes, unless someone knocked it off. If knocked off, it might do great damage. . . . Are any literary effects of this sort? Does literature ever promote ways which are "neutral" in themselves (as is the lamp), but which, depending upon other circumstances, may either give light or burn down one's house? At least we know that such is the case with moral systems. A moral attitude may be adopted by one class, for instance, to *help* them in their work, and may be promoted by another class to *keep* them at their work. Again, how accurate a gauge of response is verbalization? Consider the many questionnaires which used to fly about, in the heydey of the New Era, when philanthropists were financing all sorts of ingenious fact-finding escapades as a social-minded way of cutting down their income taxes. To what extent were the answers a just revelation of attitude? For my own part, I can only say: God pity the findings of such investigations if those persons who were interrogated were not vastly more skilled in the verbalizations of their attitudes under such conditions than I am.

For the moment, we leave the issue vague. I believe that there *are* good grounds for suspecting that man's responses are *normally* of a contradictory nature. There is a kind of "one to one" correspondence between stimulus and response which is assumed in much contemporary criticism, and I believe that it is not justified. Does antimilitarism produce antimilitarism, corruption corruption, quietude quietude, acceptance acceptance, individualism individualism, etc.? I think that the entire issue must be broadened considerably.

I wish to offer evidence for suspecting that *irrationality*, or *contradictoriness of response,* is basic to human psychology, not merely as error, but for sound biological reasons; and this particularly at those depths of human sensitiveness which are implicated in the religious, ethical, poetic, or volitional aspects of man (the four adjectives are synonymous for my purposes, but the reader may prefer one or another of them).

Continuing with the controversy over *The First World War,* I would note a dismaying paradox which arises at the beginning of Cowley's article. After matching some of Mac-Leish's statements against others, he holds that they cancel one another. On the face of it, no procedure in controversy could be sounder than that of exposing "contradictions" in the assertions of one's opponent. But where do we stand if we find these contradictions exposed in a magazine which is continually and valuably instructing us as to the "contradictions of capitalism"? Now, if our capitalist social structure contains fundamental contradictions, and the poet's imagination is piously and sensitively constructed after the environmental patterns among which he arose, how could a man born and bred under capitalism be expected to honestly and totally express his attitudes without revealing a contradiction in them? In a society plagued by contradictions, one might more justly employ the opposite kind of rebuttal, and seek to discredit a man's thinking by exposing the fact that it was poor in fundamental contradictions.

This is no plea for loose thinking. Our statements should certainly be required to meet the tests of compatibility, at least to the extent that, where they are at odds, we offer a shuttle concept for getting from one to the other. Cowley is certainly justified in exposing any point at which, to his mind, such shuttle concepts are needed and are lacking. But in so far as our statements are taken merely to indicate our underlying attitude, they should in some way or other reveal a contradiction of attitudes if they arose out of our response to an economic structure distinguished above all by the genius of the contradictory. Liberals have long suffered in silence under this curse, since they are half the time advocating reforms when they know that reforms interfere with fundamental change. And even the Communists, who in America are still living by the dictates of capitalism, became involved in a similar contradiction when they began pleading for unemployment insurance which, if adequate, might put off the Revolution forever. John Maynard Keynes once noted a similar predicament among the English socialists: put them in power in an ailing capitalist structure, and they inevitably fall into the muddle-headed position of attempting to patch up the very structure they would abolish.

I believe there is a corresponding emotional contradiction in our society which has done much to interfere with a unified moral attitude, radically splitting our ethical responses into two largely antithetical compartments. Under typical industrialized capitalism, there are important influences making for *acquiescence to* its ways and equally important influences tending to carry one *beyond capitalism*. The doctrines of "emancipation" are a case in point. It was under the aegis of "emancipation" that the commercial state arose and conquered the feudal state—yet this same stressing or emphasis threatens to endanger the commercialists' hegemony itself, once they become thoroughly entrenched in their privileges. In this sense, the very kingpin of Marxian exhortation is a virtue stressed by capitalist enterprise, a standard developing out of the very laissez-faire psychosis which Communism would abolish. It is a principle of change, hence interferes with the stabilization of any *status quo*. Similarly, a certain degree of literacy has been a necessary instrument for shaping contemporary man to his place as customer, salesman, and potential soldier—yet this same literacy has afforded all sorts of people momentous glimpses into the critical lore of mankind, thus serving again and again to hamper the processes of naïve accommodation that might otherwise have taken place. The freedom of criticism which, originally aimed at priesthood and nobles, was finally turned to practical and acquisitive purpose by the rising commercial class, tended throughout the nineteenth century to transcend this function and become a criticism of commerce itself. The writings of Marx are perhaps the purest example of this tendency in the theoretical sphere; the same trend was exemplified in the imaginative sphere by the various social satirists, Bohemians, paradoxists, romantic, neoclassical, and primitivistic poets of "refusal," culminating perhaps in the symbolizations of the Ivory Tower, writers whom Edmund Wilson has treated somewhat un-

246

fairly, as they did not content themselves with a merely negative attitude towards the contemporary state of affairs, but went aggressively to work depicting alternative existences, other and preferable worlds.

In the end, we have here "two moralities"—and the active, conscientious, well-educated member of Western culture showed himself thoroughly versed in both of them. The one prevailed largely in "glimpses," compensating by intensity for what it lacked in permanence, as earnest and uneasy young men, browsing about their local libraries in the indeterminate years before they had definitely settled down to "serious business," found opportunities and incentives to nibble at the fringes of a humanistic, cultured way of life. They even tentatively encouraged in themselves such characteristics and interests and standards as would prepare them to be decent integers in a world so constructed. Here was the possibility of poetry, which they could find substantiated in the imagery of books, and at certain moments even dared think might attain its parallels in the architecture of the state.

However, the need of a counter-morality clearly made itself felt. For a morality is but a set of attitudes and ways of thinking which enable us the better to do the things we must do—and unless one happened to be supported by unearned increment from the capitalist structure, he found it imperative that he either cultivate the "capitalist virtues" or perish. As Veblen once neatly pointed out, opportunities to get ahead are likewise opportunities to fall behind—and though one may well ask himself whether a desire to triumph in the Scramble marks a very high cultural ideal, neither is it very "cultural" to find oneself edged further and further into the ditch. Some people supported by coupon-clipping could afford to "scorn" the very virtues of salesmanship, bluster, and brass out of which their income was arising; likewise, the artists could escape to an extent, sometimes by addressing their imagery to the class of coupon-clippers themselves, but more often by writing for what might be called the coupon-clipping portion of the mind of drudges. In general, however, the entire populace had to equip itself for the demands of the Scramble by adopting a morality in keeping. This they could best accomplish by accepting a picture of the "good life" built around the ideal of the "live-wire" salesman, with culture taken to mean the maximum purchase of manufactured commodities.

The result was a moral split which became more and more sharply characterized in imaginative literature as the character of the nineteenth century took form. Out of books, out of delightful moments in one's personal life, out of sporadic voyages, out of *vacational* experiences as distinct from *vocational* ones, people got visions of a noncompetitive structure of living, a "good life" involving gentle surroundings, adequate physical outlets, the pursuit of knowledge, etc., and the very slogans of the commercial ethic assured them that they were "entitled" to all this. At the same time they had to meet the conditions of the daily Scramble—jockeying, outselling, outsmarting—demands better justified by the price they brought than by the wholesome calls they made upon mind and body. This contradiction led to the artistic phenomenon generally and inappropriately designated a "breach between art and life." It was naturally in the field of the aesthetic (the "vacational") that the opposition to practical ("vocational") demands could best be kept alive. Conditions of economic combat necessarily silenced or stunted the noncommercial morality between the hours of nine and five. Often, the problem was resolved by a man's enjoying vicious satire and the contemplation of lovely or hectic alternative worlds with the "after hours" portion of his mind while each day, grimly and cynically, buckling down to equip himself in precisely the kinds of effort and accomplishment for which he had, in his freer moments, soundly damned all mankind. Observable also is the "Faustian" split between "serious pursuits" and "dissipation." In New York, the discrepancy regularly took the form of privately playing the stock market and publicly praying for the revolution. Such was an inevitable incongruity, since capitalism fed both a capitalist morality and a morality beyond capitalism—yet I believe it has embittered a great many people's relations with one another in recent years.

In particular it has aggravated the plight of poets whose emotional, nonmechanical emphases might, even without this added burden, have made them forlorn enough in an age of intense mechanistic striving. A critic might conveniently restrict his exhortations to the "morality beyond capitalism" if he chose, but the poet is tapping deeper levels of response. If he arose under conditions of pronounced moral duality, it is not likely that the flow of his imagery can be confined to whichever of the two moral channels he happens to consider preferable. This dilemma has in particular exposed him to the purist attacks of all rationalist criticism (of either the neo-Humanist or the neo-Marxian kind) which would programmatically suppress one or another aspect of this duality by critical *fiat*. As regards certain superficial manifestations such demands can possibly be met: for instance, if a poet is sufficiently impressed by some new critical canon, he might train himself to avoid the subject of Greek Isles and select the subject of workingmen instead. Or he

249

can depict people "with or without will," depending upon which symbolic externalities the tastes of the season may deem more acceptable. But in the end, to a sharper eye, he will necessarily be found to symbolize the patterns of experience under which he was formed. At best, like the Lowlands painters, he will depict Calvary among windmills. Nor may it always be possible to say when the poet formed by capitalist contradictions is exemplifying the *acquiescent* response and when the *corrective* one. When a wild animal grows heavier fur with the approach of winter, is it "resisting" the demands of the season or "acquiescing to" them?

So much for "capitalist contradictions" and our suggestion that the "complete" response to a contradictory society should be contradictory. Not all people may agree that environments impress themselves upon the individual mind so accurately. They may even accuse me of secretly propounding much the same kind of "one to one" correspondence between social stimulus and emotional response as I had attempted to discredit—the only difference in my version being that I offer a combined "A to A and non-A to non-A" correspondence. Accordingly, I propose to consider the matter from another angle, suggesting this time certain psychological or physiological contradictions so indigenous to man that they might be expected to operate even in a thoroughly homogeneous economic or social order. In fact, the contradictory aspects of a given temporal society might even conceivably be traced back to this source, being taken as the outgrowth or social externalization of initial biologic contradictions. For contradictions are not confined to capitalism. Yeast, fermenting in the fruit mash, eventually generates enough alcohol to pickle itself in death. Or nobles under feudalism, at one point in their exploitation, presumably had to do so contradictory a thing as restrain themselves from taking all they could, in order that their serfs might live and serve. Some contradictions may be considered as purely subjective phenomena, depending for their existence upon the "point of view." The "synthetic" act of walking, for instance, might well be described by an eloquent right foot as a fluctuating battle against a contradictory left. The glands of internal secretion "cancel" the effects of one another, but from the standpoint of the body as a whole they may be said to "collaborate." Newton talked of planetary motion as a synthesis of centrifugal and centripetal forces, but he himself warned that the synthesis was the real event and the two contradictory concepts were purely mathematical conventions used in plotting it. *Das Wahre ist das Ganze,* wrote Hegel, in the backwash of whose thinking we now flounder. By the "really real" he meant the synthesis of unreal, contradictory concepts. But we need not endanger our discussion here by roaming into a region whereby even so contradictory an alignment as two armies opposed on a battlefield must seem like "coöperation" in the eyes of God. Rather, we shall confine ourselves to an attempted distinction between essayistic and poetic exhortation, attempting to show that the second necessarily carries us towards a contradiction.

Suppose that we favored the triumph of the workingman, and wrote a work embodying this attitude. Essayistically (critically, rationally) we should proceed as follows: We should line up all the reasons why the triumph of the workingman seems preferable, and we would presumably seek to refute arguments which seemed directly or indirectly to prejudice this position. But the poetic (tragic, ethical) method of recommendation would be quite different. The poet might best plead for his Cause by picturing people who suffered or died in behalf of it. The essayistic critic would win us by proving the serviceability of his Cause—the poet would seem as spontaneously to stress the factor of disserviceability. For how better recommend a Cause by the strategies of a fiction than by picturing it as worthy of being fought for? And how better picture it as worthy of being fought for than by showing people who are willing to sacrifice their safety, lives, and happiness in its behalf? Such facts must lead us to search in all deeply felt tragedies the symbol of a birth, and not of the dying we should rationally expect. I never so greatly felt the limitations of rationalist criticism applied to poetry as when I once heard Michael Gold complain about the "defeatism" in plays and novels written by labor sympathizers. He felt that there should be pictures of triumph, of glorification—perhaps somewhat as Ziegfeld found ways to glorify the American Girl. He took the tragic ending simply at its face value, despite the obvious fact that the tragedies were written by sincere labor sympathizers who were trying to commend their Cause in the symbols of art, and who did commend their Cause precisely as human Causes have ever been commended, by the symbol of the Crucifixion.

In sum, we might say that the difference between essayistic and poetic exhortation is that the essayistic can be consistent while the poetic is necessarily contradictory. "Business Christianity" is rational: it recommends religion quite simply and directly on the grounds that Church contacts help you get ahead. "Poetic Christianity" was contradictory, building its entire doctrine of salvation about the image of a god in anguish. So also, our great "tragedies of individualism" preceded the spread of individualist ethics throughout our social structure. And thus characteristically, we find so deeply ethical a poet as Baudelaire seeking to celebrate the flesh, not in the direct manner of our musical revues, but by recourse to the rationally repellent symbols of brutality, sterility, and even frigidity. And we may note the presence of this tragic device, in a more domesticated form, thus: In an age wherein the prestige of art was undergoing gradual eclipse, Flaubert tended to keep his vocation in good repute, in his own eyes at least, by forever grumbling about the annoyances caused him by the *problème du style.*

This fundamental distinction between the "rational" and "ethical" modes of exhortation or incitement seems especially apropos to the MacLeish-Cowley discussion. For it should reveal a process whereby many so-called "attacks" on war might come, through the vagaries of the sacrificial symbol, to serve pro-military ends. For such attacks generally stress the sufferings of war, and these are precisely the foremost ethical symbols of commendation. Of all the inconsistencies in which the human mind is entangled, this confusion between "goodness" and "sacrifice" seems the most unavoidable. Even were we to grant with the utilitarians that our notions of the "good" arise purely and simply from our notions of the "useful" or "usable," the fact remains that the best argument in favor of a "good" is one's willingness to sacrifice himself for it. Thus, by the ethical contradiction, categories as logically distinct as service and disservice, advantage and disaster, become fundamentally intertwined. It is not mere "compensation" that brings religion and failure together. By the "logic of the emotions" the religious feeling may *demand* failure as its symbolic counterpart. The confusion probably goes far to explain

253

why so much of the propaganda for the good of society has been carried on antagonistically instead of by wheedling. The rational method would clearly be to plead for one's Cause by the most unctuous strategy one could command —but ethical attachment makes one tend to "testify" by invitation to martyrdom.

It is this discrepancy, I believe, which lies at the bottom of Unamuno's insistence upon the "tragic sense of life." He is forever talking of plans for human benefit, while seeming to prize nothing so greatly as the thought of human suffering. His pages at times are a kind of bullfight, a gory spirituality concerned with the need to incur risk, to inflict and suffer misery, coexisting with an almost morbidly intense yearning to see mankind housed in a very pigeonry of ease. Thus, in his *Essays and Soliloquies,* he speaks of a groaning, heard at night from an adjoining room: "It produced upon me the illusion of coming out of the night itself, as if it were the silence of the night that lamented; and there was even a moment when I dreamt that that gentle lament rose to the surface from the depths of my own soul." Is not this the "connoisseur" speaking? And in the social sphere, he sees in Don Quixote the tragic symbol under the guise of the ridiculous—for it is ridicule which puts us most cruelly apart from others, hence one may poetically commend his wares by the symbol of ridicule. Martyrdom creates the creed—though out of the creed in turn may come a "rationally compensatory" codicil to the effect that martyrdom will be rewarded.

The instance of Unamuno, whose ethics so confusingly intermingles ideals of peace and ideals of anguish, may serve to help us consider the same paradox from another angle. For it is undeniably a fact that even so brutal a performance as modern warfare is ethically rooted. The neurologist Sherrington has pointed out that, whatever "consciousness" may be, it is mainly manifested in those processes involved in the seeking and capture of food; whereas, once the prize is seized and swallowed, the organism's "awareness" is of a very blunt order. Unless the digestion is impaired, there is slight sensation beyond a vague state of wellbeing, relaxation, and somnolence. Now: what do we face here if not a fundamental contradiction in human incentives? The organism has at its command a keen and adventurous equipment for attaining the wherewithal to bring about a state of security, peace, relaxation, comfort, the benign sluggishness of satiety and warmth—yet this very equipment for attaining the state of worldly Nirvana is the soul of turbulence and struggle. Here is a "militaristic-pacifistic" conflict at the basis of morals. We seek peace ever by the questionable Rooseveltian device of fighting for it. In so far as the organism attains the state of quiescence, its militaristic equipment (that is: nervous agility, bodily and mental muscle, imagination, intellect, senses, expectation, "curiosity," etc.) is threatened with decay. And in so far as this militaristic equipment is kept in vigorous operation, it makes impossible precisely the state of relaxation which it is designed to secure.

Many of the disagreements among moralists might be traced to the fact that they have selected one of these factors, rather than the other, to form the keystone of their ethical schemas. Perhaps Nietzsche was the modern thinker who plagued himself most spectacularly with this problem of the militaristic-pacifistic conflict. His madness may account for the inadequate means of communication which he sometimes adopted in his attempt to symbolize his preoccupations (as with the excesses of the "blonde beast," for instance), but this fact should not lead us to overlook the genius and fertility of his perception and the wide range of human activities which he saw implicated in this confusion. He knew that the morality of combat is no despicable thing, that morals are fists, and that we cannot stop at noting the savagery of some slayer or the greed of some financial monopolist. There is the same fanaticism, tenacity, and even pugnacity underlying the efforts of the scientist, artist, explorer, rescuer, inventor, experimenter, reformer. Militaristic patterns are fundamental to our "virtue," even the word itself coming from a word which the Latins applied to their warriors.

One could consider the matter from other points of view. In particular, for instance, I believe that a kind of "egoistic-altruistic merger" can be established whereby a man may be found honestly "devoting" himself and "sacrificing" himself to activities which are primarily pursued because they net him large profits. How many business men actually do warp and ruin their lives in the getting of fortunes which the very intensity of their devotion unfits them to enjoy? And when an ape "protects" his women, perhaps even losing his life in the effort, is that act "egoistic" or "altruistic"? It seems to be something of both. Who lives by the sword dies by the sword? In terms of the "egoistic-altruistic merger" we might restate it: If one possesses a resource or device that greatly sustains or protects him, he will even risk his life to keep it or improve it.

As possible confusions to complicate human response we have, then: the Bohemian-practical; the useful-sacrificial; the militaristic-pacifistic; the egoistic-altruistic, as effected through "devotion to work."

There is also a wide "neutral" area of response wherein such confusions do not seem to arise. Generally, if one wishes to strike a match, he simply takes it and strikes it in the most direct, convenient, rational way his experience has taught him. (Even in this field, however, I must recall an occasional "poetic" or "ethical" match-striker, particularly among those drawing-room martyrs to form who willingly endanger their health and happiness by striking matches with their thumbnails, a sacrificial technique which sometimes lodges bits of fizzing sulphur between the nail and the quick.) Science is the attempt to extend this "neutral" area to as many procedures and relationships as possible. Ideally, it would have all our responses to stimuli obey the rational pattern, so that contradictions would arise purely from "error," from "insufficient knowledge." Science hopes to impose this neutrality of approach upon a kind of mental and bodily structure which, according to Veblen, is best fitted for a state of "mild savagery." It would impose mechanistic ideals upon a non-mechanistic organism.

FREUD—
AND THE ANALYSIS OF POETRY

THE reading of Freud I find suggestive almost to the point of bewilderment. Accordingly, what I should like most to do would be simply to take representative excerpts from his work, copy them out, and write glosses upon them. Very often these glosses would be straight extensions of his own thinking. At other times they would be attempts to characterize his strategy of presentation with reference to interpretative method in general. And, finally, the Freudian perspective was developed primarily to chart a psychiatric field rather than an aesthetic one; but since we are here considering the analogous features of these two fields rather than their important differences, there would be glosses attempting to suggest how far the literary critic should go along with Freud and what extra-Freudian material he would have to add. Such a desire to write an article on Freud in the margins of his books, must for practical reasons here remain a frustrated desire. An article such as this must condense by generalization, which requires me to slight the most stimulating factor of all—the detailed articulacy in which he embodies his extraordinary frankness.

Freud's frankness is no less remarkable by reason of the fact that he had perfected a method for being frank. He could say humble, even humiliating, things about himself and us because he had changed the rules somewhat and could make capital of observations that others, with vested interests of a different sort, would feel called upon to suppress by dictatorial decree. Or we might say that what for him could fall within the benign category of observation could for them fall only within its malign counterpart, spying.

Yet though honesty is, in Freud, methodologically made easier, it is by no means honesty made easy. And Freud's own accounts of his own dreams show how poignantly he felt at times the "disgrace" of his occupation. There are doubtless many thinkers whose strange device might be *ecclesia super cloacam*. What more fitting place to erect one's church than above a sewer! One might even say that sewers are what churches are for. But usually this is done by laying all the stress upon the ecclesia and its beauty. So that, even when the man's work fails to be completed for him as a social act, by the approval of his group, he has the conviction of its intrinsic beauty to give him courage and solace.

But to think of Freud, during the formative years of his doctrines, confronting something like repugnance among his colleagues, and even, as his dreams show, in his own eyes, is to think of such heroism as Unamuno found in Don Quixote; and if Don Quixote risked the social judgment of ridicule, he still had the consolatory thought that his imaginings were beautiful, stressing the ecclesia aspect, whereas Freud's theories bound him to a more drastic self-ostracizing act—the charting of the relations between ecclesia and cloaca that forced him to analyze the cloaca itself. Hence, his work was with the confessional as cathartic, as purgative; this haruspicy required an inspection of the entrails; it was, bluntly, an interpretative sculpting of excrement, with beauty replaced by a science of the grotesque.

Confronting this, Freud does nonetheless advance to erect

a structure which, if it lacks beauty, has astounding ingeniousness and fancy. It is full of paradoxes, of leaps across gaps, of vistas—much more so than the work of many a modern poet who sought for nothing else but these and had no search for accuracy to motivate his work. These qualities alone would make it unlikely that readers literarily inclined could fail to be attracted, even while repelled. Nor can one miss in it the profound charitableness that is missing in so many modern writers who, likewise concerned with the cloaca, become efficiently concerned with nothing else, and make of their work pure indictment, pure oath, pure striking-down, pure spitting-upon, pure kill. True, this man, who taught us so much about father-rejection and who ironically became himself so frequently the rejected father in the works of his schismatic disciples, does finally descend to quarrelsomeness, despite himself, when recounting the history of the psychoanalytic movement. But, over the great course of his work, it is the matter of human rescue that he is concerned with—not the matter of vengeance. On a few occasions, let us say, he is surprised into vengefulness. But the very essence of his studies, even at their most forbidding moments (in fact, precisely at those moments), is its charitableness, its concern with salvation. To borrow an excellent meaningful pun from Trigant Burrow, this salvation is approached not in terms of religious hospitality but rather in terms of secular hospitalization. Yet it is the spirit of Freud; it is what Freud's courage is for.

Perhaps, therefore, the most fitting thing for a writer to do, particularly in view of the fact that Freud is now among the highly honored class—the exiles from Nazi Germany (how accurate those fellows are! how they seem, with almost 100 per cent efficiency, to have weeded out their greatest citizens!)—perhaps the most fitting thing to do would be simply to attempt an article of the "homage to Freud" sort and call it a day.

However, my job here cannot be confined to that. I have been commissioned to consider the bearing of Freud's theories upon literary criticism. And these theories were not designed primarily for literary criticism at all but were rather a perspective that, developed for the charting of a nonaesthetic field, was able (by reason of its scope) to migrate into the aesthetic field. The margin of overlap was this: The acts of the neurotic are symbolic acts. Hence in so far as both the neurotic act and the poetic act share this property in common, they may share a terminological chart in common. But in so far as they deviate, terminology likewise must deviate. And this deviation is a fact that literary criticism must explicitly consider.

As for the glosses on the interpretative strategy in general, they would be of this sort: For one thing, they would concern a distinction between what I should call an essentializing mode of interpretation and a mode that stresses proportion of ingredients. The tendency in Freud is toward the first of these. That is, if one found a complex of, let us say, seven ingredients in a man's motivation, the Freudian tendency would be to take one of these as the essence of the motivation and to consider the other six as sublimated variants. We could imagine, for instance, manifestations of sexual impotence accompanying a conflict in one's relations with his familiars and one's relations at the office. The proportional strategy would involve the study of these three as a cluster. The motivation would be synonymous with the interrelationships among them. But the essentializing strat-
261

egy would, in Freud's case, place the emphasis upon the sexual manifestation, as causal ancestor of the other two.

This essentializing strategy is linked with a normal ideal of science: to "explain the complex in terms of the simple." This ideal almost vows one to select one or another motive from a cluster and interpret the others in terms of it. The naïve proponent of economic determinism, for instance, would select the quarrel at the office as the essential motive, and would treat the quarrel with familiars and the sexual impotence as mere results of this. Now, I don't see how you can possibly explain the complex in terms of the simple without having your very success used as a charge against you. When you get through, all that your opponent need say is: "But you have explained the complex in terms of the simple—and the simple is precisely what the complex is not."

Perhaps the faith philosophers, as against the reason philosophers, did not have to encounter a paradox at this point. Not that they avoided paradoxes, for I think they must always cheat when trying to explain how evil can exist in a world created by an all-powerful and wholly good Creator. But at least they did not have to confront the complexity-simplicity difficulty, since their theological reductions referred to a ground in God, who was simultaneously the ultimately complex and the ultimately simple. Naturalistic strategies lack this convenient "out"—hence their explanations are simplifications, and every simplification is an oversimplification.[1]

It is possible that the literary critic, taking communica-

1 The essentializing strategy has its function when dealing with classes of items; the proportional one is for dealing with an item in its uniqueness. By isolating the matter of voluntarism, we put Freud in a line or class with Augustine. By isolating the matter of his concern with a distinction between unconscious and conscious, we

tion as his basic category, may avoid this particular paradox (communication thereby being a kind of attenuated God term). You can reduce everything to communication—yet communication is extremely complex. But, in any case, communication is by no means the basic category of Freud. The sexual wish, or libido, is the basic category; and the complex forms of communication that we see in a highly alembicated philosophy would be mere sublimations of this.

A writer deprived of Freud's clinical experience would be a fool to question the value of his category as a way of analyzing the motives of the class of neurotics Freud encountered. There is a pronouncedly individualistic element in any technique of salvation (my toothache being alas! my private property), and even those beset by a pandemic of sin or microbes will enter heaven or get discharged from the hospital one by one; and the especially elaborate process of diagnosis involved in Freudian analysis even to this day makes it more available to those suffering from the ills of preoccupation and leisure than to those suffering from the ills of occupation and unemployment (with people generally tending to be only as mentally sick as they can afford to be). This state of affairs makes it all the more likely that the typical psychoanalytic patient would have primarily private

---

may put him in a line with Leibniz's distinction between perception and apperception. Or we could link him with the Spinozistic *conatus* and the Schopenhauerian will. Or, as a rationalist, he falls into the bin with Aquinas (who is himself most conveniently isolated as a rationalist if you employ the essentializing as against the proportional strategy, stressing what he added rather than what he retained). Many arguments seem to hinge about the fact that there is an unverbalized disagreement as to the choice between these strategies. The same man, for instance, who might employ the essentializing strategy in proclaiming Aquinas as a rationalist, taking as the significant factor in Aquinas' philosophy his additions to rationalism rather than considering this as an ingredient in a faith philosophy, might object to the bracketing of Aquinas and Freud (here shifting to the proportional strategy, as he pointed out the totally different materials with which Aquinas surrounded his rational principle).

sexual motivations behind his difficulties. (Did not Henry James say that sex is something about which we think a great deal when we are not thinking about anything else?) [2] Furthermore, I believe that studies of artistic imagery, outside the strict pale of psychoanalytic emphasis, will bear out Freud's brilliant speculations as to the sexual puns, the *double-entendres*, lurking behind the most unlikely façades. If a man acquires a method of thinking about everything else, for instance, during the sexual deprivations and rigors of adolescence, this cure may well take on the qualities of the disease; and in so far as he continues with this same method in adult years, though his life has since become sexually less exacting, such modes as incipient homosexuality or masturbation may very well be informatively interwoven in the strands of his thought and be discoverable by inspection of the underlying imagery or patterns in this thought.

Indeed, there are only a few fundamental bodily idioms —and why should it not be likely that an attitude, no matter how complex its ideational expression, could only be completed by a channelization within its corresponding gestures? That is, the details of experience behind A's dejection may be vastly different from the details of experience behind B's dejection, yet both A and B may fall into the same bodily posture in expressing their dejection. And in an era like ours, coming at the end of a long individualistic emphasis, where we frequently find expressed an attitude of complete

[2] We may distinguish between a public and universal motive. In so far as one acts in a certain way because of his connection with a business or party, he would act from a public motive. His need of response to a new glandular stimulation at adolescence, on the other hand, would arise regardless of social values, and in that sense would be at once private and universal. The particular forms in which he expressed this need would, of course, be channelized in accordance with public or social factors.

independence, of total, uncompromising self-reliance, this expression would not reach its fulfillment in choreography except in the act of "practical narcissism" (that is, the only wholly independent person would be the one who practiced self-abuse and really meant it).

But it may be noticed that we have here tended to consider mind-body relations from an interactive point of view rather than a materialistic one (which would take the body as the essence of the act and the mentation as the sublimation).

Freud himself, interestingly enough, was originally nearer to this view (necessary, as I hope to show later, for specifically literary purposes) than he later became. Freud explicitly resisted the study of motivation by way of symbols. He distinguished his own mode of analysis from the symbolic by laying the stress upon free association. That is, he would begin the analysis of a neurosis without any preconceived notion as to the absolute meaning of any image that the patient might reveal in the account of a dream. His procedure involved the breaking-down of the dream into a set of fragments, with the analyst then inducing the patient to improvise associations on each of these fragments in turn. And afterward, by charting recurrent themes, he would arrive at the crux of the patient's conflict.

Others (particularly Stekel), however, proposed a great short cut here. They offered an absolute content for various items of imagery. For instance, in Stekel's dictionary of symbols, which has the absoluteness of an old-fashioned dreambook, the right-hand path equals the road to righteousness, the left-hand path equals the road to crime, in anybody's dreams (in Lenin's presumably, as well as the Pope's). Sisters are breasts and brothers are buttocks. "The luggage of a traveller is the burden of sin by which one is oppressed," etc. Freud criticizes these on the basis of his own clinical experiences—and whereas he had reservations against specific equations, and rightly treats the method as antithetical to his own contribution, he decides that a high percentage of Stekel's purely intuitive hunches were corroborated. And after warning that such a gift as Stekel's is often evidence of paranoia, he decides that normal persons may also occasionally be capable of it.

Its lure as efficiency is understandable. And, indeed, if we revert to the matter of luggage, for instance, does it not immediately give us insight into a remark of André Gide, who is a specialist in the portrayal of scrupulous criminals, who has developed a stylistic trick for calling to seduction in the accents of evangelism, and who advises that one should learn to "travel light"?

But the trouble with short cuts is that they deny us a chance to take longer routes. With them, the essentializing strategy takes a momentous step forward. You have next but to essentialize your short cuts in turn (a short cut atop a short cut), and you get the sexual emphasis of Freud, the all-embracing ego compensation of Adler, or Rank's master-emphasis upon the birth trauma, etc.

Freud himself fluctuates in his search for essence. At some places you find him proclaiming the all-importance of the sexual, at other places you find him indignantly denying that his psychology is a pansexual one at all, and at still other places you get something halfway between the two, via the concept of the libido, which embraces a spectrum from phallus to philanthropy.

The important matter for our purposes is to suggest that
266

the examination of a poetic work's internal organization would bring us nearer to a variant of the typically Freudian free-association method than to the purely symbolic method toward which he subsequently gravitated.[3]

The critic should adopt a variant of the free-association method. One obviously cannot invite an author, especially a dead author, to oblige him by telling what the author thinks of when the critic isolates some detail or other for improvisation. But what he can do is to note the context of imagery and ideas in which an image takes its place. He can also note, by such analysis, the kinds of evaluations surrounding the image of a crossing; for instance, is it an escape from or a return to an evil or a good, etc.? Until finally, by noting the ways in which this crossing behaves, what subsidiary imagery accompanies it, what kind of event it grows out of, what kind of event grows out of it, what altered rhythmic and tonal effects characterize it, etc., one grasps its significance as motivation. And there is no essential motive offered here. The motive of the work is equated with the structure of interrelationships within the work itself.

"But there is more to a work of art than that." I hear this objection being raised. And I agree with it. And I wonder whether we could properly consider the matter in this wise:

For convenience using the word "poem" to cover any complete made artistic product, let us divide this artifact

[3] Perhaps, to avoid confusion, I should call attention to the fact that symbolic in this context is being used differently by me from its use in the expression "symbolic action." If a man crosses a street, it is a practical act. If he writes a book about crossings—crossing streets, bridges, oceans, etc.—that is a symbolic act. Symbolic, as used in the restricted sense (in contrast with free association), would refer to the imputation of an absolute meaning to a crossing, a meaning that I might impute even before reading the book in question. Against this, I should maintain: One can never know what a crossing means, in a specific book, until he has studied its tie-up with other imagery in that particular book.

(the invention, creation, formation, poetic construct) in accordance with three modes of analysis: dream, prayer, chart.

The psychoanalysis of Freud and of the schools stemming from Freud has brought forward an astoundingly fertile range of observations that give us insight into the poem as dream. There is opened up before us a sometimes almost terrifying glimpse into the ways in which we may, while overtly doing one thing, be covertly doing another. Yet, there is nothing mystical or even unusual about this. I may, for instance, consciously place my elbow upon the table. Yet at the same time I am clearly unconscious of the exact distance between my elbow and my nose. Or, if that analogy seems like cheating, let us try another: I may be unconscious of the way in which a painter-friend, observant of my postures, would find the particular position of my arm characteristic of me.

Or let us similarly try to take the terror out of infantile regression. In so far as I speak the same language that I learned as a child, every time I speak there is, within my speech, an ingredient of regression to the infantile level. Regression, we might say, is a function of progression. Where the progression has been a development by evolution or continuity of growth (as were one to have learned to speak and think in English as a child, and still spoke and thought in English) rather than by revolution or discontinuity of growth (as were one to have learned German in childhood, to have moved elsewhere at an early age, and since become so at home in English that he could not even understand a mature conversation in the language of his childhood), the archaic and the now would be identical. You could say, indifferently, either that the speech is regression or that it is not regression. But were the man who had forgot the language of his childhood, to begin speaking nothing but this early language (under a sudden agitation or as the result of some steady pressure), we should have the kind of regression that goes formally by this name in psychoanalytic nomenclature.

The ideal growth, I suppose—the growth without elements of alienation, discontinuity, homelessness—is that wherein regression is natural. We might sloganize it as "the adult a child matured." Growth has here been simply a successive adding of cells—the growth of the chambered nautilus. But there is also the growth of the adult who, "when he became a man, put away childish things." This is the growth of the crab, that grows by abandoning one room and taking on another. It produces moments of crisis. It makes for philosophies of emancipation and enlightenment, where one gets a jolt and is "awakened from the sleep of dogma" (and alas! in leaving his profound "Asiatic slumber," he risks getting in exchange more than mere wakefulness, more than the eternal vigilance that is the price of liberty—he may get wakefulness plus, i. e., insomnia).

There are, in short, critical points (or, in the Hegel-Marx vocabulary, changes of quantity leading to changes of quality) where the process of growth or change converts a previous circle of protection into a circle of confinement. The first such revolution may well be, for the human individual, a purely biological one—the change at birth when the fetus, heretofore enjoying a larval existence in the womb, being fed on manna from the placenta, so outgrows this circle of protection that the benign protection becomes a malign circle of confinement, whereat it must burst forth into a different kind of world—a world of locomotion, aggression, competition, hunt. The mother, it is true, may have already been living in such a world; but the fetus was in a world within this world—in a monastery—a world such as is lived in by "coupon clippers," who get their dividends as the result of sharp economic combat but who may, so long as the payments are regular, devote themselves to thoughts and diseases far "above" these harsh material operations.

In the private life of the individual there may be many subsequent jolts of a less purely biological nature, as with the death of some one person who had become pivotal to this individual's mental economy. But whatever these unique variants may be, there is again a universal variant at adolescence, when radical changes in the glandular structure of the body make this body a correspondingly altered environment for the mind, requiring a corresponding change in our perspective, our structure of interpretations, meanings, values, purposes, and inhibitions, if we are to take it properly into account.

In the informative period of childhood our experiences are strongly personalized. Our attitudes take shape with respect to distinct people who have rôles, even animals and objects being vessels of character. Increasingly, however, we begin to glimpse a world of abstract relationships, of functions understood solely through the medium of symbols in books. Even such real things as Tibet and Eskimos and Napoleon are for us, who have not been to Tibet, or lived with Eskimos, or fought under Napoleon, but a structure of signs. In a sense, it could be said that we learn these signs flat. We must start from scratch. There is no tradition in them; they are pure present. For though they have been handed down by tradition, we can read meaning into them only in so far as we can project or extend them out of our own experience. We may, through being burned a little, understand the signs for being burned a lot—it is in this sense that the coaching of interpretation could be called traditional. But we cannot understand the signs for being burned a lot until we have in our own flat experience, here and now, been burned a little.

Out of what can these extensions possibly be drawn? Only out of the informative years of childhood. Psychoanalysis talks of purposive forgetting. Yet purposive forgetting is the only way of remembering. One learns the meaning of "table," "book," "father," "mother," "mustn't," by forgetting the contexts in which these words were used. The Darwinian ancestry (locating the individual in his feudal line of descent from the ape) is matched in Freud by a still more striking causal ancestry that we might sloganize as "the child is father to the man." [4]

As we grow up new meanings must either be engrafted upon old meanings (being to that extent *double-entendres*) or they must be new starts (hence, involving problems of dissociation).

It is in the study of the poem as dream that we find re-

---

[4] Maybe the kind of forgetting that is revealed by psychoanalysis could, within this frame, be better characterized as an incomplete forgetting. That is, whereas table, for instance, acquires an absolute and emotionally neutral meaning, as a name merely for a class of objects, by a merging of all the contexts involving the presence of a table, a table becomes symbolic, or a *double-entendre*, or more than table, when some particular informative context is more important than the others. That is, when table, as used by the poet, has overtones of, let us say, *one* table at which his mother worked when he was a child. In this way the table, its food, and the cloth may become surrogates for the mother, her breasts, and her apron. And incest awe may become merged with "mustn't touch" injunctions, stemming from attempts to keep the child from meddling with the objects on the table. In a dream play by Edmund Wilson, *The Crime in the Whistler Room*, there are two worlds of plot, with the characters belonging in the one world looking upon those in the other as dead, and the hero of this living world taking a dream shape as werewolf. The worlds switch back and forth, depending upon the presence or removal of a gate-leg table. In this instance I think we should not be far wrong in attributing some such content as the above to the table when considering it as a fulcrum upon which the structure of the plot is swung.

vealed the ways in which the poetic organization takes shape under these necessities. Revise Freud's terms, if you will. But nothing is done by simply trying to refute them or to tie them into knots. One may complain at this procedure, for instance: Freud characterizes the dream as the fulfillment of a wish; an opponent shows him a dream of frustration, and he answers: "But the dreamer wishes to be frustrated." You may demur at that, pointing out that Freud has developed a "heads I win, tails you lose" mode of discourse here. But I maintain that, in doing so, you have contributed nothing. For there are people whose values are askew, for whom frustration itself is a kind of grotesque ambition. If you would, accordingly, propose to chart this field by offering better terms, by all means do so. But better terms are the only kind of refutation here that is worth the trouble. Similarly, one may be unhappy with the concept of ambivalence, which allows pretty much of an open season on explanations (though the specific filling-out may provide a better case for the explanation than appears in this key term itself). But, again, nothing but an alternative explanation is worth the effort of discussion here. Freud's terminology is a dictionary, a lexicon for charting a vastly complex and hitherto largely uncharted field. You can't refute a dictionary. The only profitable answer to a dictionary is another one.

A profitable answer to Freud's treatment of the Oedipus complex, for instance, was Malinowski's study of its variants in a matriarchal society.[5] Here we get at once a corrobora-

---

[5] It is wrong, I think, to consider Freud's general picture as that of an individual psychology. Adler's start from the concept of ego compensation fits this description par excellence. But Freud's is a family psychology. He has offered a critique of the family, though it is the family of a neo-patriarch. It is interesting to watch Freud, in his Group Psychology and the Analysis of the Ego, frankly shifting between the primacy of group psychology and the primacy of individual psychology, changing

tion and a refutation of the Freudian doctrine. It is corroborated in that the same general patterns of enmity are
revealed; it is refuted in that these patterns are shown not
to be innate but to take shape with relation to the difference
in family structure itself, with corresponding difference in
rôles.

Freud's overemphasis upon the patriarchal pattern (an assumption of its absoluteness that is responsible for the
Freudian tendency to underrate greatly the economic factors influencing the relationships of persons or rôles) is a
prejudicial factor that must be discounted, in Freud, even
when treating the poem as dream. Though totemistic religion, for instance, flourished with matriarchal patterns,
Freud treats even this in patriarchal terms. And I submit
that this emphasis will conceal from us, to a large degree,
what is going on in art (still confining ourselves to the
dream level—the level at which Freudian coördinates come
closest to the charting of the logic of poetic structure).

In the literature of transitional eras, for instance, we find
an especial profusion of rebirth rituals, where the poet is
making the symbolic passes that will endow him with a new
identity. Now, imagine him trying to do a very thorough
job of this reidentification. To be completely reborn, he
would have to change his very lineage itself. He would have
to revise not only his present but also his past. (Ancestry
and cause are forever becoming intermingled—the thing is
that from which it came—cause is *Ur-sache*, etc.) And could

---

his mind as he debates with himself in public and leaves in his pages the record
of his fluctuations, frankly stated as such. Finally, he compromises by leaving
both, drawing individual psychology from the rôle of the monopolistic father, and
group psychology from the rôles of the sons, deprived of sexual gratification by the
monopolistic father, and banded together for their mutual benefit. But note that
the whole picture is that of a family albeit of a family in which the woman is a
mere passive object of male wealth.

a personalized past be properly confined to a descent through the father, when it is the *mater* that is *semper certa?* Totemism, when not interpreted with Freud's patriarchal bias, may possibly provide us with the necessary cue here. Totemism, as Freud himself reminds us, was a magical device whereby the members of a group were identified with one another by the sharing of the same substance (a process often completed by the ritualistic eating of this substance, though it might, for this very reason, be prohibited on less festive occasions). And it is to the mother that the basic informative experiences of eating are related.

So, all told, even in strongly patriarchal societies (and much more so in a society like ours, where theories of sexual equality, with a corresponding confusion in sexual differentiation along occupational lines, have radically broken the symmetry of pure patriarchalism), would there not be a tendency for rebirth rituals to be completed by symbolizations of matricide and without derivation from competitive, monopolistic ingredients at all? [6]

To consider explicitly a bit of political dreaming, is not

[6] Or you might put it this way: Rebirth would require a killing of the old self. Such symbolic suicide, to be complete, would require a snapping of the total ancestral line (as being an integral aspect of one's identity). Hence, a tendency for the emancipatory crime to become sexually ambivalent. Freud's patriarchal emphasis leads to an overstress upon father-rejection as a basic cause rather than as a by-product of conversion (the Kierkegaard earthquake, that was accompanied by a changed attitude toward his father). Suicide, to be thorough, would have to go farther, and the phenomena of identity revealed in totemism might require the introduction of matricidal ingredients also. Freud himself, toward the end of *Totem and Taboo,* gives us an opening wedge by stating frankly, "In this evolution I am at a loss to indicate the place of the great maternal deities who perhaps everywhere preceded the paternal deities. . . ." This same patriarchal emphasis also reinforces the Freudian tendency to treat social love as a mere sublimation of balked male sexual appetite, whereas a more matriarchal concern, with the Madonna and Child relationship, would suggest a place for affection as a primary biological motivation. Not even a naturalistic account of motivation would necessarily require reinforcement from the debunking strategy (in accordance with which the real motives would be incipient perversions, and social motives as we know them would be but their appearances, or censored disguise).

Hitler's doctrine of Aryanism something analogous to the adoption of a new totemic line? Has he not voted himself a new identity and, in keeping with a bastardized variant of the strategy of materialistic science, rounded this out by laying claim to a distinct blood stream? What the Pope is saying, benignly, in proclaiming the Hebrew prophets as the spiritual ancestors of Catholicism, Hitler is saying malignly in proclaiming for himself a lineage totally distinct.

Freud, working within the patriarchal perspective, has explained how such thinking becomes tied up with persecution. The paranoid, he says, assigns his imagined persecutor the rôle of rejected father. This persecutor is all-powerful, as the father seems to the child. He is responsible for every imagined machination (as the Jews, in Hitler's scheme, become the universal devil-function, the leading brains behind every "plot"). Advancing from this brilliant insight, it is not hard to understand why, once Hitler's fantasies are implemented by the vast resources of a nation, the "persecutor" becomes the persecuted.

The point I am trying to bring out is that this assigning of a new lineage to one's self (as would be necessary, in assigning one's self a new identity) could not be complete were it confined to symbolic patricide. There must also be ingredients of symbolic matricide intermingled here (with the phenomena of totemism giving cause to believe that the ritualistic slaying of the maternal relationship may draw upon an even deeper level than the ritualistic slaying of the paternal relationship). Lineage itself is charted after the metaphor of the family tree, which is, to be sure, patriarchalized in Western heraldry, though we get a different quality in the tree of life. MacLeish, in his period of aesthetic negativism, likens the sound of good verse to the ring of the ax in the

275

tree, and if I may mention an early story of my own, *In Quest of Olympus,* a rebirth fantasy, it begins by the felling of a tree, followed by the quick change from child to adult, or, within the conventions of the fiction, the change from tiny "Treep" to gigantic "Arjk"; and though, for a long time, under the influence of the Freudian patriarchal emphasis, I tended to consider such trees as fathers, I later felt compelled to make them ambiguously parents. The symbolic structure of Peter Blume's painting, "The Eternal City," almost forces me to assign the tree, in that instance, to a purely maternal category, since the rejected father is pictured in the repellent phallus-like figure of Mussolini, leaving only the feminine rôle for the luxuriant tree that, by my interpretation of the picture, rounds out the lineage (with the dishonored Christ and the beggarwoman as vessels of the past lineage, and the lewd Mussolini and the impersonal tree as vessels of the new lineage, which I should interpret on the nonpolitical level as saying that sexuality is welcomed, but as a problem, while home is relegated to the world of the impersonal, abstract, observed).

From another point of view we may consider the sacrifice of gods, or of kings, as stylistic modes for dignifying human concerns (a kind of neo-euhemerism). In his stimulating study of the ritual drama, *The Hero,* Lord Raglan overstresses, it seems to me, the notion that these dramas appealed purely as spectacles. Would it not be more likely that the fate of the sacrificial king was also the fate of the audience, in stylized form, dignified, "writ large"? Thus, their engrossment in the drama would not be merely that of watching a parade, or the utilitarian belief that the ritual would insure rainfall, crops, fertility, a good year, etc.; but, also, the stages of the hero's journey would chart the stages of their journey (as an Elizabethan play about royalty was not merely an opportunity for the pit to get a glimpse of high life, a living newspaper on the doings of society, but a dignification or memorializing of their own concerns, translated into the idiom then currently accepted as the proper language of magnification).[7]

But though we may want to introduce minor revisions in the Freudian perspective here, I submit that we should take Freud's key terms, "condensation" and "displacement," as the over-all categories for the analysis of the poem as dream. The terms are really two different approaches to the same phenomenon. Condensation, we might say, deals with the respects in which house in a dream may be more than house, or house plus. And displacement deals with the way in which house may be other than house, or house minus. (Perhaps we should say, more accurately, minus house.)

One can understand the resistance to both of these emphases. It leaves no opportunity for a house to be purely and simply a house—and whatever we may feel about it as regards dreams, it is a very disturbing state of affairs when transferred to the realm of art. We must acknowledge, however, that the house in a poem is, when judged purely and simply as a house, a very flimsy structure for protection against wind and rain. So there seems to be some justice in retaining the Freudian terms when trying to decide what is going on in poetry. As Freud fills them out, the justification becomes stronger. The ways in which grammatical rules are violated, for instance; the dream's ways of enacting conjunc-

[7] Might not the sacrificial figure (as parent, king, or god) also at times derive from no resistance or vindictiveness whatsoever, but be the recipient of the burden simply through "having stronger shoulders, better able to bear it"? And might the choice of guilty scapegoats (such as a bad father) be but a secondary development for accommodating this socialization of a loss to the patterns of legality?

tions, of solving arguments by club offers of mutually contradictory assertions; the importance of both concomitances and discontinuities for interpretative purposes (the phenomena of either association or dissociation, as you prefer, revealed with greatest clarity in the *lapsus linguae*); the conversion of an expression into its corresponding act (as were one, at a time when "over the fence is out" was an expression in vogue, to apply this comment upon some act by following the dream of this act by a dreamed incident of a ball going over a fence); and, above all, the notion that the optative is in dreams, as often in poetry and essay, presented in the indicative (a Freudian observation fertile to the neopositivists' critique of language)—the pliancy and ingenuity of Freud's researches here make entrancing reading, and continually provide insights that can be carried over, *mutatis mutandis,* to the operations of poetry. Perhaps we might sloganize the point thus: In so far as art contains a surrealist ingredient (and all art contains some of this ingredient), psychoanalytic coördinates are required to explain the logic of its structure.

Perhaps we might take some of the pain from the notions of condensation and displacement (with the tendency of one event to become the synecdochic representative of some other event in the same cluster) by imagining a hypothetical case of authorship. A novelist, let us say, is trying to build up for us a sense of secrecy. He is picturing a conspiracy, yet he was never himself quite this kind of conspirator. Might not this novelist draw upon whatever kinds of conspiracy he himself had experientially known (as for instance were he to draft for this purpose memories of his participation in some childhood *Bund*)? If this were so, an objective breakdown of the imagery with which he surrounded the conspiratorial events in his novel would reveal this contributory ingredient. You would not have to read your interpretation into it. It would be objectively, structurally, there, and could be pointed to by scissor work. For instance, the novelist might explicitly state that, when joining the conspiracy, the hero recalled some incident of his childhood. Or the adult conspirators would, at strategic points, be explicitly likened by the novelist to children, etc. A statement about the ingredients of the work's motivation would thus be identical with a statement about the work's structure—a statement as to what goes with what in the work itself. Thus, in Coleridge's "The Eolian Harp," you do not have to interpret the poet's communion with the universe as an affront to his wife; the poet himself explicitly apologizes to her for it. Also, it is an objectively citable fact that imagery of noon goes with this apology. If, then, we look at other poems by Coleridge, noting the part played by the Sun at noon in the punishments of the guilt-laden Ancient Mariner, along with the fact that the situation of the narrator's confession involves the detention of a wedding guest from the marriage feast, plus the fact that a preference for church as against marriage is explicitly stated at the end of the poem, we begin to see a motivational cluster emerging. It is obvious that such structural interrelationships cannot be wholly conscious, since they are generalizations about acts that can only be made inductively and statistically after the acts have been accumulated. (This applies as much to the acts of a single poem as to the acts of many poems. We may find a theme emerging in one work that attains fruition in that same work—the ambiguities of its implications where it first emerges attaining explication in the same integer. Or its full character may not be developed until a later work.

279

In its ambiguous emergent form it is a synecdochic representative of the form it later assumes when it comes to fruition in either the same work or in another one.)

However, though the synecdochic process (whereby something does service for the other members of its same cluster or as the foreshadowing of itself in a later development) cannot be wholly conscious, the dream is not all dream. We might say, in fact, that the Freudian analysis of art was handicapped by the aesthetic of the period—an aesthetic shared even by those who would have considered themselves greatly at odds with Freud and who were, in contrast with his delving into the unbeautiful, concerned with beauty only. This was the aesthetic that placed the emphasis wholly upon the function of self-expression. The artist had a number—some unique character or identity—and his art was the externalizing of this inwardness. The general Schopenhauerian trend contributed to this. Von Hartmann's *Philosophy of the Unconscious* has reinforced the same pattern. This version of voluntaristic processes, as connected with current theories of emancipation, resulted in a picture of the dark, unconscious drive calling for the artist to "out with it." The necessary function of the Freudian secular confessional, as a preparatory step to redemption, gave further strength to the same picture. Add the "complex in terms of the simple" strategy (with its variants—higher in terms of lower, normal as a mere attenuation of the abnormal, civilized as the primitive sublimated); add the war of the generations (which was considered as a kind of absolute rather than as a by-product of other factors, as those who hated the idea of class war took in its stead either the war of the generations or the war of the sexes)—and you get a picture that almost automatically places the emphasis upon art as utterance, as the naming of one's number, as a blurting-out, as catharsis by secretion.

I suggested two other broad categories for the analysis of poetic organization: prayer and chart.

Prayer would enter the Freudian picture in so far as it concerns the optative. But prayer does not stop at that. Prayer is also an act of communion. Hence, the concept of prayer, as extended to cover also secular forms of petition, moves us into the corresponding area of communication in general. We might say that, whereas the expressionistic emphasis reveals the ways in which the poet, with an attitude, embodies it in appropriate gesture, communication deals with the choice of gesture for the inducement of corresponding attitudes. Sensory imagery has this same communicative function, inviting the reader, within the limits of the fiction at least, to make himself over in the image of the imagery.

Considering the poem from this point of view, we begin with the incantatory elements in art, the ways of leading in or leading on the hypothetical audience X to which the poem, as a medium, is addressed (though this hypothetical audience X be nothing more concrete, as regards social relations, than a critical aspect of the poet's own personality). Even Freud's dream had a censor; but the poet's censor is still more exacting, as his shapings and revisions are made for the purpose of forestalling resistances (be those an essay reader's resistances to arguments and evidence or the novel reader's resistance to developments of narrative or character). We move here into the sphere of rhetoric (reader-writer relationships, an aspect of art that Freud explicitly impinges upon only to a degree in his analysis of wit), with the notion of address being most evident in oration and

281

letter, less so in drama, and least in the lyric. Roughly, I should say that the slightest presence of revision is per se indication of a poet's feeling that his work is addressed (if only, as Mead might say, the address of an "I" to its "me").

Here would enter consideration of formal devices, ways of pointing up and fulfilling expectations, of living up to a contract with the reader (as Wordsworth and Coleridge might put it), of easing by transition or sharpening by ellipsis; in short, all that falls within the sphere of incantation, imprecation, exhortation, inducement, weaving and releasing of spells; matters of style and form, of meter and rhythm, as contributing to these results; and thence to the conventions and social values that the poet draws upon in forming the appropriate recipes for the rôles of protagonist and antagonist, into which the total agon is analytically broken down, with subsidiary rôles polarized about one or the other of the two agonists tapering off to form a region of overlap between the two principles—the ground of the agon. Here, as the reverse of prayer, would come also invective, indictment, oath. And the gestures might well be tracked down eventually to choices far closer to bodily pantomime than is revealed on the level of social evaluation alone (as were a poet, seeking the gestures appropriate for the conveying of a social negativeness, to draw finally upon imagery of disgust, and perhaps even, at felicitous moments, to select his speech by playing up the very consonants that come nearest to the enacting of repulsion).

As to the poem as chart: the Freudian emphasis upon the pun brings it about that something can only be in so far as it is something else. But, aside from these ambiguities, there is also a statement's value as being exactly what it is. Perhaps we could best indicate what we mean by speaking of the poem as chart if we called it the poet's contribution to an informal dictionary. As with proverbs, he finds some experience or relationship typical, or recurrent, or significant enough for him to need a word for it. Except that his way of defining the word is not to use purely conceptual terms, as in a formal dictionary, but to show how his vision behaves, with appropriate attitudes. In this, again, it is like the proverb that does not merely name but names vindictively, or plaintively, or promisingly, or consolingly, etc. His namings need not be new ones. Often they are but memorializings of an experience long recognized.

But, essentially, they are enactments, with every form of expression being capable of treatment as the efficient extension of one aspect or another of ritual drama (so that even the scientific essay would have its measure of choreography, its pedestrian pace itself being analyzed as gesture or incantation, its polysyllables being as style the mimetics of a distinct monasticism, etc.). And this observation, whereby we have willy-nilly slipped back into the former subject, the symbolic act as prayer, leads us to observe that the three aspects of the poem, here proposed, are not elements that can be isolated in the poem itself, with one line revealing the "dream," another the "prayer," and a third the "chart." They merely suggest three convenient modes in which to approach the task of analysis.[8]

The primary category, for the explicit purposes of literary criticism, would thus seem to me to be that of communication rather than that of wish, with its disguises, frustrations,

[8] Dream has its opposite, nightmare; prayer has its opposite, oath. Charts merely vary—in scope and relevance. In "Kubla Khan," automatically composed during an opium dream, the dream ingredient is uppermost. In "The Ancient Mariner," the prayer ingredient is uppermost. In "Dejection" and "The Pains of Sleep," the chart ingredient is uppermost: here Coleridge is explicitly discussing his situation.

and fulfillments. Wishes themselves, in fact, become from this point of view analyzable as purposes that get their shape from the poet's perspective in general (while this perspective is in turn shaped by the collective medium of communication). The choice of communication also has the advantage, from the sociological point of view, that it resists the Freudian tendency to overplay the psychological factor (as the total medium of communication is not merely that of words, colors, forms, etc., or of the values and conventions with which these are endowed, but also the productive materials, coöperative resources, property rights, authorities, and their various bottlenecks, which figure in the total act of human conversation).

Hence, to sum up: I should say that, for the explicit purposes of literary criticism, we should require more emphasis than the Freudian structure gives, (1) to the proportional strategy as against the essentializing one, (2) to matriarchal symbolizations as against the Freudian patriarchal bias, (3) to poem as prayer and chart, as against simply the poem as dream.

But I fully recognize that, once the ingenious and complex structure has been erected, nearly anyone can turn up with proposals that it be given a little more of this, a little less of that, a pinch of so-and-so, etc. And I recognize that, above all, we owe an enormous debt of gratitude to the man who, by his insight, his energy, and his remarkably keen powers of articulation, made such tinkering possible. It is almost fabulous to think that, after so many centuries of the family, it is only now that this central factor in our social organization has attained its counterpart in an organized critique of the family and of the ways in which the informative experience with familiar rôles may be carried over, or "metaphored," into the experience with extra-familiar rôles, giving these latter, in so far as they are, or are felt to be, analogous with the former, a structure of interpretations and attitudes borrowed from the former. And in so far as poets, like everyone else, are regularly involved in such informative familiar relationships, long before any but a few rudimentary bodily gestures are available for communicative use (with their first use unquestionably being the purely self-expressive one), the child is indeed the adult poet's father, as he is the father of us all (if not so in essence, then at least as regards an important predisposing factor "to look out for"). Thence we get to "like father like son." And thence we get to Freud's brilliant documentation of this ancestry, as it affects the maintenance of a continuity in the growing personality.

Only if we eliminate biography entirely as a relevant fact about poetic organization can we eliminate the importance of the psychoanalyst's search for universal patterns of biography (as revealed in the search for basic myths which recur in new guises as a theme with variations); and we can eliminate biography as a relevant fact about poetic organization only if we consider the work of art as if it were written neither by people nor for people, involving neither inducements nor resistances.[9] Such can be done, but the cost is

9 Those who stress form of this sort, as against content, usually feel that they are concerned with judgments of excellence as against judgments of the merely representative. Yet, just as a content category such as the Oedipus complex is neutral, i. e., includes both good and bad examples of its kind, so does a form category, such as sonnet or iambic pentameter, include both good and bad examples of its kind. In fact, though categories or classifications may be employed for evaluative purposes, they should be of themselves nonevaluative. Apples is a neutral, nonevaluative class, including firm apples and rotten ones. Categories that are in themselves evaluative are merely circular arguments—disguised ways of saying "this is good because it is good." The orthodox strategy of disguise is to break the statement into two parts, such as: "This is good because it has form; and form is good." The lure behind the feeling that the miracle of evaluation can be replaced by a codified scientific routine of evaluation seems to get its backing from the hope

tremendous in so far as the critic considers it his task to disclose the poem's eventfulness.

However, this is decidedly not the same thing as saying that "we cannot appreciate the poem without knowing about its relation to the poet's life as an individual." Rather, it is equivalent to saying: "We cannot understand a poem's structure without understanding the function of that structure. And to understand its function we must understand its purpose." To be sure, there are respects in which the poem, as purpose, is doing things for the poet that it is doing for no one else. For instance, I think it can be shown by analysis of the imagery in Coleridge's "Mystery Poems" that one of the battles being fought there is an attempt to get self-redemption by the poet's striving for the vicarious or ritualistic redemption of his drug. It is obvious that this aspect of the equational structure is private and would best merit discussion when one is discussing the strategy of one man in its particularities. Readers in general will respond only to the sense of guilt, which was sharpened for Coleridge by his particular burden of addiction, but which may be sharpened for each reader by totally different particularities of

---

that a concept of quality can be matched by a number. The terms missing may be revealed by a diagram, thus:

Quantity	Number
Weight	Pound
Length	Foot
Duration	Hour
Quality	( )
Excellence	( )
Inferiority	( )

Often the strategy of concealment is accomplished by an ambiguity, as the critic sometimes uses the term "poetry" to designate good poetry, and sometimes uses it to designate "poetry, any poetry, good, bad, or indifferent." I do, however, strongly sympathize with the formalists, as against the sociologists, when the sociologist treats poetry simply as a kind of haphazard sociological survey—a report about world-conditions that often shows commendable intuitive insight but is handicapped by a poor methodology of research and controls.

experience. But if you do not discuss the poem's structure as a function of symbolic redemption at all (as a kind of private-enterprise Mass, with important ingredients of a black Mass), the observations you make about its structure are much more likely to be gratuitous and arbitrary (quite as only the most felicitous of observers could relevantly describe the distribution of men and postures in a football game if he had no knowledge of the game's purpose and did not discuss its formations as oppositional tactics for the carrying-out of this purpose, but treated the spectacle simply as the manifestation of a desire to instruct and amuse).

Thus, in the case of "The Ancient Mariner," knowledge of Coleridge's personal problems may enlighten us as to the particular burdens that the Pilot's boy ("who now doth crazy go") took upon himself as scapegoat for the poet alone. But his appearance in the poem cannot be understood at all, except in superficial terms of the interesting or the picturesque, if we do not grasp his function as a scapegoat of some sort—a victimized vessel for drawing off the most malign aspects of the curse that afflicts the "greybeard loon" whose cure had been effected under the dubious aegis of moonlight. And I believe that such a functional approach is the only one that can lead into a profitable analysis of a poem's structure even on the purely technical level. I remember how, for instance, I had pondered for years the reference to the "silly buckets" filled with curative rain. I noted the epithet as surprising, picturesque, and interesting. I knew that it was doing something, but I wasn't quite sure what. But as soon as I looked upon the Pilot's boy as a scapegoat, I saw that the word *silly* was a technical foreshadowing of the fate that befell this figure in the poem. The structure itself became more apparent: the "loon"-atic

Mariner begins his cure from drought under the aegis of a moon that causes a silly rain, thence by synecdoche to silly buckets, and the most malignant features of this problematic cure are transferred to the Pilot's boy who now doth crazy go. Now, if you want to confine your observations to the one poem, you have a structural-functional-technical analysis of some important relationships within the poem itself. If you wish to trail the matter farther afield, into the equational structure of other work by Coleridge, you can back your interpretation of the moon by such reference as that to "moon-blasted madness," which gives you increased authority to discern lunatic ingredients in the lunar. His letters, where he talks of his addiction in imagery like that of the "Mystery Poems" and contemplates entering an insane asylum for a cure, entitle you to begin looking for traces of the drug as an ingredient in the redemptive problem. His letters also explicitly place the drug in the same cluster with the serpent; hence, we begin to discern what is going on when the Mariner transubstantiates the water snakes, in removing them from the category of the loathsome and accursed to the category of the blessed and beautiful. So much should be enough for the moment. Since the poem is constructed about an opposition between punishments under the aegis of the sun and cure under the aegis of the moon, one could proceed in other works to disclose the two sets of equations clustered about these two principles. Indeed, even in "The Ancient Mariner" itself we get a momentous cue, as the sun is explicitly said to be "like God's own head." But, for the moment, all I would maintain is that, if we had but this one poem by Coleridge, and knew not one other thing about him, we could not get an insight into its structure until we began with an awareness of its function as a symbolic redemptive process.

I can imagine a time when the psychological picture will be so well known and taken into account—when we shall have gone so far beyond Freud's initial concerns—that a reference to the polymorphous perverse of the infantile, for instance, will seem far too general—a mere first approximation. Everyone provides an instance of the polymorphous perverse, in attenuated form, at a moment of hesitancy; caught in the trackless maze of an unresolved, and even undefined, conflict, he regresses along this channel and that, in a formless experimentation that "tries anything and everything, somewhat." And in so far as his puzzle is resolved into pace, and steady rhythms of a progressive way out are established, there is always the likelihood that this solution will maintain continuity with the past of the poet's personality by a covert drawing upon analogies with this past. Hence the poet or speculator, no matter how new the characters with which he is now concerned, will give them somewhat the rôles of past characters; whereat I see nothing unusual about the thought that a mature and highly complex philosophy might be so organized as to be surrogate for, let us say, a kind of adult breast-feeding—or, in those more concerned with alienation, a kind of adult weaning. Such categories do not by any means encompass the totality of a communicative structure; but they are part of it, and the imagery and transitions of the poem itself cannot disclose their full logic until such factors are taken into account.

However, I have spoken of pace. And perhaps I might conclude with some words on the bearing that the Freudian

technique has upon the matter of pace. The Freudian procedure is primarily designed to break down a rhythm grown
obsessive, to confront the systematic pieties of the patient's
misery with systematic impieties of the clinic.[10] But the
emphasis here is more upon the breaking of a malign
rhythm than upon the upbuilding of a benign one. There is
no place in this technique for examining the available resources whereby the adoption of total dramatic enactment
may lead to correspondingly proper attitude. There is no
talk of games, of dance, of manual and physical actions, of
historical rôle, as a "way in" to this new upbuilding. The
sedentary patient is given a sedentary cure. The theory of
rhythms—work rhythms, dance rhythms, march rhythms—
is no explicit part of this scheme, which is primarily designed to break old rhythms rather than to establish new
ones.

The establishing of a new pace, beyond the smashing
of the old puzzle, would involve in the end a rounded philosophy of the drama. Freud, since his subject is conflict,
hovers continually about the edges of such a philosophy; yet
it is not dialectical enough. For this reason Marxists properly resent his theories, even though one could, by culling
incidental sentences from his works, fit him comfortably
into the Marxist perspective. But the Marxists are wrong,
I think, in resenting him as an irrationalist, for there is
nothing more rational than the systematic recognition of
irrational and nonrational factors. And I should say that

10 There are styles of cure, shifting from age to age, because each novelty becomes a commonplace, so that the patient integrates his conflict with the ingredients of the old cure itself, thus making them part of his obsession. Hence, the need
for a new method of jolting. Thus, I should imagine that a patient who had got
into difficulties after mastering the Freudian technique would present the most
obstinate problems for a Freudian cure. He would require some step beyond
Freud. The same observation would apply to shifting styles in a poetry and philosophy, when considered as cures, as the filling of a need.

both Freudians and Marxists are wrong in so far as they cannot put their theories together, by an over-all theory of drama itself (as they should be able to do, since Freud gives us the material of the closet drama, and Marx the material of the problem play, the one worked out in terms of personal conflicts, the other in terms of public conflicts).

The approach would require explicitly the analysis of rôle: salvation via change or purification of identity (purification in either the moral or chemical sense); different typical relationships between individual and group (as charted attitudinally in proverbs, and in complex works treated as sophisticated variants); modes of acceptance, rejection, self-acceptance, rejection of rejection [11] ("the enemies of my enemies are my friends"); transitional disembodiment as intermediate step between old self and new self (the spirituality of Shelley and of the Freudian cure itself); monasticism in the development of methods that fix a transitional or other-worldly stage, thereby making the evanescent itself into a kind of permanency—with all these modes of enactment finally employing, as part of the gesture idiom, the responses of the body itself as actor. (If one sought to employ Freud, as is, for the analysis of the poem, one would find almost nothing on poetic posture or pantomime, tonality, the significance of different styles and rhythmic patterns, nothing of this behaviorism.) Such, it seems to me, would be necessary, and much more in that direction, before we could so extend Freud's perspective that it revealed the major events going on in art.

But such revisions would by no means be anti-Freudian. They would be the kind of extensions required by reason of

---

[11] I am indebted to Norbert Gutermann for the term "self-acceptance" and to William S. Knickerbocker for the term "rejection of rejection."

the fact that the symbolic act of art, whatever its analogies with the symbolic act of neurosis, also has important divergencies from the symbolic act of neurosis. They would be extensions designed to take into account the full play of communicative and realistic ingredients that comprise so large an aspect of poetic structure.

LITERATURE
AS EQUIPMENT FOR LIVING

HERE I shall put down, as briefly as possible, a statement in behalf of what might be catalogued, with a fair degree of accuracy, as a *sociological* criticism of literature. Sociological criticism in itself is certainly not new. I shall here try to suggest what partially new elements or emphasis I think should be added to this old approach. And to make the "way in" as easy as possible, I shall begin with a discussion of proverbs.

1

Examine random specimens in *The Oxford Dictionary of English Proverbs*. You will note, I think, that there is no "pure" literature here. Everything is "medicine." Proverbs are designed for consolation or vengeance, for admonition or exhortation, for foretelling.

Or they name typical, recurrent situations. That is, people find a certain social relationship recurring so frequently that they must "have a word for it." The Eskimos have special names for many different kinds of snow (fifteen, if I remember rightly) because variations in the quality of snow greatly affect their living. Hence, they must "size up" snow much more accurately than we do. And the same is true of social phenomena. Social structures give rise to "type" situations, subtle subdivisions of the relationships involved in competitive and coöperative acts. Many proverbs seek to chart, in more or less homey and picturesque ways, these "type" situations. I submit that such naming is done, not for the sheer glory of the thing, but because of its bearing upon human welfare. A different name for snow implies a different kind of hunt. Some names for snow imply that one should not hunt at all. And similarly, the names for typical, recurrent social situations are not developed out of "disinterested curiosity," but because the names imply a command (what to expect, what to look out for).

To illustrate with a few representative examples:

Proverbs designed for consolation: "The sun does not shine on both sides of the hedge at once." "Think of ease, but work on." "Little troubles the eye, but far less the soul." "The worst luck now, the better another time." "The wind in one's face makes one wise." "He that hath lands hath quarrels." "He knows how to carry the dead cock home." "He is not poor that hath little, but he that desireth much."

For vengeance: "At length the fox is brought to the furrier." "Shod in the cradle, barefoot in the stubble." "Sue a beggar and get a louse." "The higher the ape goes, the more he shows his tail." "The moon does not heed the barking of dogs." "He measures another's corn by his own bushel." "He shuns the man who knows him well." "Fools tie knots and wise men loose them."

Proverbs that have to do with foretelling: (The most obvious are those to do with the weather.) "Sow peas and beans in the wane of the moon, Who soweth them sooner, he soweth too soon." "When the wind's in the north, the skilful fisher goes not forth." "When the sloe tree is as white as a sheet, sow your barley whether it be dry or wet." "When the sun sets bright and clear, An easterly wind you need not fear. When the sun sets in a bank, A westerly wind we shall not want."

In short: "Keep your weather eye open": be realistic about sizing up today's weather, because your accuracy has bearing upon tomorrow's weather. And forecast not only the meteorological weather, but also the social weather: "When the moon's in the full, then wit's in the wane." "Straws show which way the wind blows." "When the fish is caught, the net is laid aside." "Remove an old tree, and it will wither to death." "The wolf may lose his teeth, but never his nature." "He that bites on every weed must needs light on poison." "Whether the pitcher strikes the stone, or the stone the pitcher, it is bad for the pitcher." "Eagles catch no flies." "The more laws, the more offenders."

In this foretelling category we might also include the recipes for wise living, sometimes moral, sometimes technical: "First thrive, and then wive." "Think with the wise but talk with the vulgar." "When the fox preacheth, then beware your geese." "Venture a small fish to catch a great one." "Respect a man, he will do the more."

In the class of "typical, recurrent situations" we might put such proverbs and proverbial expressions as: "Sweet appears sour when we pay." "The treason is loved but the traitor is hated." "The wine in the bottle does not quench thirst." "The sun is never the worse for shining on a dunghill." "The lion kicked by an ass." "The lion's share." "To catch one napping." "To smell a rat." "To cool one's heels."

By all means, I do not wish to suggest that this is the only way in which the proverbs could be classified. For instance, I have listed in the "foretelling" group the proverb, "When the fox preacheth, then beware your geese." But it could obviously be "taken over" for vindictive purposes. Or consider a proverb like, "Virtue flies from the heart of a mercenary man." A poor man might obviously use it either to console himself for being poor (the implication being, "Because I am poor in money I am rich in virtue") or to strike at another (the implication being, "When he got money, what else could you expect of him but deterioration?"). In fact, we could even say that such symbolic vengeance would itself be an aspect of solace. And a proverb like "The sun is never the worse for shining on a dunghill" (which I have listed under "typical recurrent situations") might as well be put in the vindictive category.

The point of issue is not to find categories that "place" the proverbs once and for all. What I want is categories that suggest their active nature. Here there is no "realism for its own sake." There is realism for promise, admonition, solace, vengeance, foretelling, instruction, charting, all for the direct bearing that such acts have upon matters of welfare.

2

Step two: Why not extend such analysis of proverbs to encompass the whole field of literature? Could the most complex and sophisticated works of art legitimately be considered somewhat as "proverbs writ large"? Such leads, if held admissible, should help us to discover important facts about literary organization (thus satisfying the requirements of technical criticism). And the kind of observation from this perspective should apply beyond literature to life in general (thus helping to take literature out of its separate bin and give it a place in a general "sociological" picture).

The point of view might be phrased in this way: Proverbs are *strategies* for dealing with *situations*. In so far as situations are typical and recurrent in a given social structure, people develop names for them and strategies for handling them. Another name for strategies might be *attitudes*.

People have often commented on the fact that there are contrary *proverbs*. But I believe that the above approach to proverbs suggests a necessary modification of that comment. The apparent contradictions depend upon differences in *attitude*, involving a correspondingly different choice of *strategy*. Consider, for instance, the *apparently* opposite pair: "Repentance comes too late" and "Never too late to mend." The first is admonitory. It says in effect: "You'd better look out, or you'll get yourself too far into this business." The second is consolatory, saying in effect: "Buck up, old man, you can still pull out of this."

Some critics have quarreled with me about my selection of the word "strategy" as the name for this process. I have asked them to suggest an alternative term, so far without profit. The only one I can think of is "method." But if "strategy" errs in suggesting to some people an overly *conscious* procedure, "method" errs in suggesting an overly *"methodical"* one. Anyhow, let's look at the documents:

Concise Oxford Dictionary: "Strategy: Movement of an army or armies in a compaign, art of so moving or disposing troops or ships as to impose upon the enemy the place and time and conditions for fighting preferred by oneself" (from a Greek word that refers to the leading of an army).

New English Dictionary: "Strategy: The art of projecting and directing the larger military movements and operations of a campaign."

André Cheron, *Traité Complet d'Echecs: "On entend par stratégie les manoeuvres qui ont pour but la sortie et le bon arrangement des pièces."*

Looking at these definitions, I gain courage. For surely, the most highly alembicated and sophisticated work of art, arising in complex civilizations, could be considered as designed to organize and command the army of one's thoughts and images, and to so organize them that one "imposes upon the enemy the time and place and conditions for fighting preferred by oneself." One seeks to "direct the larger movements and operations" in one's campaign of living. One "maneuvers," and the maneuvering is an "art."

Are not the final results one's "strategy"? One tries, as far as possible, to develop a strategy whereby one "can't lose." One tries to change the rules of the game until they fit his own necessities. Does the artist encounter disaster? He will "make capital" of it. If one is a victim of competition, for instance, if one is elbowed out, if one is willy-nilly more jockeyed against than jockeying, one can by the solace and vengeance of art convert this very "liability" into an "asset." One tries to fight on his own terms, developing a strategy for imposing the proper "time, place, and conditions."

But one must also, to develop a full strategy, be *realistic*. One must *size things up* properly. One cannot accurately know how things *will be*, what is promising and what is menacing, unless he accurately knows how things *are*. So the wise strategist will not be content with strategies of merely a self-gratifying sort. He will "keep his weather eye open." He will not too eagerly "read into" a scene an attitude that is irrelevant to it. He won't sit on the side of an active volcano and "see" it as a dormant plain.

Often, alas, he will. The great allurement in our present popular "inspirational literature," for instance, may be largely of this sort. It is a strategy for easy consolation. It "fills a need," since there is always a need for easy consolation—and in an era of confusion like our own the need is especially keen. So people are only too willing to "meet a man halfway" who will *play down* the realistic naming of our situation and *play up* such strategies as make solace cheap. However, I should propose a reservation here. We usually take it for granted that people who consume our current output of books on "How to Buy Friends and Bamboozle Oneself and Other People" are reading as *students* who will attempt applying the recipes given. Nothing of the sort. *The reading of a book on the attaining of success is in itself the symbolic attaining of that success.* It is *while they read* that these readers are "succeeding." I'll wager that, in by far the great majority of cases, such readers make no serious attempt to apply the book's recipes. The lure of the book resides in the fact that the reader, while reading it, is then living in the aura of success. What he wants is *easy* success; and he gets it in symbolic form by the mere reading itself. To attempt applying such stuff in real life would be very difficult, full of many disillusioning difficulties.

Sometimes a different strategy may arise. The author may remain realistic, avoiding too easy a form of solace—yet he may get as far off the track in his own way. Forgetting that realism is an aspect for foretelling, he may take it as an end in itself. He is tempted to do this by two factors: (1) an *ill-digested* philosophy of science, leading him mistakenly to assume that "relentless" naturalistic "truthfulness" is a proper end in itself, and (2) a merely *competitive* desire to outstrip other writers by being "more realistic" than they. Works thus made "efficient" by tests of competition internal to the book trade are a kind of academicism not so named (the writer usually thinks of it as the *opposite* of academicism). Realism thus stepped up competitively might be dis-

tinguished from the proper sort by the name of "naturalism." As a way of "sizing things up," the naturalistic tradition tends to become as inaccurate as the "inspirational"
strategy, though at the opposite extreme.

Anyhow, the main point is this: A work like *Madame
Bovary* (or its homely American translation, *Babbitt*) is the
strategic naming of a situation. It singles out a pattern of
experience that is sufficiently representative of our social
structure, that recurs sufficiently often *mutandis mutatis*,
for people to "need a word for it" and to adopt an attitude
towards it. Each work of art is the addition of a word to an
informal dictionary (or, in the case of purely derivative
artists, the addition of a subsidiary meaning to a word already given by some originating artist). As for *Madame
Bovary,* the French critic Jules de Gaultier proposed to add
it to our *formal* dictionary by coining the word "Bovar-
ysme" and writing a whole book to say what he meant by it.

Mencken's book on *The American Language,* I hate to
say, is splendid. I console myself with the reminder that
Mencken didn't write it. Many millions of people wrote it,
and Mencken was merely the amanuensis who took it down
from their dictation. He found a true "vehicle" (that is, a
book that could be greater than the author who wrote it).
He gets the royalties, but the job was done by a collectivity.
As you read that book, you see a people who were up against
a new set of typical recurrent situations, situations typical of
their business, their politics, their criminal organizations,
their sports. Either there were no words for these in standard English, or people didn't know them, or they didn't
"sound right." So a new vocabulary arose, to "give us a
word for it." I see no reason for believing that Americans
are unusually fertile in word-coinage. American slang was

not developed out of some exceptional gift. It was developed
out of the fact that new typical situations had arisen and
people needed names for them. They had to "size things
up." They had to console and strike, to promise and admonish. They had to describe for purposes of forecasting.
And "slang" was the result. It is, by this analysis, simply
proverbs not so named, a kind of "folk criticism."

3

With what, then, would "sociological criticism" along
these lines be concerned? It would seek to codify the various
strategies which artists have developed with relation to the
naming of situations. In a sense, much of it would even be
"timeless," for many of the "typical, recurrent situations"
are not peculiar to our own civilization at all. The situations
and strategies framed in Aesop's Fables, for instance, apply
to human relations now just as fully as they applied in
ancient Greece. They are, like philosophy, sufficiently "generalized" to extend far beyond the particular combination
of events named by them in any one instance. They name
an "essence." Or, as Korzybski might say, they are on a
"high level of abstraction." One doesn't usually think of
them as "abstract," since they are usually so concrete in
their stylistic expression. But they invariably aim to discern
the "general behind the particular" (which would suggest
that they are good Goethe).

The attempt to treat literature from the standpoint of
situations and strategies suggests a variant of Spengler's notion of the "contemporaneous." By "contemporaneity" he
meant corresponding stages of different cultures. For instance, if modern New York is much like decadent Rome,
then we are "contemporaneous" with decadent Rome, or

with some corresponding decadent city among the Mayas, etc. It is in this sense that situations are "timeless," "non-historical," "contemporaneous." A given human relationship may be at one time named in terms of foxes and lions, if there are foxes and lions about; or it may now be named in terms of salesmanship, advertising, the tactics of politicians, etc. But beneath the change in particulars, we may often discern the naming of the one situation.

So sociological criticism, as here understood, would seek to assemble and codify this lore. It might occasionally lead us to outrage good taste, as we sometimes found exemplified in some great sermon or tragedy or abstruse work of philosophy the same strategy as we found exemplified in a dirty joke. At this point, we'd put the sermon and the dirty joke together, thus "grouping by situation" and showing the range of possible particularizations. In his exceptionally discerning essay, "A Critic's Job of Work," R. P. Blackmur says, "I think on the whole his (Burke's) method could be applied with equal fruitfulness to Shakespeare, Dashiell Hammett, or Marie Corelli." When I got through wincing, I had to admit that Blackmur was right. This article is an attempt to say for the method what can be said. As a matter of fact, I'll go a step further and maintain: You can't properly put Marie Corelli and Shakespeare apart until you have first put them together. First genus, then differentia. The strategy in common is the genus. The *range* or *scale* or *spectrum* of particularizations is the differentia.

Anyhow, that's what I'm driving at. And that's why reviewers sometime find in my work "intuitive" leaps that are dubious as "science." They are not "leaps" at all. They are classifications, groupings, made on the basis of some strategic element common to the items grouped. They are neither more nor less "intuitive" than *any* grouping or classification of social events. Apples can be grouped with bananas as fruits, and they can be grouped with tennis balls as round. I am simply proposing, in the social sphere, a method of classification with reference to *strategies*.

The method has these things to be said in its favor: It gives definite insight into the organization of literary works; and it automatically breaks down the barriers erected about literature as a specialized pursuit. People can classify novels by reference to three kinds, eight kinds, seventeen kinds. It doesn't matter. Students patiently copy down the professor's classification and pass examinations on it, because the range of possible academic classifications is endless. Sociological classification, as herein suggested, would derive its relevance from the fact that it should apply both to works of art and to social situations outside of art.

It would, I admit, violate current pieties, break down current categories, and thereby "outrage good taste." But "good taste" has become *inert*. The classifications I am proposing would be *active*. I think that what we need is active categories.

These categories will lie on the bias across the categories of modern specialization. The new alignment will outrage in particular those persons who take the division of faculties in our universities to be an exact replica of the way in which God himself divided up the universe. We have had the Philosophy of the Being; and we have had the Philosophy of the Becoming. In contemporary specialization, we have been getting the Philosophy of the Bin. Each of these mental localities has had its own peculiar way of life, its own values, even its own special idiom for seeing, thinking, and "proving." Among other things, a sociological approach should attempt to provide a reintegrative point of view, a broader empire of investigation encompassing the lot.

What would such sociological categories be like? They would consider works of art, I think, as strategies for selecting enemies and allies, for socializing losses, for warding off evil eye, for purification, propitiation, and desanctification, consolation and vengeance, admonition and exhortation, implicit commands or instructions of one sort or another. Art forms like "tragedy" or "comedy" or "satire" would be treated as *equipments for living,* that size up situations in various ways and in keeping with correspondingly various attitudes. The typical ingredients of such forms would be sought. Their relation to typical situations would be stressed. Their comparative values would be considered, with the intention of formulating a "strategy of strategies," the "over-all" strategy obtained by inspection of the lot.

TWELVE PROPOSITIONS
ON THE RELATION BETWEEN
ECONOMICS AND PSYCHOLOGY

THE following propositions briefly state the approach exemplified in my recent work, *Attitudes Toward History*.
They are offered as a reply to Margaret Schlauch's review of
the work, in the last number of *Science & Society*. They
are an attempt to codify my ideas on the relation between
psychology and Marxism.

1. *The basic concept for uniting economics and psychology ("Marx and Freud") is that of the "symbols of
authority."*

Symbols of authority are obviously related to economic
categories, because of their connection with property rights
(ownership of productive resources), with educative, legislative and constabulary bodies, and with the guidance of a
society's practices. Symbols of authority are related to psychological categories, because of their tie-up with morals,
laws, social relationships, etc.; they overlap upon both political and intimate responses because they usually involve such
figures as parents, doctor, nurse in the "pre-political" period
of childhood, and such figures as boss or foreman or employer in commercial relationships.

2. *The two basic dichotomous attitudes toward reigning
symbols of authority are those of* acceptance *and* rejection
(with intermediate gradations, such as are to be found when

any flat logical distinction is translated into the field of psychology).

The attitude of acceptance is the most desirable way of "digesting" one's world. But the attitude of rejection is evoked in so far as the reigning symbols of authority represent ideals of ownership and modes of economic management inadequate for operating the means of production and distribution. By reason of such phenomena as "cultural lag," old values survive from periods in which they were a relatively adequate structure of meanings into periods when they are relatively inadequate.

3. The need of rejecting the reigning symbols of authority is synonymous with "alienation."

"Alienation" is thus also a concept clearly having both economic and psychological relevance. An increasing number of people become alienated by material dispossession. And an increasing number who still share some material advantages from the ailing economic structure become spiritually alienated as they lose faith in the structure's "reasonableness." One may be materially or spiritually alienated, or both.

4. The purely psychological concept for treating relations to symbols of authority, possession and dispossession, material and spiritual alienation, faith or loss of faith in the "reasonableness" of a given structure's methods and purposes and values, is that of "identity."

The individual's identity is formed by reference to his membership in a group. In the feudal structure, for instance, one was identified mainly by his membership in the Catholic Church. The reigning structure of authority coördinated this "corporate identity" with his identity as member of some economic class and his identity in a family collectivity. With the rise of the bourgeoisie, such bases of identity were progressively broken, until now we are mainly offered identification by membership in a financial corporation, or identification by membership in a political corporation seeking either to cement or to destroy the business forms of identity. The business identity is retained in the "corporate state" and destroyed in the socialist state. The vagaries of transition were revealed particularly in the vague, footloose, "poetic" identities of nineteenth-century art, with its many variants of the "Aesthetic Opposition."

5. *In this complex world, one is never a member of merely one "corporation." The individual is composed of many "corporate identities." Sometimes they are concentric, sometimes in conflict.*

For instance, one may have a job in some large financial corporation, while at the same time being a member of a party opposed to its policies. Or one may be identified with a general body of thought "oppositional" in quality, while at the same time making various attempts to identify himself with some specific political faction; and these two "identities" may conflict in varying degrees. An example of specious concentric identity is to be seen in the businessman who identifies himself with business and nation.

6. *In highly transitional eras, requiring shifts in allegiance to the symbols of authority (the rejection of an authoritative structure still largely accepted, even by its victims, who are educated in wrong meanings and values by the "priesthood" of pulpit, schools, press, radio and popular art) the problems of identity become crucial.*

Though it is men's natural tendency to make peace with their world, to "accept" it, they are forced into some measure of alienation by the inadequacy of its property structure.

Men must then throw off old and deceptive modes of identification and take on new ones.

7. *The processes of* change of identity *are most clearly revealed by analyzing formal works of art and applying the results of our analysis to the "informal art of living" in general.*

Art works, owing to their high degree of articulateness, are like "meter readings." Here all the implicit social processes become explicit. By studying them, you will discern what forms "alienation" takes as a factor in human experience, and what forms likewise arise in the attempt to *combat* alienation (to "repossess" one's world).

8. *Identity itself is a "mystification." Hence, resenting its many labyrinthine aspects, we tend to call even the* study *of it a "mystification."*

The response would be analogous to the response of those who, suffering from an illness, get "relief" by quarreling with their doctors. Unless Marxists are ready to deny Marx by attacking his term "alienation" itself, they must permit of research into the nature of alienation and into the nature of attempts, adequate and inadequate, to combat alienation.

9. *The analysis of the "strategies" by which men respond to the factor of alienation and by which they attempt to repossess their world could not be conducted without tremendous wastage of time and energy, if a writer were required, at every point, to stop and demonstrate the specific bearing of his analysis upon such matters as food, jobs, etc.*

For one thing, the relationships, so analyzed, would often be totally unreal (particularly since many of those symbolizing alienation are not materially alienated to any extreme degree). Further: the objective factors giving rise to a code of moral and aesthetic values are, of course, *economic.* They are the "substructure" that supports the ideological "superstructure." But the objective materials utilized by an individual writer are largely the *moral and aesthetic values* themselves. For instance, new methods of production gave rise to the change from feudal to bourgeois values. But Shakespeare's strategy as a dramatist was formed by relation to this conflict between feudal and bourgeois values. This "superstructural" material was the objective, social material he manipulated in eliciting his audience's response. Economic factors gave rise to the transition in values, but he dealt with the transition in values.

Or another example: Modern conditions of distribution by sale put a social value on the pushing, breezy, aggressive type of salesman. And since this "psychosis" is thus established as a social form, the dramatist may appeal (as is often the case in our popular motion pictures) by "idealizing" a character who is in general the "live wire" type.

In sum, economic conditions give form to the values; and these values, having arisen, form "objective material" with which the artist works in constructing symbols that appeal.

10. *"Style" is an aspect of identification.*

Even a materially dispossessed individual may "own" privilege vicariously by adopting the "style" (or "insignia") of some privileged class. Thus did typical poets of the age of Pope vicariously own the privileges of the squirearchy, by embodying in style the ideals that the squirearchy approved of.

Consideration of such "symbolic boasting" offers an excellent instance in support of our contention that the analysis of aesthetic phenomena can be extended or projected into the analysis of social and political phenomena in general. We see a petty clerk, for instance, who can "identify" himself either by "owning the style" of the workers or by "owning the style" of his boss. The *boss's* style often appeals the more strongly, because it symbolically promises him advancement; and in this mere symbolic *promise* he locates his notions of purpose, of his society's "reasonableness," etc. The boss is his "symbol of authority," related to his own notions of economic interest. Such a "style" may be totally deceptive. Such "identification" may get him no advancement whatever. But he may continue, through it, to get advancement *vicariously,* by merely "owning the insignia" of his boss. Such a man must change his identity if he would locate himself not by reference to his employers' "corporation," but by incorporation in a fellowship of employees. Our "proletarian" school of writers is, of course, attempting to coach a stylistic shift of this sort.

One may note another variant of "stylistic" identification when the immigrant, rich in gesture speech, seeks to "possess" the insignia of middle-class status in the most paradoxical way imaginable: by learning deliberately to *cramp* the expressiveness of the body, suppressing marked gesticulation and range of voice. For the kind of citizens with whose privileges he would seek to identify himself (in keeping with the natural human desire to "belong" by accommodating oneself to the reigning authoritative structure) are inexpressive in the language of gesture mainly because they have so little to express in any language, and have been sedentary too long. So the insignia here acquired "stylistically" are hardly more than the laborious attainment of zero.

11. Human *relations should be analyzed with respect to the leads discovered by a study of drama.*

Men enact rôles. They change rôles. They participate. They develop modes of social appeal. Even a "star" is but a function of the total cast. Politics above all is drama. Anyone who would turn from politics to some other emphasis, or vice versa, must undergo some change of identity, which is dramatic (involving "style" and "ritual"). People are neither animals nor machines (to be analyzed by the migration of metaphors from biology or mechanics), but actors and acters. They establish identity by relation to groups (with the result that, when tested by *individualistic* concepts of identity, they are felt to be moved by "deceptions" or "illusions," the "irrational"—for one's identification as a member of a group is a rôle, yet it is the only active mode of identification possible, as you will note by observing how all *individualistic* concepts of identity dissolve into the nothingness of mysticism and the absolute). If you would avoid the antitheses of supernaturalism and naturalism, you must develop the coördinates of socialism—which gets us to coöperation, participation, man in society, man in drama.

Both Freud and Marx were "impresarios." Marx's concept of the "classless" stage following a maximum intensification of class conflict is precisely in line with the Aristotelian recipe for the process of dramatic "catharsis." The shock value of Freudian analysis exemplified the same process in tiny "closet dramas" of private life (the facing and burning-out of conflict). Forms like the lyric (to employ an excellent word used by Ben Belitt in a recent number of *Poetry*) are analyzable as "monodrama."

The value, the normative basis of reference, proper to this approach is "communication." It is "hortatory" in that it implicitly postulates communication as a good. It is "diagnostic" in that it invites us to note the psychological and material factors *furthering* communication (the coöperative act) and psychological and material factors *obstructing* communica-

311

tion (the competitive act). The corresponding abstract ideal might be sloganized ethically (in terms of combined opposites) as: "Unity without Conformity."

12. *The difference between the symbolic drama and the drama of living is a difference between imaginary obstacles and real obstacles.* But: *the imaginary obstacles of symbolic drama must, to have the relevance necessary for the producing of effects upon audiences, reflect the real obstacles of living drama.*

Modes of coöperation (production and distribution) give form to modes of communication. The modes of communication thus refer back to the modes of coöperation. Much "symbolic action" in works of art deals with conflicts within the communicative or superstructural realm (conflicts among social values)—but these conflicts have their grounding in economic conflicts (as the clashes in Congress represent corresponding clashes among business interests).

To an extent, also, they arise from the fact that men cannot be a complete fit for *any* historical texture (which necessarily encourages some possibilities and discourages others). Hence, to some degree, solution of conflict must always be done purely in the symbolic realm (by "transcendence") if it is to be done at all. Persons of moral and imaginative depth acquire great enterprise and resourcefulness in such purely "symbolic" solutions of conflict (by the formation of appropriate "attitudes"). Hence, at times they try to solve symbolically kinds of conflict that can and should be solved by material means. A writer who has invested deeply in symbolic resourcefulness is threatened with a kind of "psychological unemployment" ("alienation") when his structure of meanings invites him to "solve" by symbolism alone a conflict requiring material solution.

312

It is of great importance to study the various strategies of "prayer" by which men seek to solve their conflicts, since such material should give us needed insight into the processes of prayer ("symbolic action," "linguistic action," "implicit commands to audience and self") in its many secular aspects, not generally considered "prayer" at all. Such insight should make precise the nature of the resistance encountered by those interested in engineering shifts in allegiance to the reigning symbols of authority.

And it should offer a *ground in common* between propagandizer and propagandized, whereby the maximum amount of readjustment could be accomplished through the "parliamentary" (discourse, discussion). That is: it should avoid the coaching of *unnecessary* factional dispute by considering modes of response applicable to *all* men and it could confine differences solely to those areas where differences *are* necessary. Such procedure is especially to be desired in the propagandist, since humaneness is the soundest implement of persuasion. For it contributes towards the general humanization of policies, even should bad policies prevail.

THE NATURE OF ART
UNDER CAPITALISM

THE present article proposes to say something further on the subject of art and propaganda. It will attempt to set forth a line of reasoning as to why the contemporary emphasis must be placed largely upon propaganda, rather than upon "pure" art. The general procedure to be followed is: (a) some basic considerations as to the relation between work and ethics are offered; (b) the attempt is made to show that this integral relationship between work and ethics is violated under capitalism; (c) by reference to the psychology of art, and to the connection between art and ethics, I attempt to show why the breach between work and ethics, indigenous to capitalistic enterprise, requires a "corrective" kind of literature. The article is in the form of seven propositions, with a brief demonstration of each.

1. Work-patterns and ethical patterns are integrally related.

The teachings of naturalism and religion seem united on this point. The great monastic orders were invariably founded upon a scheme of practical duties. "Virtue," however far into the infinite it might range, was always grounded upon the performance of specific earthly tasks. In India the four castes seem to be corruptions of four original occupational patterns, four kinds of *duties* or *obligations* having decayed into distinct categories of *privilege* and *privation*. Duty, or social function, was the synthesis out of which the two decadent antitheses, privilege and privation, have arisen. The fervor with which religions extolled the "sweat of the brow" was even so convincing to the general populace that it served admirably as a method of preëmption by the cunning, who could harness this deep piety for their private ends. Finding people ethically prepared to respect themselves and one another for their toiling, the cunning could manipulate this obedience for individual gain. Yet the fact remains that the "exploited" often seem to have had a better time of it than the "exploiter," for to be ethical is a deeply contenting thing. This may in part explain the fact that so much genuine folk culture has arisen out of unfair circumstances—or that it is precisely the descendants of slaves who, as a race in America, have been most given to song.

In its secular trappings, the respect for the ethics of work may be seen in the American's deep devotion to his business, or in the Marxian cult of the proletariat as the bearer of the new ethics. Again, we have such notions as John Dewey's concept of the "occupational psychosis," his thesis that a society's patterns of thought are shaped by the patterns of livelihood, that "spiritual" values get their authority because they reinforce the ways of thinking and feeling by which man equips himself to accomplish the tasks indigenous to his environment. The entire Darwinian point of view, in fact, emphasizes the growth of moral systems out of practical needs, the ways of "survival," and in human societies these ways of survival are fundamentally methods of producing and distributing goods.

Hence, in either naturalistic or transcendental thought we find the same tendency to accept an integral relationship between work and ethics.

315

2. The ethical values of work are in its application of the competitive equipment to coöperative ends.

Recall the symbol of the "Village Blacksmith." What is so "ennobling" about this man? Or Whitman's symbol of the broad-ax. It is in the fact that the basically destructive equipment, the military weapons of the body, are here used not to plague mankind but in social service. Such figures are "ethical" because they represent a fusion of the combative and the charitable. By work, the muscular and mental endowments which originally made for survival by the destruction of competitors are turned wholly into the channels of the coöperative. Work thus fuses the two aspects of the ethical: morals-as-implements, or morals-as-fists, and morals-as-social-cohesion. In the psychology of service the individually competitive capacities are sublimated into a coöperative enterprise. It has been suggested that the primitive group dance is so highly satisfying "ethically" because it is a faithful replica of this same coöperative fusion. It permits a gratifying amount of muscular and mental self-assertion to the individual as regards his own particular contribution to the entire performance, while at the same time it flatly involves him in a *group* activity, a process of giving and receiving.

3. Under capitalism this basic integration between work-patterns and ethical patterns is constantly in jeopardy, and even frequently impossible.

By far the most valuable work by Thorstein Veblen was his *Theory of Business Enterprise*. Here he reminds us that we tend to take "business" and "industry" as synonymous, whereas they are fundamentally distinct. Throughout the recent depression our financial Genghis Khans have managed again and again to uphold and strengthen this confusion. We must worry ourselves as to "what is good for business," rather than ask the more fundamental question, "What is business good for?" And the trick whereby our people so spontaneously ask themselves the first of these questions rather than the second lies precisely in the capitalistic assumption that business and industry are synonymous. Veblen shows that, far from being synonymous, they can often be radically at odds. It is considerations of *business,* not of *industry,* which keep our productive plant in a state of partial paralysis today.

But the objection to capitalism does not stop at the interference with our work-patterns, and the consequent decay of morals and morale, which it offers in times of depression. The profit motive is equally suspect under conditions of prosperity. By its emphasis upon the competitive aspect of work as against the coöperative aspect of work, it runs counter to the very conditions by which the combative equipment of man is made ethical—or social. It tends to leave man's capacities for "force and fraud" too purely capacities for force and fraud. Hence it is no accident that the racketeer and the crooked promoter-director have arisen as the culmination of our business philosophy. ("You'd do the same thing if you were in his place." Imagine trying to get a morality out of that!) Racketeers and promoters are frequently put forward as preying upon "legitimate business," but as a matter of fact they are the logical conclusion of business's failure to provide adequate charitable outlets for the combative man. (The tendency has usually been manifested compensatorily in the "philanthropic" activities by which the predatory frequently attempt to convert the fruits of their conquests back into social services. But this makes two antithetical stages of a process which is morally sound only

317

when it is synthetic. It is not moral to seize and give back—it is moral to convert the act-of-seizure itself into an act of public benefit.)

How can people go on publishing reports as to the many billions of dollars a year which racketeers cost "business" without taking the next obvious step, and noting how many more billions of dollars a year "business" costs "industry"? And how can they fail to note that in industry alone is the competitive ability, the muscle and mind of man, given a wholly coöperative fusion? Business, to be "moral," would be nothing more or less than the distributive end of industry. In so far as it is not this, it is vowed to a fundamental moral decay.

The church, ever acquiescent to the advantages of the hour despite its underlying philosophy of the Immutable, has of course stressed the aspects of its doctrine which seem to corroborate the fabulous acquisition and retention of private gain. Hence it has largely been the naturalists, the scientific skeptics, who have contributed to the distrust of the commercial ethic. But it must be recalled that the entire commercial exaltation was developed in opposition to the church's deepest teachings. If the Communists cared to do so, they could find many astonishing parallels between their own doctrines, which come at the end of the commercial upswing, and the church doctrines, which began to pale at its beginning. And even the Rotarians at the height of the New Era felt the profound moral need of a *coöperative* philosophy, precisely at the time when the drive to sell one's full quota, to put one's rival agents out of business, was at its psychotically intensest. The back-slapping of Babbitt was a hollow performance, but it represented a profoundly honest yearning. It attempted to do by a sheer ritual act, after hours, what one's entire efforts during the day were necessarily straining to deny.

4. Such a frustration of the combative-coöperative fusion under capitalism is a grave stimulus to wars.

If the coöperative genius is fundamentally frustrated or vitiated in civil life, men are still "moral" enough, still alive enough to the feeling that in *working together* lies virtue, for war to recommend itself to them in its best guise. War *is* cultural. It *does* promote a highly coöperative spirit. The sharing of a common danger, the emphasis upon sacrifice, risk, companionship, the strong sense of being in a unifying enterprise—all these qualities are highly *moral,* and in so far as the conditions of capitalistic peace tend to inhibit such expressions, it is possible that the thought of war comes as a "purgation," a "cleansing by fire." If the function of work fuses morals-as-implements or morals-as-fists with morals-as-social-cohesion, this same fusion is performed by war. Hence it seems natural that any radical impairment of this fusion under conditions of peace would instigate the search for a similar fusion in war, where it can indeed be attained. The non-professional character of modern war, the fact that the entire populations, even unto the gentle old ladies, contribute so avidly to its maintenance, would seem to indicate that it does satisfy deep emotional need. It is natural that, when the coöperative patterns are vitiated in peace, the moment war is declared it is found to be an "adequate" emotional solution to the difficulty, since it promptly brings the coöperative genius to the fore. Of course there are the profiteers who approach the entire matter from the standpoint of their private gain. But I doubt whether the ghoulish delights of this group could account for the exaltation of the people as a whole. It is the moral side of war which draws them to it, the fact that it brings their group together, if only for the dismal purpose of slaughtering or oppressing a common foe.

5. "Pure" art tends to promote a state of acceptance.

The group dance, as previously described, would seem to be a case in point. It carries the social patterns into their corresponding "imaginative" pattern, hence tends to substantiate or corroborate these patterns. The aesthetic act here maintains precisely the kind of thinking and feeling and behaving that reinforces the communal productive and distributive act. Or, to consider the question of tragedy, we may accept in a general way the psychoanalytic thesis, backed by such critics as Aristotle, that the tragedy makes for a state of resignation, or acceptance. By the psychoanalytic thesis this state of resignation is produced through fusing, in aesthetic symbols, mental conflicts which cannot be fused in the practical sphere. The maintaining of a strict family pattern, for instance, gives rise to certain proscriptions or taboos which conflict with desires arising out of the same pattern. One could not practically destroy these taboos without breaking up the family pattern. Hence, by symbolic fusion in tragedy, an ability to "accept one's fate" is established. This, in a general way, is the explanation of the "catharsis" of tragedy, which is the essence of "pure" art. It enables us to "resign" ourselves by resolving in aesthetic fusion trends or yearnings not resolvable in the practical sphere. And this same tendency to promote acceptance is to be seen likewise in "pure" humor. Pure humor is not protestant but acquiescent. It enables us to accept our dilemmas by belittlement, by "humanization." A good humorist does not want to "make us go out and do something about it." Rather, he makes us feel,

"Well, things may not be so bad after all. It all depends on how you look at them."

6. "Pure" art is safest only when the underlying moral system is sound.

Since pure art makes for acceptance, it tends to become a social menace in so far as it assists us in tolerating the intolerable. And if it leads us to a state of acquiescence at a time when the very basis of moral integration is in question, we get a paradox whereby the soundest adjunct to ethics, the aesthetic, threatens to uphold an unethical condition. For this reason it seems that under conditions of competitive capitalism there must necessarily be a large *corrective* or *propaganda* element in art. Art cannot safely confine itself to merely *using* the values which arise out of a given social texture and integrating their conflicts, as the soundest, "purest" art will do. It must have a definite hortatory function, an element of suasion or inducement of the educational variety; it must be partially *forensic*. Such a quality we consider to be the essential work of propaganda. Hence we feel that the moral breach arising out of capitalist vitiation of the work-patterns calls for a propaganda art. And incidentally, our distinction as so stated should make it apparent that much of the so-called "pure" art of the nineteenth century was of a pronouncedly propagandist or corrective coloring. In proportion as the conditions of economic warfare grew in intensity throughout the "century of progress," and the church proper gradually adapted its doctrines to serve merely the protection of private gain and the upholding of manipulated law, the "priestly" function was carried on by the "secular" poets, often avowedly agnostic.

7. Our thesis is by no means intended to imply that "pure" or "acquiescent" art should be abandoned.

There are two kinds of "toleration." Even if a given state of affairs is found, on intellectualistic grounds, to be intolerable, the fact remains that as long as it is with us we must more or less contrive to "tolerate" it. Even though we might prefer to alter radically the present structure of production and distribution through the profit motive, the fact remains that we cannot so alter it forthwith. Hence, along with our efforts to alter it, must go the demand for an imaginative equipment that helps to make it tolerable while it lasts. Much of the "pure" or "acquiescent" art of today serves this invaluable psychological end. For this reason the great popular comedians or handsome movie stars are rightly the idols of the people. Likewise the literature of sentimentality, however annoying and self-deceptive it may seem to the hardened "intellectual," is following in a direction basically so sound that one might wish more of our pretentious authors were attempting to do the same thing more pretentiously. On the other hand, much of the harsh literature now being turned out in the name of the "proletariat" seems inadequate on either count. It is questionable as propaganda, since it shows us so little of the qualities in mankind worth saving. And it is questionable as "pure" art, since by substituting a cult of disaster for a cult of amenities it "promotes our acquiescence" to sheer dismalness. Too often, alas, it serves as a mere device whereby the neuroses of the decaying bourgeois structure are simply transferred to the symbols of workingmen. Perhaps more of Dickens is needed, even at the risk of excessive tearfulness.

READING WHILE YOU RUN

An Exercise in Translation from English into English

EVERY once in a while, in the orthodox press, there is an article in which, at almost every step, you find something said one way and must read it another way. It is something like the "dramatic irony" of classic tragedy: Some character in the play is interpreting the signs to mean *plus,* but the audience with a different frame of reference knows that the signs should be interpreted to mean *minus.* Thus, Oedipus sees cause for boasting in the very disclosures that, as the audience realizes, foretell his downfall.

There is much of such dramatic irony in the news—with the highly unpleasant additional fact that the audience who would read this news differently than it is written is itself implicated in the threatened debacle of capitalist *hubris.*

A news story on the first page of the *Herald Tribune* seems to me especially rich in dramatic irony of this disturbing sort. Nearly every passage requires retranslation. A mass of interpolations extensive as *Das Kapital* would be required to make the job complete. I here merely suggest a few of those most obviously called for.

My purpose is to illustrate a situation that we understand in a general way but do not always note in the particular, to show how thoroughly the merest commonplaces of language serve to confuse the criticism of capitalist methods. Propaganda? Capitalist propaganda is so ingrained in our speech that it is as natural as breathing.

323

Political War
Declared by
Industry to
Halt New Deal

"Industry" is here used as the synonym of "big business." Thus, the most necessary distinction of all is automatically obliterated at the very start. By using "industry" where you mean "big business," you stack the cards to perfection. People know that factories have to be managed; and by using "industry" when you mean "the gatherers of excess profits," you imply that factories can be managed only by adepts in the art of "legal" shakedowns.

Nation's Manufacturers
End Convention Ready
to Fight for a Return
to "American System"

Same device at work in the use of the word "manufacturers." It is a vital boon to capitalism—that delicate usage (graceful and tactful) whereby the man who operates a manufacturing machine is *not* a manufacturer while the man who does *not* operate a manufacturing machine but juggles the dividends for himself and his kind *is* a manufacturer. The confusion gains additional sanctification by being put forward as an essential feature of America. Implied in the "Fight for a Return to 'American System' " there is some such argument as this: If you are wholesome, you love your country; your country is capitalist; therefore, to be wholesome, you must love capitalism. The form looks less convincing if thus made explicit, since it can so easily be parodied: If you are

324

wholesome, you love your country; your country has slums; therefore, to be wholesome, you must love slums.

Platform Calls for
Restoration of Gold

The emotional pull behind the shibboleth of gold goes deep. That profound worshiper of the golden calf, Carter Glass, will be singing of the gold standard in one paragraph, and in the next, before you know it, he is talking about God. Gold would at least be as good a standard as wampum, shells or any other conventionalized form of national IOU promising a man goods in exchange for services. But by devoutly plugging for the standard per se, without examining too closely the one-way profit system that makes any standard of promises to pay unworkable, we effectively center the attack upon a symptom and ignore the ill that causes the symptom.

Freedom for Enterprise
Is Demanded as Effort
to Balk Dictatorship
and Collectivism Gains

Here the needs for translation come thick and fast. First note that the phrase "freedom for enterprise" is an effective variant of the "industry-business" identification. If "business" equals "industry," then "promoters" become the same as "managers," and opportunity for excess profits is thus enshrined as "enterprise." Now, since every right-minded person desires freedom for enterprise, we are subtly invited to salute the great monopolists as the guardians of freedom.

"Balk dictatorship." Among the surest devices by which the interests of monopolists are upheld in the name of laissez faire is the use of this word "dictatorship" when you mean "social legislation." Carry it through, and you get miraculous results. You will find that even a feeble attempt, on the part of our constitutionally elected legislators and administrators, to mitigate distress, raise wage levels, improve housing conditions and the like becomes the work of a Hitler or a Mussolini. Watch Walter Lippmann, if you would see how rich a mental life can be built upon this simple confusion. See this suave magician daily put the kerchief of "social legislation" into his hat, make a few magic passes, and lo! out comes the rabbit of "dictatorship."

At the word "collectivism" in the headline my plodding patience fails. It is hard to believe that, in a democracy, such a word could ever be used as the synonym of evil. And it is hard to believe that even the most slovenly of tricksters should try to suggest that the New Deal is collectivist. The roots of the matter, I think, reside in this: *No* administration can, over a long period, conceal the fact that the needs of business are basically at odds with the needs of national welfare. Hence the fascist turn, implicit in the ability to use as a term of reproach so essentially democratic a word as "collectivism." One would expect the demagogues to do exactly the opposite; one would think that even the most reactionary advocates of special privilege would mask their policies under such a word as "collectivism." It is a grim sign when they don't.

Alas! we have only got through the headlines. Obviously, to translate the whole article, brief as it is, would require an encyclopaedia. We shall simply give samples of the article itself. It begins:

326

> Government has gone into business, so business will invade the field of politics, it was determined yesterday by 1,500 industrial leaders and business executives attending the final session of the annual convention of the National Association of Manufacturers at the Commodore.

The effrontery of the notion that business, after patiently suffering in silence through a hundred and fifty years of the Republic, has finally decided to "invade the field of politics" is almost breath-taking. The reporter was doubtless in a hurry. He simply wanted some sort of introduction that would serve to make the oldest story in American history look like something new—but it is disturbing to think that a man whose life work is the collecting of "facts" could begin a story in a great metropolitan daily with so brutal a violation of fact.

> Among those concurring in the decision, which aligns the most powerful commercial interests in the country against the Roosevelt administration, were business men of international reputation, representing billions of invested capital, millions of stockholders and employees.

"Representing billions of invested capital, millions of stockholders and employees." Again variants of the master confusion between "business" and "industry." From this source all capitalist apologetics flow. Later in the piece, by means of this identification, we find these gentlemen "representing" not only the flesh and blood whose services they command in their factories, but also even the unemployed, the flesh and blood they keep out of their factories.

327

But we shall not go on. My theme is an old one, well understood by many. I simply thought of showing by painful literalness how incessant the barrage against the criticism of capitalism is. The truly effective work is not done by some crude blast in an editorial by Hearst; that helps, to be sure, but the real confusion is kept alive by this modest tithing, this gentle, almost imperceptible choice of words. The surest way to balk action is to choose words that draw lines at the wrong places. And the very core of the strategy, I think, as Veblen made clear and Karl Marx before him, resides in the identification of "business" with "industry." Thus, we can have incessant palavers by business men about the ways of getting our factories going. They can be perplexed and earnest and noble and organization-loving and resolve-making, all for the good of the country, and the country can sit trembling and praying that they will make wise decisions for us. And all the time the one basic fact goes unregarded: The fact that, if their special interests as *business men* were ruled out today, our factories could resume operation at capacity tomorrow. But once you allow a *promoter* to look like a *manager,* once you allow the *channelization of profits* to mean the same thing as *control of production,* you are in for the same old fabulous swing from Republicans to Democrats and from Democrats to Republicans.

And the words by which they advocate the swing from one to the other are precisely the words that keep the people from getting rid of them both. History is a skilled dramatist, with dramatic irony as the main feature of the plot.

ANTONY IN BEHALF OF THE PLAY

AT times when the standards of criticism are set by a *receptive* class, as in the decadent stages of feudalism, the emphasis of the critic tends to be placed upon *consumption*. Matters of "appreciation" and "enjoyment" are the touchstones. Conversely, in the Art for Art's Sake movement of recent decades, we find the emphasis placed almost wholly upon *production*. Our practical inventors and business promoters of this period tended to emphasize the productive factor, assuming that in the large the matter of consumption would take care of itself —and there was a corresponding trend in aesthetics, with the essence of art being seen in the "self expression" of the artist.

Today, in nonliterary fields, we are stressing neither production nor consumption, but the *integration* of the two. And in the aesthetic field, this emphasis might be paralleled by a tendency to consider literature, not as a creator's device for self-expression, nor as an audience's device for amusement or instruction, but as a communicative relationship between writer and audience, with both parties actively participating. In such an approach, the poet's "self-expression" or the audience's "appreciation" will necessarily figure, but the main emphasis will be elsewhere.

This reader-writer relationship is emphasized in the following article, which is an imaginary speech by Antony. Instead of addressing the mob, as he is pictured in the third act of *Julius Caesar*, he turns to the audience. And instead of being a dramatic character *within* the play, he is here made

329

to speak as a critical commentator *upon* the play, explaining its mechanism and its virtues. Thus we have a tale from Shakespeare, retold, not as a plot but from the standpoint of the rhetorician, who is concerned with a work's processes of appeal.

Act III, Scene ii. *Antony has entered with the body of Caesar. Brutus has made his defense before the people, has won their sympathies to the cause of the conspirators, and has departed.*

Antony: Friends, Romans, countrymen . . . one—two—three syllables: hence, in this progression, a magic formula. "Romans" to fit the conditions of the play; "countrymen" the better to identify the play-mob with the mob in the pit —for we are in the Renaissance, at that point when Europe's vast national integers are taking shape, and all the wisdom that comes of the body is to be obscured by our putting in place of the body the political corpus, while we try to run this bigger hulk with the instincts for the little one—the Hobbesian metaphor—and the gloomy error has exalted us, so that no word handles as much, and as quickly, and as inexpressibly, as this word "countrymen," which must really mean, if pragmatic results are the test, that there is glory solely in being outdone by those within our own borders. Anyway, consider how much better my one-two-three arrangement is than was the opening salutation in Brutus' speech: "Romans, countrymen, lovers." He is an orator—but because you of England have thought the untrustworthy Latins eloquent, and because you don't think you are nearly so clever as you'd like to be, I shall seem closer to you if I apologize for bluntness. Yet how much more competent my opening syllables are: how much *truer,* since true to the processes of a spell, stressing a charm's *threeness.*

My Elizabethan audience, under the guise of facing a Roman mob I confront you at a most complicated moment. As a matter of fact, up to this point in our play you have been treated most outrageously. It can honestly be said that, in no major particular, have you been granted those clear and simple responses to which, as customers, you might feel yourselves entitled. Instead, your author has kept you in as vacillating a condition as this very Roman mob you have been watching with so little respect. I doubt if he distinguishes between the two of you. All that I as Antony do to this play-mob, as a character-recipe I do to you. He would play upon you; he would seem to know your stops; he would sound you from your lowest note to the top of your compass. He thinks you as easy to be played upon as a pipe.

Oh, there have been signs you recognize quickly, that you might feel familiar with the road upon which you have been stumbling. The conspirators have met during storms and in the "vile contagion of the night." They have pulled caps over their eyes. One plucked at another's sleeve. Such labels are easily read by anyone. The streets of Rome have bristled with bad omens. Caesar's wife has cried in sleep that they are murdering Caesar. Outlandish astronomical and biologic marvels have occurred—to point the direction of our plot and give it weight by implicating the very heavens. And finally, Caesar was struck with daggers. Yet these standard things have lured you into a region where you are not competent at all.

Consider the burden you now carry, as I step before the play-mob with the fresh-murdered body of Caesar. We have established a Caesar-principle and a Brutus-principle, though

I blush to consider some of the devices whereby the two principles have been set into your minds. Realize for what slight reasons you have been willing to let Caesar die. (The conspirators would not so much as touch him until you also had been brought into their band. And when Casca shouted, "Speak, hands, for me!" stabbing great Caesar, those homicidal hands spoke for you also.) First, we had the portents, beginning with the soothsayer's admonition that Caesar beware the Ides of March. In showing how things were going, these signs prepared you somewhat to go in the same direction.

But in addition, *your sympathies have been poisoned.* Caesar a conqueror, a monarch by reason of his attainments? Yet he was deaf in one ear. He had the falling-sickness, and "swounded" from the intense strain of refusing a crown he coveted. "He had a fever when he was in Spain," cried out "like a sick girl," his feebleness amazing Cassius. Cassius was a better swimmer than Caesar—and when the two of them had leaped into the Tiber on a dare, Cassius had to pull out Caesar, to whom he must "bend his body if Caesar carelessly but nod on him." His wife is barren. For all his determination to be bold, there is a timid and superstitious trait in him. And worst, for an emperor, on a night of storm and portents he appeared on the stage in his nightgown—so let him die. For such reasons as these you are willing to put a knife through the ribs of Caesar.

Still, you are sorry for Caesar. We cannot profitably build a play around the horror of a murder if you do not care whether the murdered man lives or dies. So we had to do something for Caesar—and you would be ashamed if you stopped to consider what we did. I believe we made Caesar appealing by proxy. That is: I, Antony, am a loyal follower of Caesar; you love me for a good fellow, since I am expansive, hearty, much as you would be after not too heavy a meal; and as one given to pleasure, I am not likely to lie awake at night plotting you injury. If such a man loves Caesar, his love lifts up Caesar in your eyes.

I serve a double purpose. Not only do I let Caesar shine a bit warmly by his reflection of my glow, but when the actual *persona* of the Caesar-principle is dispatched by daggers, the principle lives on in me, who continue the function of Caesar in the play. In the next act, the fourth, the *persona* itself will reappear momentarily as a ghost in Brutus' tent—but on the whole, after Caesar's death, I am the plot-substitute for Caesar. No wonder Brutus, in his address to the play-mob but a short time ago, told them that only Caesar's vices had been slain, while his virtues lived on, still active. So they do, in me, whom you like because I am marked by so serviceable a trait as loyalty. And when this play is over, Antony alone of the major characters will live; for you like to have about you such a man as might keep guard at the door while you sleep. Given certain conceptions of danger, I become the sign of safety. A little sunshine-thought, to take home with you after these many slaughterings. Only as much of the Caesar-principle as will let you relax, is left to bid you good-night—and the Brutus-principle will have died to purchase you this handsome privilege.

I grant that on this last score I am not the perfect recipe. My author has provided purer comfort-recipes for you elsewhere. I show a little too much aptitude at deception, but you should not hold that against me. This trait was merely a by-product of my place in the story: it arose from the fact that upon me fell the burden of keeping things going, and the plottiness of our drama makes naturally for plotting. Besides, recall that I was wholly the reveler as long as Caesar lived. Once he is dead, it is no longer so necessary that I be likable in Caesar's behalf and warm him by my warmth. Henceforth I am no mere Caesar-adjunct, but the very vessel of the Caesar-principle. So, in expanding to my expanded rôle, I must break the former mold somewhat. Let *savants* explain the change by saying that carefree Antony was made a soberer man, and a bitter one, by the death of Caesar. But it is an obvious fact that if an important cog in the plot vanishes in the very middle of our drama, something has to take its place. In deputizing for Caesar, I found it impossible to remain completely Antony. Let *savants* explain my altered psychology as they will—*I* know it was a playwright's necessity.

You have been made conspirators in a murder. For this transgression, there must be some expiative beast brought up for sacrifice. Such requirements guided us in the mixing of the Brutus-recipe, for it is Brutus that must die to absolve you of your stabbing an emperor who was deaf in one ear and whose wife was sterile. But let us be fair. There is also the fact that you wrested certain political prerogatives from King John, and have been taught to cherish them. Here also was a source of conviction to be tapped as an ingredient in our formula. We discredited Caesar from the very opening of the play, even before he had appeared (significant timing), by letting you see the tribunes angry with certain commoners who were too cordial in their preparations for the return of Caesar after victory. Caesar, it seems, would try to retract your *Magna Carta* from the Romans. Conversely, it is the Brutus-recipe that would prevent this threatened undoing of English political emancipation. So we make Brutus honorable in your eyes by starting his conduct primarily from this fear, which is always your fear as regards conditions in the contemporary state. He is virtuous because he does for Romans what you want your popular leaders to do for you. He takes on the nobility that comes of being good for private enterprise.

On the other hand, he is a conspirator; hence from the general censure takes corruption. For tough Casca is a Brutus-adjunct; and lean, envious Cassius; and Decius the flatterer. Here are qualities which, if lodged in any but yourselves, are not comforting to contemplate—hence are "vices." Brutus' acts, though done in a good cause, have shadiness. One cannot be stealthy as a thief without partially earning the kind of judgments that are laid against thieves. Nobleness, yes, but dirty business. And if his wife, Portia, speaks for him by her deep affection (as I obediently did for Caesar), note that she is allowed to show this affection only at those moments when he is sinisterly engaged, and answers her evasively. That is: her *love* is conveyed by her *misgivings,* as she worries because her once regular husband roams about at night, in "rheumy and unpurged air" sucking up "the humours of the dank morning," so that even the quality of swamps is drawn upon to discredit Brutus a little, right when Portia is loving him. All told: a fit expiative offering for our offense of murder: worthy, since he was noble and aroused affection, yet yieldable on good legalistic grounds, since he was a conspirator, like a bog. In weeping for his death, you will be sweetly absolved.

At this particular point in the play, however, as I rise to address you, accompanied by Caesar's corse, Brutus has just confronted the play-mob, stated before them the case of the conspirators, and been exonerated. They have clamored their approval. They are convinced that Caesar would have been a tyrant. And they have shouted to the Brutus-principle, who must die for you, "Live, Brutus! live! live!" It is my task, as I stand before the play-mob, to contrive a *peripety* for my audience, reversing the arrows of your expectations. When my speech is finished, we must have set you to making the preparations for Brutus' death.

Well, a dramatist is a *professional* gambler. He prefers playing with loaded dice. And don't think that we should try to bring about this reversal without first making sure that we had furtively dealt ourselves some trumps. We have stacked the cards a little—not so shamelessly as some of our rival Shake-scenes might have done, but enough. Here, I believe, we have drawn from the well of magic. As follows:

Recall how, in the early rites of communion, whereby one man's interests were made identical with another's, the risks of competitive harms were eliminated by a partnership, a partnership established by three distinct symbolic acts: the sharing of one's wife, the exchanging of blood, the sitting down together at table. Of these, the sharing of the wife is dead, buried beneath notions of virtue that go with later concepts of ownership. Yet we give you something similar, in Caesar's dying words, *"Et tu, Brute?* Then fall, Caesar!"* which suggests that in Caesar's pain there is more than the pain of knives, there is the pain of wrenched intimacy, eliciting a rebuke almost Christlike in its replacing of vengefulness with sorrow, as the victim saw that "Caesar's angel" was among his slayers. At this moment Caesar becomes great— for he must die well, at the expense of Brutus. They had shared affection; hence a promise contracted within the deep-lying terms of magic had been violated.

As for the rites at table: When the conspirators had come, to make sure that Caesar would be on hand at the Senate to be murdered, Caesar welcomed them heartily: "Good friends, go in, and taste some wine with me." And lastly, as for the blood-communion, how grimly it is vivified and mocked (in pious profanation) when the conspirators, at Brutus' word, bathe in the blood of Caesar's wounds. Three magic formulae, outraged—thus Shakespeare speaks to you in accents you had heard while not listening.

I now stand before you, assigned to the definite task of contriving our peripety, turning the arrows of your future while apparently engaged only in turning those of this unruly play-mob. I shall, by what immediately follows, proclaim myself in all thoroughness the Caesar-principle perpetuated. Here I fulfill the pledge I gave when first I came upon the stage after Caesar's murder. I came ostensibly to reassure the conspirators that I was ready to make peace with them, now that the offense was definitely beyond reparation. I shook hands with them, one after the other—but in the very act of doing so, I forgot them, and fell to musing aloud upon the destroyed magnificence of Caesar. In this way I signaled you to the effect that I was not turning against Caesar, even while "shaking the bloody fingers of his foes." (You wanted me to remain with Caesar, since that has been established as my part in this play. I have been given my label—and like children, you insist that a thing's *true* name is the name you first heard it called by. In your insistence that I remain allied with Caesar, repeating my number, you are grateful for the little cue I give you by my absent-minded musings over Caesar's body. In your satisfaction at receiving from me this sign, to restate my identity even as I make peace with the conspirators, you do not stop to ask why the conspirators should not interpret this sign precisely as you do. Your concern with your own aesthetic problem leads you to overlook this straining of verisimilitude, as we thought you would. We judged that, in your eagerness to receive the clue, you would not be overexacting as regard our manner of conveying it.)

Brutus, you will remember, had asked the mob to weigh what he said, and to judge his statements as critics. But, as a matter of fact, he gave them no opportunity to follow his advice. He told them to choose, then stated the issue in such a way that there was no choice. Those that love Rome, he said, must agree that Caesar should have been killed. Those that do not love Rome, should object. If there are any that do not love Rome, let them step forward in protest. No move —hence, the killing is endorsed.

And now, my countrymen, hear me ask the play-mob to lend me their ears, as I proceed to lay before you a plot in miniature. It will not be a very difficult pattern that I ask you to appreciate: a rudimentary piece of translation, by which I awaken in you the satisfactions of authorship, as you hear me say one thing and know that I mean another. "I come to bury Caesar, not to praise him"—whereat I praise him so roundly that all the vigor of the Caesar-principle is brought to life again.

> . . . if I were dispos'd to stir
> Your heart and minds to mutiny and rage,
> I should do Brutus wrong, and Cassius wrong, . . .

Whereat I stir hearts and minds to mutiny and rage. And as the pattern grows clear, I can subtilize it, making Brutus and his band dishonorable by calling them all, all honorable men. And by the time I mention Caesar's will, saying that I would not read it because it would inflame the people, in accordance with the pattern you wait to hear me read the will. You hear them entreat me, you hear me refuse. Then you observe me stepping down, to be among them, that I may better "realize" Caesar's death for them, and make them tearful coroners while I appraise the wounds:

If you have tears, prepare to shed them now.
You all do know this mantle: I remember
The first time ever Caesar put it on;
'Twas on a summer's evening in his tent,
That day he overcame the Nervii.
Look! in this place ran Cassius' dagger through:
See what a rent the envious Casca made:
Through this the well-beloved Brutus stabb'd;
And, as he pluck'd his cursed steel away,
Mark how the blood of Caesar follow'd it,
As rushing out of doors, to be resolv'd
If Brutus so unkindly knock'd or no;
For Brutus, as you know, was Caesar's angel:
Judge, O you gods! how dearly Caesar lov'd him.
This was the most unkindest cut of all;
For when the noble Caesar saw him stab,
Ingratitude, more strong than traitors' arms,
Quite vanquish'd him: then burst his mighty heart;
And, in his mantle muffling up his face,
Even at the base of Pompey's statua,
Which all the while ran blood, great Caesar fell.
O! what a fall was there, my countrymen;
Then I, and you, and all of us fell down,
Whilst bloody treason flourish'd over us.
O! now you weep, and I perceive you feel
The dint of pity; these are gracious drops.
Kind souls, what! weep you when you but behold

> Our Caesar's vesture wounded? Look you here,
> Here is himself, marr'd, as you see, with traitors.

You see my "transference," as I turn from the mantle to
the dead man that had worn the mantle. You see the play-
mob grow *inflamed* under my talk of *pity* (remember our
pattern). There is loud talk of mutiny; the people are about
to rush away in anger—but we would "consolidate" our
position. And now, rounding out the pattern, I return to
the matter of the will, which I had refused to read:

> Why, friends, you go to do you know not what.
> Wherein hath Caesar thus deserv'd your loves?
> Alas! you know not: I must tell you then.
> You have forgot the will I told you of.

Whereupon I read them the will of a rich philanthropist—
and their vindictiveness against the conspirators is complete.
You have been engrossed—faugh! you demons, how you do
love plottings, for all your censure of plotters. Or is it machinery that delights you—and are you pleased with joining
me to make a smoothly running engine of fatality?

Cassius was right in proposing that they slay me, along
with Caesar. But Brutus held it was enough to slay the
persona of the Caesar-principle, on the ground that the *adjunct* would subside through want of its source:

> Our course will seem too bloody, Caius Cassius,
> To cut the head off and then hack the limbs, . . .
> For Antony is but a limb of Caesar.
>
> .   .   .   .   .
>
> And, for Mark Antony, think not of him;
> For he can do no more than Caesar's arm
> When Caesar's head is off.

So the Brutus-principle slays half the Caesar-principle, and spares the other half that will in turn destroy it.

Recall these steps: How first, after the murder, I had sent word by a servant offering to join the cause of the conspirators, if they would guarantee me safety. How I fell to musing over the body of Caesar. How, after *exeunt all but Antony,* I had let loose my full-throated venom:

> O! pardon me, thou bleeding piece of earth,
> That I am meek and gentle with these butchers;
> Thou art the ruins of the noblest man
> That ever lived in the tide of times.
> Woe to the hand that shed this costly blood!
> Over thy wounds now do I prophesy,
> Which like dumb mouths do ope their ruby lips,
> To beg the voice and utterance of my tongue,
> A curse shall light upon the limbs of men;
> Domestic fury and fierce civil strife
> Shall cumber all the parts of Italy;
> Blood and destruction shall be so in use,
> And dreadful objects so familiar,
> That mothers shall but smile when they behold
> Their infants quarter'd with the hands of war;
> All pity chok'd with custom of fell deeds:
> And Caesar's spirit, ranging for revenge,
> With Ate by his side come hot from hell,
> Shall in these confines with a monarch's voice
> Cry "Havoc!" and let slip the dogs of war;
> That this foul deed shall smell above the earth
> With carrion men, groaning for burial.

Then, in my speech before the Romans, I fulfilled my promises, starting those processes by which the Brutus-

341

principle, which killed the Caesar-*persona*, is driven to his death by the Caesar-adjunct.

Thank us for this growing thing by growing with it—and in the following scene we shall allow you to squeeze the last available sum of emotion from the mounting sequence, causing it to drip, not by still hotter pressure, but by a sudden cooling. Prominent among the conspirators, there was a certain Cinna. Now another Cinna comes upon the stage, Cinna the poet, ludicrous, the cartoon of a poet, the aesthete, such as you have long before now been taught to laugh at (our author is treading on safe ground here). He is an earnest but ineffectual wretch, who probably knows a good line when he sees it, and would doubtless have been entranced to write just such verses as Shakespeare wrote; and perhaps he might even have written them had he known, like Shakespeare, how to draw finesses from toughnesses. Yet our dramatist betrays him for the delectation of you, my stinking audience, makes him your laughing stock, ridicules one of his own Guild for your benefit, though you have no desire whatever to write like Shakespeare, would much rather eat beef than hear a play, but cannot go on eating beef forever, and so come here occasionally, demanding firm, beefy diction. The mob stumbles upon this Cinna, overwhelming him. First Citizen, Second Citizen, Third Citizen, and Fourth Citizen each ask him a different question, all at the same time, insisting imperiously that he answer without delay. It is all quite hilarious, as Cinna is in a daze, comically. And when they ask him his name, and he says with assurance, "Cinna," they start pawing at him in earnest—and when he begs them for a little accuracy, insisting that he is not Cinna the conspirator but Cinna the poet, they unanswerably answer that they abominate the name, and so will pummel him for his verses, and the act ends with the brawling group moving from the stage. You somehow know that the poetic Cinna will suffer no fundamental harm. He will merely be slain-notslain, like a clown hit by cannon balls—yet by this let-down we have re-affirmed in another way the grim intentions of the mob. We have clinched the arrows of your expectancy, incidentally easing our obligations as regard the opening of Act IV.

You will be still more wisely handled by what follows, as our Great Demagogue continues to manipulate your minds. I think particularly of the second scene of the next act, weighted by the steadily organized pressure of events. You will witness a startling quarrel between Brutus and Cassius. After this violence and the sad reconciliation (these men are disintegrating), there will be a contrasted descent to soft tearfulness, as Brutus' drowsy servant plays him a disconsolate little tune in the dead of night (Portia is dead)—and the servant is drowsy, that he may fall asleep as Varro and Claudius have done; then with three men sleeping (and you drooping in sympathy) and Brutus alone awake, there will be, all about, a sleepiness, and a Brutus-loneliness—whereat the Caesar-*persona*, now as a ghost, may return to indicate, by a vague prophecy, that all will be ended for Brutus at Philippi.

TRIAL TRANSLATION
(FROM TWELFTH NIGHT)

ACT I, Scene i—*A room in the Duke's palace. Enter Duke, Curio, Lords; Musicians attending.*

Duke: As the first speaker in a well-formed drama, I shall begin significantly—in the sense that I shall give the audience some inkling of my "program" forthwith—suggesting the *quality* which the subsequent events are to *quantify.* In his responsiveness to beginnings, man lays cornerstones, distributes souvenirs when a new enterprise is opened, pronounces "valedictories," and even (ironically enough) treats *burial* as the symbol of a birth-in-heaven. So I shall not violate the implicit confidence of my audience, a confidence which they place in me without their even themselves knowing that they do so. I shall point the arrows of their expectations thus promptly: my very opening words will proclaim an aspect of this work:

If music be the food of love, play on . . .

As cells absorbing sunlight, as the fetus basking in its womb-heaven, *receiving* nutriment; not venturing forth aggressively, predaciously, as with those jungle animals that stalk, leap, and capture before they eat, and thus must do hating and injuring—but simply as larvae feed, let me take in gentle music. You, the poet's audience, even now have it placed more clearly before you, what I have in mind. There

344

are "musicians attending"—they have played somewhat, encouraging you to rise and fall in *Einfühlung* with their melody, setting you so early into a mood of acquiescence. You too have laid yourselves open, as cells are filled, as the fetus prospers by merely having bounty forced upon it. The ground lies stretching beneath fine rain—not an assailment, but a gently-falling mist, blotted by the soil (I refer not to the weather, but to a way of feeling). We are recipient. Play on.

> Give me excess of it, that, surfeiting,
> The appetite may sicken and so die.

Which modifies my first statement considerably. For if, in the hearing of soft music, there is a basking, a larval-feeding, we have now introduced an element alien to such absolute recipience. In laying us open to clemency, music lays us open in general—and thus may also lay us open to inclemency, if there is inclemency about. You northerners, skilled in love-fictions and their melancholies, know that by our mentioning the "food of love" we have introduced a theme of melancholy. So quickly you experts detect the signs, and decide why your Duke is gloomy. We have suggested two ways at once: how, in the nutriment of music, there is an added hunger started up. I shall not bewilder you on saying that, as I have laid myself open to this "food of love" (music), I may in surfeiting close myself. You Elizabethan gluttons can grasp this trope quite readily—hence I intermingle things so widely separated in their range as faint music and gut-knowledge, for even in our frailest imaginings we must imagine with our bodies.

> That strain again! it had a dying fall.

A "dying fall" is simply a "cadence" (from *cadere,* to fall)—so I here use a purely technical designation for whatever sentimental increment it may carry. If notes drop to a semi-close, let us drop with them—so altogether: our melody, our verbal images, and our tyrannical yet gullible audience. Consider all that "down"-thoughts contain for people who picture ambition and victory as *up,* to whom careers are a climbing of hills, who would struggle towards the head-waters, who place their *heels* upon a *neck,* whose heaven is *above* them, and who are put to rot six feet *under.* I have just been talking of a relinquishment so total that it becomes protective. I have really proposed carrying the blessedness of larval-feeding into that further stage of *stereotypy* wherein humble things protect themselves by becoming *motionless.* See: they have no stouter defense than that—a mere rigidifying, a turning-off of the register, a method integral to such as might derive their scheme of happiness, not from a snatching of pulsant meat, but as a swimming in tepid water, a being-tubularly-fed from a manna-placenta. Accordingly I would, under danger, merely shut away the recordings of danger—so the music at this point, to do outside me what I would make it do within, falls dying.

[Novelist: To close oneself is to attempt "protection by immobility." I mean: these things that larval-feed will usually, at the threat of danger, fall into a stiffness, making themselves nonexistent by rigidity. Lacking predatory weapons, their defense is in their simulation of deadness, which we see from without, as we observe only the curled-up irresponsiveness of their forms, when we have touched them, with a stick or something—but which obviously has its deadness-counterpart in the stopping of their emotions, the stilling of their little caterpillar thinkings. So this Duke is a gentle one, who

346

would strike at no one, but asks only that he be able to "turn off" his entire experience, to protect himself by becoming a living nothing.]

> O, it came o'er my ear like the sweet sound,
> That breathes upon a bank of violets,
> Stealing and giving odour!

As you, the audience, already suspected, my prayer for "surfeit" was somewhat metaphorical. You know I wanted the music to continue (in the sense that I would not turn off my sensitiveness to the sweetly unhappy situation "behind" the music). But an important change has occurred—and I mention the stimulating waft of a scent to the nostrils. Did I talk of larval-feeding, with its "pure receptivity," its mere lying prone—and did I describe defense, in this order, as a similarly nonaggressive process, a shutting-within? Then stop to realize that I am speaking in Elizabethan England, to a turbulent nation of brawlers and huntsmen. To such, even an ecstatic praise of passiveness cannot go long without becoming *invitation*, rather. You cannot take my gloom to mean that I am, in that which concerns me, without a future, as there is not one single member of this entire audience that is without a future (without an image of something like that which is, in the sixteenth century, vaguely deemed available in America). [Novelist: When speaking of a "sweet sound, that breathes upon a bank of violets, stealing and giving odour," he has put many signs together, starting from the standard one that violets both are prudish and do bloom in the emergent stages of the rutting season. Adolescent, incipient love, upon which our adult English poets have doted, is best symbolized by vernal things (by an adolescent season). It is southern races, accustomed to the glare of sunlight, that seem most pleased

347

with the glaring, high-noon aspects of attachment. But the north, awaiting spring, is schooled in awaiting the incipient, hence the paradox of these mature fellows who especially prize a mere burgeoning of affection, and write noble rôles to be played by boys wheezing falsetto . . . Note also how a discreet synæsthesia has occurred—not pointedly as with Rimbaud's sonnet in which he states the color-equivalents of vowels—but with an imperceptible shifting whereby, without knowing it, the audience has let itself be taken from sound to scent, has been told that the music *sounds* as violets *smell*. But if sound was for larval receptivity, scent is a goad to more aggressive ways of thinking; to the nostrils there is wafted the promise of prey. No basking fetus now—but a huntsman—though the change come in the disarming guise of a bank of violets! Process: beginning with the receptive, he turned to a tentative interest in the protection of immobility, next to that promise of a future which would ever arise in those men when you talk to them of a resigning; and lastly, a going-forth.]

Enough, no more:
'Tis not so sweet now as it was before.

The filmy fabric I had built around my notion of pure receptivity is ripped by ambition. Scent, however tactfully I have introduced it here, is a more businesslike matter—and when sound has become scent, the meanings shift accordingly. That which was like soft rain sinking upon me is now like something to be sought. Whereas my rhythm heretofore has been undulant, a merely breathing or imbibing rhythm, it now fittingly makes a saltation, as of those that snatch (abruptly snapping "enough, no more"). In talking only of violets, I reveal myself predacious. Then I fall to musing in a different vein:

> O spirit of love, how quick and fresh art thou!
> That, notwithstanding thy capacity
> Receiveth as the sea, nought enters there,
> Of what validity and pitch soe'er,
> But falls into abatement and low price,
> Even in a minute!

[Novelist: He began moonily, and here he has got to sheer diagnosis. Diagnosis is the "aesthetic," it is "pure inquiry," it is a mere "abstract interest" in things, 'tis "idle curiosity," —arising from the primordial jungle hunt, when anything might be the prey, hence anything was worthy of inspection, hence organisms simply "looked about," hence they became "speculative." So, the Duke has gone complete from larval thought to the predatory (they are both in our tissues)—and is now critical, diagnostic, in quest—in such chaste quest as their lustful, lusty, unpolitical, beddy minds would most readily consider questing.]

Curio: Will you go hunt, my lord?
Duke: What, Curio?
Curio: The hart.
Duke: Why, so I do, the noblest that I have.
       O! when mine eyes did see Olivia first, . . .
Et cetera.

CALDWELL:
MAKER OF GROTESQUES

ERSKINE CALDWELL'S most revealing work is a "sport." I refer to the last story in *American Earth,* "The Sacrilege of Alan Kent." It is divided into three sections, with wholly non-Caldwellian titles, "Tracing Life with a Finger," "Inspiration for Greatness," and "Hours Before Eternity." In these words we catch a tonality of brooding which, though so much a part of America as to have been pronounced by Poe, is more generally associated with the pious satanists who developed the ways of Poe in Europe: Baudelaire, Rimbaud, Lautréamont, and the early Gide. This work is as unique to Caldwell in manner as it is in mood. Whereas his other stories, long or short, are written with the continuity of the undulations along a moving caterpillar's back, "The Sacrilege" is a chain of brief numbered paragraphs, each bluntly set off from the rest. Done with the solemnity of a farewell or a testament, they contain a kind of aphoristic rhetoric, except that the aphorisms are less ideas than tiny plots. We note here a formal resonance, a stentorian quality, obtained by a swift recital of plagues, monstrosities, horrors, obsessions, disasters and gigantesque imaginings, set against a tender counter-theme: "I never heard a girl whose face and body and eyes were lovely say anything but lovely words." Here we have the symbol of the wanderer, driven by unnamed sins and called by vague visions of a homecoming in female sweetness. The swift segments shunt us back and forth between brutality and wistfulness. Perhaps

350

the grandiose, the violent, and the gentle qualities of the piece are all fused in this bit of purest poetry: "Once the sun was so hot a bird came down and walked beside me in my shadow." A section in *Pagany* containing this item was the first thing by Caldwell I ever saw. For days I was noisy in my enthusiasm—but I could not understand how it went with some of his other work.

Now that we have five books to examine, the connections are more easily discernible. It seems to me that Caldwell has elsewhere retained the same balked religiosity as distinguishes "The Sacrilege," but has merely poured it into less formidable molds. We may detect it, transformed, as the incentive leading him to blaspheme and profane for our enjoyment. We may glimpse this balked religiosity in the symbolic transgressions and death penalties that give shape to the plots of *Tobacco Road* and *God's Little Acre*. It is the explicit subject matter of much conversation in all his novels. It is revealed by an almost primitive concern with sexual taboos, and with fertility rites rising in opposition to the theme of castration. In its temperate, more social aspects, it shows as a tendency to deny humans their humaneness, as though the author, secretly abased, wanted to "drag others down" with him. Entertainingly, it appears in still more attenuated form as caricature and humor, the mental state of "refusal" here inducing extravagant incongruities that sometimes can be received with laughter, but are frequently so closely connected with degradation and acute suffering that the effect is wholly grim. Towards the end of his longer works, the goad of balked religiosity provokes grandiloquent moralistic passages wherein his subnormal mannikins, strangely elated by the story's symbolism, transcend themselves and speak of vital purpose with almost evangelical fervor (plus a slight

351

suggestion that they had read D. H. Lawrence). And in an unexpected episode of *Journeyman,* his latest book, Caldwell has even gone so far as to introduce a quality of other-worldliness into the very midst of his human rabbit hutch— for in no other way can I interpret the section (which Horace Gregory has selected for approval) where three men take turns at peering out through a crack in the wall of the barn, while one sermonizes: "It's sitting there and looking through the crack at the trees all day long that sort of gets me. I don't know what it is, and it might not be nothing at all when you figure it out. But it's not the knowing about it, anyway—it's just sitting there and looking through it that sort of makes me feel like heaven can't be so doggone far away."

In taking balked religiosity as the underlying theme upon which his successive works are the variations, I do not want to imply that Caldwell, like Hemingway, is preparing himself for a return to Rome. His powerful story "Kneel to the Rising Sun" indicates that he can make the change from negativism to affirmation by choices usually called secular. In so far as he is moved by the need of salvation, he seems minded to find it in the alignments of political exhortation, by striving mainly to see that we and he take the right side on matters of social justice. But as partial vindication of my proposal that his cult of incongruity seems to stem from the same source as his social propaganda, I should note that, precisely in this story of a lynching, his emphasis upon the playful scrambling of the old proprieties abates: instead of the humorist's refusal, as shown in his earlier zest to garble the conventions, we get a sober assertion of positive values. He does not merely act to outrage an old perspective by throwing its orders of right and wrong into disarray: he subscribes to an alternative perspective, with positive rights and wrongs of its own, and with definite indications as to what form he wants our sympathies and antagonisms to take. Incidentally, this development suggests the ways in which a motivation essentially nonpolitical or noneconomic can be harnessed in the service of political or economic criticism.

Whether one so apt at entertaining us by *muddling* our judgments will be equally fertile in *stabilizing* judgments remains to be seen. My guess would be that he won't, since he would have to master a whole new technique of expression. His very abilities tend to work against him. Recently I heard one man complain that Caldwell "has yet to learn that the revolution begins above the belt." And I incline to suspect that, in the learning, he may begin to find himself psychologically unemployed. A literary method is tyrannical—it is a writer's leopard-spots—it molds what a writer can say by determining what he can see; hence I should imagine that Caldwell would have to develop by satirizing more complex people rather than by pleading unmistakably for simple ones. But that is a guess about tomorrow's weather.

When I say that Caldwell's particular aptitude has been in scrambling or garbling propieties, I refer to his deft way of putting the wrong things together. An unendowed writer, for instance, might strain to engross us by lurid description of the sexual act—and the result would be negligible. But such an uninventive writer would probably be quite "proper" in the sense that he accepted the usual conventions as to the privacy of this act. Caldwell can be much more stimulating by merely so altering the customary situation that people are looking on and commenting in the blandest fashion, as in the comically inappropriate episode of this nature in *God's Little Acre*. Or he may have Ty Ty say, without confusion, such things to his daughters and daughter-in-law as would "properly" be said only under the greatest of morbid intensity. By an astounding trick of oversimplification, Caldwell puts people into complex social situations while making them act with the scant, crude tropisms of an insect—and the result is cunning, where Lawrence, by a variant of the same pattern, is as unwieldy as an elephant in his use of vulgar words for romantic love-making. Probably only in the orgy at the end of *Journeyman* does Caldwell become so undiplomatic in his treatment. Here, with almost the literalness of an inventory, he has us observe in each member of the congregation that phenomenon which so mortified Saint John of the Cross, the fact that, since the body has less channels of expression than the mind, acute religious ecstasy may be paralleled neurologically by sexual orgasm.

In the psychology textbooks, we read accounts of experiments whereby the higher centers of an animal's brain are removed, with the result that the animal's responses to stimuli are greatly simplified. A frog, so decerebrated, may jump when prodded, eat when fed, and croak when caressed—but it is evident that with the operation the poor fellow's personality has vanished. He has become less like a living organism, and more like a doorbell, which rings when you press the button. He has lost the part of himself that is sometimes called free will and which Bergson names the "center of indetermination." And his ways, as compared with the ways of a whole frog, are distinctly grotesque. Caldwell often seems to have performed such an operation upon the minds of his characters. As Ty Ty Walden complains in *God's Little Acre,* "There was a mean trick played on us somewhere. God put us in the body of animals and tried to make us act like people." It is a just complaint of Ty Ty's, as the creature of his own private creator. What the decerebrated frog is to the whole frog, Caldwell's characters are to real people. In view of which, it is positively incredible that his extravaganzas, imagined in a world essentially as fantastic as Swift's should ever have passed for realism.

Pearl, the image of better things in *Tobacco Road*, does not even *speak*. Anderson's gropers stuttered, but in this book the golden-haired child wife who is charged with the novelistic duty of upholding a little corner of glory in the midst of degradation, is totally inarticulate. For her there is no such verbal key as that with which the great sonneteer unlocked his heart. Though married, she sleeps alone; she will not look at her uncouth husband; she refuses to discuss his appetites with him (she cries when he beats her, but "Lov did not consider that as conversation"); and in the end, still wordless, she vanishes, doubtless to become a prostitute in Augusta. Silk stockings in the city, we feel, is her noblest conceivable utopian negation of the physical and spiritual impoverishment all about her; but to her understanding of this little, she will bring a deep, innate delicacy, invisible to all but the novelist and his readers.

In this discussion of Pearl, I may seem to have involved myself in a contradiction. For I speak of Caldwell's sub-human characters, yet I credit them with great delicacy. Here we come to the subtlest feature of Caldwell's method. Where the author leaves out so much, the reader begins making up the difference for himself. Precisely by omitting humaneness where humaneness is most called for, he may stimulate the reader to supply it. When the starved grandmother in *Tobacco Road* lies dying, with her face ground into the soil, and no one shows even an onlooker's interest in her wretchedness, we are prodded to anguish. When these automata show some

355

bare inkling of sociality, it may seem like a flash of ultimate wisdom. I suspect that, in putting the responsibility upon his readers, he is taking more out of the community pile than he puts in. Perhaps he is using up what we already had, rather than adding to our store. He has evoked in us a quality, but he has not materialized it with sufficient quantity. In any event, the silence of Pearl in *Tobacco Road* and the sober burlesque of the men peering through the crack in *Journeyman* are of a piece with the strange albino of *God's Little Acre,* the "conjur" who makes the simple, lyrical declaration to Darling Jill (herself graced with one of the loveliest names in all fiction):

> "I wish I had married you," he said, his hands trembling beside her. "I didn't know there was a girl so beautiful anywhere in the country. You're the prettiest girl I've ever seen. You're so soft, and you talk like birdsong, and you smell so good. . . ."

I have denied that Caldwell is a realist. In his tomfoolery he comes closer to the Dadaists; when his grotesqueness is serious, he is a Superrealist. We might compromise by calling him over all a Symbolist (if by a Symbolist we mean a writer whose work serves most readily as case history for the psychologist and whose plots are more intelligible when interpreted as dreams). In *The Saturday Review of Literature* a few months back, Dr. Lawrence S. Kubie took as particularly significant the absence of the motherly woman in Caldwell's fictions, with attendant cult of sterility. And his article gave many relevant clues as to the *nonrational* linkages involved in the imagery of *God's Little Acre.*

In books of complex realistic texture, such as the great social novels of the nineteenth century, we may feel justified in considering the psychologist's comments as an intrusion when he would have us find there merely a sublimation of a few rudimentary impulses. The important thing is not the base, but the superstructure. With fantastic simplifications of the Caldwell sort, however, the symbolic approach has more relevance. Thus, the selection of extreme starvation as a theme for *Tobacco Road* is found to take on a significance besides that of realistic justification when we link it with passages in *God's Little Acre* where Ty Ty, admiring Griselda, declares that the sight of her "rising beauties" makes him feel inspired to "get down and lick something." How possibly explain as mere reporting the episode in *God's Little Acre* about the girls who have replaced the men in the factory, and of whom we read the dreamlike statement, "When they reached the street, they ran back to the ivy-colored wall and pressed their bodies against it and touched it with their lips. The men who had been standing idly before it all day long came and dragged them home and beat them unmercifully for their infidelity"? A factory that could induce such surprising antics must have peculiar connotations not realistically there. And perhaps we come closer to them when recalling how, in this same factory, where the rebellion of the workers takes very unreal forms, Will finally fulfills his determination to "turn on the power," but only after his perverted rape of Griselda. When the old grandmother dies, the sight of her face in the dirt simply reminds her son Jeeter that the soil is right for planting. Immediately after, he is destroyed by fire.

The symbolic relations submerged here begin to suggest themselves when we recall the following facts: In both *Tobacco Road* and *God's Little Acre* we are told that there are two types of people, those who stay on the farm and those who go to the factory. Both Jeeter of *Tobacco Road* and Ty Ty of *God's Little Acre* are the kind that stay on the farm, the first hoping to plant again (a frustrated hope) and the second digging in the bowels of the earth for gold (an exceptional obsession to motivate an entire book about contemporary Georgia, though we may legitimately remember here the golden-haired Pearl of *Tobacco Road*). In one of the short stories, "Crown Fire," we learn from the course of the plot that the fire symbol is linked with partial female acquiescence; and in "The Sacrilege," where the "offense" is unnamed, we are told, "My mother saw from her bed the reflection in the sky of red wind-fanned flames. She carried me out into the street and we sat in the red mud shivering and crying"—sitting in this same soil with which Jeeter is so impotently preoccupied (since he cannot buy the seed for planting) and which Ty Ty turns into sterility by digging there for gold. After Will carries out in actuality the perverse inclination Ty Ty speaks of, Will can "turn on the power" in the factory. But though Will here seems to deputize for Ty Ty, Ty Ty's son commits a murder and must run away. Ty Ty moans that blood has been spilled upon his land, whereupon he is freed of his obsession to dig gold; and as the son is leaving, Ty Ty wills that God's little acre be always under him. Both books are thus permeated with symbolic sins, symbolic punishments, followed by symbolic purification. At the end of each, and following the orgy in *Journeyman*, there is the feeling that a cleansing had taken place, that the character who, at the last transformation, is the bearer of the author's identity, is free to "start anew." All this is magic, not reason; and I think that we are entitled to inspect it for the processes of magic. The balked religiosity of which we spoke is evidently linked with the devious manifestations of

358

"incest-awe"; the plots are subtly guided by the logic of dreams.

I am not by any means satisfied by the psychoanalytic readings of such processes to date, though I do believe that in moralistic fantasies of the Caldwell type, where the dull characters become so strangely inspired at crucial moments, we are present at a poetic law court where judgments are passed upon kinds of transgression inaccessible to jurists, with such odd penalties as no Code Napoléon could ever schematize.

The short stories (republished in *American Earth* and *We Are the Living*) as a whole seem too frail. They are hardly more than jottings in a diary, mere *situations* that Caldwell, with his exceptional turn for narrative and his liquid style, manages to palm off as plots. I call them diary jottings because they often give the impression of having suggested themselves to him in this wise: If you were sitting alone in a strange room, you might think, "What if someone knocked at the door?" If Caldwell were similarly placed, such a thought might occur to him, and there he would have his story.

He has a sharper sense of beginnings than most writers, as witness in the long story, *Journeyman,* Semon Dye's formal entrance in the lavishly balky and noisy car. Here is a mock announcement of the hero's approach, done with such a blare and fanfare of brasses as Wagner summons to herald the approach of Siegfried. Thus, the author tends to begin with some oddity of situation, which as likely as not suggested itself without a resolution, so that the story merely fades away rather than closes. He shows a surprisingly naïve delight in all the possible ramifications of the thought that girls may be without panties, and he seems to have searched the length and breadth of the country for new situations whereby some

359

significant part or parts can be exposed for us. The basic formula seems to be the use of two unrelated orders of events until they are felt to be related. He gets very appealing pictures of adolescent love—but his most successful venture in the shorter form is probably "Country Full of Swedes," where a family returns to their house across the road after a couple of years' absence, and their sudden prevalence in the locality is amusingly magnified until, for all their obvious peacefulness, they take on the qualities of a vast invasion.

Caldwell's greatest vice is unquestionably repetitiousness. He seems as contented as a savage to say the same thing again and again. Repetition in his prose is so extreme as almost to perform the function of rhyme in verse. In analyzing the first four chapters of *Tobacco Road,* I found that it was simply a continual rearrangement of the same subjects in different sequences: Jeeter wants Lov's turnips, Lov wants Jeeter to make Pearl sleep with him, Jeeter's own turnips all have "damn-blasted green-gutted turnip-worms," hair-lipped Ellie May is sidling up to Lov, Dude won't stop "chunking" a ball against the loose clapboards, Jeeter hopes to sell a load of wood in Augusta—about ten more such details, regiven in changing order, make the content of forty pages. Sometimes when reading Caldwell I feel as though I were playing with my toes.

THE NEGRO'S PATTERN OF LIFE

RUN, LITTLE CHILLUN! as played at the Lyric
Theatre in New York City, seemed to me a deeply impressive
event within simple operatic outlines. I had not seen the play
which may have been its prototype, *The Green Pastures,* but
I have read the cold words—and though they are fresh, and
even sweet, I believe that *Run, Little Chillun!* is a richer
work. The appeal of *The Green Pastures* may have arisen in
part from the fact that, for all the honest pleasantness in its
dialogue, it did contrive to exploit the old minstrel show conception of the Negro (naïve, good-natured, easily put upon)
which would naturally provide an endearing symbol for the
eliciting of White warmth. Nothing is so expansive as comfort—and such childlike fancies were highly comforting. By
the *Green Pastures* picture of heaven, amusingly absurd in
its anachronisms and solecisms, there was regiven, in brightly
new symbolization, the old simplicity and innocuousness of
the "Black-face" comedian. One could safely bestow one's
love upon such essentially ineffectual foibles and imaginings.
They had the lovableness of the incompetent.

Americans, driven by some deep competitive fear, seem to
open their hearts most easily to such symbols of "contented
indigence." Note how their darling comic heroes are all trans-
parent, outspoken, ineffectual fellows, too scatter-brained to
be dangerous, too prompt in tomfoolery for expertness in the
grim ways of jockeying one out of a job or getting the better

361

of one in a deal. Psychoanalysts used to situate the appeal of child stories for adults in the ability to "carry them back"— but literature is always carrying people somewhere or other, so maybe the carrying, rather than the regression, is the important factor. In any case, the child symbol is the symbol par excellence of innocence (*innocentia:* "harmlessness"; thence derivatively, "blamelessness"; thence, lo! "integrity"). And the Negroes of *The Green Pastures,* with their heavenly clambakes, mildly disconsolate "Lawd," the incongruous Africanization of the Biblical legends, can carry one into a region of gentleness that is, in contrast with the harsh demands of our day, caressing.

We emphatically imply no censure of *The Green Pastures* in attributing much of its appeal to the tapping of such a vein. The feeling is honest—and any work that can manipulate symbols for arousing this feeling in us is honest. But the point may serve somewhat to account for the sluggishness of the general public's interest in *Run, Little Chillun!* as compared with the vogue of *The Green Pastures*—for the new play, written "from within," by a Negro, Hall Johnson, brings out an aspect of the Negro-symbol with which our theater-going public is not theatrically at home: the power side of the Negro. One White playwright, Eugene O'Neill in *Emperor Jones,* did partially stress this power emphasis, as distinct from the child-symbol Negro of the minstrel show tradition. But only as a kind of "powerful persistence in error." In *Run, Little Chillun!* one sees a Negro genius, an attractive positive ability, exemplified with a conviction, a liquidness, a sense of aesthetic blossoming, and a gift for spontaneous organization which is capable, I believe, of actually setting the spectator aquiver as he participates in the vocal and mimetic exhilaration taking place before him. No amusing picture of heaven here—nor "backward superstition" corrosively suggested by the unending nag of a drumbeat—but an insight, a well-rounded biological pattern, a "way of life." And there was an impromptu integrative capacity as one might find it, laboriously planned, in the Prelude to Wagner's *Meistersinger,* where the themes are ultimately welded together with such strength that the composer, in his triumph, grows martial, and the piece ends with the boastfulness of firmly coördinated marching men.

We shall concern ourselves mainly with the two choric scenes, which seemed to us soundly operatic, utilizing the characteristic operatic devices not as mere conventions, but as the correct resources for the attainment of the ends in view. We have perhaps come to think of opera as a vast set of semaphore signals for wigwagging communications from the stage to the pit. The two choric scenes of *Run, Little Chillun!* restore our understanding of what the writer of "music-drama" must have intended: a kind of performance in which the visual and the auditory aspects of an event would be completely integrated, so that the tone of the voice and the flexions of the body would seem interchangeable.

There were many such integrated moments in *Run, Little Chillun!* Indeed, the second choric scene, which allowed for considerable improvising beyond the specified trend of the plot, so combined the planned and the spontaneous as to offer the fullest opportunity for the workings of those hypnotic processes by which the cast, like migrating birds, could fall into a unity, and this unity in turn could absorb the spectators, precisely as one might, in observing the birds' movements, veer and deploy with them. The other choric interlude, the scene of the Baptist service, was a succession of these "one-time" flashes, doubtless differently constituted

363

with each performance. There are the typical experiences of the Faith: temptation, sinning, repentance, confession, redemption, elation—and for each of these experiences fixed phrases have arisen. In time, these phrases have been set to music, the spirituals. Accordingly, in the Baptist ceremony, as members rose to tell of their religious moments, they would naturally fall into these "technical expressions," the "nomenclature for a special science," whereupon the accompanying melodies would suggest themselves, so that bars of song popped forth here and there among the congregation to fit the half-spoken, half-chanted recitals—or at times when all converged upon the same phrase and melody, we had a choral number—and this process, the singling out of a particular spiritual from among the accompanying chaos of suggestions, was invigorating—it was like getting hold of great complexities, or perhaps it was like seeing little flowers come up out of the ground, swiftly grow big, and blossom, in less than a minute.

Negro voices have an almost orchestral range of timbres. They do not vary merely as ordinary tenor, soprano, bass, but as viola, 'cello, flute, horn. And the Negroes' interest in the nonrecordable aspects of rhythmic and tonal subtlety leads them naturally into coördinations between the skeletal muscles and the voice which are beyond paraphrase. There were all kinds of miniature departures, permissible variations within the fixed theme of the plot. When the turbulent scene was abruptly reduced by the death of Sulamai to horrified rigidity, the patness of the device was found to have justified itself completely. One was made equally rigid—thereafter to ease gently from stoniness into something malleable, wholly pliant and submissive, as the members of the Baptist congregation softly joined the Voodoo plaint and the curtain descended.

I went away asking myself questions. For if the performance could leave one aglow, what dismaying event would come next, as one stepped into the street? Where does this fit? What does it apply to, as you elbow your way towards home? True: if you are weary enough from the intense exercising of your "motor imagery," with the soarings, brandishings, and interweavings in which you have "empathetically" participated, you may be rewarded by hearing the subway wheels grind out pure notes, in voices almost angelic. But that is a mere waywardness, making the city acceptable by a subterfuge. One is not quite at rest with his art unless he can feel it related to his environmental issues acquiescently, and not by some mere "elsewhere" quality relevant to our present life only in the sense that any evocation of faraway things, in time or space, is somewhat of a corrective to too gloomy a view of the present.

I had seen a cartoon by George Grosz. It was a picture of a New York street, with a clutter of shop signs extending over the pavement. As one looked along the street one saw them chaotically beckoning, each partially hidden by another, straining to get clear of the rest, vaguely and impersonally recommending something to whoever might pass. They were bunched together in a kind of frozen scramble —and they seemed to me the very opposite of this "folk drama" which had somehow got to Broadway, there to run for a month or two.

The situation seemed, roughly, this: I had been witnessing a work which revealed at times a remarkably complete kind of biological adaptation (for I hold sound art to be precisely

365

that). Here were ways of shuttling indeterminately between bodily processes and their "spiritual equivalents" which could repeatedly provoke, under new guise, "internal-external correspondences" as correct as may be felt, say, in the Processional and Recessional of the orthodox service. Here was an emotional organization maintained by the suggestiveness of pronounced muscular and neural functionings. A "communion" took place, in front of us, by reason of an exhibitionism so genuinely felt as to eliminate the professional aspects of performance. This was vocation, not as a job, but as a calling—and I can imagine no more thorough integration than that of suddenly feeling "called" to do what one is in the act of doing. On the other hand, was it not biological fitness for an environment which had passed? It was a survival, existing vestigially from an era to which it had been accurately adapted—and it in no way seemed to "equip" one in the subtleties of the commercial ethic which had meanwhile slowly risen and spread itself throughout our thinking. Here was a type of organization which, when it flashed across to us, was far removed indeed from the kinds of knowledge that generally go with political organization or sales organization, the coöperative stressings which seem more apropos to our environment, as the struggle for life has changed into a struggle for livelihood. I do not mean that this vestigial insight absolutely unfits one for the commercial-competitive forms of understanding and exertion. I mean simply that a race gifted with such cultural emphasis is at a disadvantage when forced to fit this wholesome pattern to an environment peopled by a race whose imagery, training, and form of ambition are more accurately set for the acquiring of "success" by the new rules.

Where, then, do we find ourselves? A people have developed, and carried down from an agrarian past, an aesthetic understanding which is complex, subtle, and gratifying, this emphasis tending naturally to promote concepts of the "good life" which turn attention and effort into channels to which the demands of commercial and financial conquest are almost wholly irrelevant. Then they are "cursed by a gift, handicapped by an endowment," checked in the competitive struggle by a deeply imaginative pattern whose very fullness and satisfactoriness endangers its adepts under the shifting of the "environmental rules." So this mode of adaptation, inspiriting as it is, may be doomed to extinction, undermined by irrelevance. Already the "advance guard" of Negroes are teaching their suffering people to "organize" in ways more suited to these nasty times—and I am sure there is much in *Run, Little Chillun!* which they must consider with distrust, attempting to stamp it out of their people: it survives there, in its purity, only by reason of the poet's conscientiousness, which keeps him close to the roots of his folk-music. If they must "learn," they will learn, burying even these profound kinds of satisfaction thoroughly, until they have fitted themselves for forms of scheming more serviceable to our era, focussing their imagery accurately within the narrower range of purposes bounded on the right by anti-Marxian business and on the left by Marxian anti-business.

In the meantime, the Caucasians who have made the new rules find themselves with problems of their own. The thorough grasp of the commercial ethic, the complete specialization in ways of feeling, thinking, striving, and repressing which would best equip one to meet competitive demands of this sort, are found to have pledged them to ambitions which often make for emptiness as regards basic cultural or religious gratifications, and for a compensatory secular expansiveness which often involves them in deadly quarrels with one another. Thus, the White ethic seems also endangered, as equipping the individual by imaginative devices which menace both himself and his group.

I guess it is a sorry time. One hates to think that such insight as is evident in *Run, Little Chillun!* must be abandoned, as "unequal" to the tincans of the glorious present. Yes, we may confidently expect these Negroes, if they are plagued consistently enough, to cast aside their endowment from a directer past, developing instead a dry hysteria, a steely counter-running-amok, to match the hysterical running-amok of their starved and desolate competitors. It will be difficult to abandon ways so accurately attuned to the organism, so close to the orthodoxies of the body, but punishment enough will finally make them grim, and competent in grimness—be sure of it. Meanwhile, we have in *Run, Little Chillun!* a sample of the values they will lose—and perhaps we may even some day hope, should there be any of us left, to regain a skill in processes analogous to these. Perhaps after we have "gone all the way round the circle." And perhaps should there be any of us left, and with spirit enough to care whether we regained anything, we may console ourselves with the thought that in a repossession we shall be more soundly entrenched. We shall then possess not "vestigially," not with the instability of a mere "survival," but with the documentary warnings that come precisely of our having gone round the circle, the critical equipment accumulated from a rich store of error, so that we may be not merely "primitive," but "astutely" or "cunningly" so—whereat we might perceive a way of cultural (religious, aesthetic) emphasis which no parched secular ambitions could ever again tempt us to abandon.

ON MUSICALITY IN VERSE

HAVING had occasion to linger over the work of Cole-ridge,[1] I came upon this problem: There were many passages that seemed to have a marked consistency of texture; yet this effect was not got by some obvious identity of sound, as in alliteration. For instance, the sequence of words, "bathed by the mist," seemed to justify a bracketing together, as a kind of unified event, for other than purely grammatical reasons. They seemed to have an underlying consistency that gave them an appeal as musicality. The following observations are offered to the Guild, for what they may be worth, as an explanation of such effects.

Let us ground our speculations upon thoroughly orthodox phonetics. If you place the lips in the position to make the sound m, from this same position you can make the sounds b and p. Hence, when looking for a basis of musicality in verse, we may treat b and p as close phonetic relatives of m. The three are all in the same family: they are "cognates."

Now, if we take into account this close phonetic relationship between b and m as phonetic cognates, we find that "b— b— the m—" is a *concealed* alliteration. "B— b— the b—" would be blunt, and even relatively tiresome. But in deflecting the third member from a b to an m, the poet retains the same phonetic theme, while giving us a variation upon this theme. And were "mist" to be replaced by some word be-

[1] This material was originally presented in a course on Coleridge, given at the University of Chicago during the summer session of 1938.

369

ginning with a phonetically disrelated sound, such as *w, z,* or *k,* the particular kind of musical bracketing that the poet got here would be lost.

Another orthodox set of cognates is *n, d, t,* with *d* and *t* bearing the same relation to *n* as *b* and *p* bear to *m.* Thus, the *d* in "bathed" and the *t* in "mist" are cognates. So we find that the first and last words of the bracketed sequence both end on members of the *n* family. Or you could make the relationship still more apparent by noting that *d* is but a voiced *t,* and *t* an unvoiced *d.*

The corresponding aspirate of *t* is *th* as in "tooth." The corresponding aspirate of *d* is *th* as in "this." Accordingly, the *th* of "bathed" and "the" may be considered as variations upon the sound *d.*

In sum: *n* moves into *d* and *t;* and *d* and *t* move respectively into voiced and unvoiced *th.* The whole design would be

$$n \begin{cases} \text{—d———th (voiced, or hard)} \\ \text{—t———th (unvoiced, or soft).} \end{cases}$$

Similarly, the *m* family could be designed as

$$m \begin{cases} \text{—b———v} \\ \text{—p———f.} \end{cases}$$

If, now, with these designs in mind, we inspect the underlying consonantal structure of "bathed by the mist," we find that it is composed of two concealed alliterations: one, "b— b— — m—"; the other, "—thd — th— —t." [2] And I would suggest that the quality of musicality is got here by this use of cognate sounds.

[2] We could differentiate the second kind by some such word as "colliteration." Thus, the bracketing, "soft and silent spot," could be said to alliterate *s* and colliterate *t* (with *t* extended into *nt* in "silent" and into *nd* in "and").

Perhaps, in the line, "Fainting beneath the burthen of their babes," there is an overstressing of the *b*'s, though the wide range of shifting among the *n* cognates helps greatly to redeem this effect, as you get *n, t,* both voiced and unvoiced *th,* and the *n* nasalized: *ng.* Except for the one *r,* this line contains, as regards consonantal structure, solely cognates of *m* and *n.* (For though the distance from *m* to *f* is great, the distance from *b* to *f* is much closer, since *p* is *b* unvoiced, and *p* leads directly into *f.* Hence, the *f* in "fainting" is a tenuous variant of the *b* theme.)

The notion of concealed alliteration by cognates seems obvious enough to require no further treatment or illustrations. However, before dropping this aspect of the subject, we might list other phonetic cognates by which the effect could be got. *J* is cognate with *ch* (as voiced and unvoiced members of the same family). Hard *g* is cognate with *k.* And *z* is cognate with *s,* from which we could move to a corresponding aspirate pair, *zh* (as in "seizure") and *sh.*

We may next note an acrostic structure for getting consistency with variation. In "tyrannous and strong," for instance, the consonant structure of the third word is but the rearrangement of the consonant structure in the first: *t-r-n-s* is reordered as *s-t-r-ng.* In the line previously quoted, "beneath the burthen" has a similar scrambling: *b-n-th*(unvoiced), *b-th*(voiced)-*n.* Perhaps the most beautiful example of the consonantal acrostic in Coleridge is the line from "Kubla Khan": "A damsel with a dulcimer," where you match *d-m-z-l* with *d-l-s-m*-plus *r.*

This acrostic strategy for knitting words together musically is often got by less "pure" scrambling of the consonants. The effect is got by a sound structure that we might name by a borrowing from the terminology of rhetoric: chiasmus, i. e., "crossing." Chiasmus, as a form in rhetoric, is much more often found in Latin than in English, owing to the greater liberty of word order permissible to Latin. It designates an a-b-b-a arrangement, as were we to match adjective-noun with noun-adjective, for instance: "nonpolitical bodies and the body politic." This reversal, however, is quite common in music (where the artist quite regularly varies the sequence of notes in his theme by repeating it upside down or backwards)—and the *musicality* of verse is our subject.

The most effective example of tonal chiasmus I have found happens to be a reversal of vowels rather than consonants: "Dupes of a deep delusion," which is *"oo of an ee ee oo."* In the consonantal usage, the chiasmus is usually to be discovered by using the theory of cognates. Thus, in "beneath the ruined tower," the last two words are chiastic in their consonantal reversal, *r—nd t—r* (with *t* as a variant of *nd*). We may thus see why "The ship drove fast" seems so "right" in sound. The surrounding structural frame of "drove" (*d—v*) is reversed in "fast" (*f—t*), with the variation of a shift from the voiced *d* and *v* to the corresponding unvoiced *t* and *f*.

Since we are on the subject of musicality, could we not legitimately borrow another cue from music? I refer to the musical devices known as "augmentation" and "diminution." Thus, if a theme has been established in quarter notes, the composer may treat it by augmentation in repeating it in half notes. And diminution is the reverse of this process. In poetry, then, you could get the effect of augmentation by first giving two consonants in juxtaposition and then repeating them in the same order but separated by the length of a vowel. Thus in

> She sent the gentle sleep from Heaven,
> That slid into my soul,

you find the *sl* progression in "sleep," "slid," and "soul," but it is varied in its third appearance by augmentation: *sl, sl, s—l.* (One should also note the many repetitions and variations of sound in "she sent the gentle sleep.")

As an instance of the contrary process, diminution, we have

> But silently, by slow degrees,

where the temporal space between the *s* and *l* in "silently" is collapsed in "slow": *s—l, sl.* (Also involved here are an alliterated *b* and colliterated *s.*)

To sum up: we have the repetition of a sound in cognate variation, acrostic scrambling, chiasmus, augmentation, and diminution.[3] If one now applies this whole set of coördinates, one may note the presence of one or several, in different combinations. To select a few examples at random, for trial analysis:

"In Xanadu did Kubla Khan" is found, by reason of the cognate relationship between *n* and *d,* to be much more closely knit, on the phonetic basis, than would otherwise be supposed. One might make this apparent by imagining himself pronouncing the line with a head cold, thus: "Id Xadadu did Kubla Khad." "Drunken triumph" would be a modified

---

[3] A major factor that has kept a consideration of musical reversion, augmentation, and diminution out of our standard prosodies may be this: that the prosodies have been disposed to confine themselves within the grooves set by Greek-Roman models, and these three devices for melodic development were not so methodologically exploited in Greek and Roman music as in Western music from Bach to Schoenberg. But I do not know enough about early theories of music to be sure that this explanation is correct.

alliteration, with *dr* (voiced) varied as *tr* (unvoiced). "So fierce a foe to frenzy" contains, besides the obvious alliteration, a diminution of the distance between *f—r* in "fierce" and *fr* in "frenzy." "Beloved from pole to pole" contains a cognate augmentation (that is: voiced *b—l* becomes unvoiced *p—l*, and the temporal distance in pronouncing the *o* of "pole" is greater than that in pronouncing the *e* of "beloved").

"Terms for fratricide" contains chiasmus and diminution: *t—r, f—r, fr, tr.* "The sails at noon left off their tune" contains a modified repetition of *ft* (in "left" and "off their"), while "noon" and "tune" are not merely internal rhymes, but are constructed of cognates, *n* and *t.* In "dote with a mad idolatry," the *d—t* of "dote" becomes augmented by a two-syllable interval in "idolatry." "Midway on the mount" gives us *"mount"* as cognate variant of *"mid."* In "only that film, which fluttered," you get a diminution from *f—l* to *fl.* In "the minstrelsy that solitude loves best," we find chiasmus with augmentation, as per the *ls* of "minstrelsy" and the *s—l* of "solitude."

There is quite a complexity in "steamed up from Cairo's swamps of pestilence," where the *s—m* of "steamed" is repeated in *"swamps,"* while the *ps* of "swamps" is in turn augmented in *"pestilence."* In "green light that lingers," the *g-r-n-l* of "green light" is acrostically reordered as *l-ng-r* in "lingers." In "the spirit and the power," you get the temporal distance between the *p* and *r* in "spirit" augmented in "power." "Luminous mist" gives us *m-n-s, m-s-t* (cognate of *n*). "Sleep, the wide blessing" contains *"sl—p the wide bl—s,"* which is to say (recalling that *b* and *p* are cognates): 1,2,3 = 3,2,1.

374

Coleridge also occasionally used the *ablaut* form (the Hopkins "heaven-haven" kind of punning got by the changing of vowels within a constant consonantal frame) as per his "loud lewd Mirth." And very frequently he obtained modified consistency by repeating one consonant while varying its partner with a noncognate variant. Thus: "*gl*immers with *gr*een light"; "*fl*uent *phr*asemen"; "in *gr*een and sunny *gl*ade." "*Bl*ooms most *pr*ofusely" carries this process farther afield, in that the initial alliteration is by cognates, the voiced and unvoiced mutes. An exceptionally complex line of this sort is "blue, glossy green, and velvet black," where you have *bl, gl, gr, v—l, v—t, bl*. Here the second and third are paired, with the first consonant of this pair alliterated and the second noncognately varied—while the *l* of "glossy" appears as a correspondingly placed member in three of the other four pairs: *bl, v—l, v—t, bl*. The *bl* design is augmented, by cognate, in *v—l*. And the design of "*glossy green*" is augmentatively matched by the design of "*velvet*," one member being an alliteration and the second a noncognate variant. It may be cumbersome to state these manifold interrelationships analytically, but the spontaneous effect can be appreciated, and the interwovenness glimpsed, by anyone who reads the line aloud without concern with the pattern as here laboriously broken down for the purposes of anatomic criticism.

People to whom I have suggested the use of these coördinates (obviously they could be applied to other poets) usually ask me whether I think that Coleridge employed them consciously. I doubt whether it makes much difference. For instance, one may sense the well-knittedness of a popular cliché like "team mate" without explicitly noting that its structural solidity is due, in large measure at least, to the chiastic progression $t—m = m—t$. There is an indeterminate realm between the conscious and the unconscious where one is "aware" in the sense that he recognizes a special kind of event to be going on, and yet is not "aware" in the sense that he could offer you an analytic description and classification of this event. The first kind of awareness we might call a consciousness of method, the second a consciousness of methodology. And I presume that we should not attribute the second kind to an artist unless explicit statements by the artist provide us with an authorization. Furthermore, even where such explicit statements are available, we need not describe the awareness as wholly of the methodological sort. Very often in writing, for instance, one is conscious of using a tactic that seems to him like a tactic he had used before (that is, he feels that both instances could be classifiable together on the basis of a method in common). Yet he may sense this kinship quite accurately without necessarily finding for it a corresponding analytic or methodological formulation.

And even if he does arrive at an explicit formulation of his tactic, the fact remains that he developed the tactic and used it with awareness long before this explicit stage was reached (a stage, incidentally, that either may lead him into a more "efficient" exploitation of the method, so that his manner threatens to degenerate into a mannerism, or may start him on the way towards totally new methodical developments: from method, to methodology, to post-methodological method).

In Coleridge's case, we do have evidence that he was "aware" of his consonantal practices at least to this extent: he was "consonant-conscious." Thus, in *Table Talk:*

Brute animals have the vowel sounds; man only can utter consonants. It is natural, therefore, that the consonants should be marked first, as being the framework of the word; and no doubt a very simple living language might be written quite intelligibly to the natives without any vowel sounds marked at all. The words would be traditionally and conventionally recognized, as in short-hand; thus: *Gd crtd th hvn nd th rth.*

In the case of a passage like "my bright and beauteous bride," I doubt whether any poet or reader is sufficiently innocent of methodological awareness to miss the *b—t, b—t, b—d* structure of tonality here. As for the chiastic arrangements, the closest I can come to finding some explicit recognition of its operation is in his sensitivity to reversal of direction in general, as with the turn from "The Sun came up upon the left" to "The Sun now rose upon the right" (the reversal of direction following the crime). "Asra," his cipher for Sarah Hutchinson, was built acrostically. In "flowers are lovely, love is flowerlike," the grammatical chiasmus is obviously pointed, while the attendant "fl l-vl, l-v fl-l" structure of *"flowers lovely, love flowerlike"* is almost as obtrusive to the ear as the grammatical reversal is to the thought. And we may glimpse methodical concern behind the title "To the Autumnal Moon," which is more of an event musically than "To the Autumn Moon" would have been, since the use of the adjective form gives us an augmentation, from *mn* to *m—n*. (In effect, he explicitly pronounces "moon" once, but implicitly or punningly pronounces it twice.)

In all of the examples and speculations I have offered, I have made no attempt to establish any correlation between musicality and content. The extra burdens I should take on, if I attempted to deal with this controversial realm, would be enormous. Lines like "Black hell laughs horrible—to hear the scoff," and "Where the old Hag, unconquerable, huge" seem to profit expressionistically by their reliance upon gutturals. But I have here been offering coördinates for the analysis of musicality pure and simple, without concern for the possible expressionistic relation between certain types of tonal gesturing and certain types of attitude.

But though I shall fight shy of expressionistic correlations for the present, before closing I would like to append some observations bearing upon the call of the owl as Coleridge finally decided to form it in "Christabel": "Tu—whit!—Tu—whoo!"

In "Frost at Midnight," the "owlet's cry" is mentioned, and though the sound is not explicitly given, may we not discern it there, implicitly, two lines below, as the poet, after mentioning its cry, announces that he has been left to "that solitude, which suits abstruser musings"? The sound also appears in "Fears in Solitude," where the reference is to the "owlet Atheism, Sailing on obscene wings athwart the noon." For *w* is but *oo* pronounced quickly—and the line might be transcribed phonetically: "oo-ings athoo-art the noon." Incidentally, as this passage proceeds, we may get a glimpse into a possible translation of the nonsense syllables in "Christabel." I refer to the lines in "Fears in Solitude," where the owl's cry is given as an explicit question containing the sounds of both "whoo" and "it":

> And hooting at the glorious sun in Heaven,
> Cries out, "Where is it?"

GEORGE HERBERT MEAD

THE publishers of these posthumous documents print Whitehead's endorsement as follows: "I regard the publication of the volumes containing the late Professor George Herbert Mead's researches as of the highest importance for philosophy. I entirely agree with Professor John Dewey's estimate, 'A seminal mind of the very first order.' " The editors rank Mead, in the pragmatist movement, "as a thinker of the magnitude of Peirce, James and Dewey." And though the reader will probably feel that a philosophy is here mulled over, rather than formed, I cannot see why he should want to disagree with the above testimonials. Anyone who would cherish with gratitude what of great value may have been piled up in this country, must study these books (the journalistic remaining, as always, for those who prefer the like-water-off-a-duck's-back mode of reading, and will not work over the printed page except when doing puzzles, rebuses and cryptograms).

In search of a text, as a handy way of getting at the gist of these 1,700 or so pages, I should select from the good book, under "Voice—middle":

> Middle voice (*Gram.*), that form of the verb by which its subject is represented as both the agent, or doer, and the object of the action, that is, as performing some act to or for his advantage.

Mead's philosophy of the act, in other words, takes its start in the idealist's concern with the identity of subject and object. The concept of the Self is pivotal, the very word "Self" suggesting the reflexive form, a subject that is its own object. The strategy of romantic philosophy (which Mead likens to the beginnings of self-consciousness at adolescence) was to identify the individual Self metaphysically with an Absolute Self, thereby making the reflexive act the very essence of the universe, a state of affairs that is open to lewd caricature. But Mead, turning from a metaphysical emphasis to a sociological one, substitutes for the notion of an Absolute Self the notion of mind as a social product, stressing the sociality of action

379

and reflection, and viewing thought as the internalization of objective relationships.

Mead calls his social psychology behavioristic, while distinguishing clearly between his brand of behaviorism and that of Watson. The individual's responses are matured by such processes of complication and revision as arise from coöperative and communicative factors. The communicative, in turn, is formed by language, out of which arises the "universe of discourse," and rational self-consciousness is framed with reference to this universe of discourse.

We have been hearing much of "democracy" and much of "dialectics"—and surely Mead's approach helps us to understand the integral relationship between these concepts. For dialectics deals with the converse, the conversational, while democracy is the ideal of expression in the market place, the dramatics of the forum. The truth of the debate arises from the combat of the debaters, which would transform the competitive into the coöperative (somewhat as competitors in a game "coöperate" to make it a good game).

So Mead would envisage the act of reflection as the holding of conversation with oneself—of seeking to contain within oneself, dialectically, the entire drama—of asserting in the form of an incipient act, which is delayed, to be corrected from the standpoint of the "generalized other" ("the attitude of the generalized other is the attitude of the whole community")—and of thus waging this internal dialogue back and forth, in search of truth matured by the checking of an imaginary opponent. It is by this ability (implemented by the character of language) to put oneself in the rôle of the other, that human consciousness is made identical with self-consciousness, that the subject can see itself as object (an "I" beholding its "me"), and that the subject can mature by encompassing the maximum complexity of rôles.

The metaphor of the conversation (uniting "democratic" and "dialectical" by the *forensic* element common to both) is systematically carried throughout Mead's view of human relations. "The parry is an interpretation of the thrust," as one even "converses" with objects, coöperating with them to his benefit only in so far as he allows them to have their say, takes their rôle by telling himself what their modes of assertion are, and corrects his own assertions on the basis of their claims. To "silence" them by the use of one's dictatorial opportunities is to deny oneself the opportunity to gauge their resistances correctly, an imposing of the quietus that would take its vengeance upon him by restricting his available knowledge of reality. Or again, when discussing two phases of universal societies (the religious, which are treated as extensions of neighborliness, and the economic, which are treated in the spirit of Adam Smith's apologetics, as the exchange of surpluses to the mutual advantage of the exchangers), he writes: "One cannot complete the process of bringing goods into a market except by developing means of communication. The language in which that is expressed is the language of money"—where the philosopher presumably so carries out his conversational metaphor as to say, without irony, that "money talks."

The general tenor of Mead's social psychology is in keeping with the promissory mood that went with the happier days of progressive evolution. Here man the problem-solver looks with Whitman-esque delight upon the state of affairs wherein each solution is the basis of a new problem. Mead considers the possibility that, in seeking to encompass the total conversation, one might make of oneself an internal wrangle, with more of heckling than discussion (particularly where he would identify himself with a society in which subgroups are at odds)—but characteristically, he treats this as a complicating factor, as something to look out for and try to guard against, rather than as a basic element of discord in his picture.

The book covers a vast range of material. *Mind, Self and Society* is the volume in which Mead's sociological pattern is developed. *The Philosophy of the Act* deals with his devices for transferring his concepts of sociality and perspective into cosmological interpretations, wherein he uses the physicist's theories of relativity to his purposes. And *Movements of Thought in the Nineteenth Century* is a highly serviceable historical treatment of trends since the Renaissance, mainly centered upon matters of science and revolution. It is a great loss to the quality of discussion in America that the volumes were not publicly available during the period of upheaval and recasting that went with our attempts to refurbish our individualism for collective necessities after 1929. One might conceivably sometimes want to put pluses where Mead put minuses, and vice versa, particularly where Mead considers social developments, in promissory fashion, as a straight line towards a kind of ideal League of Nations. Again and again, one misses Veblen. But particularly in his remarks on attitudes as incipient acts, on modes of identification, on personality and abstraction, on the relations between the biological and the social,

381

and on thought as gesture, his writings seem to map out the field of discussion for forthcoming years.

Unfortunately, the piety of Mead's disciples has worked against him somewhat, as they sought to preserve for us his every word rather than to seek condensation and saliency. For there is another sense in which these books hinge about the metaphor of the conversation. They are composed mainly of transcripts from classroom discussion, so that much is repeated, and is said loosely. As a result, there are many paragraphs, but no sentences.

INTELLIGENCE AS A GOOD

PHILOSOPHERS, after long telling us what the universe is and commiserating with the blunt majority of mankind too brutelike for such refined insight, next began to question their own possibilities of knowledge. The focus shifted from "What is the universe?" to "How can we know what the universe is?" Each new discovery of science put such knowledge farther from us. The world's most thoroughgoing body of information threatened to block out that cosmological vision which seemed sharpest when the data were sparest—until now, in pragmatism, a third stage is reached. The pragmatist says simply: "The universe is." And, the universe being, it does—so the pragmatist will situate his knowledge, not in *what* the universe is, but in *how* it works. He will seek to understand operations, to find in what order things generally precede and follow one another. He will also consider himself as involved in the process, will recognize that one discovers "reality" in accordance with one's terminology, that a shift in the vocabulary of approach will entail new classifications for the same events. He will renounce what Professor Dewey aptly calls the "spectator theory of knowledge," the notion that the universe is something like an insect under glass in a museum, and that to know it we must merely go and look at it. Knowledge he will see as arising from an interaction between an organism and its environment. Knowledge is not knowledge of what things are, but a knowledge of when and how they happen.

APPENDIX

In the present volume (*The Quest for Certainty*), Professor Dewey has traced this course of thought with great clarity and critical keenness. He has pictured mankind, in its quest for certainty, turning to some rigid metaphysical or theological structure as compensation for the contingencies of actual life. Man fortified himself against the irregularities of life by imagining the perfect regularity of heaven. The consistency, justice, dependability which he could not feel assured of in his intercourse with nature, he relegated to some supernatural realm of "antecedent Being," where it lies intact, an absolute good, truth and beauty. These absolutes are "reality," and they are but obscured by "appearances." The dialectic juggling of these concepts, the vast intellectual legerdemain by which "reality" is first obscured by "appearances" and then traced back through "appearances" to "reality," the strenuous effort required to show how a thing both is and is not, has given rise to the grandiose structure of metaphysics, an imposing monument, but one regrettably rotten at the base and kept standing only by hasty replacements which soon crumbled in turn.

I fear that metaphysics, gentlemen, is a living lie. What does the metaphysician do? He begins, like any artist, with himself and his corresponding set of values. Then he figures out that the world *ought to be* such and such if these values are to be imbued with universal validity. So much has been done under cover. He next comes forward with the assertion that not until now is his process of investigation to begin. Under our very eyes he examines the nature of the universe; he finds the universe to be such and such; and then he says triumphantly, since we have found the universe to be such and such, it follows irrefutably that these values which I am about to sell you have universal validity. Having thought from Z to A, he poses as thinking from A to Z.

Now, Professor Dewey situates the fallacy of the metaphysician's A in the doctrine of "antecedent Being," the notion that there is a fixed reality to be known as it really is, that there is an equation between the thing to be known and the thing as we know it. He holds that we do not perceive in this sense, but translate. An object is perceived as a food is taken into the stomach; it is acted upon in accordance with the capacities and requirements of the equipment receiving it. Further, what would be the gain in knowing what reality *is?* Our whole interest would reside in how to *use* such knowledge—and the progress of science and invention is evidence that we have already gone far in the *use* of reality, while metaphysicians still lag behind, wrangling over their first principles. While they were asking whether or not we could possibly know, the pragmatism of science was steadily increasing its knowledge. And if science, in the newest paradoxes of physics, now reaches what it considers an impasse, so that the old cry of "Can we know?" begins to arise in these new quarters, this is only because science has become metaphysically speculative, and had begun attempting with its instruments to discover what the universe is instead of how it works. But whatever the cosmological difficulties of science, it continues to amass pragmatic certainties. It can, for instance, *use* electrons without even being sure that they exist.

The Quest for Certainty is an ideology of science. Professor Dewey, looking over the history of the progress of physical science, discovers that its knowledge has been the knowledge of processes. He sees that, while man tended to retreat from the world of contingencies, compensatorily building a structure of immutable absolutes in the mind, and thus combating the uncertainty of life by getting at least the *feel* of certitude (whistling to keep up his courage), science went ahead with its study of processes and succeeded in greatly increasing the actual certitude of living. One does not depend upon a chance stroke of lightning for his fire, upon the chance dropping of a seed for his crops. Nonmetaphysical certainty, pragmatic knowledge, knowledge of the processes by which fires are lighted and seeds grow, has increased the certainty of living. Scientific knowledge is of this sort. The theological or metaphysical system gets certainty by affirming dogmatically how things *are,* how they *must be;* it erects a set of vested interests, which cannot be questioned without imperiling its precious certainty; it cancels by decree the actual fluctuations in human livelihood. So here, in the doctrines of antecedent Being, were certainties which left the world uncertain. Whereas pragmatic knowledge is erected out of doubt, questioning, experimentation. It has no vested interests; to have one of its beliefs undermined is a gain, an aid in the better understanding of processes. It defines as truth *what works.* Possessing no certainties in itself, it has undeniably increased the certainties of living.

Having got so far, Professor Dewey would now argue by analogy. Since the scientific (pragmatic, experimental, instrumental) method has produced such good results despite the many cases of misuse for private ends, he would have us apply this same method to the criticism of values. Values, too, should be grounded, not upon the authority of antecedent Being, but in accordance with their workings. We should not necessarily turn against traditional values because they have been derived from the past. Their survival may in many cases be some proof of their adequacy. But they can be tinkered with, improved like any other process, and these improvements are made by looking to their possibilities. Values, in other words, are to be tested by experiment, experiment either in actuality or in thought (since thought is a kind of deferred, or symbolic, action). The past of a value is used as the past of a laboratory experiment—it is neither glorified nor condemned, but interpreted in accordance with the problem at hand.

Approached in this way, the argument for an analogous application of experiment to the study of values (the ultimate aim of all philosophy) seems quite cogent. But should we situate the success of science in its perfection of measurement, it is harder to see that the application of its method to a criticism of values is analogous. Science owes much to experimentation, to pragmatic knowing, but this method has been reinforced by an instrument equally important —mathematics, the instrument of quantification, of measurement. This instrument enables us to test an operation by means which minimize the opportunities for differences of opinion. When people can look at the scales and agree that they say twenty, or look at the thermometer and agree that it says forty, the experiment is proved. It is not always quite so simple as that; the process of proof itself is often brought into question. But in contrast with an argument about the workings of a value, it is exactly as simple as that.

How do we test the success of a value? Values undeniably work— but they don't necessarily succeed or fail. We have monogamy, bigamy, polyandry, polygyny, and a dozen other systems of marriage. They have all *worked,* since people seem to have lived and sung under each of them. Taboo against murder works, since societies flourish where this taboo is prevalent; a systematic killing of aging parents also works. The latter custom is more necessary where food is scarce and existence is hard; perhaps to that extent it is even a pragmatic value. Values are all somewhat pragmatic, since they have arisen to serve human needs, though they undeniably may become a menace when they survive the situation for which they were invented, and the knowledge of the processes by which they arose can do much to break the force of their authority in the minds of those who still hold them. The understanding of processes can clearly contribute greatly to the elimination of such outgrown values.

But the matter is different with the erection of new values by the experimental method. The experimental method would derive its values, not by authority, not by any theory of antecedent absolute good, but by test. It seems, however, that when carried to its logical conclusion, this method of evaluating values presents difficulties of its own. When judging the effectiveness of a value, for instance, we have to utilize some other value to appraise it. Though we may know the processes whereby people are made fat, lean or middling, we still have to decide whether we *ought* to make them fat, lean or middling; for there is no judgment inherent in a process. Suppose that we decide to make them lean in order that they may run faster. Then we have founded our value of leanness upon the value of speed in running, which must in turn be founded upon another value, and so on. Where then is our "key value"? By the experimental method there could obviously be no key value, in the sense of its antecedent existence, its acceptance on authority. Even a key value must be dependent upon experiment for its justification, and its worth could be tested only by the adoption of some other value by which to test it. Eddington has already discussed this circular chase in the definitions of physics, each phenomenon being defined in terms of another until you get back to the first. Thus, it should not be surprising if we found the same situation in the evaluating of values when values are treated by an analogous method.

It is interesting to see how Professor Dewey handles this difficult matter. He must necessarily avoid a key value, yet must have evaluations. How does he satisfy both needs? By his writings on the nature of intelligence, in which he praises the function of intelligence, tact, taste in the formation of our judgments. For intelligence is not a value; it is a process, a functioning. Still, it is more than a process; it is a good process. Intelligence, if I correctly interpret Professor Dewey's chapter, both *is* and *is good* (or, more accurately, both *becomes* and *becomes good*). It thus serves as substitute for the key value. For if intelligence is good, it will naturally choose good values. So, being a value in itself, it does the work of a key value in grounding a criticism, for all other values can issue from it.

I am not competent to judge whether this is a wholly justifiable step, though I do feel that it is the crux, or fulcrum, of Professor Dewey's philosophy. If Intelligence is good by definition, we need not be surprised that a system of good can be drawn from it. In the older systems there was something which, by definition both *is* and *is good,* and with so much given all the rest could be deduced, down to the divine authorization of imprisonment for failure to salute the sheriff.

Further, if the arbiter of success is Intelligence, evaluating out of itself, creating the values by which it measures its own success, is this not an intrusion upon the relativistic thinking of pragmatism? Would it not be much like "pure" Intelligence, an absolute? We have done away with the unmoved mover; but do we have in its stead the self-judging judger, the self-measuring measure, a good so good that it perceives its own goodness? Do we face a choice between the circular chase from value to value, and the treatment of Intelligence as an absolute evaluator?

Also, the goodness of the Intelligence, so far as the pragmatic evidence goes, seems much more like goodness in a technical sense, like the goodness of one's liver. Its goodness as an *ethical* good, a good for society in general, is less apparent. For though the functioning of a liver be accounted a good, the functioning of mine enemy's liver is not good for myself. The evidence shows more clearly its goodness from the standpoint of the organism than goodness for all.

The reader may or may not agree with these tentative objections, which seem to me the difficulties arising if we carry experimentalism to its farthest implications and seek to find in it a mechanism for the erection of values without relying upon the existence of a prior good. In any event, my zeal to discover the bare bones of Professor Dewey's logic has led me into a major act of unfairness. For I have failed to convey any notion of the sensitivity, learning and vitality contained in *The Quest for Certainty.* Its incidental sidelights on the history of philosophy constitute, to my mind, a constant succession of scores. The total lack of authoritarianism in his thinking is forever leading Professor Dewey into the expansive and adventurous. The book is tolerant and inquisitive. Its extension of strict dialectic by borrowings from psychology, anthropology, history, sociology, economics, fits it into a wider scheme than mere matters of dogma and makes it an important contribution to our culture. We see that pragmatism in such hands can disclose its social value without going so far into the subject of the rock that supports the rock that supports the world. And Professor Dewey's good is certainly no tax upon our good will. It is not hard for us to accept that the Intelligence both is and is good, for we act upon this assumption daily, and it brings results. These results are tested by values which just are, regardless of how they came about, or how many no longer fit, or how many should be remedied, or how many would be incapable of empirical proof. Whether or not the scientific attitude could provide the grounding for a world of values, once values are given it can certainly contribute to their better guidance. And it can always play one value against another, relying upon a kind of relative antecedent Being, since it can take values which are generally accepted as good and use them to argue for values not yet so accepted. If the world prizes justice or happiness, for example, we need not seek the justification for these values; but we can use them to prove that some practice is reprehensible because unjust, or because it leads to misery.

In this respect the pragmatist is strongest when he is more like the artist than like the metaphysician. It is not gratuitous that Professor Dewey has written so brilliantly of art, both in this present volume and in his *Experience and Nature*. The artist says, in substance: "I make this exhortation in the terms of what has already been accepted. Once these terms are accepted, I can go a little beyond them. But I shall argue only for my addition, and assume the rest. If people believe *eight,* I can recommend *nine;* I can do so by the manipulation of their *eightish* assumptions; I need not justify my *nine* by arguing for *one.*"

LIBERALISM'S FAMILY TREE

DR. DEWEY'S *Liberalism and Social Action* is divided into three chapters: on the history of liberalism, on the crisis in liberalism, and on "renascent liberalism." About the topic of liberalism, the author groups the cultural values he most admires. His book is written to show with what important and desirable traits liberalism can be identified. He goes through a cycle of virtues, such as peace, liberation, "the development of the inherent capacities of individuals made possible through liberty," tolerance, reintegration, science, rationality, education, charity, courage and hope—and he pleads that liberalism, as he conceives it, can be included in this cycle.

388

APPENDIX

As a way of beginning his series, he selects an ancestry for liberalism. He sketches its history briefly and suggests a theory of origins:

> The use of the words liberal and liberalism to denote a particular social philosophy does not appear to occur earlier than the first decade of the nineteenth century. But the thing to which the words are applied is older. It might be traced back to Greek thought; some of its ideas, especially as to the importance of the free play of intelligence, may be found notably expressed in the funeral oration attributed to Pericles. But for the present purpose it is not necessary to go back of John Locke, the philosopher of the "glorious revolution" of 1688. The outstanding point of Locke's version of liberalism is that governments are instituted to protect the rights that belong to individuals prior to political organization of social relations.

In this citation, Dr. Dewey seems to bring up the possibility that we have the choice of two different family trees in charting the history of liberal manifestations. If we mean by liberalism a "particular social philosophy," the author finds that "for the present purpose it is not necessary to go back of John Locke." But if we mean simply "the thing to which the words are applied," he finds it possible to begin the family tree with classic Greece. Indeed, since he situates such liberalism in "ideas as to the importance of the free play of intelligence," and since such ideas can obviously be found in periods antedating Greece or in cultures independent of Greece, the attempt to chart all the ancestors in this second family tree might carry us far beyond the "funeral oration attributed to Pericles."

In Dr. Dewey's first chapter he is concerned solely with the briefer, historic ancestry of liberalism. Here he shows the organic connection between liberalism and the rise of business enterprise. He recounts the negativistic, atomistic, "muckraking" elements in liberal thought, demonstrating why the liberal philosophies were much better fitted for sweeping away old resistances than for building up a new positive integration. He traces the ways in which the liberals' doctrines of individual rights were made negotiable in removing the restrictions upon profit and trade. He shows why such theories can be called liberal despite the tremendous cramping of opportunity they necessitate at present. But when admitting that liberalism, as so conceived, is now owned and managed by the reactionaries of the Liberty

389

League, he notes a "split" in liberal philosophy. This split was caused in part, he shows, by the surprising contributions which various brands of Tories made to the maturing of liberal philosophy "in alliance with evangelical piety and with romanticism," and later with the institutionalism, traditionalism and collectivism in German idealistic thought. In contrast with the older liberalism, the coöperative aspects of society were now stressed, and the demand for control through social legislation became uppermost. One may question whether this revision of liberal emphasis could properly be called liberalism at all. But it is what the author advocates as liberalism, and the names of historic phenomena are not ordained.

The important consideration from my point of view is that, precisely where this "split" occurs, we covertly shift from the short family tree to the long family tree as the basis on which liberalism (the collective, social-legislation kind) is advocated. For somewhat in line with Veblen's distinction between business and industry, we are told that the really dynamic factor in the development of modern history is not business, or capitalism, with its attendant problem of the "class struggle," but scientific method as objectified in technology. Behind this method lies the functioning of "intelligence" in general. The function of intelligence is, among other things, to integrate old material and new material (to "mediate" the change of status), and this integrative or mediating function is called upon at every period of history. Now, if "liberalism," as "intelligence," is identified with an integrative or mediating function that operates in *every* period of history, we have obviously gone from the short family tree to the long family tree, plus extensions far beyond or beneath Periclean Athens. The implied origin is not temporal, but universal, as the integrative work of intelligence goes on, *mutandis mutatis,* in all eras.

I think too that the ancestry undergoes still deeper extensions without avowal on the author's part, as his conception of scientific method becomes colored with connotations of love or charity. When one notes that a prizefighter's skillful left swing to the jaw may be good intelligent pragmatic science, one questions just how Dr. Dewey manages to introduce nonviolent, noncoercive requirements into his notions of scientific method. He *implies* a difference in kind between the use of a chemical to eliminate vermin and the use of a chemical to eliminate human rivals, but his *explication* is vague at this important juncture. Particularly in view of the fact that Dr. Dewey

390

usually celebrates scientific achievement as a "conquest," we become aware that, when applied to people, his idea of scientific method is not merely that of a *power* but adds hidden connotations of charity or solidarity usually connected with religion, ethics or poetry.

Again, when Dr. Dewey celebrates liberalism as the opportunity for the "development of the inherent capacities of individuals," we realize that there is some such adjective as "good" or "wholesome" implied before the word "capacities." If the adjective were explicitly there and if the attendant steps made necessary by its explicit presence were inserted, or if the author's merging of science as technique with science as a charitable attitude towards people were made the express subject of analysis and rationalization, Dr. Dewey's volume would be more enlightening. As it stands, it seems essentially Ciceronian. It serves primarily as a lawyer's brief, in that it persuades without exposing the crucial steps in its persuasion. Philosophic tracts, if they are of worth, seek to persuade; but the difference between them and Ciceronian exhortation, it seems to me, is that they try at the same time to expose their methods of persuasion. I question whether Dr. Dewey could be said to meet this test fairly so long as the ambiguity as regards "family trees" remains at the keystone of his treatise.

However, as Dr. Dewey warns us in his introduction, a writer cannot say everything at once. And certainly the present book becomes far less "Ciceronian" if one considers it, not in itself, but as a kind of final chapter to such fuller books as *Experience and Nature* and *The Quest for Certainty*, books that, for this reader at least, did a lot of eye-opening. Yet some of the same ambiguity seems to lie at the roots of these also. When one talks of "functions," one necessarily brings in nonhistoric assumptions of structure. The "function of intelligence" belongs to the long family tree, quite as does the "function of the heart." History may tell us how the heart beat faster on a given day. But behind the effect of that given day, there lies a property of hearts, a "heart function," that is not historical in the same sense at all. The attempt to divorce philosophy from metaphysics will always, I suspect, be merely a protective screen for the setting up of metaphysical assumptions.

MONADS—ON THE MAKE

IN a review of John Dewey's *Logic* (*New Republic*, November 23, 1938) Mr. Weiss writes:

> He grounds the acts of inquiry in the movement of the organism from a state of disequilibrium to one of recovered equilibrium with respect to an environment. But if that pulsational process did not have its roots in the nature of inorganic things as well, his basic "principle of continuity" would be violated and organisms would be made into a special kingdom within a kingdom of nature, forcing a radical break between the sciences of biology and physics.

Mr. Weiss here touches upon a basic problem of philosophic strategy, and from an angle that may help us to characterize his own book. For in *Reality,* his ingenious work on epistemology and ontology, he would confront the issue that he accuses Professor Dewey of slighting. He would move by transformations from the realm of physics to the realm of biology, and would do so without violating the *lex continui* (that is, without the intervention of a miracle, a mutation veiled in an ambiguity).

I can think of but two ways of fulfilling such conditions. You can keep the two realms together by either physicizing your biology or biologizing your physics. Mr. Weiss seems to prefer the latter. And having put a biology implicitly into his physics at the start, he has no trouble in drawing it forth explicitly at the appropriate moment. He contrives this by treating both physical and biological processes in terms of a biological metaphor: the metaphor of eating, of digestion, of assimilation. Individuals, both organic and inorganic, seek to attain self-completion by incorporating external beings.

We might add a third realm: the realm of ethics. And applying our pattern, we should then hold that the philosopher may preserve continuity of realms by ethicizing physics and biology, physicizing biology and ethics, or biologizing physics and ethics. Mr. Weiss seems to

392

remain loyal to his biological metaphor, by applying it to this third realm as well.

"To be is to be incomplete." And to be incomplete is to strive to be complete by the assimilation of all others than oneself. "The universe is one where multiple unique beings endeavor to become the Absolute in unique and opposing ways." Every being, either organic or inorganic, "at every instant is at a stage analogous to that ascribed by Leibniz to his monads, but every one endeavors to pass beyond that stage in the effort to achieve the state ascribed by Leibniz to his God."

This monadology differs significantly from Leibniz's in that there is no harmony among the monads, preëstablished by God. Perhaps we might even say that Mr. Weiss has replaced this by a kind of "preëstablished disharmony," with each individual enterprise seeking to become a universal monopoly, within a marketplace of mutual checks and balances provided by all the other individuals similarly striving, within the means or limitations peculiar to their natures.

Leibniz characterized his monads as "without windows." Their development was internal, with God accounting for the harmonic interrelationships whereby these internal developments amounted to external interaction. Mr. Weiss, considering this introduction of a common ground as a mere *deus ex machina* to save an otherwise faltering explanation, gives us instead a plurality of individual universes interacting by an overlapping of their "virtual regions." Also, in this way, he avoids the picture of the world as illusory, that arises in such philosophies as Schopenhauer's, positing a single, absolute striving of which each individual will is but a fragment. The individual's striving is real, independent, unique, in accordance with its intrinsic nature. Hence, these are monads with windows, with a view, even a point of view, looking out upon a public world, and seeking to get along in the real opportunities and resistances that the world offers.

Though Mr. Weiss would ground his structure of thinking on the law of contradiction, this does not prevent him, as he approaches ethical problems, from introducing a very cute concept, "privational possession," composed by an incongruity. One can "privationally possess" what one does not have. And, conversely: "It is perfectly possible to eat one's cake and have it too." By knowledge we attain vicarious perfection, as we may, in knowing the structure of the universe, thus vicariously or privationally possess nothing less than this universe entire. But one must *live* his knowledge in action, "until one's mind permeates one's body." Only by thus "infecting ourselves with our knowledge" can we "achieve the only possible perfection open to man."

I regret that, in thus trying to report the main features of Mr. Weiss's picture, I have been unable to exhibit the many subtle and suggestive details encountered en route. I refer to such matters as his advance from quest to question; his treatment of the circularity in the relation between epistemology and ontology; his systematic placing of the arts and sciences with relation to his total scheme; and his crucial chapter on "Mellontological Causation." But the book is hard going. Mr. Weiss spins a very fine web of internally adjusted descriptions, and the reader must work very hard if he would be caught in this web—otherwise, he will rip the fabric with inattention and fall through, like a clumsy wasp that blundered into a trap laid for gnats.

QUANTITY AND QUALITY

STANDARD procedure: You find a sentence, expand the sentence into a paragraph, the paragraph into a chapter, and the chapter into a book. You start by stating what you're going to prove, you proceed, "now I'm proving it," and for a grand finale you summarize.

To turn from such mighty projects in deforestation to Otto Neurath's *Modern Man in the Making* is to realize how much filibustering takes place, where we were never taught to look for filibustering. As against a species of historiography that resembles the worst kind of naturalistic novel (wherein two hundred thousand details are twice as great as one hundred thousand) you have here an essay in *reduction,* and a splendid one.

The contemporary cult of "the facts" must gain strength in part because, by this cult, systematic plagiarism has been made the norm. "The facts" are a species of quotation which one can appropriate without the quotation marks. They are collections by Bartlett, signed as though Bartlett had made them up himself. "The facts" are, to be

394

sure, the basis of Neurath's book—but he establishes his right to them by a fresh act.

It is his intention to locate the modern world for us by comparing and contrasting quantitative aspects of today with quantitative aspects of the past, sometimes with intermediate points showing the rate at which these quantitative changes occurred. And he has sought to translate his exposition into the idiom of visualization, his so-called "isotypes," a picturizing method that is hardly new with him, but is employed so deftly and methodically as to give one always the feeling of newness, both in the isotypes themselves and in the succinct kind of text that, in being designed to accompany them, became imbued with the same reductive genius.

The reduction to quantities necessarily eliminates important qualitative ingredients. Neurath has an isotype, for instance, visualizing the changed proportions of work, leisure and sleep in a day "formerly" and "now." The sleep quantity remains the same; the leisure quantity has greatly increased and the work quantity greatly decreased. But we are left with the important possibility that many ingredients in the quality of work in the past have been shifted to the quality of leisure now. And though the quantity of sleep is the same for both periods, anyone who has slept (a) by a traffic-laden street after a day at the office and (b) in a mountain cabin after a day of physical exercise, knows that there may be important differences in the quality of sleep.

The author, fully aware of this problem, attempts by a method of "silhouettes" so to combine quantities as to give us an inkling of quality. We are shown, for instance, the silhouette of a town in the Middle Ages and in modern times. In each we see a church surrounded by secular buildings. In the Middle Ages, the church overtops a little cluster of dwellings, in about the proportion of a hen to her chicks. In his visualization of modern times, we see the same church, now surrounded by skyscrapers, in about the proportion of the hen to a batch of electric refrigerators. And the same qualitative question is approached from another quantitative answer by indicating loss of religious influence thus: By coupling a rise in the suicide rate with the fact that religious authority is generally against suicide, Neurath interprets this change as a quantitative indicator of a change in the quality of religious authority.

But though the beginnings of a statistical approach to quality are made here, with great ingenuity, I question whether the problem

395

has been completely solved. Look at one of the isotypes, for instance, with its neat rows of little standardized men, all alike, and each "representing" some tens, or hundreds, or thousands of his fellows. Is there not an important omission in the very concept of representation that is embodied here? We may recall an alternative kind of representation, a culminative sort, such as we might get in the culminative quality of a great portrait painter. Or otherwise put: we might distinguish between the kind of representation that sums up an era and the kind that strikes the average of an era. As for the average-man sort, statistically disclosable by little regimented figures, often left uncompleted to indicate that they represent the portion of a quantity, I am always uneasy when noting that this "average man" marries the fraction of an average woman, together they get some fraction of a job, in time they produce the fraction of a child, and they all go riding in two wheels and the bumper of an automobile.

SEMANTICS IN DEMOTIC

IN *The Tyranny of Words,* Stuart Chase has given us a very entertaining and easily read account of a study that is still in the course of mapping out its territory, and may some day have a chair all its own in our colleges, probably called the chair of "semantics." Semantics deals with the subject of communication, meaning, the interpretation of signs.

Sometimes the students of semantics seem to be stressing the genetic, psychological or historical aspects of the question: they observe and speculate to determine how meanings arise. Anthropologists like Malinowsky throw special insight upon this aspect of the subject, as do experimental psychologists like Pavlov and Watson, Koffka and Koehler. Psychoanalysis also makes a distrusted, but probably necessary, contribution here. Sometimes the emphasis seems to be primarily upon an attempt to perfect an accurate system of signs or pointers, regardless of the ways in which our meanings, or lack of meanings, or muddled meanings, arise and operate in everyday vocabulary. The speculations of the logical positivists, stemming largely from the symbolic logic of the "Principia Mathematica," seem to stress this aspect. Sometimes semantics seems to be mainly a new weapon for the debunker who, revolting at the balderdash meted out daily in the press, pulpit, radio, political exhortation, goodwill advertising, legal and economic theory, etc., wants to find some quick and efficient way of dissolving said balderdash.

In *The Tyranny of Words*, Stuart Chase, like Thurman Arnold in *The Symbols of Government* and *The Folklore of Capitalism*, is interested primarily in this third emphasis. He is looking for a solvent, a corrosive, that will dispatch verbal obstacles with as much speed as possible. To do this, he first picks some salient moments from writers like Korzybski, Malinowsky, Ogden, Richards, and Bridgman that give one an inkling of fields one and two—and then he plunges into a varied assortment of case histories where he debunks with zest the thinking of right, center, and left.

By the use of his rough and ready instruments he does good work in making hash of the well-paying verbosities uttered by the priesthood of the right. That is all to the good. But unfortunately, the same instruments also dissolve (as Chase explains on pp. 191–3) a definition like this by Harold Laski:

> I suggest the conclusion that fascism is nothing but monopoly capitalism imposing its will on the masses which it has deliberately transformed into slaves. The ownership of the instruments of production remains in private hands.

Though conceding that this statement *seems* clear to "a reader of the *New Republic* living in New York," Chase contends that the enlightened student of semantics "is not disposed to argue with Mr. Laski, because the apparent meaning has faded into a series of semantic blanks. Laski is not necessarily wrong; he is saying nothing worth listening to. Knowledge cannot be spread, sensible action cannot be taken, on the basis of such talk."

To arrive at this conclusion, Chase suggests that many necessary ramifications and modifications are omitted from Laski's *definition*. Completely overlooking the fact that a definition is, by the necessities of the case, a *summary*, and that Laski has written a great deal giving explicit body to this summary, he finds the definition itself meaningless. Chase has warned, at many points in his book, against taking words at their face value, without reference to their place in a total context of thought and situation. Yet here he seems to be doing pre-

397

cisely what he warns against. And I do not see how any just theory of meanings could require that a writer give a summarization of his thought without omitting all the ramifications and modifications of that thought.

There must surely be something wrong with instruments of analysis that can debunk so drastically. Chase is dubious about the word "slaves," for instance, recalling that it falls in with "a stock phrase in socialist propaganda." Yet, applying the same enlightened test, we might question the word "tyranny" in Chase's own title, if we simply jumped on this *summary* of his book without reference to the material with which he gave it body. And he notes that the enlightened student of semantics "never saw an 'ism' imposing its will," thereby debunking Laski's metaphorical shortcut as though it were intended to be taken literally as a completely and explicitly filled-out statement. To show that a summary requires filling out is not per se to show that the summary is nonsense. We do not know whether the summary is nonsense until we have examined the ways in which the author himself has given it body.

The difficulties arise, I think, from the overly empirical bias which Chase adopts in his approach to the subject of meaning. Empiricism is, of course, a philosophy—one among several—but Chase begins by adopting it under the "down with philosophy" slogan. *Other* philosophies are philosophies—*his own* is just sound "fact." He proposes to try meanings by the reassuring test of seeing, touching, feeling, weighing, smelling. Hence, since many meanings are *interpretations* of *relationships* as disclosed from a certain *perspective* or *point of view*, you are going to find a lot of very necessary meanings dissolved, once you permit a man to impose a naïvely empiricist philosophy in the name of anti-philosophy.

Chase also bolsters up this approach appealingly by borrowings from Bridgman's philosophy of physical science, called "operationalism." According to this, the meaning of a concept is to be tested by some actual operation performed in a laboratory, or recorded on a meter reading. There is no point here in attempting a critique of Bridgman's theory. (The reader is referred to a very stimulating article on the subject by R. B. Lindsay in *Philosophy of Science*, October, 1937.) My present point is that, even if we granted its validity for the physical sciences (despite several centuries of fruitful scientific development done largely in violation of it), we could still legitimately demand that Chase offer explicit reasons why one may forcibly induce the migration of this perspective from the realm of physics to the realm of social relationships. The migration may be justified, but the justification is not offered. Chase, by the unconscious ruse of putting forth his philosophy in the name of anti-philosophy, spares himself the trouble; a perspective is simply made to migrate from one realm to another, with no discussion of this migratory process itself, no discussion of the metaphorical function that arises when such migration takes place.

It is my suspicion that, if you would seek an "operation" or a meter reading, or a test of seeing, feeling, tasting, when you come to the interpretation of a relationship as disclosed from a given perspective, you are going to debunk meanings with a vengeance. So thoroughly, in fact, that whenever you want to stop debunking, and would adopt a positive policy of your own, you can do so only by pulling your punch and not applying to yourself the solvent you apply to your opponents. Thus, when in a pure debunking mood, Chase dismisses "the going canons of philosophy, theology and the rest" on the ground that they deal with "ideas and purposes." He distrusts a concern with such matters as "purposes," because you can't see them, touch them, test them "operationally." But when he is in a normative, hortatory mood, he writes, "The controlling issue, the real task for statesmen, is to find the human purpose to be accomplished in a given situation." So far as I can see, you could not do this unless you offered, implicitly, a philosophy of human purpose.

So I question whether it is legitimate for a writer to save himself embarrassment by putting forward a philosophy under the name of no philosophy, a device that enables him simply to avoid the issues at every important point. I question whether a theory of meanings can be put forward simply in the reassuring name of "the facts." Rather, the student of communication must evolve an explicit critique concerned with the processes of making judgments, of putting forth structures of judgments, or rationalizing these structures (by tests of internal consistency), of showing their scope and relevancy to human situations, of verbalizing the rôle played by metaphorical migrations (transplanted perspectives) in the interpretative process. References to apples, skins, cats, caterpillars, and meter readings sound homey, and as such contribute solace by making a complex field look simple. But those who would banish philosophy from the study of meaning must simply make a show of throwing out by the front door what they covertly smuggle in again by the back door.

CORROSIVE WITHOUT CORRECTIVE

ARNOLD'S *The Folklore of Capitalism* is a continuation and amplification of his *The Symbols of Government*. Perhaps it is more profitably to be approached as a lexicon than as an argument. For it is attempting to chart some hitherto uncharted areas of speculation, particularly as to the relations between business and politics; and such attempts are necessarily more concerned with the rounding out of a point of view, suggesting a perspective by giving examples of its major aspects, than with rigorous advance from premise to conclusion. Arnold himself names this perspective "Political Dynamics," which is probably as good a trade name as any. But for purposes of general location, I think we could class it, with Mannheim's *Ideology and Utopia*, as a contribution to the *sociology of politics*.

Arnold's analysis of capitalism's dilemmas and antics seems at once *on* the track and *off* the track. And it is not easy to differentiate one phase from the other, without relying merely on appeal to prejudice. Above all, a reviewer should not allow his reservations to obscure his obligations as a mere reporter of the book's contents. For to my mind, everyone interested in the techniques of propaganda should read *The Folklore of Capitalism*, quite as he should read Jeremy Bentham and Thorstein Veblen.

Attempting to simplify a complex volume, I should reduce *The Folklore of Capitalism* to two main strands: the one that, by my notion, puts it *on* the track, and the one that puts it *off*. Both exemplify the use of planned incongruity for interpretative purposes.

By planned incongruity I mean a rational prodding or coaching of language so as to see around the corner of everyday usage. Impressed by the great development of machinery, for instance, many thinkers have sought to explain the workings of human beings after the analogy of the machine. Or others, impressed by the documents of biological evolution, have sought to explain the workings of human beings after the analogy of apes. Such modes of interpretation would be examples of planned incongruity, whereby the thinker

400

coached the migration of a perspective from its special area into a wider area. This would be a kind of metaphorical projection.

One can very easily coach words in this way, by subjecting them to a *functional* test. For instance, not many years ago, when men spoke of morals or ethics, they meant only good morals, good ethics. But suppose you apply a purely functional approach to some term like moral code. You say, "morality *is* as morality *does*," whereupon you may with propriety speak of criminal ethics, the moral code of gamblers, etc. By simply passing over the barriers of the word, as built up in the pieties of everyday usage, and rationally using it instead to name a function or process, you may coach it to migrate beyond its customary barriers, often with valuable interpretative results.

Arnold's book seems to gravitate about two such metaphorical projections. One is the mode of interpretation obtained by projecting (and then toning down) the perspective of the psychiatric institution until it covers all human relations. This leads to a picture of society as a farce, hilarious on the surface but somewhat grim in its ultimate implications. I should call this the dubious aspect of Arnold's book, though it contributes much to its value as entertainment. The dramatic and ritualistic elements he notes in the historic process are, I think, given a radically false interpretation, by reason of the quality of indictment inherent in this psychiatric perspective itself.

The *useful* projection, for interpretative purposes, is in the amply documented transformation he performs upon the word "government." In the pieties of popular usage, business and government are usually treated as *opposites*. Arnold, by subjecting the words to a functional treatment, sees beyond this piety. As you read, in particular his ironic chapters on "The Benevolence of Taxation by Private Organization" and "The Malevolence of Taxation by Government," you find accumulated a mass of clearly pointed material that is perfectly designed to dissolve the quackery of such writers as Walter Lippmann, Mark Sullivan, and Dorothy Thompson. Arnold makes it apparent that business is purely and simply a government, and a nondemocratic form of government at that, even having its own regularized modes of taxation. In fact, he clearly shows how this business government has repeatedly resorted to the *capital levy*, despite the fact that such a notion strikes horror into the hearts of our conservatives when presented in political forms.

I should also salute a chapter like "The Ritual of Corporate Reorganization," in which Arnold amasses from many contemporary sources the evidence disclosing the unreal and filmy nature of the concept of property under finance capitalism, and the ways in which this breach between legalistic ideals and practical actualities is manipulated to the advantage of insiders.

Again and again, however, the author's showmanship leads him to overstress the part played by ritual in the judicial pronouncements of our legal and economic priesthood. The picturesqueness of his farce, for instance, is greatly heightened, at the expense of interpretative accuracy, by playing down the factor of *interests* behind the continual shifting of principles and ideals. Suppose, for example, you were to give a general picture summarizing, through the course of American history, the continual shifting back and forth between state's rights and federalism. You would find the same group on one side of the issue one day and on the other side the next. Then suppose that, for purposes of farce, you simply made a composite picture of all such shifting. By simply playing up the verbal and logical contradictions, and playing down the consistent pressure of the interests behind them, you might put on a good show that entertained by making people look extremely irrational. But your result at this point would be more valuable as entertainment than as diagnosis.

When reading Arnold's composite picture of such endless shifting, and hearing him explain it by stressing it as a purely ritualistic act, you make a paradoxical discovery. You find that a man who continually refers such antics to the pressure of interests, no matter how mean these interests may be, would actually enable you to receive a much less desolating picture of human motives than the one Arnold paints. For you at least have a process essentially rational, however complicated it may become as the result of other factors. But Arnold's version of human motivation, by attributing mainly to ritual the cause of men's "inconsistent, irrational, and illogical" shifts in thinking, makes even downright hypocrisy on the part of our reactionaries seem an almost wholesome motive, by comparison.

Arnold justifies his farce on ritual in an appealing way, I must admit. He contends that history, being a dramatic process, must be approached as drama. And since ritual is an aspect of drama, we seem to get from such a view a justifiable ground for playing up the ritualistic and playing down the factor of interests in his picture of the human drama. The deception here arises, I think, from the fact that Arnold does not base his dramatic metaphor upon a preparatory analysis of drama itself. A couple of passing references to hero and villain in melodrama, with passing references to the dramatic nature of trial by combat in the law court, are the nearest he comes to explicit dramatic criticism, as a basis for the remarks about drama and ritual that flicker about the edge of his book throughout. As it is, you get here a glancing reference to art without an explicit study and philosophy of art.

The dramatist is not only a ritualist. Or rather, ritual itself is not merely a lot of passes in the air. The dramatic ritual *materializes*, and does so by reference to an audience's interests. Arnold is apparently a rationalist who has simply kicked over the traces, getting a flat irrationalist antithesis. His version of drama is simply legal principle in reverse. In going from the *ideals* of law to drama, he got farce (i. e., legal ideals turned upside down). Had he begun with drama, I think that both the uses and misuses of law could have fallen into place, with more definite relation to the rational pressure of interests.

Toward the end of the book there is a noticeable chastening, as Arnold begins to feel the necessity for a more positive statement. So, what in his earlier work he had made ludicrous as principles, and in the earlier portion of this one is taken for a ride as abstract ideals, is subsequently restored to good favor, by an apparently unconscious subterfuge, in the name of propositions and a philosophy. Thus, to keep his universal corrosive from corroding everything, he must cheat a bit. So he resorts to a little contraband, as he begins to discern the fact that not only do organizations play their part in twisting ideals, but also that ideals play their part in guiding the rise of new organizations. But they are brought back, not as ideals, since that would spoil the symmetry of his book (he had already made perfect hash of ideals). So he brings them back in the name of propositions, thereby saving face.

All told, there are several countermovements going on at once in this book, as is probably inevitable in an investigation of this sort at this time. And Arnold's great respect for administrative tribunals in contrast with courts very well might, if carried out, tend to perfect and regularize an N.R.A. economic structure that perpetuated the present privileged status of business leaders rather than deposing them. On this point, however, the book is vague, since there is also a general tendency favoring the increase of political government's activity, which would probably entail a corresponding atrophy of private, business government. Such elements in the book are as uncertain as they are in the contemporary scene itself. In short, the vacillations in the book reflect the present economic conflicts, so that *The Folklore of Capitalism* is more valuable in picturing for disintegrative purposes the breach between capitalism's slogans and capitalism's realities than in developing a positive program. But the main reason why I think it should be read is for its shrewd comments on the practices of both our business leaders and their ideological priesthood. The book is certainly not to be considered an alternative to Marxism, as many reviewers have proposed; but if read by readers who will discount it from the angle of a Marxist critique, it is very serviceable indeed.

THE CONSTANTS OF SOCIAL RELATIVITY[1]

DISCOURAGED by the ways in which the perspectives of different people, classes, eras, cancel one another, you may decide that all philosophies are nonsense. Or you may establish order by fiat, as you bluntly adhere to one faction among the many, determined to abide by its assertions regardless of other people's assertions. Or you may become a kind of referee for other men's contests, content to observe that every view has some measure of truth and some measure of falsity. If they had asserted nothing, you could assert nothing. But in so far as they assert and counterassert, you can draw an assertion from the comparison of their assertions.

Professor Karl Mannheim's "sociology of knowledge" is a variant of the third of these attitudes. He would begin with the *fact of difference* rather than with a *choice among the differences*. But in erecting a new perspective atop the rivalries of the old perspectives, he would subtly change the rules of the game. For the new perspective he offered would not be simply a *rival perspective;* it would be a *theory of perspectives.* In so far as it was accurate, in other words, its

[1] A review of *Ideology and Utopia*, by Karl Mannheim.

contribution would reside in its ability to make the *perspective-process* itself more accessible to consciousness.

Faction A opposes Faction B. To do so as effectively as possible, it "unmasks" Faction B's "ideology." Faction B may talk nobly about "humanity" or "freedom," for instance. And Faction A discloses the "real meaning" of these high-sounding phrases in terms of interests, privileges, social habits, and the like. Faction B retaliates by unmasking Faction A's ideology.

Each faction exposes, as far as possible, the conscious and unconscious deception practiced by the ideologists of rival camps. But in the course of exposing the enemy, a faction comes upon principles that could be turned upon itself as well. Hence, it can spare its own members from the general censure only by "pulling its punch." And precisely at this point there enter the opportunities for a "sociology of knowledge," if only the sociologist can so change the rules of the game that he finds no embarrassment in completing and maturing this "unmasking" process.

This he does in the easiest way imaginable. Whereas the ideologists of the opposing factions "point with alarm" to the fact that there is a difference between the face value of an opponent's idea and its real value in social commerce, the sociologist starts out by taking such discrepancies for granted. He begins with the assumption that an idea must be "discounted" by the disclosure of the interests behind it. Hence, he can treat the difference between the face value of an ideology and its behavior in a social context not as an "unmasking" but as an "explanation" or "definition" of the ideology. Thus, instead of being startled to find that an idea must be discounted, and taking this fact as the be-all and end-all of his disclosures, he assumes at the start the necessity of discounting, and so can advance to the point where he seeks to establish the *principles of discounting*.

Such, at least, is the reviewer's way of understanding Professor Mannheim's point in tracing a development from the "unmasking of ideologies" to the "sociology of knowledge." And his book presents a great wealth of material to guide the sociologist who would define ideologies in terms of their social behavior. Incidentally, in his gauging of the case, he suggests reasons why members of the intelligentsia are not a perfect fit for strict political alignment. Their working capital is their education—and in so far as they accumulate this capital to its fullest, they venture far beyond the confines of some immediate political perspective. He does not use this thought, however, to disprove the value of political affiliation. On the contrary, he suggests that there are ways in which this somewhat "classless" ingredient in the "capital" of the intelligentsia may serve to broaden and mature the outlook of the stricter partisans, and enable them to take wider ranges of reality and resistance into account.

As for the key terms, ideology and utopia, their "discounting" in social textures makes it impossible for the reader to follow them as absolute logical opposites. In general, the term ideology is used to connote "false consciousness" of a conservative or reactionary sort —while utopia stresses the same phenomenon in the revolutionary category. If conditions have so changed, for instance, that the landed proprietor has become a capitalist yet "still attempts to explain his relations to his laborers and his own function in the undertaking by means of categories reminiscent of the patriarchal order," he is thinking by "ideological distortion." And the "spiritualization of politics" in the thinking of the Chiliasts is treated as a typical utopia, surviving even in the thought of anarchists like Bakunin. However, although the conservative is not naturally given to utopian imaginings, being content to accept the *status quo*, the competitive pressure of revolutionary utopias spurs him to the construction of counter-utopias. Hegel's romantic historicism, erected in opposition to the liberal idea, is given as a prime example. Perhaps the following quotation illustrates the difference most succinctly:

> As long as the clerically and feudally organized medieval order was able to locate its paradise outside of society, in some otherworldly sphere which transcended history and dulled its revolutionary edge, the idea of paradise was still an integral part of medieval society. Not until certain social groups embodied these wish-images into their actual conduct, and tried to realize them, did these ideologies become utopian.

The book is concerned with the ramifications and subtilizations of this distinction, and with a theory of knowledge to be drawn from the plot of history as charted in accordance with these terms. The discussion being conducted largely in abstractions, the book will probably not endear itself to the general reader—but anyone interested in the relation between politics and knowledge should find it absorbing. Perhaps we could venture to summarize the case this way: whereas the needs of the forum tend to make sociology a subdivision of politics, Professor Mannheim is contributing as much as he can toward making politics a subdivision of sociology.

THE SECOND
STUDY OF MIDDLETOWN

IF one had to find a quick slogan for summarizing the way in which science is effective, I should propose the formula: stooping to conquer. Such is the experimental method at its best. In so far as is humanly possible, it begins by *listening* rather than by *asserting*. It is postponed assertion, somewhat as investment is said to be postponed consumption.

The Lynds are expert listeners. Their method makes of us all their laboratory. They use the representative town of Muncie, Indiana, as their specific field of study, and as control, their study of the same town ten years ago. One man figures out, let us say, that "everything will turn out well in the end." And so does the next man, and the next. But an important qualitative change takes place when you have added up all these quantities, thereby getting a kind of statistical view of this homely little invention.

The Lynds have done, without the note of guying, what Mencken and Nathan used to do in their collection of Americana. And the omission of this note makes considerable difference. What Mencken and Nathan did polemically, and Sinclair Lewis did inspirationally, they complete by the strategy of stooping to conquer.

As a result, they have given us two books (the earlier and present studies of "Middletown") contributing greatly to the charting of American mores. We already had the topographical maps surveying the hills and valleys of America. Here we get a survey of the country's mental contours.

The findings could hardly be saluted as new. Anyone who has surveyed America either from the standpoint of the earlier aesthetic criticism (culminating in expatriation, actual or symbolic) or from the standpoint of current political emphasis will probably feel, in reading *Middletown in Transition,* that he is more often being re-

407

minded than informed. The general outlines of the map are already known. The service of these authors is (a) in giving it greater precision and (b) in the working attitude which their study embodies. The second is particularly of value as a hint to our formal and informal propagandists. For the criticism, radical as it seems in its implications, is voiced by investigators who are eager to make sure that the bonds of participation between investigators and investigated are not broken. The emphasis, in other words, is not upon exposure, but upon analysis, with the result that, although the analysis is in effect a drastic exposure, the stylistic change in emphasis prevents the breaking of contact. I can imagine Middletown being troubled by the work; but I cannot imagine it being furious.

The book being over five hundred pages in length, and being largely an assemblage of graphs and statistics written out, I shall not make a pretense of giving it in summary. What one sees, on the whole, is the spectacle of a people attempting to handle new situations by symbols developed under past and different situations, people who still tend to look upon the dislocations of capitalism as an "act of God," who have worked out a bewildering hash of religious and secular coördinates, who strive hard to be friendly under an economy that too often makes for anger (and thereby become all the angrier when their friendliness is frustrated), whose weakness for scapegoats is resisted mainly by lack of some rationalization speciously complete (a lack making it awkward for them to deflect all their resentment upon one fixed symbolic victim). One sees in the main the struggle to form the mind by the acceptance of ailing institutions. This is a disastrous struggle, since the tendency of the individual to locate himself with relation to an institutional frame is in itself *natural* and *wholesome* enough—you can safely think of changing institutions only when you have some *alternative* institutional basis upon which to erect your purposes, as for instance the basis you may derive from the body of anti-capitalist criticism, a criticism rooted in organization and method—but the ailing institutions, as the Lynds make obvious, themselves serve to perpetuate lines of thinking that obscure the issues.

There is one fundamental problem in a book of this sort. The investigators are, by the very nature of their investigation, looking for the typical. And when you have finished, you begin to ask yourself whether there might be some important difference between the typical and history. Middletown, for instance, went 59 per cent for Roosevelt in the last election. Yet this shift from Republicanism is not adequately foreshadowed in the Lynds' survey. In so far as "Middletown" is typical of America, and this survey is typical of Middletown, the material would have led you to expect a national sweep for Landon.

We are left with two possibilities. Perhaps the choice of Roosevelt over Landon was more spectacular than significant. The individual voter, for instance, may have been *almost* undecided whether to vote one way or the other, and *just barely did* finally decide for Roosevelt (this tenuousness adding up, in the deceptiveness of statistical aggregates, to a landslide, quite as the small difference in percentage of votes adds up to a blunt all-but-Maine-and-Vermont in the electoral college). Or else: there may be something about the typical that is itself misleading, as a way of historical gauging and forecasting.

I propose that the second of these possibilities should be considered, in approaching all surveys of this sort. The typical is, in a sense, the relatively *inert*. It is *what people answer when presented with a questionnaire*. It is a *quantitative* rather than a *qualitative* test, since it assigns to everyone the same rating, regardless of his activity. And though history is moved by quantities, is not this movement accomplished by those people, rare rather than typical, most awake to new *qualities* which the changing quantities have brought forth? In other words, might not the *single song of one poet,* under certain conditions, put us on the track of something that the *typical platitudes of a group* could give us no inkling of?

In any case, one thing is certain: those hired to sing for the Landon perspective had a painful job of it—and those hired to sing for the Roosevelt perspective had a much easier time of it. The unhired songs further to the left went practically unheard—but one may believe that they will gradually make themselves heard, and that they will act *precisely because they are not typical,* containing rather the *emergent* factors, such all-important trends of history as the inertly typical conceals from us.

Another problem is suggested by the subtitle, "a study in cultural *conflicts.*" Following leads provided by Bergson, we may note that every state of moral or social "balance" can, by the very nature of language, be analyzed as a conflict between opposing tendencies. Thus even Newton moralistically plotted the curve of planetary motion in terms of opposing centrifugal and centripetal tendencies. And Aristotle, by dint of patient thinking, made the phenomenal discovery that when something is just right in its proportions, it is neither too big nor too small. All moral journeys go between Scylla and Charybdis.

Are not conflicts, in this technical sense, inevitable and everywhere? Can you possibly analyze *any* social manifestation except in terms of a conflict? Many of the conflicts noted by the Lynds seem to me of this linguistically engendered sort. Every state or local portion of a state, for instance, must face in some form a conflict between the attempt to keep down the tax rate and the attempt to promote public enterprises by taxation. Or every state must face a conflict between ideals of work and ideals of leisure, between individual preferences and group necessities, etc. Many of such conflicts noted by the Lynds do not seem to me quite on the same plane with the inner contradictions engendered by capitalism's dilemma in trying to develop mass production without reordering its property relationships to facilitate mass consumption.

An explicit acceptance of the Marxist analysis would, it seems to me, form a sounder basis upon which one might proceed to make distinctions between these two kinds of conflicts, the conflicts caused by a system working against itself and the conflicts arising linguistically from the fact that *any* adjustment must be expressed, in analytic terms, as the juggling of opposites. Once we have carried out such a weeding, it is true, we may very well find that the essential contradictions of capitalism serve greatly to aggravate conflicts all along the line, causing dislocations that turn all consciousness into dilemmas (a theme that Norbert Guterman, in collaboration with Lefebvre, has exploited strikingly in *La Conscience Mystifiée*). But we may be warned that not even socialism can alter the nature of analytic speech in accordance with mystical ideals of nonconflicting unity. The balance of the tight-rope walker, as translated into analytic terms, is attained by adjusting the opposing weight of the right and left sides of the body. And so, in any mature society, there will be balancings of individual and group, manual workers and brain workers, industry and agriculture, or among regional divisions. A "good" state is not one that can eliminate them (the notion of eliminating them is meaningless, unless you are proposing to eliminate language itself as an instrument for the analysis of interrelationships). A "good" state is one that can eliminate some of the obviously man-made contradictions as contained in the capitalist distribution of profits. The others, arising from our position as mere parts of a universal totality, will remain, to form the stimulus for the "symbolic bridges" erected by thinkers and poets. The Lynds show us a people who instinctively grasp this necessity, who know that man's proper enterprise must be expended in developing modes of thought that enable him to *accept* the world, but who are tragically engaged in trying to extend such modes of acceptance to institutions that can and should be *rejected*. The descriptive and admonitory value of such a study cannot be praised too highly.

A RECIPE FOR WORSHIP

IT is not likely that many readers will find the primary thesis of this book (*The Hero: A Study in Tradition, Myth, and Drama,* by Lord Raglan) its most notable aspect. The author is very eager to prove that the figures and events of myth have no basis in history. Even a character like Robin Hood, for instance, would seem to dissolve under his analysis—particularly when we recall the material on The King of the Wood in Frazer's *Golden Bough*, are reminded that there was a Continental story of Robert des Bois, and that "hood" is the word for "wood" in several English dialects. Even the historicity of the Trojan War is brought up for severe and drastic questioning, while the author hurls many amusing darts at the pious savants who would attest their respect for Greek enclitics by believing that there was a real prototype in history for the heroes and events celebrated in *The Iliad*, despite the fact that even the stratagem of the horse appears in variation in the myths of other peoples.

When you finish you can still, if you prefer, persist in your belief that there was some actual flood to form the basis of the account in Genesis—and you may still satisfy your hankerings to seek some naturalistic account of Moses's feat in guiding his people across the Red Sea that later closed to swallow up the soldiers of Pharaoh. (You may hang on, regardless of the author's evidence indicating that such magical strewing of obstacles in the path of the enemy was the stock in trade of mythic leaders.) For as the author himself admits, it is impossible to prove absolutely that myths lack a grounding in

411

historicity. Nevertheless he does attain a high degree of inference.

But whether you are convinced of his main thesis or not, I think you will find that, in the course of maintaining it, he turns up an enormous amount of valuable material. It is his contention that the figures and events of myth owe their origin to the ritual dramas of initiation and propitiation (rites for the installation of kings, for rain-making, fertilization, and victory in war). The origin of myth, therefore, is in drama, and in drama of a purely *ceremonial* sort (such as we saw in the recent coronation). He traces the rôle played by king-god-hero in these magic rituals for the securing of prosperity. And he holds that tradition was written *backward*, with these dramas providing the perspective for interpretation. In fact, he gives ample reasons to conclude that history in the annalist's sense of the term could not exist prior to literacy. The primitive lives in the "pure present," his rituals linking past, present, and future into one (as they seek scrupulously to reënact a past ceremony in the present, for future efficacy, and their past persists in their present quite as the Catholic will tell you that every day Christ is crucified—the event being not merely "historical," but continuous).

But even though, when you finish, you may still tend to feel that there was an "actual someone" who provided the polarizing principle for the accumulation of mythic details (as Mae West is now the broad basis of Mae West stories), you do feel the important point to be the way in which they were reshaped for ritual purposes. In the course of his argument the author works out a recipe of twenty-two points for the typical hero. Among these might be cited: "At birth an attempt is made to kill him"; "he is spirited away and reared by foster-parents in a far country"; "on reaching manhood he returns or goes to his future kingdom"; "after a victory over the king and/or a giant, dragon, or wild beast, he marries a princess . . . and becomes king"· he "prescribes laws, but later he loses favor . . . and is driven from the throne and city, after which he meets a mysterious death, often at the top of a hill." The author cites as examples Hercules, Perseus, Bellerophon, Dionysus, Joseph, Moses, and Siegfried; and their fidelity to the pattern is quite convincing.

We should make but one major objection to his book. Noting that the details of the hero's life are not realistic, but ritualistic, he seems to underestimate the rôle of the people in the development of mythic figures. The author seems to assume that, since the details of the dramatic rituals deal with kingly ceremonies rather than with everyday life, the people beheld them merely as onlookers, their participation residing mainly in the fact that they had a share in the successful outcome of the rite.

This emphasis would, I think, imply a false relationship between drama and audience. The spectator, I believe, could not have been attached to these dramas merely because they were spectacular but mistaken ways of doing what is now done by irrigation and reforestation. The dramas could retain their hold only in so far as the spectators were "glued" to them—and one is glued to a work of art only when that work is reliving for him some basic pattern of his own experience, with its appropriate "medicine." The *curriculum vitae* symbolized in the dramas must have paralleled their own, despite the kingly symbols. In their heroic-ritualistic translation, these experiences were, to be sure, "writ large," but the underlying processes of transition charted by the mythic hero's life must have been a replica of their own processes. Thus the author accounts for the fact that so many of the ritual dramas have a doorway or gateway as setting by attributing it to a mere technical convenience of stage presentation; but could we not rather note the relevance of this "Janus" symbol for objectifying rebirth, such changes of identity as investigators have noted in totemic initiation? From this standpoint we might hold that, despite absence of realistic, everyday detail in the rituals, they symbolized the experience of even the most lowly, though expressed "transcendentally," in "stylistic dignification" (as when Shakespeare dignified his own concerns in *King Richard II* and *Prince Hamlet*).

The author is strongly antagonistic to Euhemerus and all his modern variants. He does not believe with that genial old debunker of 300 B. C. that the gods and heroes of mythology were merely deified mortals, with their real acts amplified by the imagination. Perhaps my reservation is but another brand of Euhemerism, though with a difference. I am suggesting that, despite the absence of realistic detail in the rituals, it was not the *king's* life but their *own* lives that the onlookers were reliving—and these lives were being made acceptable, or "negotiable," by transmogrification into royal attributes.

HYPERGELASTICISM EXPOSED

MR. LUDOVICI (in *The Secret of Laughter*), having "creatively" noted the fact that we laugh or smile under a wide range of circumstances, looks for a *lex continui* that might apply to all of them. He reviews past literature on the subject, but finds it wanting, except in the case of Hobbes, who held that laughter had its genesis in self glory, thus: "The passion of laughter is nothing else but sudden glory arising from some sudden conception of some eminency in ourselves, by comparison with the infirmity of others, or with our own formerly." And again: "Sudden glory is the passion which maketh those grimaces called laughter; and is caused either by some sudden act of their own [the laughers'] that pleaseth them or by the apprehension of some deformed thing in another by comparison whereof they suddenly applaud themselves. And it is incident most to them that are conscious of the fewest abilities in themselves; who are forced to keep themselves in their own favour by observing the imperfections of other men."

The author shows that this formula of Hobbes' can be startlingly developed if we supplement it with a behavioristic description of laughter. For when you have listed the significant aspects of the *act* of laughing (elevation of the head, baring of the teeth, emission of harsh guttural sounds) you have given us the symptoms, not of laughter, but of an animal enraged. Such would suggest that laughter has a jungle origin, in the "showing of teeth" as an indication of challenge or threat. However "civilized" the situations at which we laugh, there will be observable in them a pronounced superior-inferior relationship (are there many other relationships?) such as would characterize the encounter of two jungle beasts, displaying their weapons and conveying their ominous attitudes.

If the reader applies for himself this Hobbes-Darwin-Behaviorism device of Mr. Ludovici, he will find that the most disparate kinds of laughter-situations and smile-events can, with a little squeezing, be made to fit. We may expect pleased laughter when some discrepancy, discordancy, or defect exalts us by a feeling of "superior

414

adaptation"; conversely, we may expect a man to laugh or smile "dishonestly" when he is on the under side of such a disproportion and would suggest "superior adaptation" by "bluff." The author tries his formula on fifty or sixty different laughs, with helpful results. Thus: a child laughs when, running from a mock-pursuer, it reaches the haven of its mother's skirts. Or the condescending gods of Olympus laughed at the sight of lame Hephaestos. Or the villain laughs a mirthless, you-are-in-my-power laugh. Or we laugh if a portly and pompous squire, such as might foreclose our mortgage, has his dignity punctured. We laugh when tickled, for the most neurologically direct reason of all: because we must bare our teeth as the attacks upon our body produce inevitably in us the stimulation of our defense reflexes. We laugh at our own pun, buoyed up by that proud conquest of the syllables we have mangled; and we are generally quite greedy to laugh at another's pun if we perceive it through the fog of a foreign language with which we should like to appear at home. Mr. Ludovici saw a young woman slip on a wet pavement; her clothes were soiled, and she laughed and laughed, though it is hard to imagine that she thought the episode really funny, and much easier to suppose that she was covering her embarrassment by a nervous mechanism ("showing of teeth"—"display of weapons") which gave her a compensatory "superior adaptation" for a situation otherwise humiliating. And Mr. Ludovici's formula would explain our delight in stage characters whose stupidity is total, as though nothing less than *sheer nonsense* could now serve to provide us with that wholesome feeling of *superiority* which we so greatly need.

The formula is also very useful as a conversion mechanism. For the combat patterns, as spiritualized or "sublimated" into corresponding social modes, will naturally lack jungle "purity," and may yield their secret only through the exegesis of Evolutionism. In the Jungles of Society we may more likely discover, not alignments involving life and death, but the subtler calls upon our machinery of competition which are to be found in the Battle of Wits. Though one woman, it is true, may break into irrepressible giggles at the sight of her husband tumbling down stairs, we usually have to track our jungle far: to the good Professor, perhaps, with his faintly ironic guying of a student's faulty answer (the cultivated and widely documented perception of the delicately comic). This Professor might "show teeth" when his student slipped on a question—yet he would not deign to show teeth, like a mere savage child, had this same student slipped on a banana peel. The concept of "superior adaptation" would explain the laughter of a girl well-dressed and courted (she would seem to live among great wits); and "bluff superior adaptation" would explain the strained frozen twitching smiles of nervous people who really ought never to see one another, but who happen to be compelled by the usages of society to sit down at table together, and so proceed dutifully in a circle to show teeth on the slightest provocation.

It does seem to me, however, that in the interest of his thesis the author is more thoroughgoing than he need be. One might hold completely to the jungle origin of laughter, without attempting so strenuously to interpret each laugh or smile by carrying them back to their jungle equivalent. The socialized snarl of laughter may often be due to what we might call "secondary" or "derived" meanings. That is: if we grant that verbal speech probably originated in the mimetic, in bodily posture, we might conversely find occasions in which the mimetic is still used exactly as verbal speech is used. Some laughter might then have to be explained "lexically." To illustrate: Suppose that A had laughed just because he "felt good." Such a phenomenon would be strictly accountable within Mr. Ludovici's formula—since to "feel good" is to "feel superior adaptation" in a general way, and one in an expansive mood might properly show teeth at the entire universe. But if A, in his burst of smiling, had smiled upon B, note how a new kind of "meaning" for this smile might arise. For B might whisper to himself, "This is obviously the time to ask a favor of A. A's mere sense of physical wellbeing will be superiority enough for him today. He will do me no damage with teeth, or with their social counterparts." In other words, A's laughter of good health may suggest to B nothing other than a *promise of sufferance or service*. And as bearded savants, studying the preferences of babies, have discovered that bottle-fed babies bestow upon the bottle the love that would, with breast-feeding, have been bestowed upon the mammae, we may experimentally establish it that from a *promise of service* arises a *judgment of value*—the *lovable*. And once we have established a recurrent type of situation in which laughter, by being a promise of service, takes on connotations of the *lovable,* we may expect subsequently to find occasions wherein a man, employing this derived or "conditional" meaning, will show teeth purely as a sign that he would like to be deemed lovable. To explain the use of the smile-sign on such an occasion wholly by its snarl-origin would be exactly as though one were to discover a "socialized snarl" lurking in some actual verbal equivalent, such as "I want you to like me." This charitable reservation will be seen for the pacifistic thing it is when we attempt to exegetize the smile of a defeated opponent. We should be cruel in calling his smile simply a "bluff superior adaptation" to conceal chagrin. Rather, we might take it as gesture-speech for saying, more economically and fleetingly than words, "This is to indicate that our contest will not be carried by me beyond the limits of the game."

With such a minor reservation as a way of guarding against that "fallacy of origins" to which nineteenth-century science erected all its altars, I think the author's thesis can be followed with much profit. And his closing suggestions that the sense of humor is especially prized today (hypergelasticism) because it offers us a ready "disguised inferior adaptation" to the many perplexities and indignities besetting us, may not tell the whole story, but they certainly tell much of it. Here would be trench humor, to maintain trench morale (which might incidentally suggest that we state the laughter-disproportions the other way round, calling the purpose of laughter not so much a glorifying of the self as a minimizing of the distresses menacing the self).

Somewhat tangentially to Mr. Ludovici's thesis, I was led to speculate on the fact that precisely *Hobbes* was the first thinker who attributed laughter to "self-glory." For it was precisely Hobbes who, alone of English philosophers (and perhaps alone of important philosophers, except Schopenhauer) was "distinguished" by an extraordinary willingness to display vanity, self-importance, self-esteem, etc. Some might say, "His vanity so marked him that it even led him to find vanity and selfishness in the abnegatory and companionable activity of laughing." For my own part, in view of the man's great insight on many matters, I should credit him with a much more complicated process. Practically all cultivated Englishmen were schooled against the obvious show of self-glory in its conventionally recognized forms (as in boasting), so it would not be asking a great deal of Hobbes to expect that he should be equally sensitive to this convention, and to the kinds of censure and handicap that might come of violating it. My explanation accordingly would run somewhat as follows:

Hobbes appreciated, as well as the next man, the social proscriptions with relation to overt self-glory. He saw that his countrymen

417

had a rigid code concerning such matters, and were obedient to it. On the other hand, since they did not detect the covert self-glory of laughter, their prizing of the sense of humor would enable them to gratify the impulses of boasting, vaunting, etc., while apparently complying with the most rigorous code of modesty and polite self-effacement. With his theory of laughter as self-glory, he naturally saw them as forever glorifying themselves in varying degrees of supercilious smilings while thinking of themselves as the very soul of retirement. Hence, he lived in a world where everyone was a monster of incessant boastfulness. What more natural than that he also should be contaminated finally, by this general orgy, and begin boasting himself? And what more natural than that, being a good metaphysician and recognizing the *deviousness* of smile-boasts, he would prefer to take his boasting straight, with that consistency, that thoroughness, that quality-of-seeing-a-thing-through-to-the-end, which is the most distinctive feature of the metaphysician's calling?

MAINSPRINGS OF CHARACTER

IN seeking a key term for the pattern of thought underlying the works of Anatole France, Mr. Chevalier (in *The Ironic Temper: Anatole France and His Times*) holds that an insistence upon France's irony as a central fact makes possible "an organic account of the contradictory elements in the man himself." By his interpretation, not only was France ripe for irony, but the times were ripe for irony. That is: France's irony is "explained" as a pattern peculiar to the author as a person, manifesting itself in emergent forms long before he could have accurately gauged the issues of the day; yet the issues of the day were also such as to encourage an ironic stressing. Hence France, like a kind of Leibnitzian monad, could be obeying wide social patterns while obeying his own. This lock-and-key fit between a society naturally making for ironists and a man with many traits of character naturally making for irony resulted in a writer who, subjective, personal, impressionistic, concerning himself with his own particularities of experience, became a popular writer symbolizing trends of thought and feeling which ran through the entire reading public of his day.

Mr. Chevalier's documentation seems to me thoroughly convincing. It is no accident that irony was brought up for deep consideration by the romantics at the beginning of the nineteenth century and became an attribute of many lively writers as the century progressed. His remarks on the nature of irony enable us to understand why the nineteenth century, of all centuries, a century inferior in great drama, should be concerned with a device so integral to drama. As Mr. Chevalier points out, dramatic irony arises from a relationship between the audience and the play. The audience knows that certain tragic events are destined to take place. It also hears some figure on the stage boasting of the good times to come. And in the audience, as *spectator*, arises dramatic irony. The audience is powerless to affect the course of events; at the same time, its sympathy for the characters makes it long to alter the course of events—and this divided attitude, a sense of being *with* the people as regards one's sympathies but *aloof* as regards one's ability to forestall the movements of destiny, this awareness of a breach between one's desires and one's understanding, this is ironic.

Hence it becomes clear why the nineteenth century, of all centuries, reapplied irony by transferring the spectator attitude from the audience to the writer. Hence the irony of men like Renan, France, Henry James. Here was a century in which the men of intellect saw the people headed eagerly towards so many ambitions which these men despised. Feeling that the authority of this movement was irresistible, yet having always a strong desire to change the course of events if they could, they became *spectators*, with the divided, ironic attitude that comes of seeing people headed with confidence towards desolate ends.

The ironic attitude was complicated by the dual position which science played in the life of the century. In the speculations of pure science there was everything which a lover of the "aesthetic" could admire: enterprise, independence, spiritedness, imaginativeness, critical keenness. Applied science on the other hand (the adventurous speculations harnessed for business purposes) seemed to make for the very opposite type of mind, with more and more demands upon our acquiescence, our obedient repeating of such parrotlike things as one says to a parrot, our loss of fluid, physical, "earthy" living, our development of cogwheel thoughts to match the cogwheel methods of production. This was cause enough for irony: a sense that the most brilliant aspects of human thought were being steadily converted, by men of a different order, into human impoverishments. The situation was further complicated by the fact that pure science had robbed the social critics of a stable basis upon which they might erect a system of protest, such completely relativistic sciences as psychology and anthropology having destroyed the underpinnings of absolute judgment. Only those who remained staunch Catholics were able to write sturdy invective. They could still base their thunderings upon the old ideology of horrors, thus deriving "strength," but the "new men" had weakened: they could not say, "It is wrong in the eyes of God," nor even, "It is wrong in the eyes of human justice," but simply, "I do not like it." Thus, pure science had not merely put them in a divided attitude as the result of its harsh commercial application; it had also impaired the authoritative, "metaphysical" judgments upon which they could frame an attack against this harsh commercial application. Hence their complaints about the "disillusionment" of science—complaints, be it noted, which never turned them against scientific speculation, for as men of spirit they were necessarily vowed to breadth of inquiry, regardless of where it led.

There was a strong attempt to avoid their dilemmas by making ethics a branch of aesthetics. As a matter of fact, the criteria of the beautiful were as fundamentally impaired as the criteria of the good. But ethical crumblings were naturally more noticeable, so a definition of goodness as a subdivision of the beautiful seemed to point in the direction of an area still partially intact. This was, I believe, a move in the right direction, and might eventually have led to such a biologic or psychologic basis of judgment as, "It is wrong because it outrages needs of the mind and body, because it interferes with the felicitous working of the human organism." As a matter of fact, however, all that it did generally lead to was an ultimate realization that beauty also was relative, so at the close of the century this double frustration was in evidence: applied science driving the world towards ways of living and thinking which required the elimination of many past amenities; and pure science having corroded the basis of judgment upon which the disorders of applied science could be attacked.

Mr. Chevalier clearly shows Anatole France at the center of these issues. He shows how certain personal elements, of indolence, of irresponsibility, permitted him to stress this ironic, spectator attitude to the limits, allowing him to remain at home (as regards his page) in these many contradictions, inducing him to live by an "as if" philosophy which could restore the classic amenities once more by permitting oneself on paper to feel "as if" they were still with us, and yet grew apologetic at the awareness of its own subterfuge.

It is customary today to be repelled by the thought of this spectator attitude. There are no spectators. All men, though they have done no more for a living than to exhaust themselves by clipping coupons, are a-tremble. There is no haven, no elevation above the century, from which one can look out calmly upon the hideous Manichean battles that are to be fought between the principle of goodness and the principle of evil during the next decades. So it can be made to seem that there was something cold, something unfeeling, in the ironic temper. Yet whatever else we may hold against it, we must dismiss this charge entirely. As Mr. Chevalier very pointedly says of France in his closing summation:

> That which he expressed—often with profound sophistication —was the naïve, the fresh, the immature approach to experience, the first contacts with life, the budding emotions, the tentative intellectual discoveries that each youth must make anew. Life remains for him always clothed with mystery and enchantment, fraught with danger. It is an ecstatic youth's vision of life, even when his reactions are those of a disabused old man. . . . Some of the most appealing human traits are magically evoked —tenderness, compassion, and childlike wonder, a perpetual fresh surprise before objects of beauty and grandeur.

For all his guise of "complexity," France managed all this by a very simplified kind of poetry. He wrote his books on the top of other books, that his might share the quality of theirs; he found that by "scribbling upon the margins of books," he could restore for us some of the gentler existences out of which these other books had arisen. Like an archeologist, he found a calm Atlantis, which had heaved a huge geologic sigh and sunk slowly to the bottom of the sea, where it now lay, its temples still standing, its marbles posturing, and mournful fishes peering upon these dead splendors. It is not the most "usable" attitude for today—neither is it an attitude which could be dismissed from the mind without great loss.

EXCEPTIONAL IMPROVISATION

WILLIAM EMPSON'S *Some Versions of Pastoral* is unquestionably one of the keenest, most independent, and most imaginative books of criticism that have come out of contemporary England. Since Eliot has been encumbered with so much troublesome extra baggage in recent years, his value for us is lessened. And the three most fertile works on literature since *The Sacred Wood* are I. A. Richards' *Principles of Literary Criticism*, Caroline Spurgeon's *Shakespeare's Imagery*, and this new book by the author of *Seven Types of Ambiguity*.

The step from *Seven Types of Ambiguity* to *Some Versions of Pastoral* is considerable. Empson is still, unfortunately, inclined to self-indulgence, as he permits himself wide vagaries. But presumably that is his method—so the reader, eager to get good things where he can, will not stickle at it. He will permit Empson his latitude, particularly since it seems to be a necessary condition for the writing. He will take what he gets, and will proceed to *delve* there. He will enjoy the author's suggestions, looking elsewhere for four-square schematizations.

By the "pastoral" Empson appears to designate that subtle reversal of values whereby the last become first. They do this, not by assuming the qualities of the first, but by suggesting the firstness implicit in their lastness. Hence, we get the long literature of transvaluation whereby humble rustics, criminals, children, and fools are shown to contain the true ingredients of greatness. They are uplifted, not by renouncing their humbleness, but by affirming it, until out of it there arises the prophetic truth.

We can discern the workings of this process in thought as superficially divergent as primitive Christian evangelism and Marx's "proletarian" morality. We may note it in the reshaping of the Parsifal legends, where the knightly half-wit becomes transformed into the saint of the Holy Grail, his earlier Quixotic *credulousness* being metamorphosed into *insight*. Empson chooses, for his examples, *The Vision of Piers Plowman*, Spenser's *Faery Queen*, Gray's *Elegy in a*

APPENDIX

Country Churchyard, Marvell's *Garden, The Beggar's Opera,* Swift, and *Alice in Wonderland.* Apparently stimulated by sources so different as the propounders of "dialectical materialism" and Frazer's *The Golden Bough,* he makes explicit many of the complex psychological ingredients implicit in "pastoral" revolutions.

"If you choose an important member the result is heroic; if you choose an unimportant one it is pastoral." But also: "In my account the ideas about the Sacrificial Hero as Dying God are mixed up in the brew," the "unimportant member" becoming, by pastoral transformation, the really "important member," and hence the heroic redeemer. There is much here that is necessarily tenuous, and that a rigorously schematizing mind might not have thought of.

The book is also made valuable by many incidental passages opening up new resources of literary "appreciation." We should mention, for instance, the author's acute way of appraising the appeal in a poem on the ways of fish, by Rupert Brooke. And as a sample of his improvising powers, we might close by citing his exegetic comments on the passage from Gray, about the flower that "is born to blush unseen":

> Full many a gem of purest ray serene
> The dark, unfathomed caves of ocean bear;
> Full many a flower is born to blush unseen
> And waste its sweetness on the desert air.

What this means, as the context makes clear, is that eighteenth-century England had no scholarship system or *carrière ouverte aux talents.* This is stated as pathetic, but the reader is put into a mood in which he would not try to alter it. . . . By comparing the social arrangement to Nature he makes it seem inevitable, which it was not, and gives it a dignity which was undeserved. Furthermore, a gem does not mind being in a cave and a flower prefers not to be picked; we feel that the man is like the flower, as short-lived, natural, and valuable, and this tricks us into feeling that he is better off without opportunities. The sexual suggestion of *blush* brings in the Christian idea that virginity is good in itself, and so that any renunciation is good; this may trick us into feeling it is lucky for the poor man that society keeps him unspotted from the world. The tone of melancholy claims that the poet understands the considerations opposed to aristocracy, though he judges against them; the truism of the reflections in the churchyard, the universality and impersonality this gives to the style, claim as if by comparison that we ought to accept the injustice of society as we do the inevitability of death.

One will look long among the writings of most self-professed "Marxist" critics before he finds such profoundly Marxist analysis of literature as this.

EXCEPTIONAL BOOK

THE colyumist's dream is of a book that lays down its thesis in the opening sentence, expands it through the entire introduction, repeats it with variations through several hundred pages, and winds up by summarizing it in an epilogue. By such a test, the superb literary analysis of William Empson would be the colyumist's nightmare. I have read this book three times, and each time I find more in it to reward the attention. In fact, I should like, if I am able, to make this review simply a plea, a "come and buy," recommending *English Pastoral Poetry* [1] to those readers who are also frugal purchasers, and who would thus prefer a work of literary criticism that they can live with to one that they can hurry through.

Empson, who is an offshoot of I. A. Richards, is an honor both to his *magister* and to himself. He has made Richards' teachings his own, and thereby has been able to give them new developments, particularly in laying more stress upon the historical-transitional aspect of literary psychology, which Richards tends more to consider in its arrested, or "flat" aspects. His feeling for literature as a social manifestation is acute, fertile and well documented. There are few psychological novels that have the appreciation of nuance, the ironic pliancy, in which Empson is a specialist. You may legitimately complain that often his perceptions are too refined, leading him into a welter of observations that suffer from lack of selectivity and drive.

[1] *English Pastoral Poetry* is the American title of the book published in England as *Some Versions of Pastoral*.

He is far better at marginalia than at sustained exposition. Obviously, this critic could write an intelligent gloss upon every single line of a long work—and often he seems to have proceeded in precisely this way.

The underlying concern of *English Pastoral Poetry* reflects Empson's response to the salubrious effects that the "proletarian school" has exerted upon the course of literary criticism. To turn from Empson's earlier volume, *Seven Types of Ambiguity,* to his present book, is to realize the importance of the new dimension that the Marxist emphasis has given to his work. Here the balloons of his earlier pure aestheticism are effectively tied to a social basis of reference; the later work has a kind of "gravitational pull" in which the former is lacking. Yet he has by no means abandoned the liquidity of his previous volume—the happy result being that there is here no sociological simplism.

The opening chapter, on "Proletarian Literature," considers some representative statements of the proletarian school, and offers reasons why, for the author's purposes, the aesthetic of proletarian literature should be considered as part of a wider literary strategy, named by him the "pastoral process." Some quotations from this chapter may serve to characterize the general tenor of his approach:

"The essential trick of the old pastoral, which was felt to imply a beautiful relation between rich and poor, was to make simple people express strong feelings (felt as the most universal subject, something fundamentally true about everybody) in learned and fashionable language.

"The usual process for putting further meanings into the pastoral situation was to insist that the shepherds were rulers of sheep, and so compare them to politicians or bishops or what not; this piled the heroic convention onto the pastoral one, since the hero was another symbol of his whole class.

"The praise of simplicity usually went with extreme flattery of a a patron (dignified as a symbol of the whole society, through the connection of pastoral with heroic). . . . It allowed the flattery to be more extreme because it helped both author and patron to keep their self-respect. So it was much parodied, especially to make the poor man worthy but ridiculous, as often in Shakespeare; nor is this merely snobbish when in its full form. The simple man becomes a clumsy fool who yet has better "sense" than his betters and can say things more fundamentally true.

"The realistic sort of pastoral . . . also gives a natural expression for a sense of social injustice. So far as the person described is outside society because too poor for its benefits he is independent, as the artist claims to be, and can be a critic of society; so far as he is forced by this into crime he is the judge of the society that judges him.

"My own difficulty about proletarian literature is that when it comes off I find I am taking it as pastoral literature; I read into it, or find that the author has secretly put into it, these more subtle, far-reaching, and I think more permanent, ideas."

The author then proceeds, first to the analysis of double plot, with the ironic complexities arising from the juxtaposing of the central heroic thread with its burlesqued counterpart, and thence to many variants of his paradox, in the figures of poets, fools, children, madmen, rogues, who are in subtle and devious ways the bearers of sharp social criticism. Thus, we have the "Twist of Heroic-Pastoral Ideas into an Ironical Acceptance of Aristocracy" (elucidated by reference to Shakespeare's Sonnets); "The Ideal Simplicity Approached by Resolving Contradictions" (Marvell's "Garden"); "The Pastoral of the Innocence of Man and Nature" (Milton); "Mock-Pastoral as the Cult of Independence" (*Beggar's Opera*); "The Child as Swain" (*Alice in Wonderland*).

One may, if he chooses, insist upon the important element of *difference* between this general "pastoral" category and its manifestations in books of specifically proletarian cast. For my own part, I much prefer Empson's way of considering the matter, by seeking the permanent forms that underlie changing historical emphases. Indeed, I should contend that one could not properly define the qualities of specifically proletarian works until he had first placed them in some such *genus* as Empson here proposes. Let us first see the whole line, in its long historical continuity, before attempting to differentiate the particular characterizations at any one stage along this line. Trying this approach, in this book by a man who has a most delightful sensitiveness to the fluctuant ways in which the tactics of compliment and insult (coupled with bids for immunity) are managed in works of imaginative scope, you will, I submit, get here an analysis highly provocative.

PERMANENCE AND CHANGE

THIS first volume of Thomas Mann's trilogy, *Joseph and His Brothers,* carries us, as down a deep shaft, to old Biblical regions across which lie peaceful and pastorally melancholy landscapes. Down into the big black hole of the past we drift, until we come upon a world that lived three thousand years ago and is now, by Orphic conjuring, made to live again. The book has about it a quality that has almost vanished from contemporary fiction. It is contemplative, or ruminant—so perhaps one could speak more intelligently of its effects after a long interim of silence during which one returned to it only in memory. One must judge Mann, not as an adept in quickly caught and quickly forgotten impressions—his value resides rather in a subtle, patient and skillfully sustained evangelism which produces changes in us capable of developing through decades.

Mann is a very thorough writer—and surely this melancholy volume, with its astonishingly complex morality, is the end-product of his thoroughness. As one reads it, one understands the solemn note that has gained prominence in his later critical writings. It seems clear that, in a pre-scientific era, Mann would have become a priest —or still farther back, in more primitive groups, he would have taken his place in the college of elders who carefully scan the tribal archives that all new acts may be judged and shaped by precedent. Indeed, as we read this reworking of the Biblical legends clustered about Isaac, Jacob, Esau, Leah, Rachel and Joseph, we get a new understanding of the part played by precedent in the matter of human motives. In earlier days, we feel, precedent was not the purely legalistic device it has since become, a way of preventing new decisions by reference to past decisions made under different conditions and for different purposes. The reference to precedent was *revealing* rather than *obstructive,* precisely because the conditions and purposes had remained constant. Again, these precedents were not the individualized events we meet when we go back to the records of 1929 to find out what the Supreme Court ruled in the case of Johns vs. Johns. They were *mythical* precedents: they were group products—they were "right" because they took their form as a col-

427

lective enterprise. They were selective and interpretative, the results of long revision at the hands of many people through many years. They were the "key" situations of the tribe that had evolved them, after all that could be forgotten had been forgotten and all that could not be forgotten had been made salient. They were not "facts," as legalistic precedents are, but communal works of art. And when the individual understood his own rôle by reference to them (saying, "I am like Jacob," or "This situation is like Leah's") he was being himself and a member of his group simultaneously. It is in this sense that Mann sets about to write of "people who do not know precisely who they are," and "the phenomenon of open identity which accompanies that of imitation and succession."

At least, whether one agrees with the suggestion or not, it is the feeling that one takes away with him from the reading of Mann's latest piously ironic novel. What one can do with it, I do not know. The author has simplified and idealized his point of view by eliminating attempts at modern parallels. He is not concerned with strict modern-ancient correspondences like Joyce, who would chart the new equivalents to the old wanderings of Odysseus. In the altered ways of life which technology has brought, perhaps the situations are so radically changed from those earlier pecuniary or stock-breeding days that we must abandon the attempt to understand ourselves by reference to the precedents of myth. Again, the myths are bewilderingly intermingled: they are not living art, but art in a museum. Yet even for this state of affairs, perhaps, there is a mythical parallel— for is there not everywhere the legend of the Tower of Babel that arose to confound primitive men when they were elated by such ambitions as have in recent centuries elated us, and the vast projects of building were confused by a multitude of tongues quite as our specialized vocabularies continually threaten to confuse us?

"Without passion and guilt nothing could proceed." If I chose the word "thorough" as the label that might most briefly characterize this book, it is because *Joseph and His Brothers* profoundly pursues the ramifications of this thought. The strange intermingling of kindness and cruelty which animates it could all, I believe, be shown to flow from this statement. The pervasive imagery of the pit, the phenomena of indentured service which he considers with insistence, his constant concern with the psychology of waiting, his almost fierce emphasis upon the cult of fertility, his remarks on the "upper and lower half of the sphere," his deliberate affronts to the mechanistic concepts of causality, his ironic sympathy with opportunism, his somewhat awestruck pondering on the subject of recurrence—all this, I believe, could be shown to follow, directly or indirectly, from his care as to the part which the "problem of evil" plays in the civic, or historic process. An author in search of metaphor, he makes us feel that life itself is metaphorical.

I have probably said enough to suggest that another word might replace my adjective "thorough." Mann's new book is "mystical." It brings us to the edge of things, to that fearful dropping-off place which, before the feat of Columbus, could be geographically imagined but has since usually been relegated solely to a disposition of the mind under duress, though it is brought back once more in the physical sense perhaps by the contemporary physicist's suggestion that electronic activity is like a radiation from a nonexistent core (as were it to well up from some other region like water quietly moving the sand at the bottom of a spring). It is an eschatological book, dealing with the "science of last things." As such, it is disturbing, and will perhaps be rightly repudiated by happier fellows who prefer to shape their acts by contingencies alone. To live by contingencies alone is unquestionably the most comforting way to live— and contented ages have probably been those in which the concepts of duty were wholly of this specific sort, harvesting when the crops were ripe, shearing when the sheep were heavy, and coupling when the body felt the need of its counterbody. But the world of contingencies is now wholly in disarray. In our despicable economic structure, to do the things thus immediately required of us is too often to do despicable things. It is at such times, I imagine, that the question of duty naturally becomes more generalized, and attempts at defining the "ultimate vocation" seem most apropos. Mann's new book is written in this spirit.

BY ICE FIRE, OR DECAY?

AFTER having been led, by the explicitly formulated objections of some dissenters, to expect that I would dislike Odets' *Paradise*

Lost, I finally went to see it, and liked it enormously. I even found that the scandalous number of entrances and exits did not bother me, except in a few instances where the action was not paralleled by a similar movement in the lines themselves. And though I had in the past complained against propagandists who compromised their cause by the depiction of people not worth saving, and had been led to believe that Odets transgressed on this score, I found on the contrary that the characters, for all their ills, possessed the ingredients of humanity necessary for making us sympathetic to their disasters. To me there was nothing arbitrary about the prophetic rebirth in Leo's final speech. And as I had witnessed, not pedestrian realism, but the idealizations of an expert stylist, I carried away something of the *exhilaration* that good art gives us when, by the ingratiations of style, it enables us to contemplate even abhorrent things with calmness.

The opportunity to examine the play in print has even heightened my admiration, by revealing the subtlety, complexity and depths of the internal adjustments. For all his conscious symbolism, the author has not merely pieced together a modern allegory. His work seems to embody ritualistic processes that he himself was not specifically concerned with—and I want to discuss them briefly.

At the close of Act I, as the characters listen to Pearl playing the piano upstairs, Gus says: "And when the last day comes—by ice or fire—she'll be up there playin' away." I consider this the "informing" line of the play. "By ice or fire." It is interesting that, in *The Partisan Review,* James T. Farrell, who wrote a book called *Judgment Day,* should have objected to a work having this eschatological theme as its point of departure. But Farrell is in the stage of pure antithesis, turning his old Catholicism upside down—and hence preferring, for the time at least, the simple, hard-boiled reversal of his religious past. Odets may be more complex, admitting elements that Farrell could not admit without a corresponding expansion of his aesthetic frame. Farrell's resistance is justified on the grounds of self-preservation, rather than as a mature act of critical appraisal.

Along with the "ice or fire" epigram, I should note the significant credo of Pike who, within the conditions of the play, comes nearest to the "proletarian" philosophy: "I'm sayin' the smell of decay may sometimes be a sweet smell." And taking these two passages as seminal, I should say that the play deals with three modes of "redemption"—redemption by ice, fire, or decay—and finally chooses the third. Like certain ancient heresies, it pictures the "good" arising from the complete excess of the "bad," as the new growth sprouts from the rotting of the seed.

The first act rejects "redemption by ice." In its simplest objectivization, we find the situation placed before our eyes in the form of Ben's statue on the stage. The friends, Ben and Kewpie, had been under ice together; they had been skating with a third boy, when the ice broke and their friend had drowned. The spell of this "life-in-death" is still upon them. As Ben formulates it later: "We're still under ice, you and me—we never escaped!" And again: " 'Did we die there?' I keep asking myself, 'or are we living?' " The first act establishes this situation—and Acts II and III show us the author's attempts to shape a magic incantation whereby the spell is broken.

Act II, by my analysis, considers and rejects "redemption by fire." It is in this way that I would locate the symbolic element underlying the remarkable realism of Mr. May, the professional firebug. Leo refuses to accept his impotent partner Sam's proposal that they solve their financial troubles by employing this man. But Pike, the proletarian furnace tender (who would thaw the ice), had proclaimed his belief in "redemption by decay." He is thus the bridge between Sam's fire solution and Leo's rebirth from decay. And we complete the pattern in the third act where, as the process of decay is finished, Leo's prophecy of rebirth sprouts from the rotted grain, and the curtain descends.

I might note other features of the internal organization. Thus, Pike's mere entrance at times foreshadows the "fatality" of the plot. For he knocks at the door (1) just as Julie has said, "When the time comes—" (2) when Gus has said he would like to "go far away to the South Sea islands and eat coconuts," and (3) when, Clara having asked "Is it the end?" Leo has answered, "Not yet." At these crucial moments, Pike's message is in the offing. But whereas the message remains the same throughout the play, Leo (the "father") must assimilate it in his own way, as he does by conscientiously completing the symbolism of the rotting grain. (The same basic pattern of thought may be seen in the "conscientious corruption" of André Gide, who has significantly entitled his autobiography *"Si le grain ne meurt."*)

Approached from this angle, Krutch's doubts as to the play's statistical value (its actuarial truth as a survey of the bourgeoisie) may seem less relevant. If a poet happens to have the sort of imagination

431

that revivifies an old heresy in modern details, how would he go about it to put this imaginative pattern into objective, dramatic form? At other times, he might have externalized the pattern as a struggle between angels and demons, or between Indians and settlers, or between patriot and foe, or in the "war of the sexes," etc. At present, in keeping with current emphasis, he may symbolize it with relation to an interpretation of historic trends, where its "prophetic" truth is enough. Incidentally, the *subjective* origin of the pattern need not impair the *objective* validity of the symbols used. If the bourgeoisie is oppressed by loss of certainty, one may have many good objective reasons for externalizing the pattern of his imagination in this form, particularly as the pattern itself may have been established in the individual poet precisely by the effects of the same frustrating process.

Our approach also may have bearing upon the comments of Stanley Burnshaw, who observed in *The New Masses* that the play erred as political strategy. Inasmuch as the proletariat must expect the petty bourgeoisie to become its allies, he asks, how could people so decayed have the vitality to assist in the tremendous work of establishing a new order? This objection is justified only if one does not believe in the Odets formula for redemption, remembering only the ash and not the Phoenix that arises from the ash. But if one follows the Odets ritual to the end, the objection is weakened. By the Marxist formula, the complete "proletarian" would require no process of rebirth. He would grow up with his morality. He and it would be one. But the bourgeois would have to "come over," dropping the morality that made him and taking another in its place. Converting the situation into drama, we should require rebirth, the ritualistic changing of identity, rather than merely a superficial matter of climbing off one bandwagon and climbing on another. And we should require the dramatist to deepen and broaden the process as greatly as possible.

Thus, I question whether we can appreciate the play by a simple "scientific" test of its truth, as in Farrell's naturalistic bias, Krutch's census-taking requirements or Burnshaw's question of united-front tactics. A more integral test is to be found, I submit, in a consideration of the play as ritual. And those who respond to its ritual will be enabled to entertain drastic developments, without drawing simply upon a masochistic desire to be punished.

FEARING'S NEW POEMS

"THE alarm that shatters sleep, at least, is real" . . . Before you have finished one stanza in a poem by Kenneth Fearing, you have felt the trend of its stimulus, and have set yourself to the proper mode of expectation and response. I know of no poet who can swing you into his stride with greater promptness. Taking as his characters the stock situations of modern history's problem play, he offers us a slogan-laden "science of last things," in imagery found among the piles of the metropolis. Confronted by all the alloys, substitutes, and canned goods that are offered us by the priesthood of business, the catch phrases of salesmanship and commercialized solace, Fearing has put the utilitarian slogans to a use beyond utility, as he rhythmically sorrows, with their help, assigning them an interpretative function in his poems that they lack in their "state of nature."

By his method, you may peer beyond some trivial advertisement to discern despair, migration, even "Amalgamated Death" (since the poet, after a secular fashion, is given to carrying out the churchman's injunction: "Thou shalt live a dying life"). The handwriting in a letter becomes the handwriting on the wall; and I feel sure that, with his expressive resources, he could readily transmogrify a pat salutation like "Dear Sir" into a prognosis of the vast collapse of Western culture.

Perhaps the quickest way to characterize his book (*Dead Reckoning*) is by a paragraph of cullings, one from each poem, that convey the quality of the poet's burden: "shadows that stop for a moment and then hurry past the windows" . . . "the phone put down upon the day's last call" . . . "until then I travel by dead reckoning and you will take your bearings from the stars" . . . "it is late, it is cold, it is still, it is dark" . . . "fill in the coupon" . . . "how the moon still weaves upon the ground, through the leaves, so much silence and so much peace" . . . "Lunch With the Sole Survivor" . . . "is it the very same face seen so often in the mirror" . . . "not until we've counted the squares on the wallpaper" . . . "on the bedroom floor with a stranger's bullet through the middle of his

433

heart, clutching at a railroad table of trains to the South" . . . "It is posted in the club-rooms" . . . "a privileged ghost returned, as usual, to haunt yourself?" . . . "CAST, IN THE ORDER OF DISAPPEARANCE" . . . "tomorrow, yes, tomorrow" . . . "soothed by Walter Lippmann and sustained by Haig & Haig" . . . "if now there is nothing" . . . "the empty bottle again, and the shattered glass" . . . "as armies march and cities burn" . . . "ask the family on the illuminated billboard" . . . "the stones, so often walked" . . . "the natives can take to caves in the hills, said the British MP" . . . "wages: DEATH" . . . "Take a Letter" . . . "with the wind still rattling the windows" . . . "why do you lay aside the book in the middle of the chapter to rise and walk to the window and stare into the street" . . . "Dance of the Mirrors" . . . "this house where the suicide lived" . . . "something that we can use, like a telephone number" . . . "Wait, listen."

There is a risk here, in the "statistical" quality of the perspective by which the poet sizes up the "thousand noble answers to a thousand empty questions, by a patriot who needs the dough." There is such limitation of subject matter as may come of taking the whole world as one's theme. All people look like ants, when seen from the top of a skyscraper—and the poet's generalized approach often seems like the temptation of a high place. Connected with this is an overreliance upon accumulation and repetition, traits that derive also from his disposition to establish a very marked pattern, which he expands as a theme with variations. Hence, for my part, the items I liked best were "Pantomime" ("She sleeps, lips round, see how at rest" . . .), a poem of tenderness and meditation that is very moving, and the opening "Memo" ("Is there still any shadow there, on the rainwet window of the coffeepot" . . .)—where the generalized plaint is introduced in less head-on fashion. "Devil's Dream" (a kind of "There but for the grace of God goes our author" theme) is another poignant accomplishment, by reason of the more personal note. The author's rhetoric of attack ranges from the slap to a tearing of the hair (with perhaps his "En Route" among the most successful of the generalized statements); and all his lines bear convincing testimony—in speech swift and clear—of estrangement in a world awry, where many are asked to face the emptiness of failure in order that a few may face the emptiness of success.

GROWTH AMONG THE RUINS

THOSE who believe that history-in-the-making is only what comes over the wires, for front-page headlines, are advised to read no farther in this article. For I would here salute a happening of a deeper, more solemn order. This happening concerns the processes of history, after they have been strained through the consciousness of a sensitive, imaginative and resourceful artist. I refer, in brief, to Peter Blume's new painting, "The Eternal City," now on exhibit at the Julien Levy galleries, in New York City.

For those who have not seen the reports in the press, revealing the excitement of both aesthetic and political cast the picture has aroused, I might record the fact that this is not merely a one-man exhibit, but a one-picture exhibit, comprising one large canvas and six draw-ings of details made preparatory to work on the ensemble. The oil is thus composed of many remarkably executed miniatures, each an event in itself, but all brought within a larger frame of reference. The picture is the result of nearly four years' concentrated application. It has subtleties of pigment and draughtsmanship, and solidities of architectural construction that are purely visual experiences, beyond the reach of verbal description. Blume knows how to flood his canvas in a strange light. And all such qualities one could not verbalize with any greater justice than one could verbalize the taste of an orange.

I shall here discuss only the material in Blume's new work that does lend itself to verbalizing. To label bluntly: we might call "The Eternal City" the painting of a surrealist, turned social propagandist. But one must hasten to modify. It does not trifle with enigmas, as so much of surrealism does. And, as propaganda, it extends its range until a total personality is encompassed; the propagandist element merely takes its place as one function in a broad texture of conscious-ness, having much more scope and complexity than the artist could possibly include if he conceived of propaganda as a purely utilitarian act (to "sell" this policy as against that policy).

To suggest the quality of the total texture, I propose as subtitle: "Growth among the Ruins." In the scattered bits of architectural

435

fragments, vestiges of different styles and periods, surviving in various stages of decomposition, we see the clutter and accumulation of past ages. And out of this a strikingly ambivalent *vita nuova* is emerging. There is "growth" in two senses: there is malign growth, in the repulsive head of Mussolini, a salient popping-forth across the picture like a Jack-in-the-bandbox with spring released. And for benign growth, there is a stately and calmly assertive tree. The head and the tree (a "tree of life"?) are at once linked and divided: for both are done in green—the one green benign, and the other malign.

The tree and Mussolini, on the right, are countered on the left by a different lineage. We see an agonizing Christ, crucified with honors (the wrong honors—mainly gifts of wealth and military symbols). Perhaps he even bears a literal cross, in the swords crossed upon his knees. Beneath him is an alms box—and lower in the picture is a beggar woman, soliciting alms, *degraded* with poverty.

Seen from another angle: the picture may be divided roughly like a medieval stage. In the foreground is the pit (hell), with its two plotting figures (racketeer and gangster, summarizing perhaps "crimes of cunning" and "crimes of violence"). These figures are *active;* their faces reveal *intention;* their placing on the canvas puts them under the aegis of Mussolini, who is himself springing from pit sources. There are other figures, moving to emerge from this pit to the level of earth—a level on which a peculiar kind of panic is taking place. People confront soldiers agonizingly; while two Cossack-like soldiers, mounted, are allowing women to slip beneath the bellies of their horses. This panic is obviously, in "dream-logic," associated with the one popping eye of Mussolini, who casts a spell of "evil eye" upon the scene. In the background, you reach the "heavenly" level: remote mountains rise on the left, while houses of an unpeopled city (tomblike, suggesting a "city of the dead") are banked against the slope of a nearer mountain on the right. We should also note in the immediate foreground, raised above the level of the pit, the marble replicas of two lovers, in sexual embrace, and broken into fragments. It is on one of these fragments that the artist signs his name, in letters like carving on a tomb.

The state of panic in the central drama suggests action at cross purposes, an agitation not "organized," but balked. In the foreground, sniffing tentatively at the broken statuary, is a dog, "spectator" of this breakage (a breakage that none the less perpetuates a point of crisis). And on a balcony there is an American tourist viewing the central drama (the clash between people and soldiers) with a *collector's* interest (it is a grotesque touch: this inadequacy of her response, as she squints through a lorgnette, lest she miss anything, whereas one knows that she could not possibly fail to miss it all). Meyer Schapiro called to my attention how much of such perception-at-one-remove there is in this picture, notably in the many miniatures of art-objects, while the tourist is observing the central upheaval itself as though it were a picture.

When I say that "The Eternal City" is "propaganda-plus," I have in mind the complex way in which political means have been fused with other elements, religious, sexual and naturalistic. A psycho-analyst might even omit the political elements altogether, with re-vealing and relevant results. The Mussolini head could be easily treated as a menacing kind of super-ego in phallic guise (an invita-tion censorially rephrased as a "thou shalt not") surveying the scene with an evil eye that blasts, causing disintegration and petrifaction of the lovers and leading to the midway state of panic. And the author's choice of bogeyman is certainly drawn from a deep child-hood level of experience, since it is in early childhood that we first learn to be jarred and fascinated by the sudden leer of such a puppet, leaping from his dark box.

The possible interconnections are endless; for there is "dream-logic" in this painting, as well as conscious ideology, and the interaction of the two is what gives it its depth and scope. If you draw a diagonal line from upper left to lower right, for instance, you will find that above this line all is in brightness (buildings, mountains, the central scene, the tree, and the salient head); below the line there is darkness, even in some areas double darkness, except for a focus of illumination about the figure of Christ. Here are the pit, the fragmentary lovers and the beggar woman. All beneath the diagonal seems to symbolize an out-of-which; above the diagonal, an into-which.

Is it not "history" too ("basic" history) that there is, in this picture, no human figure of benignity? The Christ and beggar woman are outraged; even the man and woman in devotional posture in the shadows are bringing no elevated attitude, but only *some* of their concerns. There are the beautiful, unpeopled, tomblike buildings, the austere mountains, the ruddy earthen light and the tree—but there is no corresponding *human* vessel of such elements. Is this depersonalization of the benign inevitable, after so many centuries intelligently spent upon the questioning of human motives? So that,

437

for us, benignity is not in the smith, but in the spreading tree beneath which the smithy stands.

LETTERS TO THE EDITOR

1. ON PSYCHOLOGY

MRS. MALAMUD'S article [1] is so suggestive and engrossing that one would be doing the right thing by simply registering his thanks and calling it a day. But I guess all writers are ingrates; and when asked to comment on another writer's work, they end by objecting because the work was not done precisely as they would have done it (if they could have done it!). So I shall shamefacedly proceed to offer some reservations of a niggling sort. Since I cannot "put in my oar" by going Mrs. Malamud one better, all that is left is for me to go her one worse.

With regard to the "macrocosm-microcosm" relationship between the artist-spokesman and his group: It is, of course, a possibility that experience undergoes some important change of quality as we turn from the practical world to the aesthetic world. We may, with Mrs. Malamud, work on the assumption of a continuity whereby there is a single line of responses, intense at one end and tenuous at the other, a graded series "more or less accentuated" as we move from the preoccupied toward the trivial end of the spectrum, but the same in quality throughout. Yet there is the other possibility: that intense aesthetic engrossment really is a change in the quality of experience, that there is a "critical point" at which the shift from practical action to aesthetic meditation becomes more like the closing of one door and the opening of another. This is the thesis of those who hold out for a "special aesthetic sense." However, while remaining on the lookout for such possible changes in quality (discernible perhaps in the fact, for instance, that Andreyev seems to have had quite a gift for humor in his intimate conversation, but dropped it when entering the chamber of his characteristic aesthetic productions, somewhat as

[1] *American Journal of Sociology,* XLIII (January, 1938), 578–602.

though he had closed one door and opened another) we may find it necessary to abide by Mrs. Malamud's "macrocosm-microcosm" assumption, incidentally an assumption about the relationship between group and spokesman that is shared by our greatest contemporary novelist, Thomas Mann.

In any case, there is a level at which the artist cannot "vote." That is, he does not ask himself, "Shall I cast my ballot for *this* or for *that?*" For, even where there is some such fluctuancy as to specific policies discernible on the surface, look beneath it and you will find an underlying level of firm conviction. For instance, at one point in his reminiscences of Andreyev, Gorki tells of a plot that occurred to Andreyev on the spur of the moment. Gorki had just described an acquaintance as "a tiger out of a fur shop." The phrase struck Andreyev's fancy, and he proceeded to improvise:

> I must describe a man who has convinced himself that he is a hero, a tremendous destroyer of all that exists, and has become frightful to himself even—yes! Everybody believes him,—so well has he deceived himself. But somewhere in his own corner,—in real life,—he is a mere miserable nonentity, is afraid of his wife or even of his cat.

The thing that strikes one about this project (if we may assume that Gorki reported it correctly) is a spontaneous equating of "hero" with "a tremendous destroyer of all that exists." Here would be the underlying level of unquestioned values. And if we could assume a "macrocosm-microcosm" continuity between writer and audience, we could detect the tremendous social "programs of action" implicit in such equations.

It is possible, however, that Jung's terms, "introvert" and "extravert," are too broad for purposes of accurate analysis along such lines. Mrs. Malamud writes: "For Jung a symbol is that which expresses a relatively unknown fact in the best possible way." And so might Jung's own terms be somewhat too "symbolic"? And might a study of underlying equations (such as the traits a writer regularly links with his notions of hero and villain, success and failure, purpose and frustration, interest and boredom, indictment and consolation) make such analysis more precise? Perhaps Jung's dichotomy would still apply as a summarizing classification for our results; but that would remain to be disclosed afterward, after the critic had attempted to

439

locate, by specific analysis, the different types of character-recipe embodied in art works and the correspondingly different kinds of conclusions or exhortations implicit in them. There seem to be overly fatalistic implications in Jung's dichotomy, leading in the end to a kind of "a man is what he is" attitude. But by attempting to disclose and discuss concrete equations of value (what specific traits equal "hero," "failure," etc.) we might not only disclose different *types* of strategy, but might be able to adopt relevant educative measures for bringing up for conscious criticism, and so counteracting some-what, implicit equations that lead to faulty means-selection.

"Within recent years there has been a noticeable trend in the direction of a psychological approach to the study of groups and group behavior in the literature of both sociology and psychology," Mrs. Malamud writes. The study of psychology, of course, requires by definition that the main emphasis be upon psychology. But, when considering a full statement of sociological factors, surely we should also be grateful for the admonitions of Mr. William F. Ogburn, in his article, "The Influence of Inventions on American Social Institutions in the Future," in the *American Journal of Sociology* for November, 1937, pointing to the important part played by technological invention in affecting social change. Might we be justified in playing off these two articles against each other somewhat, noting their differently directed emphases and speculating as to what might be the resultant emphasis from the combining of the two?

Mrs. Malamud stresses the importance of psychological factors in social response; Mr. Ogburn stresses the importance of technology as an informative environment. But Mr. Ogburn tends to consider this environment in the lump, as though it had the same general value for all. Is it not a different environment, with corresponding difference in psychology, depending upon one's relationship to it? And is there not a tremendous difference in relationship, to be broadly classified with reference to the distinction between those who can approach the technological changes as possessors and those who must approach them as dispossessed? The works of both Gorki and Andreyev may be analyzed, for instance, as different strategies developed in response to the factor of alienation (a situation having both economic and psychological aspects). If a distinction between possession and alienation were considered admissible, it would somewhat fall afoul of both Mrs. Malamud's and Mr. Ogburn's articles. It would tend with Mrs. Malamud to suggest that we must lay tremendous importance upon a factor of psychological differentiation in the charting of social change—but it would also tend to employ Mr. Ogburn's stress upon technological environment as a way of suggesting further doubts about the accuracy of the "introvert-extravert" distinction for analyzing the structure of psychological strategies. Would not explicit reference to matters of property (both material property and its spiritual counterparts, one's sense of "having a property in" a society's enterprises) serve as a bridge to unite the Malamud-Jung psychological emphasis and the Ogburn economic emphasis?

In both Andreyev and Gorki, I have said, we find aspects of alienation and organized responses to the state of alienation. Andreyev's response suggests some such metaphor as "life a nightmare." Gorki's suggests "life a vagabondage." (We may note a parallel in the "life a flight" metaphor implicit in the response of the German *Wandervögel*, whose "push away from" preceded the "pull toward" of Nazism, if we may borrow a distinction employed by Bertrand Russell in his *Analysis of Mind*. Or we may note a contrast in the almost "touristic" connotations of the "life a pilgrimage" metaphor implicit in Chaucer—the difference in emphasis between Chaucer's perspective and Gorki's perspective reflecting a difference in their objective situations.)

Perhaps we should add an important modification to our version of the Gorki metaphor, amending it to: "life a vagabondage, *with cronies*," in contrast with Andreyev's "life a nightmare, *alone*." Gorki in his reminiscences of Andreyev reports him as saying: "I wish you were aching with my pain; then we should be nearer to one another." Here we note a most drastic "equation" affecting the development of the artist's strategy, the strategy of a man who spontaneously assumed that one counteracted loneliness not by *helping* others but by *pulling others down* to his own level of discomfort. A similar strategy is revealed in Gorki's account of the frightful bedtime story (about Death stalking little children) that Andreyev told to his son at a time when Andreyev himself was obsessed with suicidal despair; and it seems to be present as a motive behind such bogeyman pictures of ubiquitous and omnipotent death as we get in Andreyev's *Life of Man* (with the general public here being invited to take the place of the terrified child as scapegoat for the author's relief). Could we be accurate enough in discussing such matters in terms of the "extravert-introvert" dichotomy?

Incidentally, in Gorki's reminiscences there is also a very striking account of a quarrel between Gorki and Andreyev, revealing the same kind of "crisis situation" in the personal relations of these two writers as Mrs. Malamud would reveal through the occasion of social revolution itself. For, according to Gorki, this incident produced resentments that were never afterward removed. The quarrel was over the way Andreyev had reworked, in one of his stories, an incident that occurred in real life. The two men quarreled, according to Gorki, because Andreyev had not sought to appreciate "the manifestation of a good honest feeling" (as the real episode seemed to Gorki to contain), but had instead refurbished it by introducing "weird details" and "agonizing and foul mockery at man."

> I could not help pointing out to Andreyev the meaning of his action, which was to me equivalent [incidentally, Gorki seems to be touching, in uncodified form, upon the matter of "equations"] to murder for a mere whim. He reminded me of the freedom of the artist, but this did not change my attitude—even now I am not convinced that such rare manifestations of ideally human feelings should be arbitrarily distorted by the artist, for the gratification of a dogma he loves.

Later we find it is Gorki who expressed misgivings about the Russian people, while Andreyev falls into an excessive vindication of them (in accordance with a paradoxical apologetic of the sort revealed in Andreyev's remark, "the pearl only grows in a diseased shell"). Andreyev's excessive "anathema" led to an equally excessive compensatory "hosannah" (as Gorki phrased his fluctuancy); whereas we see in Gorki the strategy of a man who, through being less efficient in indictment, is also the more able to consider good grounds for *some* indictment. Such treatment of literary strategies would, I suppose, fit within the distinction between "extraversion" and "introversion"; but might it not, in inviting us to codify the specific ingredients of symbolic constructions (the interrelationships of meanings that authors put together for the acceptance and rejection of reality, and their implicit selection of the "reality" they will encounter), be more prolific in "leads" for further analysis of the purely literary events from which sociological deductions would be made?

In particular, it seems to me, the study of literary work for purposes of social analysis should look for "equations" that reveal modes of *combat* and *solace* (i. e., the implicit commands to audience and self that an author's works exemplify). There seems to me an essential difference in strategy, or program, between communion by pulling others down to one's own level of misfortune (leading to solace of the "indictment" sort, to "foul mockery at man") and communion through attempts to establish human solidarity by salvaging what we can. Both are responses to situations featuring alienation, and both are "ways of getting along" in such situations. But the "extravert-introvert" distinction, as a "way in," seems somewhat askew as an instrument for charting the specifically literary quality of such literary events.

The distinction also seems to me somewhat deficient in "programmatic" properties. That is, I question whether it itself spontaneously contains the kind of "implicit commands" required for a sociological enterprise. Though we might find that a charting of writer's and audience's equations would in the end reveal something classifiable by the "extravert-introvert" distinction, I wonder whether an approach to them as "strategies," or modes of *means-selection*, might not more readily invite us to disintegrate and reintegrate equations with specific reference to criteria of social action?

My assumption here probably is that a complete science of social analysis would not be merely diagnostic, but hortatory. I realize that many readers will not share this assumption, especially when I admit my belief that, if carried to its logical conclusion, it would demand a "science as handmaiden of faith" point of view, however much the notion of "faith" might be secularized.

2. ON DIALECTIC

THANK you for inviting me to participate in the discussion of Dr. Kilpatrick's engrossing and stimulating article,[1] embodying a spirit so sensitive and humane that one could have full confidence in a world educated in its image. And in commenting on so valuable a statement, I should dare to tinker with it but slightly.

In a few spots the argument seems to be settled by epithet. Where "propaganda (bad sense)" is pitted against "education (full sense)," all men of goodwill must necessarily vote for the second. But though Dr. Kilpatrick occasionally treads about the edges of this temptation,

[1] On education and indoctrination, in *The American Teacher*, November, 1939.

his essay as a whole is obviously concerned with much deeper issues. To approach those, I should begin by adding one more term to his "education-ethics-intelligence-personality-freedom-democracy" equation (as against the "propaganda-indoctrination-authoritarianism" equation). This added term would be "dialectics." In conformity with Mead, as I understand him, I take democracy to be a device for institutionalizing the dialectic process, by setting up a political structure that gives full opportunity for the use of competition to a coöperative end. Allow full scope to the dialectic process, and you establish a scene in which the protagonist of a thesis has maximum opportunity to modify his thesis, and so mature it, in the light of the antagonist's rejoinders.

I wish I knew in advance whether Dr. Kilpatrick concurs in my proposal that "dialectics" be added to the benign side of his *agon*. For I believe that the addition might make a slight but important difference in the nature of his argument. Hence, I should properly not proceed until I had assurance that he consented to my offer (particularly since the offering is made with mildly Trojan-horse designs).

For I should want to insist that the all-important desirability of full opportunity for the enacting of the dialectic process *should be absolutely affirmed and indoctrinated*. In fact, is not Dr. Kilpatrick in effect doing precisely this in pleading so persuasively for "the free play of intelligence"? Yet he is unnecessarily handing advantages to the enemy in trying to avoid the "charge" of indoctrination, for he thereby gives the impression that the educator would retire from his proper rôle as guide to the uninitiated in offering them the fruits of his greater maturity and knowledge.

I should contend, therefore, that the dialectic process *absolutely must* be unimpeded, if society is to perfect its understanding of reality by the necessary method of give-and-take (yield-and-advance). And on the basis of this absolute, I should next absolutely and undeviatingly place dictatorship as an imperfect medium whose imperfections are heightened to a maximum by organizational efficiency. Only if all reports were in and if there were no vital questions still unanswered, could a social body dispense with the assistance of a vocal opposition in the maturing of our chart as to what is going on, which social functions are helpful and which harmful. Dictatorships, in silencing the opposition, remove the intermediary between error and reality. Silence the *human* opponent, and you are brought flat against the *unanswerable* opponent, the nature of brute reality itself. In so

444

far as your meanings are incorrect, and you spawn them and maintain them by organizational efficiency without the opportunity of correction, you are hurled without protection against the unanswerable opponent, the opponent that, not speaking, cannot be quashed by the quietus. This "unanswerable opponent" is the actual state of affairs that is of one sort while the authority would decree it another. Let the gradual sifting and selection of persons best fit for pivotal rôles in the authoritarian situation progress sufficiently, and the dictator that began by saying only what he would like most to say ends by hearing only what he would like most to hear—whereat of a sudden the fatal heckler enters, and he must hear what he would like least to hear.

With so much affirmed absolutely, as gospel, I should next move into the area of "complicating factors." Such an area would be exemplified by Dr. Kilpatrick's observations about the propaganda of the public utilities. This would be placed as an instance of the way in which our doctrinal absolute is violated. One could note other violations. Thus, when our press, radio and newsreels play up the doctrines of some factions and play down the doctrines of others, we are again confronting the dictatorial function, with its risks. And in so far as these dictatorial functions gain organizational efficiency, making partial truths act as whole truths, they too move us closer to the unanswerable opponent.

As part of the dialectic process, this unanswerable opponent takes social embodiment in the vessel of a *counter-dictatorship*. Two forms of efficient overemphasis break into dissociates—and the debate, being balked on the parliamentary plane, moves to the plane on which an interchange is still possible, the plane of force (with its own dialectic of parry and thrust, and its ramparts "disputed").

I do not flatter myself that, by repeating this old story here, I am informing anyone of anything. My point is simply to emphasize that, from this approach, got by the addition of "dialectics" to his cluster of terms, the educator's message can be presented in terms of positive indoctrination (with all the psychological advantages of such a mode) as against the tonalities of tentativeness in Dr. Kilpatrick's strategy of presentment. And its affirmation is based squarely on a body of thought and information, that is, on a *tradition*. Yet, though affirming his position as a doctrine, to be indoctrinated, the indoctrinator need not encumber himself with the claim that his doctrine is a finished product as regards accuracy and scope in the filling-out of its implications and the tracing of its ramifications (the road to further development thus being left open).

Dr. Kilpatrick would even concede that democracy may, at some future time, need to be abandoned, or at least to be so modified as to have a radically different meaning from the meaning it has for us. But need he make this concession, through fear of "indoctrination" and its absolutes? Even if times were such as to convince a reasonable man that, within the dialectic process as institutionalized in a given structure of property, parliament and publication, a large degree of dictatorship had arisen in function (regardless of what it might be called in name) and if he felt that, within the limitations of the scene, this error-breeding function could be removed only by the act of a counter-dictatorship, he could still, as an educator, acclaim as his ideal directive the reëstablishment of full dialectic opportunity. And thus, even in raw times, he would affirm a *doctrine*, grounded in *tradition*, that tugged in the direction of maturity, towards the abating of the rawness.

And where he could not do this greatly, he could do it somewhat.

There are several passages in Dr. Kilpatrick's essay that implicitly embody this position in favor of doctrine based on tradition, for all his reluctance to subscribe explicitly. Thus, having equated democratic freedom with ethics, he observes that his ideal "is no higher than our best morals has taught for some thousands of years, and it is no higher than scientists now sternly exact of each other" (whereat we see a past tradition and a contemporary tradition merged). Or when he speaks of "decent ethics" and "proper democratic standards," he is again referring to public, or traditional, matters that impose restrictions upon the individual. Nor, if this tradition, or doctrine, is a good one, need we consider its restrictions as an infringement of an individual's liberties; hence we need not feel that an educator would be imposing his will upon the educated in indoctrinating it—a free act, a good act, and a rationally motivated (i. e., *induced*) act being the same. Dialectically, the individual's freedom depends upon the traditions of the collectivity.

What, in brief, is the function of doctrine? Doctrine is employed in the attempt to coach or induce a reasonable act which, without doctrine, could take place only through spontaneous illumination on the part of the individual. And without either doctrine or spontaneous illumination, the act could be induced only by force or threat of force (which impairs the freedom, or full rationality, of the act).

446

The doctrinal device, as localized for particular scenes, does to be sure become irrelevant in proportion as the scene undergoes change. Or the doctrine remains relevant, too relevant, relevant malignly, as it is employed by authorities consciously or unconsciously to block the development of doctrine more socially useful (doctrine better suited to chart the scene). But to attempt eliminating the problem of bad doctrine by eliminating doctrine per se is like trying to eliminate heart disease by eliminating hearts. Only by doctrine could one "act on thinking," for only by doctrine could one describe the nature of the scene in which the act is to take place. However, the dialectical, historical processes by which good doctrine becomes bad doctrine should certainly be studied, and the results of this study patiently indoctrinated, as a "doctrine of doctrines."

A perennial embarrassment in liberal apologetics has arisen from its "surgical" proclivity: its attempt to outlaw a malfunction by outlawing the function. It is happier when in the sign of "emancipation" than when in the sign of "control." But since it has so many just claims to its rôle as the repository of much "good" doctrine, why should it take on unnecessary handicaps by allowing "bad" doctrines to enjoy alone the strategic advantages that go with the doctrinal act?

DIALECTICIAN'S HYMN

A VERY clear way to illustrate the meaning of an act is to say, "The actor, by this act, is saying, in effect . . ."—then give the equivalent in a declarative sentence. Thus the practice of shaking hands after a game says in effect: "There are no hard feelings. The rivalry does not extend beyond the confines of the game."

A declarative sentence, in turn, may often be best illustrated by the optative, as in resolutions and petitions. Thus, the function of the statement, *"There are* no hard feelings . . . etc." can be most clearly conveyed by translation into a different grammatical idiom, *"Let there be* no hard feelings . . . etc."

In the following lines, we have tried to illustrate some key processes of metaphysics by use of the optative style, in this case the style of prayer. Here the distinction between belief, make-believe, and mock-belief is left fluctuant.

In a work of metaphysics, there is some term that has a "god-function." That is: its meaning derives from its rôle as a summation of all the other terms. In this technical sense, the term "dialectical materialism" is no less a "god-function" than any other title would be. The philosophy of dialectical materialism is the definition of this title, i. e., its tautological restatement. Quite as the events in Flaubert's novel, *Madame Bovary*, are the narrative definition of the novel's title. The events restate explicitly what the title contains implicitly: they draw out, in temporal arpeggio, all that is struck simultaneously, as a chord, in the title itself.

> Hail to Thee, Logos,
> Thou Vast Almighty Title,
> In Whose name we conjure—
> Our acts the partial representatives
> Of Thy whole act.
>
> May we be Thy delegates
> In parliament assembled.
> Parts of Thy wholeness.
> And in our conflicts
> Correcting one another.
> By study of our errors
> Gaining Revelation.
>
> May we give true voice
> To the statements of Thy creatures.
> May our spoken words speak for them,
> With accuracy,
> That we know precisely their rejoinders
> To our utterances,
> And so may correct our utterances
> In the light of those rejoinders.
>
> Thus may we help Thine objects
> To say their say—

Not suppressing by dictatorial lie,
Not giving false reports
That misrepresent their saying.

If the soil is carried off by flood,
May we help the soil to say so.
If our ways of living
Violate the needs of nerve and muscle,
May we find speech for nerve and muscle,
To frame objections
Whereat we, listening,
Can remake our habits.
May we not bear false witness to ourselves
About our neighbors,
Prophesying falsely
Why they did as they did.

May we compete with one another,
To speak for Thy Creation with more justice—
Coöperating in this competition
Until our naming
Gives voice correctly.
And how things are
And how we say things are
Are one.

Let the Word be dialectic with the Way—
Whichever the print
The other the imprint.

Above the single speeches
Of things,
Of animals,
Of people,
Erecting a speech-of-speeches—
And above this
A Speech-of-speech-of-speeches,
And so on,
Comprehensively,

Until all is headed
In Thy Vast Almighty Title,
Containing implicitly
What in Thy work is drawn out explicitly—
In its plenitude.

And may we have neither the mania of the One
Nor the delirium of the Many—
But both the Union and the Diversity—
The Title and the manifold details that arise
As that Title is restated
In the narrative of History.
Not forgetting that the Title represents the story's Sequence,
And that the Sequence represents the Power entitled.

For us
Thy name a Great Synecdoche,
Thy works a Grand Tautology.

INDEX of Proper Names

INDEX OF PROPER NAMES

INDEX OF PROPER NAMES

453

INDEX OF PROPER NAMES

454

INDEX OF PROPER NAMES

INDEX of Topics

456

INDEX OF TOPICS

INDEX OF TOPICS

INDEX OF TOPICS

INDEX OF TOPICS

INDEX OF TOPICS

461

INDEX OF TOPICS

INDEX OF TOPICS